Multinational Investment
in Modern Europe

NEW HORIZONS IN INTERNATIONAL BUSINESS

General Editor: Peter J. Buckley
Professor of Managerial Economics
Management Centre, University of Bradford

This important new series is aimed at the frontiers of international business research. Each volume tackles key problem areas in international political economy. The study of international business is important not least because it gives researchers the opportunity to innovate in theory, technique, empirical investigation and interpretation. The area is fruitful for interdisciplinary and comparative research. The series will rapidly become established as a lively forum for presenting new ideas in international business studies.

Multinational Investment in Modern Europe

Strategic Interaction in the
Integrated Community

Edited by
John Cantwell

Reader in International Economics
University of Reading, UK

Edward Elgar

Published by
Edward Elgar Publishing Limited
Gower House
Croft Road
Aldershot
Hants GU11 3HR
England

Edward Elgar Publishing Company
Old Post Road
Brookfield
Vermont 05036
USA

HG
5430
.5
M84

A CIP catalogue record for this book is available from the British Library

A CIP catalogue record for this book is available from the US Library of
Congress

ISBN 1 85278 421 0

Printed and bound in Great Britain by
Biddles Ltd, Guildford and King's Lynn

Contents

Contributors

Nicola Acocella is full Professor of Economic Policy at the University of Rome 'La Sapienza' and Director of Graduate Studies in the Department of Public Economics. His research interests include oligopoly, foreign direct investment and multinational corporations, and public enterprises. For some years he has directed a prominent research group working on Italian multinationals.

P.A. Campayne completed his doctoral studies at the University of Reading and is the author of a book on the locational strategies of multinational banks, due to be published soon by Routledge. He is a researcher in the North America and Japan Division of the Bank of England.

John Cantwell is Reader in International Economics at the University of Reading. He has been a Visiting Professor at the University of Rome 'La Sapienza' and the University of the Social Sciences, Toulouse. His main research areas are the economics of technological change and international production, and he is director of an Economic and Social Research Council project on the historical structure of innovative activity in Europe and the US. He is currently the President of the European International Business Association.

John H. Dunning is ICI Research Professor in International Business at the University of Reading, and State of New Jersey Professor of International Business at Rutgers University. He is probably the best-known scholar in the world in the field of direct investment and multinational firms, having published extensively in this area since his pioneering study of American investment in Britain in the 1950s.

Juan José Durán Herrera is Professor of Business Economics and Dean of the Faculty of Economics and Business Administration in the Autonomous University of Madrid. He is known for his writings on the internationalization of Spanish companies and on business finance.

He is the director of the Carlos V International Centre and a former President of the European International Business Association.

Edward M. Graham is Research Fellow at the Institute for International Economics in Washington D.C., having previously held positions at the Massachusetts Institute of Technology, the US Treasury Department, the OECD and the University of North Carolina. His field of research includes transatlantic direct investment flows and oligopolistic reaction, and US policy towards inward investment. His contribution with Paul Krugman on foreign direct investment in the US has received much acclaim.

Ph. De Lombaerde is a researcher and doctoral candidate at the State University of Antwerp.

Terutomo Ozawa is Professor of Economics at Colorado State University. He is one of the foremost scholars of Japanese multinationals since his early investigation of Japan's technological challenge to the West. His research interests include the role of direct investment in industrial restructuring in Japan, and the recycling of Japan's surpluses for the developing countries.

Francesca Sanna Randaccio is Senior Researcher at the University of Rome 'La Sapienza'. She is the author of numerous articles on international investment, and is especially known for her work on European direct investment in the US and the growth of multinationals in oligopolistic industries.

Julien Savary is Lecturer in Economics at the University of the Social Sciences in Toulouse, where he is a member of the industrial organization research team, LEREP. His main field of research is the economics of multinational firms, and especially the international strategies of industrial groups. His work on French multinationals is well known.

Vitor Corado Simões is a Lecturer in the Institute of Economics and Management at the State University of Lisbon, having formerly been Deputy Director of the Institute for Foreign Investment in Portugal. He has become the best-known author on the international investment position of Portugal, and his interests also include technology transfer. He is currently President-Elect of the European International Business Association.

D. Van Den Bulcke is Professor of Economics and Director of the Centre for International Management and Development at the State University of Antwerp. He is the leading authority on direct investment in Belgium, and is also well-known for his work on European integration and the location of regional headquarters. He is a former President of the European International Business Association.

George N. Yannopoulos is Reader in Economics and Chairman of the Graduate School of European and International Studies at the University of Reading. His research interests span a wide range of topics in international and regional economics, with particular reference to the trade policy of the European Community. At various times he has acted as an adviser to and representative of the Greek government.

Preface

The background to this study can be traced back to a European research network formed by a group of us working on international business issues. At an informal level this network has operated for a number of years, with acquaintance being renewed at relevant seminars and conferences, through occasional exchange visits, and at the annual meetings of the European International Business Association. The arrangement was formalized in 1989 when support was obtained from the European Community's Stimulation Plan for Economic Science (SPES) for a network to co-ordinate our research efforts in the area of multinational corporation activity in Europe and the completion of the single market in 1992. The SPES team brought together nine economists from six European countries: John Cantwell, John Dunning and George Yannopoulos from Reading; Nicola Acocella and Francesca Sanna Randaccio from Rome, Danny Van Den Bulcke from Antwerp; Julien Savary from Toulouse; Juan José Durán Herrera from Madrid; and Victor Simões from Lisbon. John Cantwell co-ordinated the project from Reading.

The group met under the auspices of the SPES award for the first time at a meeting in Reading in November 1989. We decided to gear our project to the launch of a book at the end of 1992, and discussed the structure that this book would take to best bring together the issues that we agreed needed to be addressed. As is explained further in the Introduction, the structure of the book combines our interests in the rise in cross-investments between countries, the restructuring of multinational operations in Europe, the development of new forms of strategic interaction between companies, and the consequent impact of multinationals on the national structure of production and technological capability. These are all matters of great significance to the workings of the new European economy, yet so far they have hardly been tackled in the existing literature on European integration or elsewhere. Our planning in Reading also benefited from the attendance and comments of others working in related areas who wished to maintain contact with members of the network: Mark Casson, Tony Foley, Grazia Ietto Gilles and Dimitri Mardas.

In the following year a number of exchange visits were organized and papers were prepared. Edward Elgar provided us with a contract for the book and Peter Buckley agreed to include it in the *New Horizons in International Business* series for which he has responsibility. It was also decided to launch the book at the Annual Meeting of the European International Business Association to be held in Reading in December 1992. The presentation of our findings there would mark the conclusion of the SPES project.

The next step was to organize a seminar to bring the whole group together again to discuss the first drafts of our chapters for the book and to integrate our thinking more closely. This seminar was held in May 1991 in the most attractive setting of the Institute for Scientific Studies in Cargèse, Corsica. The seminar was made possible by an award from the Regional Institute of Trade, Innovation and Management (IRCIG), a representative organization of the Corsican Congress.

The support of the IRCIG, together with a grant from Nestlé, also enabled us to invite three other scholars to participate in the seminar and contribute to the book. Their involvement has usefully broadened our perspective. While the SPES group concentrated on intra-EC investments, the contributions of Monty Graham of the Institute of International Economics and Terutomo Ozawa of Colorado State University have allowed us to relate activity within Europe to the inter-regional cross-investments between the US and Europe, and between Japan and Europe. Furthermore, while the SPES team had decided to focus mainly on investments in manufacturing (even if sometimes considering their changing relationship with financial and other service activity), Paul Campayne of the Bank of England has explicitly extended our coverage to include banking.

Also present at the seminar in Corsica were Michelle Gittelman, who has organized work in this field at the UN Centre on Transnational Corporations, Pilar Barrera from Reading, and Charles Straboni of the IRCIG. We are grateful to all of them for their comments. We also wish to thank Pilar Barrera for organizing our transport around the island, and Marie-France Hanseler, the Director of the Institute for Scientific Studies in Cargèse, who did so much to make our stay an enjoyable one.

The participants at the seminar acted as discussants of one another's papers and provided the authors with feedback on their work. Together with comments from the Editor and the general discussion in Corsica, this feedback was taken into account by the contributors in revising their chapters in the months following the seminar. As many members of the network commented on many other chapters, the list of acknowledgements is too long to mention in full; suffice to say that the end product is a team effort. Other particular acknowledgements are mentioned in individual chapters.

We would like to thank Linda Graves, who acted as secretary to the project in Reading and whose efforts have kept the team as a whole regularly informed of the progress being made by other members of the network. We also wish to thank Mr J.D. Cantwell, who compiled the index to the book. Finally, we must once again pay tribute to our major sponsors, without whose support the book would not have been written: the European Commission (under the SPES initiative), the Corsican Regional Institute of Trade, Innovation and Management (IRCIG), and Nestlé SA.

1. Introduction

John Cantwell

1.1. THE OBJECTIVES AND STRUCTURE OF THE BOOK

If there is one question that provides the inspiration for this volume it is this: why has direct investment within Europe, and the international production that it finances, been rising rapidly at a time when the economies of Europe are becoming more closely integrated? Many of the conventional theories or models of direct investment and international production would suggest the reverse. The approach these models have typically followed is to treat direct investment as one method or mode of servicing a final product market. Direct investment can then be compared with the alternative modes of exports by the home country firm (trade in final products), or non-equity contracts such as licensing agreements with host country firms (trade in intermediate products including intangible assets). Now consider the application of this framework to a situation in which economies that are geographically quite near one another are becoming more closely integrated, so that the costs of trade and transport between them fall, trade barriers are reduced, and cross-border markets work more efficiently. With trade and contractual agreements being easier to arrange and less costly than ever before the usual discussion of alternative market-servicing modes suggests that direct investment would be replaced by trade and licensing.

There is a variety of possible answers to the question of why in these circumstances direct investment in Europe has been increasing so dramatically, and many of these answers are to be found interspersed among the chapters of this book. One such answer is that the European picture is simply part of a worldwide trend; direct investment between the industrialized countries has grown substantially since the early 1980s. This issue is explored in the chapters by Terutomo Ozawa and Edward M. Graham which deal with direct investment in the Triad as a whole – Europe, Japan and the US. Of course, this can only be part of a broader story since it begs the question of why

it is that direct investment has recently been rising faster than trade
in the world as a whole; and in any case, direct investment has tended
to rise fastest of all (like trade) in Europe.

Another answer is that trade and direct investment need not be
substitutes, but may instead be complements. That is, the growth of
international trade and production may help to facilitate one another.
This idea is implicit in Terutomo Ozawa's chapter, given the parallel
that he draws between the growth of intra-industry trade and the
growth of intra-industry direct investment (mutual flows of trade and
investment in the same sector). The trend he has described might lead
to a state of the world in which in a given industry certain products
or brands are produced in Europe (by European as well as Japanese
firms, with the European companies exporting to Japan) while other
products are produced in Japan (by European as well as Japanese
firms, with the Japanese group exporting to Europe). For each set of
firms trade in one type of product and direct investment in another
are mutually supportive. This kind of answer, emphasizing the complementarity of international trade and production, is also to be found
in Juan Duran's analysis of direct investment in Spain. He notes that
foreign-owned affiliates in Spain are substantial importers, and their
servicing of local markets consists of both trade and local production.
The direct presence of these affiliates has helped to increase the local
market-share of foreign firms, which is then serviced by trade and
technology licensing as well as from the production of the affiliates
themselves.

A further explanation of the growth in intra-European international
production is that in the current process of European integration trade
has been facilitated by a reduction in non-tariff barriers rather than
in tariff barriers, and the effects of these two barriers are not always
analogous to one another. Tariff barriers discriminate strictly in
accordance with the location of production (plants located within the
country are favoured at the expense of those located outside it), while
non-tariff barriers may discriminate in accordance with ownership
(some firms are favoured, for instance in government contracts, at the
expense of others). Once non-tariff barriers are reduced, the local
market shares of firms that were formerly discriminated against, often
principally foreign-owned firms, is increased. The greater scope for
foreign firms to serve such markets offers them a further means to
increase their local sales by way of both trade and direct investment.
This possibility is examined in greater depth in the chapter by John
Cantwell and Francesca Sanna-Randaccio.

Another element in the rise in European direct investment is the strategic behaviour of firms. This theme is taken up by Nicola Acocella. As originally argued by Hymer, direct investment may be a means to achieving increased market power. This is especially the case when investments finance mergers and acquisitions, which raise the market power of the group in question. As Acocella observes, there has been a substantial increase in cross-border mergers and acquisitions within Europe since the mid–1980s. They constitute one of the important institutional forms of the recent growth in European direct investment. These mergers and acquisitions might be viewed as in part a response to the greater international competition within Europe that has resulted from freer trade. Again, higher levels of trade are associated with increased investment, in this case to preserve an oligopolistic balance of power. This type of corporate restructuring in European industries has also taken the form of a significant spread of strategic alliances, which could be thought of as merely one step short of a merger or acquisition.

The restructuring of productive activity across national boundaries by multinationals has occurred through rationalization within companies as well as by changes in inter-firm relationships. This provides an additional dimension to the encouragement of direct investment by a better environment for trade. Where trade is freer multinationals have more scope to organize an international division of labour, and Julien Savary, Danny van den Bulcke and Philippe de Lombaerde, Vitor Simões and George Yannopoulos are among those who provide evidence of the general shift towards regionally integrated corporate networks within Europe. The advantage which this form of co-ordinated multinationality confers upon a firm places a competitive pressure on other companies to engage in direct investment as a means towards the establishment of their own regional networks. The affiliates in such a network engage in substantial trade, both in terms of imports and exports. This type of direct investment is not aimed solely at servicing the market of the country to which it is directed but is instead part of a wider system of related investments that together serve the common regional market. In this case, the simple model of alternative modes of market servicing between countries in the same region is not relevant; each affiliate acts to promote trade as a kind of export platform for its own specialized product range, and as an importer of all other products related to that company's business.

This chapter does not seek to provide a comprehensive summary of the contents of the remainder of the book. What it does instead is to show briefly how the various chapters, although they can each be read independently for their own particular focus of interest, between them help to address certain central or unifying themes. This is therefore a somewhat selective introduction to the issues raised in the book, drawing attention to the areas of overlap between authors and how their specific concerns relate to one another. It also aims to whet the appetite of the reader and give him or her an indication of the changing perspective of the book as different aspects of multinational investment in Europe are addressed in moving from chapters that appear at the beginning to those that are placed at the end.

Aside from the general growth of multinational corporation (MNC) activity in Europe, two aspects of this growth in particular stand out as having been accelerated by the greater regional integration associated with the single market in the European Community (EC). First, cross-investments between MNCs in the same industry (intra-industry production) have been steadily rising. To a lesser extent, an increase in this kind of intra-industry investment applies between regions (Europe, North America and the Pacific Rim) as well as between countries within Europe, but the motivation and effect of these cross-investments are different within the EC. Secondly, as was also mentioned earlier, MNCs already established in the EC have been reorganizing their European operations. This restructuring has tended to increase the degree of geographical specialization of production across affiliates in each MNC, but it has also been changing inter-firm relationships. Cross-investments and network reorganization have altered both the structure of European industries and the location of technological and productive activity in the EC.

The structure followed by the book is to focus initially on the analysis of cross-investments and MNC reorganization in their own right, before gradually shifting attention towards the study of their impact upon countries and industries. The discussion begins with a general consideration by Terutomo Ozawa and Edward M. Graham of cross-investments between MNCs from the industrialized or Triad regions (the US, the EC and Japan). Closer regional integration within the EC also provides the context for an increasing interaction through direct investment between these groups of firms. It has been argued, for example, that the completion of the EC's internal market has acted as a catalyst for a substantial growth of Japanese investment in the EC. The relationship between the restructuring of industries in Europe and Japan, and the connections between restructuring in each area that have been established through cross-investments, are discussed by Terutomo Ozawa. Edward M. Graham confronts the interchange between firms from different parts of the Triad by examining instead the motives for recent changes in the pattern of cross-investments between the EC and the US.

From here, attention is turned to cross-investments within the EC. A distinction is drawn between cross-investments which are linked to the creation of regional networks, such as those developed in response to technological competition or co-operation, and cross-investments associated with mutual market access. The former type of cross-investments are more important within the EC while the latter are more important between regions. In the case of the operation of European networks there is also an internal regional implication, namely, the extent to which the cross-investments of MNCs are promoting a new geographical pattern of specialization in the EC. John Cantwell and Francesca Sanna-Randaccio discuss the cross-border location of technological activity associated with cross-investments and how this is affected by the locational hierarchies that exist in many European industries. Investments running from a centre of excellence to a more peripheral location have a different purpose from those which run in the opposite direction, and this is reflected in the types of technological activity with which they are each associated. Different patterns in the international division of labour that characterize MNC networks controlled from different countries may therefore underpin an apparently symmetrical system of cross-investments.

Subsequent chapters examine some case-study evidence on cross-investments and network reorganization in the cases of Belgium, France and Italy. These studies provide for a more detailed consideration of the workings of cross-investment and corporate restructuring in the EC at the level of particular industries (Danny van den Bulcke and Philippe de Lombaerde investigate the Belgian metal-working industries) and particular companies (Julien Savary looks at the largest French and Italian industrial groups). Both these chapters provide well-documented accounts at a microeconomic level of the close association between cross-investments by the largest industrial groups and the organization of a more refined regional division of labour in the EC within the same firms. The extent of cross-investment reflects the significance of the locations involved as centres and the competitive strength and strategies of indigenous firms. Hence, there are substantial cross-investments between France and Italy but less between Belgium and the rest of the EC, since local Belgian firms are relatively minor players in Europe by comparison with the importance of Belgium as a central location.

Cross-investments between EC countries and the greater degree of strategic interaction between companies that they entail are not only related to the reshaping of affiliate specialization across the major centres. An increase in competition through the more extended geographical overlap in the dispersion of the productive activity and markets of the major firms, when combined with slower average rates of growth in aggregate demand since the mid–1970s, have also led to rationalization. Within firms this has taken the form of plant closures and a greater focus on their own core business activities. Between firms there have been a growing number of attempts to arrive at strategic partnerships or alliances, and a substantial rise in the number of cross-border mergers and acquisitions in the EC. This issue is addressed in Nicola Acocella's chapter. While these mergers and alliances may take advantage of technological and managerial complementarities between firms, they also help to contribute to rationalization and an increase in market power as a means of offsetting the greater degree of international competition. Nicola Acocella emphasizes the role of this latter kind of strategic behaviour by MNCs in Europe.

It is at this point that the book begins to shift more clearly from the motives for cross-investments and corporate restructuring towards the study of their effects. This is of particular interest in the Iberian Peninsula which until recently was excluded from the process of European integration, but in which we would expect any increase in a geographical division of labour to have an especially marked effect. While economic conditions are more favourable than in Greece, the industrialization of Spain and Portugal still lags behind that of much of the rest of Europe, and so there would seem to be much scope for regionally integrated firms to locate assembly types of production in Spain and Portugal and more-sophisticated production elsewhere (such as in Germany). The Spanish case is considered by Juan Duran, and Vitor Simões looks at Portugal.

From somewhat different perspectives both these authors paint pictures which suggest that this process of a restructuring of investments has begun but that until now the benefits to the local economies have been matched by costs, although it seems there are now encouraging signs for the future. In Spain the closer integration of foreign-owned affiliates into European networks has initially increased imports more sharply than exports, contributing to a Spanish trade deficit and a greater technological dependency. However, direct investment has increased despite a significant rise in wages, and there is some evidence that foreign MNCs will play their part in upgrading the structure of local production within the industries by which they have been especially attracted to Spain. This may lead exports to rise faster than imports in due course. In Portugal the shift in the nature of activity conducted in foreign-owned firms has been less dramatic, but there is still a clear switch towards more-integrated types of affiliate, and some of the most recent investments seem likely to provide positive spillover effects for local industry.

The Spanish and Portuguese studies also take into account the implications of the interaction between indigenous and foreign firms for the development of domestic technological capacity and competitiveness. A distinction can be drawn between industries in which the impact is generally beneficial and those in which it is detrimental. The implications of this distinction are explored in the context of national goals for industrial restructuring and the effect of foreign MNCs on the structure of inter-industry and intra-industry activity in the local economy.

While the bulk of the discussion is concerned with cross-investments and technological development in manufacturing, Paul Campayne's chapter provides a comparison of this with investments in the provision of financial services. This is fitting, as it can be argued that with the new regional integration the pace of change of multinational bank activity is especially dramatic. A number of other chapters also touch on the ramifications of the linkages between multinational groups in the manufacturing and financial sectors and how this has affected corporate restructuring. Paul Campayne's chapter is also connected with the rest of the book through his focus on the locational specialization of financial activities associated with cross-investments, and the reorganization of the networks of multinational banks. Multinational banks have chosen to concentrate certain of their activities in particular centres.

The discussion is concluded by looking at the changing business–government relationship in the EC and at possible policy responses. George Yannopoulos addresses the issue of the single European market as such, and relates it to the strategic response of MNCs it has helped to induce, with reference to the network reorganization and merger wave discussed in earlier chapters. In the light of increased cross-investments and a greater strategic interaction between firms, John Dunning's concluding examination of policy implications gives consideration not only to the impact of inward investment on local industries, but also to the need for governments to take account of patterns of outward investment. Industrial restructuring at home and selected technological and other co-operation between firms involves outward as well as inward investment. Governments and the EC Commission now need to take explicit account of the various influences of

MNC structures and strategies on the course of industrial development.

1.2 SOME FURTHER COMMON THEMES

There are a number of other common themes which run throughout much of the book. It is worth distinguishing six of these in particular.

First, the increase in cross-investments in the EC suggests that *there is some interaction between inward and outward investment*. This is obviously emphasized in models of oligopolistic reaction, but the interplay between inward and outward investment can take other forms as well, and the form of this interaction varies a good deal between countries. The wide geographical coverage of the book allows us to make some assessment of the variation between EC member states in the form of association between inward and outward investment. John Cantwell, Francesca Sanna Randaccio and Paul Campayne concentrate on evidence from the UK, Germany and, to a lesser extent, France (and in the case of banking, Denmark); Julien Savary covers France and Italy; Danny Van Den Bulcke and Philippe De Lombaerde focus on Belgium; Juan Duran discusses Spain; and Vitor Simões looks at Portugal. Hence, overall detailed evidence is assembled on eight of the twelve current member countries of the EC.

The degree of intra-industry interaction between the inward and outward investment of the largest firms seems to be greatest between the largest countries; for example, between Britain and Germany and between France and Italy. Smaller countries such as Belgium tend to be characterized by net inward investment. However, Belgium has also become a focal point for the regional networks of foreign MNCs, to the extent that inward investment directly promotes outward investment as foreign affiliates undertake significant outward investments of their own. In Portugal and Spain the interaction between inward and outward investment is at a much earlier stage, particularly in Portugal which has little outward investment. In Spain, though, there is now already a significant interplay between foreign-owned firms and indigenous companies, and the more-advanced local firms are under some pressure to internationalize their own activities.

Secondly, *the increase in intra-Community trade is quite closely related to the restructuring and greater integration of MNC networks in the EC*. As affiliates turn from the servicing of local (national) markets and become integrated into the regional network of their multinational group then they become increasingly involved in trade. Consequently, at least within the EC, direct investment is now more of a complement to than a substitute for trade. At an earlier stage of internationalization, cross-border competition progressed between bilateral groups of MNCs serving one another's domestic markets either by direct investment or trade. In the more-developed stage of regional corporate networks and alliances today, strategic interaction has developed at a wider level in a number of industries, an interaction that involves MNCs from a range of national origins serving a common EC market. This process is creating new patterns of specialization among EC trading partners as well as helping to increase the overall level of intra-EC trade.

Thirdly, *within most MNCs integration is increasingly intra-regional (intra-EC) at the expense of inter-regional integration.* Corporate networks have normally been constituted at a regional level, integrating affiliates located in the EC, sometimes in place of linkages that they may previously have enjoyed with affiliates located in other regions. Consequently, MNC trade and specialization is developing fastest within the EC. However, partly because of the establishment of such intra-regional networks, direct investment flows between the Triad regions have increased. These inter-regional investments are motivated in large part by defensive considerations: wishing to avoid being closed out of markets and to take advantage of the opportunities for the formation of local networks in the other integrating regions. Triad linkages between regions are thereby increasingly due to direct investment rather than to trade.

The literature has come to refer to these trends as 'globalization', and to call the strategies of the MNCs responsible for this type of geographical reorganization 'global strategies'. However, these terms are potentially misleading. The element of these strategies which is indeed global is the requirement on most of the major MNCs to invest in operations in all the Triad regions. Yet these investments across regions tend if anything to be less integrated and no more interdependent than they were in the past. The international integration of affiliate networks has essentially involved a process of 'regionalization' and has entailed the development of regional strategies. This is not to rule out the possibility in the future of a more genuine global integration between the networks that are currently being formed at a regional level, but simply to acknowledge that this has not happened generally as yet.

Fourthly, *the geographical structure of regional MNC networks in the EC reflects and reinforces patterns of locational hierarchy across centres.* This theme recurs in various forms in a number of chapters.

Terutomo Ozawa suggests that Japanese MNCs operating in Europe have tended to locate their most-sophisticated activity (the 'brain' of the operation) in Germany; the assembly of medium and high technology-intensive products in the UK; the assembly of low technology-intensive products in Spain; and the functions of distribution and co-ordination in the Netherlands and Belgium. Danny Van Den Bulcke and Philippe De Lombaerde confirm the role of Belgium as a co-ordination centre for foreign MNCs. John Cantwell and Francesca Sanna-Randaccio examine the influence of locational hierarchies on the different patterns of technological specialization of MNCs from home centres of different levels of importance, while Paul Campayne carries out a similar exercise in assessing the locational strategies of multinational banks of different national origins.

Juan Duran and Vitor Simões discuss the place assigned to Spain and Portugal in the newly emerging regional division of labour. Due to their earlier stage of development, they have attracted affiliates specializing in less technologically sophisticated types of activity. Some additional evidence on this has recently been gathered by another Spanish economist, Montserrat Casado, in her study of the locational specialization developed by German MNC's in the EC with reference to their operations in Spain in the chemicals and motor vehicles sectors. German chemical firms have specialized in Spain in petrochemical products, which are exported to the Mediterranean area; while they locate the more research-intensive pharmaceutical production in Northern Italy. In the motor vehicle industry German companies produce in Spain certain medium-sized cars and small vans which are exported to the entire regional EC market, although this is organized through a central German distributor. Again, affiliate production in Spain is concentrated in less technology-intensive areas than in the German parent company, although a reasonable selection of components are produced locally in Spain.

Fifthly, *the greater extent of strategic interaction between MNCs in the EC as a result of the process of closer European integration is related to cross-investments and network restructuring.* For one thing, greater interaction between MNCs based in competing centres has increased the propensity to engage in cross-investments through mergers. This then tends to be followed by network reorganization as a result of the process of post-acquisition integration. Where the leaders and followers in an industry are more evenly matched, cross-investments and restructuring are increased, especially when (as in 1992) the catalyst is a reduction in non-tariff barriers rather than in tariffs. However, where a hierarchy of centres remains after integration the locational strategies of MNCs from higher-order centres may differ from the strategies of MNCs from centres of the lower order. Firms originating from the most important centres are likely to develop a more extensive and refined range of geographical specialization among their affiliates, such as in the types of technological activity that the affiliates are given responsibility for.

The greater role of financial interests and of capital market considerations in the decisions of manufacturing companies has also exercised an influence on the restructuring of European industries. The new linkages between industry and finance help to account for a greater strategic awareness of international competitors, and an increased willingness and capacity to enter into mergers, alliances, cross-investments and the rationalization of individual plants and networks. The different nature of these linkages between industry and finance across countries (for example, between Britain and Germany) also helps to explain different rates of expansion of outward direct investment. This is a point taken up and explored further by Edward M. Graham and Julien Savary in their chapters.

Sixthly, *the changing location of production by MNCs in the EC interacts with the growth of the firm.* This requires an analytical framework which allows for such interaction. The standard theory of the firm supposes that location considerations are a quite separate matter determined *a priori*. These locational factors are recognized as influencing the geographical distribution of the activity of the firm and its industry. However, very few studies have so far examined the reverse, namely, the influence of the growth of the firm on the locational attractiveness of alternative sites and on patterns of international specialization. Although it is clear that a broader locational analysis should be invoked when examining the geographical division of labour of the firm and how it reorganizes this over time, the existing literature on MNCs has usually followed the approach of the theory of the firm in treating locational factors as exogenous.

The role played by economies of agglomeration in each location, which go beyond the individual firm, now needs to be addressed in this context. It is also important to acknowledge the interaction between the geographical reorganization of MNC networks within Europe and the composition of activity or degree of specialization in each country. While there has been a tendency in work on MNCs to take locational factors as given, various chapters in this book call attention to the interplay between the growth of the firm and the changing location of different types of production.

An overall unifying theme of the book is the growth of cross-investments and their impact on European technological capacity and competitiveness under the conditions of a steady increase in regional integration. The strategic interaction between MNCs, including the interdependence of inward and outward direct investment, is regarded as central to an understanding of this process. In this respect this book examines a number of themes which have not been properly explored in other recent literature but which it is important to assess when dealing with the current development of MNCs in Europe.

The book also fills a gap in the empirical literature. Comparatively little work has so far been done on intra-industry production or on the reorganization of industries by MNCs. These are especially important questions in Europe, and they are steadily increasing in importance as regional integration is reinforced.

2. Cross-Investments between Japan and the EC: Income Similarity, Technological Congruity and Economies of Scope

Terutomo Ozawa*

2.1 INTRODUCTION

Japan's foreign direct investment (FDI) in Europe, especially in manufacturing, is a very recent phenomenon. It began in earnest as late as 1987 when its annual flow of manufacturing investment to Europe suddenly soared in comparison with the previous year, from $3,302 million to $6,259 million. Another record of $8,855 million was set in 1988.[1] These three years' new investments alone account for more than half of the cumulative total of Japanese investments made in Europe over the entire 1951–88 period. Why this sudden rush to Europe? No doubt the EC 1992 single market programme has been the most important inducement (an immediate 'pull' factor), but other favourable developments have similarly contributed to it. One can easily think of such 'push' factors as the dramatic appreciation of the yen (since the Plaza accord of 1985), Japan's low interest rate policy (until 1989) and the abundant supply of funds made available for overseas investments by the Japanese banking community (partly to prevent any further rise in the value of the yen).

As will be analysed and demonstrated below, a yet more fundamental and structural factor in making such advances into Europe commercially worthwhile and profitable is an *emerged compatibility* of – an *emerged basis* for – direct business activities between Japan and Europe, *the economic opportunities that can be more effectively exploited through various forms of local production rather than the*

*I am grateful to John Cantwell for his detailed incisive comments on an earlier draft of this chapter which led to many improvements in my analysis, and to Monty Graham for his stimulating discussions at the Cargese conference.

13

conventional route of trade. Until recently – say, the end of the 1970s – Japanese industry had hardly any significant common structural basis for profitable local production in Europe. It had some investments, to be sure, but mostly in local marketing facilities and distribution channels – all intended to support exports from Japan – and scarcely any in localized manufacturing.

Moreover, what makes this recent development doubly fascinating is that European multinationals too have been, all of a sudden, stepping up their investments in Japan since 1987. Europe's new investments in Japan were $235 million in 1986, $448 million in 1987 and $817 million in 1988, thus nearly doubling each year.[2] Why this European gallop to Japan? Furthermore, increases in the flows of US investments to Japan are similarly noticeable ($488 million in 1986, $938 million in 1987, and $1,774 million in 1988, again nearly doubling each year). A convergence of criss-crossing investments among the tripolar regions of the world is definitely in the making. One must, then, surmise that only in the recent past there must have emerged some mutually profitable *common* basis for FDI between Western and Japanese corporations.

My analysis proceeds in the following five sections. Section 2.2 identifies a triumvirate convergence in *per capita* income, technological capacity and taste diversification between Japan and the West. Section 2.3 contains a discussion of the recent emergence, most rapid in Japan, of flexible manufacturing that promotes multi-variety, small-lot production. Section 2.4 then examines the evolutionary basis of FDI in terms of relevant existing theoretical frameworks. Section 2.5 explores the historical configurations of scope economies against which three major categories are extracted. This typological conceptualization is subsequently applied, in Section 2.6, to the stage-based process of Japan's overseas investment in the postwar period, a conceptualization useful in explaining a variety of new strategic forms of investment adopted by Japanese multinationals. Section 2.7 presents concluding observations.

2.2 STRUCTURAL COMPATIBILITY IN INDUSTRIAL CAPACITY AND DEMAND CONDITIONS

So what is the compatible basis for trilateral flows of FDI? A common denominator of this mutual penetration among the three economic powers is the recent convergence in *per capita* income and technological sophistication mainly brought about by Japan's catching-up economic growth and technological upgrading.

Japan's GNP *per capita* now ranks second (at $21,020 in 1988), next to Switzerland's ($27,500) in nominal terms. Only 10 years earlier Japan was twelfth. When adjusted for purchasing power at home (if not overseas via exchange rates), Japan is about the same as France, ahead of Britain, yet still behind the United States and Germany.[3] On either measure, however, Japan's catch-up is impressive. This rapidity of Japan's income growth to such a high level, undreamed of only a few decades ago, has been accompanied by an equally rapid successive introduction of new products and new varieties at home, and simultaneously into Western markets as well through exports.

Similarly phenomenal has been Japan's technological progress. Back in the 1960s, as shown in Figure 2.1, Japan's technological capacity, measured in terms of its world share of patent registrations, those made outside the patentees' home countries, was way below the European standard, but it has reached a high level, comparable – or even superior in some areas – to that of Europe. Technological accumulation and diversification have recently been identified as the key determinant of FDI in the 'technological competence' theory introduced by John Cantwell (1990, 1991a). The role of technology in multinationalism is also explored by John H. Dunning (1988). Japanese and Western technological trajectories are fast converging, creating opportunities for both competition and co-operation, since such a convergence in technological capacity means greater possibilities for technological fusion and synthesis.

The swift rises in Japan's *per capita* income and technological capacity have also been accompanied by industrial structural upgrading. This process made Japanese industry very similar in composition to the advanced Western economies, providing a strong common basis for mutual interaction and penetration through FDI. As shown in Table 2.1, Japanese and European multinationals are, for the most part, setting up shop in each other's market in three *identical* major manufacturing sectors. European multinationals in Japan locally produce chemicals and pharmaceuticals (44.9 per cent of the total number of European ventures), non-electric industrial machinery (18.1 per cent), and electric/electronic machinery (7.9 per cent). Similarly, Japanese multinationals in Europe are most actively involved in electric/electronic machinery (26.3 per cent of the total number of Japanese ventures), non-electric industrial machinery (16.6 per cent), and chemicals and pharmaceuticals (18.3 per cent), though Japan is, in addition, strongly active in transportation equipment (7.2 per cent).

*Figure 2.1   Shares of major industrial countries in patents registered
outside their home country, 1965–85*

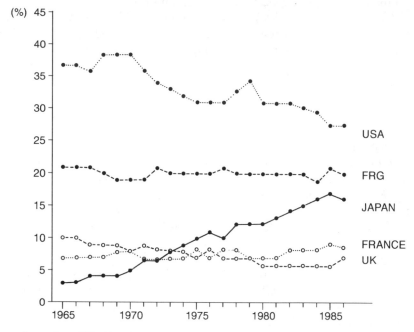

Source: Patent Office (Japan), *Annuals of the Patent Office*, as reproduced in Saito (1990).

Source: Patent Office (Japan), *Annuals of the Patent Office*, as reproduced in Saito
(1990).

American multinationals in Japan, too, are likewise deeply involved
in the same three manufacturing sectors. Thus, the three economic
powers are, on the whole, engaged in *intra-industry* FDI. Japanese
multinationals, however, are more active in the variety-orientated,
consumer-goods industries where they currently enjoy technological
advantages. On the other hand, European multinationals are especially
competitive in chemicals and pharmaceuticals, as are American multinationals.

  These structural similarities and intra-industry manufacturing investments could not have appeared back in the 1960s nor in the 1970s.
Japan's industrial structure then was not quite mature enough technologically and demandwise to interact with its Western counterparts in
mutually profitable local production. The present pattern of intra-

Table 2.1 Sectoral concentration of manufacturing investments by European, American, and Japanese multinationals

(A) European and American manufacturing investments in Japan (number of ventures at the end of 1988)

	European	American
Manufacturing industries	227 (100.0%)	356 (100.0%)
Chemicals & pharmaceuticals	102 (44.9%)	112 (31.5%)
Non-electric machinery	41 (18.1%)	57 (16.0%)
Electric/electronic machinery	18 (7.9%)	71 (20.0%)

(B) Japanese manufacturing investments in Europe (number of ventures at the end of January 1990)

Manufacturing industries	529 (100.0%)
Chemicals & pharmaceuticals	97 (18.3%)
Non-electric machinery	88 (16.6%)
Electric/electronic machinery	139 (26.3%)
Transport equipment (including parts & components)	38 (7.2%)

Source: Data in A are from Toyo Keizai (1989) and in B from JETRO (1990).

industry cross-investments has only recently emerged as a direct consequence of Japan's fast industrial catching-up and upgrading.

2.3   A NEW ERA OF MULTIVARIETY, FLEXIBLE MANUFACTURING

How has the Japanese economy evolved since the end of the Second World War to reach heights comparable to the West? What have been the salient characteristics of its industrial evolution and overseas investment activities that have finally and only recently culminated in the stage of close interaction with Europe in particular? As presented elsewhere in the 'industrial restructuring' theory of FDI (Ozawa, 1991a, 1991b, 1991c), the Japanese economy has expeditiously gone through three distinctive phases of structural upgrading, while accompanied by equally distinguishable stages of multinational operations, and is presently on the threshold of another new phase. The theory captures the phenomenon of overseas investment as a function of the *evolutionary* stages of industrial structure at home, each stage

giving birth to a distinctive stage-specific pattern of FDI, both inward
and outward.

The past three phases of industrialization and FDI are: (a) labour-
intensive industrialization and the 'elementary' stage of overseas
investment (1950 to the mid–1960s); (b) heavy and chemical
industrialization and the 'resource-seeking' – and later, the 'house-
cleaning' – stage of multinationalism (the late 1950s to the mid–1970s);
and (c) assembly-based industrialization and the 'assembly-transplant-
ing' stage of multinationalism (the late 1960s to the present). Japan
is currently at the end of the third phase and on the threshold of
entering (d) a new era of flexible manufacturing and the 'strategic-
localization' stage of global operations.

In this new phase, revolutionary changes are taking place in both
Japan's manufacturing system (supply side) and its consumption
behaviour (demand side). On the supply side, Japanese industry is
metamorphosing itself into an ever-more-efficient system characterized
by computer-guided, production process technologies (computer-integrated manufacturing or CIM) – what is popularly known as 'flexible
manufacturing' or 'smart factories'. In 1990 'one third of Japanese
manufacturers have completed their introduction of CIM, with the
remaining two thirds in the process of putting in such systems or
studying the feasibility of doing so.'[4] Japan is leaving behind the era
of limited-variety, large-lot mass manufacturing and plunging into the
new era of multi-variety small-lot flexible manufacturing (Ozawa,
1991c).

The competitive implications of this revolution are clear: Japanese
industry will be able to compete in the world market in terms of
many more product varieties, higher quality and a speedier delivery of
products, rather than – or in addition to – lower prices. This latest
industrial revolution will enhance Japan's capacity to differentiate to
a much more finely calibrated extent the physical, functional and even
psychological attributes of products so as to suit the varied needs and
wants of customers and to offer them in a more timely manner. The
thrust of Japan's industrial technology is thus definitely to build 'smart
factories'.

On the demand side, Japan's domestic market is booming, especially
for high-income products, with the fast-rising disposable income of
Japanese consumers and the ever-greater diversification and sophistication of their tastes. They have long been known for their rather
thrifty way of life, but they have lately begun spending with a ven-
geance to satisfy their pent-up demand. Their real income is rising,
not only because of the continuous hefty increases in their wages made

possible by economic prosperity and labour shortages at home but also because the sharply appreciated yen and import liberalization enables them to purchase foreign goods, services and assets at bargain prices, previously unknown to them. Japan has suddenly developed into one of the most affluent, upscale markets in the world.

This emergence of an affluent domestic market is an unexpected boon to innovation-seeking Japanese enterprises. They used to innovate new products for foreign consumers in higher-income Western countries. Nowadays, their initial targets are in their own home markets; they are innovating no longer outward but inward – first for domestic consumers, and then, having been successfully test-marketed at home, the new product is exported overseas in a 'trickle-down' fashion. Japanese stores are full of brand-new products such as DAT (digital audio tape) recorders and players, instant playback camcorders with a colour liquid-crystal display, voice-activated cameras, and 'fuzzy-logic-based' elevators, washing machines and vacuum cleaners; but these novelties have not yet been marketed overseas. Japan is thus becoming a major initiator of the product-cycle of many new products. The diversified tastes of affluent consumers, combined with flexible manufacturing, are giving Japanese entrepreneurs a double advantage in gaining from the *economies of scope*, in addition to the *economies of scale* they have been so effectively exploiting.

2.4 PRODUCT DIFFERENTIATION, TECHNOLOGICAL DIVERSIFICATION AND INTERNATIONAL BUSINESS

It is now clear that the fundamental basis for mutually stepped-up penetration of each other's market through FDI by Japanese and European multinationals is the emerged similarity or compatibility in industrial sophistication and *per capita* income; hence the common denominator shared by Japan and Europe in interacting over the prevailing ranges of technological applications and diversified tastes of consumers. Their economies have become structurally so congruent that each other's market can easily serve as an *extension* of the home market and each other's products and technologies can be quickly and efficiently adopted – and adapted to their own local market conditions.

The upshot of this enhanced opportunity for profitable interaction is the availability of a wider range of product lines (varieties and models) for consumers in each economy, who can therefore exercise greater choice among substitutable varieties but make their compatriot *domestic* producers more exposed to the competitive discipline of the market. The *gains from varied consumption* accrue to consumers, since they can select the most desirable combination of attributes embodied in a particular variety or model to suit their own tastes, instead of being compelled to consume a limited set of attributes. Here, the 'new' theory of consumption (Lancaster 1966; Baumol 1967) is relevant. In short, then, greater varieties involve economies of scope, and these economies are enjoyed not only by producers and distributors but also by consumers in the form of economies of differentiated consumption (optimizing an idiosyncratic combination of product attributes).

It was Stephan Buremstam Linder (1961) who first pointed to this 'income similarity' factor as a new determinant of international trade in manufactures, particularly as the key determinant of the volume of such trade. His analysis showed a widening range of 'representative demand' (namely, a widening range of diversified tastes) as a direct function of *per capita* income. He demonstrated that what determines the volume of trade between two countries is an *overlapping* common portion of their demand structures; that is to say, when the *per capita* incomes of two countries are equally high, the range of their taste diversification is equally wide – and the greater is the overlap of their demand structures, hence the larger is the volume of trade in manufactures between them. Yet a closer analysis of the overlap shows that trade becomes less and less desirable, while local product development and manufacturing via overseas investment are increasingly necessitated in order to satisfy the distinct preferences of local consumers, as will be discussed below.

Implicit in Linder's model also is a similarity in technological sophistication; higher *per capita* incomes are causally related to higher levels of industrial technology, and higher-income countries have greater technological capabilities, hence larger supplies of mutually tradable technologies. For technology, by its nature, always possesses an 'excess' capacity – hence a potential to be 'exported' – because of its intrinsic 'public good' characteristics, in the sense that one party's use of knowledge does not preclude its use by others. Yet as John Cantwell (1990) emphasized, technology is basically of two types: the explicit and codifiable type, and the tacit and non-codifiable type (containing 'private good' elements). It is the latter that forces the firm to adopt an internalized form of technology transfer (that is, direct investment) instead of an externalized form (such as licensing). Furthermore, the path of technological progress is context-specific and location-differentiated – and usually socioculturally and -historically moulded (Kogut, 1988). This motivates the firm to extend its technological activity beyond and across national borders in search of a larger opportunity set of complementary technologies that can lead to the synthesizing of many more innovations (Cantwell, 1990). Setting up technological facilities abroad is an eventual outcome of innovation-seeking activities which are initially home-grown. Indeed, many Japanese MNCs in Europe are now at this stage of operations, searching for the rich cultural diversities and creative human resources in local economies (Ozawa, 1991a). Overseas technological resources can be captured through FDI to serve as complements for domestic ones.

In addition to the above supply-side considerations related to technological activities, demand-side factors reinforce the need for direct local manufacturing, particularly when the product involved is highly differentiated in accordance with distinctive local tastes and requirements. In this connection, Richard E. Caves (1971) identifies product differentiation in an oligopolistic industry as the key determinant of FDI by empirically basing his theory on American experience:

> For the United States a high rank correlation seems to exist between the extent of product differentiation and the proportion of firms in an industry having foreign subsidiaries. If we calculate the portion of the larger firms in various American industries having foreign subsidiaries, the list is headed by automobiles, other consumer durables, scientific instruments, chemicals and rubber. At the bottom come primary metals, leather, lumber, paper and textiles. (Caves, 1971, p. 8)

But how does differentiation promote FDI instead of export? What are the sources of advantage created by it? Caves explains:

> Differentiation does not encompass all forms of rent-yielding knowledge available to the firm, but – and this helps greatly to explain *why differentiation and direct investment occur in the same industries* – it probably does include most forms for which local production *per se* increases the rents yielded by a market. For instance, knowledge in the form of process patents or unique managerial skills in the securing of inputs (e.g., finance) or the organizing of production creates neither differentiation nor any complementarity between local production and rents per unit of sales. *Transferable knowledge about how to serve a market* (and differentiate a product) probably accounts for most of the advantage which Servan-Schreiber describes as the organizational skill of American corporations in *The American Challenge*. Pure organizational skill would explain the successful foreign investments by American management consulting firms, but not by American manufacturing firms; and enterprise blessed with managerial excess capacity and organizational skills not related to a particular product market would tend to prefer conglomerate expansion at home, since alien status always imposes some penalty on managerial effectiveness. (Ibid., p. 6, emphases added)

In his analysis of FDI determinants, Caves thus dismisses 'pure organizational skills' and considers 'unique knowledge about marketing the product and adapting it to users' tastes' (p. 6) as the major driving force behind the firm's move to local production, though it is 'not the only industrial attribute explaining the incidence of direct investment' (p. 8). Yet he treats the existence of scale economies as a constraint on – and a trade-off variable for – FDI, and he does not explicitly mention scope economies:

> the likelihood of scale economies in national sales promotion (for differentiated products) suggest that a firm would not invest abroad while profitable opportunities remained for the exploitation of scale economies in production or sales in the home market.   (Ibid., p. 12)

It is unfair, however, to say that Caves did not take into account scope economies; it was only after the mid–1970s that the term was explicitly introduced, conceptualized and popularized for the first time by J. Panzar and R. Willig (1981) and David Teece (1980). Nevertheless, Caves overemphasizes the 'marketing' ('how to serve a market') side of product differentiation and pays scant attention to the 'technological diversification' side that can be achieved when the firm engages in cross-border technological accumulation and differentiation (Cantwell, 1990). Hence, 'how to serve a market' needs to be restated as 'how to innovate a product by employing location-specific technological resources and demand conditions as *additional* inputs in a complementary fashion with the firm's own resources'. Thus, only when linked up with the locus of technological accumulation *à la* Cantwell, does Caves's theory become more plausible and convincing.

This Caves–Cantwell linkup is all the more relevant now that the path of R&D and manufacturing has reached the evolutionary stage of scope-focused innovation and flexible manufacturing, as will be detailed below. This latest phase of manufacturing technology that can cost-effectively exploit scope economies in product differentiation connects the supply and demand sides operationally as one *unitized* activity. It can no longer be classified as supply-sided; it is demand-and-supply-interfaced. This characteristic is described well by Harald B. Malmgren (1990, p. 98):

> the most significant effect of the transformation of industrial activity is the ability to adjust products continuously, tailoring them to continuous changing requirements of individual users. The closer interaction between user and producer. It allows, and even requires, producers to work directly with

users in the design and application of products, interweaving engineering and other services with the provision of hard goods.

Thus, timely customer-specific differentiation will require manufacturers to be in constant communication and close proximity with their customers as well as with the local technological resources. There is, hence, a decisive inducement to direct local production in those markets critical for the manufacturers' operations.

Before we proceed to examine how scope economies that thrive on differentiation of products have emerged as a key determinant of international production, it is necessary to analyse the nature and concept of scope economies, since they have evolved with the historical process of industrialization and accordingly have exhibited different forms at various stages of industrial evolution.

2.5 THE EVOLUTIONARY CONFIGURATIONS OF SCOPE ECONOMIES

In essence, the economies of scope derive from the evolving economic conditions of industrial capitalism. As illustrated in Figure 2.2, three possible basic classifications are conceivable. The first type represents cases in which scope economies are causally tied with, and dependent on, scale economies; the second type is involved with situations in which scope economies are totally independent of scale and based on learning-by-doing benefits; and the third in which scope economies are linked with – and enhanced by – flexible manufacturing. These three classifications can be presented as the stylized distinctions; in reality, however, we are likely to see a number of hybrid cases.

2.5.1 Scale-based Scope Economies

In this first classification, economies of scope presuppose, are incidental to and are derived from the simultaneous existence of economies of scale. This is, in fact, the phenomenon historically observable during the pre-Second World War period of modern capitalism. This type of scope economies is stressed by Alfred D. Chandler (1990). He identifies the traditional economic concept of 'economies of joint production and distribution' with 'the increasingly popular term "economies of scope" ' (p. 17), and goes on to observe:

It was the development of new technologies and the opening of new

Figure 2.2 Evolutionary sources of scope economies

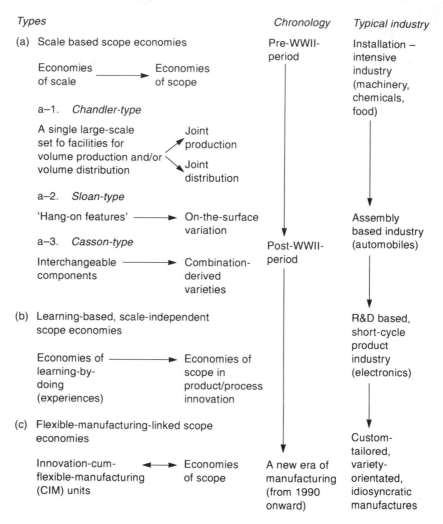

markets, which resulted in economies of scale and of scope and in reduced transaction costs, that made the large multiunit industrial enterprise come when it did, where it did, and in the way it did. These technological and market changes explain why the institution appeared and continued to cluster in certain industries and not in others, why it came into being by integrating units of *volume production* with those of *volume distribution*, and finally, why this multifunctional enterprise continued to grow (though not in all cases) by becoming multinational and multiproduct. (Ibid., p. 18, emphases added)

In Chandler's view, then, both geographical (multinational) expansion and product diversification (multiproduct operation) are by-products of the growth process of a firm and are founded on the infrastructural ('lumpiness') capacities of large-scale fixed investment or overhead capital. This interpretation is quite similar to Edith T. Penrose's (1959) theory of the growth of the firm. Chandler (1990, pp. 24, 28–9) explains:

> The economies of joint production, or scope . . . brought significant cost reduction. Here the cost advantage came from making a number of products in the *same* production unit from much the *same* raw and semi-finished materials and by the *same* intermediate processes. The increase in the number of products made simultaneously in the *same factory* reduced the unit costs of each individual product. . . .
>
> The intermediaries' cost advantage had resulted from exploiting the economies of both scale and scope. Because they handled the products of many manufacturers, they achieved *a greater volume and lower costs per unit* than did any one manufacturer in the marketing and distribution of a *single* line of products (scale). Moreover, they increased this advantage by the broader scope of their operation – that is, by handling a *number* of related product lines through a single set of facilities (scope). (Emphases added)

A single large-scale set of facilities thus creates opportunities for joint production or joint distribution that can economize on overhead costs per unit of product up to a point at which net diseconomies of scope set in; the larger a set of facilities to exploit scale economies, the greater the opportunity (or need) for producing or marketing additional products – hence, a greater variety of products. This way of defining scope economies is rather traditional, in the sense that a spreading of infrastructural costs over as many units or varieties of output as is practical is the cause of multiproduct operations; it is also static, as it stresses *physical* aspects of existing facilities.

Scale-based scope economies are most typically observable in physical-capital-intensive heavy industries such as chemicals, industrial machinery, petro-chemicals, shipbuilding and automobiles, industries that came into existence in the pre-Second World War days but some of which are now 'rust-belt' or 'sunset' industries. Since scale-based scope economies are built on a combination of scale and scope, local production becomes desirable only if the optimal size of a plant is small and the size of a local market relatively large.

This was indeed the case with American manufacturers of 'branded and packaged' food and consumer chemicals who set up subsidiaries in Europe, particularly in the interwar period (Chandler, 1990, pp. 157–61). They made FDI in different national markets, 'because the optimal size of plants was small and, therefore, required less capital, because the penalties of operating below scale were less costly than in more capital-intensive industries, and because tastes, distribution channels, and advertizing media different from country to country' (p. 157). They also wanted to achieve 'greater flexibility in adjusting products to local taste, and further utilization of the enterprise's technical and managerial skills' (p. 160). The whole process of production was thus duplicated in the host economy.

The Chandler type of product variation was thus severely constrained by scale and was rather shallow or skin deep in differentiation. In fact, a similarly shallow type of variation soon became widespread in the automobile industry, an industry that grew increasingly component-based and accessories-added. It was introduced by General Motors under the leadership of Alfred Sloan in the interwar period:

> Sloan's innovative thinking [resolved] the conflict between the need for standardization to cut manufacturing costs and the model diversity required by the huge range of consumer demand. He achieved both goals by standardizing many mechanical items, such as pumps and generators, across the company's entire product range and by producing these over many years with dedicated production tools. At the same time, he annually altered the external appearance of each car and introduced an endless series of 'hang-on features', such as automatic transmissions, air conditioning, and radios, which could be installed in existing body designs to sustain consumer interest.   (Womack, Jones and Roos, 1990, pp. 41–2)

Thus, cars began to be marketed with different combinations of optional features and add-on accessories to solve the conflict between scale and scope. Sloan also introduced a multi-divisional form of organization to deal with the managerial problems of multi-model manufacturing and marketing.

This shallow variation gradually became more and more deeply constituted as the vertical process of assembly manufacturing was further subdivided into many more components and sub-assemblies in search of specialization efficiency, especially in the post-Second World War period. This development is stressed by Mark Casson (1990, p. 18):

> A major factor promoting the post-war growth of the off-shore processing has been the redesign of goods for mass production. In the motor industry, for example, standardized components are put together as subassemblies, and the subassemblies then combined to produce the finished vehicle. Product differentiation is facilitated by the fact that different subassemblies can be interchanged to generate different variants of the product. Thus

scale economies in component production can be retained while models can be proliferated *to suit different niches of the market at the final product level.* (Emphases added)

Indeed, the application of assembly techniques was soon widespread not only in automobiles but also in many other modern manufactures, notably electronics, where component building and fabrication were pursued relentlessly in efforts to reduce production costs and simultaneously to offer a greater variety at the component level – rather than or in addition to at the accessory level. Yet this component-manipulated differentiation remains merely differentiation as such and does not offer an entirely new product.

2.5.2 Learning-based, Scale-independent Scope Economies

A second type of scope economy can be delineated as one whose existence is free from and independent of scale economies. It has emerged as a result of a rapid rate of innovation made possible by investment in research and development (R&D). This second type is an *intertemporal* and more *dynamic* phenomenon than the first. The costs of producing an additional product (or model) decline not so much because of an increased sharing of overhead costs but mainly because of the previous experiences (the economies of learning-by-doing) gained from producing the existing product. This perspective is emphasized by Chris DeBresson (1989, p. 6):

> Technical know-how is cumulative. Incrementally, slowly, but always irreversibly, the level of technical know-how increases. Occasionally, the accumulation of prior know-how elicits synthesis, which in turn allows leaps to be made. Like fixed capital, technical know-how is a capital and a stock.
> Many economic implications have already been drawn from learning-by-doing; but not yet in terms of the *clustering of innovation*. In particular, learning curve research has centered on *one product and economies of scale*; very little has been said on *product variation and economies of scope*. We will suggest that learning-by-doing will induce innovative endeavors to cluster around past innovations. (Emphases added)

In this interpretation, scale and scope economies are essentially separate; they are no longer 'joint economies' – nor are the economies of scope 'derived' from the economies of scale as by-products, as implied by Panzar and Willig (1981) and Chandler (1990). In other words, the phenomenon of scope economies has changed from that observable in connection with the production and marketing of existing products to that directly related to technological diversification. In fact, the existence of a large set of physical facilities and an accompanying large hierarchical managerial structure aimed at scale economies is likely to stand in the way of attaining learning-based economies of scope, economies that can be exploited only in quick and timely response to the changing demand conditions, and hence that require more flexible, more information-flow-facilitating organizations. This second type of scope economies, not dependent on physical scale, is closely related to a fast rate of technological progress – hence to R&D activities (intangibles). These economies are currently exploited most notably by R&D-intensive, short-product-cycle industries such as electronics in general and consumer electronics in particular.

To illustrate the cumulative clustering of innovations (new products or models introduced) based on previous learning-by-doing benefits, DeBresson makes a distinction between two cases; one case in which the learning benefits from one product are *transferable* to 'another at technical proximity', and the other case where no such transfer is present. The difference is illustrated in Figure 2.3. The evolution of unit price over time for a first product (introduced at time 1) is traced out by curve PP. Curve P'P' is for a second product which does not benefit from the learning effect of the first product; hence it starts out at the same unit cost, CO, at time 2, as incurred by the first product. On the other hand, curve P"P" is for a second product that can capture learning-by-doing benefits from the first product; its initial unit cost is C*O, the same lower cost attained by the first product at time 2, because of the transferability of the acquired skills and experiences from previous production.

Learning-based scope economies thus derive from the past experiences and the accumulating stock of knowledge. The economies involved are essentially the first-mover advantages continuously recycled by avoiding the costs of starting from scratch:

> Instead of designing every component of a new product from scratch, Japanese engineers reach instinctively for the parts catalogue. By using off-the-shelf components wherever possible, they devote their most creative engineering skills to fashioning a product that is 90% as good as a product designed from scratch might be – but only half the price of a completely original version. (*Economist*, 1991)

Very active use is made of this type of parts recycling in Japan, contributing to its impressive pace of new product development. It is said that the same strategy is vigorously adopted in developing computer software; the Japanese have 'capitalized on the American con-

Figure 2.3   Learning-based scope economies

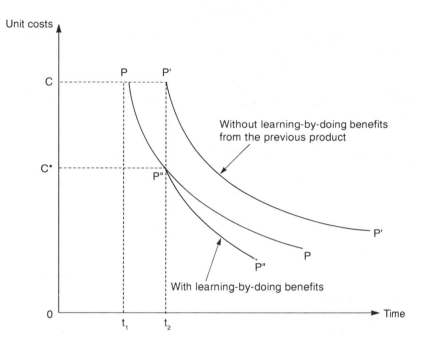

Source: Adapted with modifications from DeBresson (1989).

cept of reusable code, which involves saving chunks of commonly used code instead of programming from scratch every time'.[5]

2.5.3   Flexible-Manufacturing-Linked Scope Economies

As mentioned earlier, Japanese industry is eagerly adopting a new factory system of flexible manufacturing capable of meeting the rising sophistication of consumers and corporate customers and their ever-diversifying tastes and needs, both at home and abroad. A firm's capability to respond speedily to the changing demand conditions is becoming one of the most crucial determinants of competitiveness, especially in advanced countries' markets where their income elasticity of demand for mass-manufactured, off-the-shelf products is on the wane, while that for custom-tailored, idiosyncratic variety-based, high-end manufactures is on the rise. Time-based competition (how quickly firms can identify customers' needs and develop a product with those attributes that specifically satisfy them) is clearly a new element in global corporate strategy (Stalk and Hout, 1990).

Indeed, the emergent factory system of flexible manufacturing – the CIM system referred to earlier – is devoted to the new 'product variation and economies of scope' approach instead of the conventional 'one product and economies of scale' approach.

It is only very recently that the power of flexible manufacturing has been discovered and exploited by manufacturers – perhaps so far most vigorously in Japan. This is revealed in a study conducted by a group of researchers at Massachusetts Institute of Technology on what they call 'lean production' in automobiles:

> [A question that] crops up when we review our survey findings with companies is product variety and complexity. The factory manager . . . who maintained he could compete with anyone if he could only focus his factory on a single standardized product, is typical of many Western managers . . .
>
> However, in our survey we could find no correlation at all between the number of models and body styles being run down a production line and either productivity or product quality. We tried a different approach by comparing what was being built in plants around the world in terms of 'under-the-skin' complexity. This was a composite measure composed of the number of main body wire harnesses, exterior paint colors, and engine/ transmission combinations being installed on a production line, plus the number of different parts being installed and the number of different suppliers to an assembly plant. The results were even less assuring to those thinking that a focused factory is the solution to their competitive problems; the plants in our survey with the highest under-the-skin complexity also had the highest productivity and quality. These of course were the Japanese plants in Japan.   (Womack, Jones and Roos, 1990, p. 98)

The age of mass production based on the crude principles of component proliferation and vertical specialization is just about over; flexible manufacturing requires an integrated or holistic framework for production in which workers themselves, as well as machinery, need to be *interchangeable* between different job assignments – in addition to parts and components being interchangeable for different product lines or models. The arrival of this new era of manufacturing is well-summarized in the following observation:

> We assume that the benefits of simplifying individual tasks and parceling them out exceed the cost of weaving the separate pieces back together to form a whole cloth. (We often fail to see the paradox in simultaneously accepting that the whole exceeds the sum of its parts and that the whole

can be reconstructed from its parts.) This implicit assumption is rarely questioned and almost never subject to scrutiny: experienced executives . . . confronting a task too large to handle on their own move instinctively to break it down into smaller pieces and assign them to specialized individuals whose performance is then monitored and coordinated by other specialists.

The business success of today is starting to march to a different drummer: multipurpose machinery, multifunctional workers, flexible organization, multifunctional parts, knowledge orientation, and systems approach. In short: integration. (Hessel, Mooney and Zeleny, 1988, p. 123)

Flexible manufacturing enables manufacturers to escape from the 'tyranny' of scale economies that constrain the full development of variety. Interestingly enough, Japanese industry serendipitously stumbled upon the stage of flexible manufacturing as it strove to perfect the factory system of limited-variety, mass manufacturing by rationalizing work flows and inventory management and adopting computer-controlled robotics. These efforts have turned out to be the vital prerequisite steps to build 'smart factories' (Ozawa, 1991c). Flexible manufacturing is no doubt making its debut as the dominant *modus operandi* for industrial production.

We can summarize, in terms of a historical loop (Figure 2.4), the evolutionary struggle to resolve the conflict between the need to reduce unit production costs and the ever-rising demand for product variety. Here we can tie our analysis of scale and scope economies to the three-stage sequential development of 'craft production', 'mass production', and 'lean production' (Womack, Jones and Roos, 1990).

2.6 SCOPE-ECONOMIES-MOTIVATED FORMS OF MULTINATIONAL BUSINESS

In this section the preceding typology of scope economies will be used as a framework within which to analyse mainly the behaviours of Japanese multinationals in Europe, though some reference will be made to European multinationals in Japan.

As stated earlier, postwar Japanese industry has evolved since the end of the Second World War through three distinct phases of industrialization and is currently in a new phase of metamorphosis. And its restructuring pattern has *coincided* with the evolutionary changes in the source of scope economies. In fact, because of the rapidity and momentum of industrial catching-up, Japan seems to have out-metamorphosed Europe, and has consequently evolved to reach

*Figure 2.4   A historical loop of tradeoff between variety and unit pro-
         duction cost*

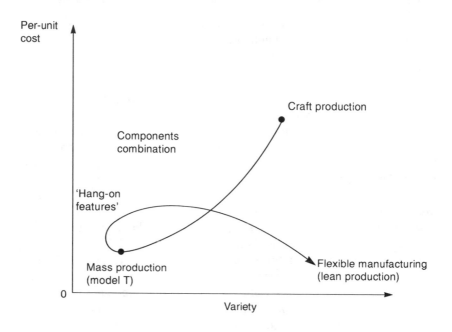

Source: The idea of depicting this historical trend is borrowed from Womack, Jones and
       Roos (1990, Figure 5.7, p. 126) who illustrate relationships between 'volume per
       product' and 'number of products on sale'.

a somewhat more advanced phase where scope economies are taking
on new characteristics.

When Japan was in the phase of heavy and chemical industrialization
(the late 1950s to the mid–1970s), *inter-industry* trade was clearly the
most desirable form of international business; Japan imported raw
materials, processed them at home and shipped back finished goods
to the world market. Japan was an 'open-economy' processing
workshop. Its overseas investments were therefore confined to the
extractive industries (*resource-seeking* investments in the exploration
and mining of mineral resources and the extraction of oil and natural
gas) on the upstream end of the workshop activities, and to the
overseas marketing facilities (*trade-supportive* investments by trading
companies and manufacturers in sales and procurement networks) on

the downstream end. Little interest was shown by Japan's heavy and chemical industries in overseas manufacturing investment (though they did make some such investments in Brazil as early as the late 1950s, but these investments were relatively limited in value and were exceptional). Nor were the European firms which had comparative advantages in such scale-dependent industries as fine chemicals, pharmaceuticals and industrial machinery attracted to Japan as a site for manufacturing investment. Europe did, however, license modern technologies to Japanese firms. International businesses were thus confined largely to exporting and licensing, namely, the market-orientated, 'flow-based' forms of exchange. Both sides were thus constrained by the existence of scale economies at home from FDI, except in trade-supportive marketing facilities.

Indeed, Japanese enterprises pushed the limit of scale economies in these industries to new heights. Some of them, such as Nippon Steel Corporation and Mitsubishi Heavy Industries, soon emerged as among the world's largest corporations in terms of physical assets and output capacities. Consequently, Chandler-type scope economies (joint production and joint distribution based on a large set of physical facilities) did come into existence but they were exploited at home whenever any additional linkage opportunities appeared – not only because of the geographical fixity of such economies associated with infrastructural physical inputs but also because of the policy of the Japanese government to foster industrialization at home. Thus Chandler-type scope economies exerted *all the more* pressure for export promotion – and *all the less* pressure for overseas manufacturing. Japanese industry was thus able to develop scale-competitive exports in steel, chemicals, ships and machinery. These exports were mostly intermediated by their general trading companies which opened marketing subsidiaries, branches and representative offices in Europe and elsewhere throughout the world.

It should be noted, however, that the success of heavy and chemical industrialization, a development process intensive in the use of physical capital (plant installation), did cause a sharp rise in wages and labour shortages, thereby compelling Japan's labour-intensive industries, notably textiles and sundries, to set up subsidiaries (mostly joint ventures) in lower-wage developing countries, the first postwar wave of Japanese manufacturing investments to transfer abroad comparative advantage in labour-intensive goods (Kojima, 1978; Ozawa, 1979). The appreciation of the yen that occurred in the early 1970s was an additional incentive. In fact, these manufacturing investments occurred at the end of Japan's labour-intensive industrialization, marking the 'elementary' stage of Japan's multinationalism. At this phase of Japan's industrial evolution Europe remained the export market and was clearly not an appropriate host for this genre of Japanese investments.

Soon afterwards, assembly-based, components-combining industries, notably automobiles, began to grow phenomenally in Japan, creating opportunities for Casson-type scope economies. At the same time, innovation-driven, yet assembly-based industries, especially semiconductors and consumer electronics, likewise began to appear successfully in Japan, thriving on learning-based scope economies. Japan was thus ushered into an era of assembly-based industrialization (the late 1960s to the present) – to a much deeper extent than Europe which, in comparison, tended to fall behind in a competitive struggle to develop the mass production of automobiles and electronics.

The Japanese manufacturers launched their first exports to the American market so swiftly that trade conflict soon arose and they had to divert them to the European markets. In Europe, too, the success of their exports caused friction, and before long Japanese exporters of assembly-based goods – first, electronics, and more recently, automobiles – had no choice but to set up local production.

Given the fact that these assembly-based industries are characterized by Casson-type scope economies, the Japanese exporters initially transplanted only the final stage of assembly operations on to Europe to cling to their export markets for the most successful models. Subassemblies, parts and components continued to be exported from Japan. No wonder, then, that final-assembly or 'screwdriver' plants became so prevalent. These plants have been built rather more frequently by Japanese multinationals than by others, but this development is not unusual to anyone familiar with the nature of the modern assembly technologies and the export competitiveness of Japan's assembly-based industries. In this regard, Richard E. Caves (1971, p. 13) makes an incisive observation:

> If scale economies are significant but prevail at only one stage of fabrication, the foreign firm may be able to carry out that process at a single location and transplant only the others ('assembly operations') to its subsidiary. Thus, foreign subsidiaries are typically less integrated vertically than the domestic firms with which they compete, and the manufacturing operations of subsidiaries less integrated than home production by the parent enterprise.

The lack of vertical integration in overseas subsidiaries inevitably leads to the demand for procurements of locally produced parts and components, hence local-content requirements. In short, Casson-type scope economies are responsible for the appearance of 'screwdriver' plants and subsequent controversy on local content.

Understandably, local reactions to these final-assembly plants are unfavourable so long as they are owned and operated by foreign manufacturers, especially by those who have injured local competitors through exports. Yet, interestingly enough, 'screwdriver' plants are less controversial when they are owned and ran by local interests. Hence, various forms of strategic alliance have been employed. *Consignment production* or a production agreement is such an arrangement, under which a local firm assembles imported subassemblies ('knockdown' kits) of a foreign competitor's model – and most often markets it as its own product line under its own brand.

This form of strategic alliance is essentially a scheme to *share* in scale-based scope economies between foreign multinationals and local producers; that is, the former retain scale economies in components production, while the latter gain from scale and scope economies (joint production and joint marketing) by utilizing the existing local assembly lines and marketing facilities. Honda Motor Co., for example, had a consignment production contract with the Rover Group in the UK under which the latter assembled Honda's Ballade cars and marketed them as Rover 200s. Suzuki Motor and Daihatsu Motor also have production consignments in Italy.

Another variant of strategic alliance is local production through a new joint venture of a hitherto-imported model to be marketed separately under partners' different brand names. For example, Mitsubishi Motor, AB Volvo and the Dutch government reportedly signed a letter of intent to transform Volvo's Dutch venture (Volvo Car BV is currently 70 per cent owned by the Dutch government) into a three-way joint venture with the participation of Mitsubishi Motor. The Japanese partner expects to secure 30 per cent of the Dutch venture to produce, by the mid–1990s, 70,000 Mitsubishi Mirage autos annually alongside the 130,000 Volvos currently manufactured by the Dutch plant. Their future plan includes a joint production of 'vehicles with different bodies but similar insides' (an arrangement homologous to the Mitsubishi–Chrysler venture in Illinois and the GM–Toyota venture in California). They plan to replace the old engines currently supplied by Renault of France with clean-burning Mitsubishi engines, but Renault itself may join the Volvo–Mitsubishi project.[6]

This 'production-sharing, separate marketing' arrangement is a conflict-avoiding scheme designed to renovate and reactivate idle physical facilities (scale) that exist in the host economy and simultaneously to exploit scope economies in marketing. Mazda and Ford are similarly taking this approach. Honda and the Rover Group are, however, setting up a new plant in Swindon, UK, along with a stock swap of 20 per cent interest, to deepen their ties in R&D and production-sharing.

In addition, another tack to avoid trade friction is being employed by many Japanese manufacturers of photocopiers, video cassette recorders (VCRs), colour TV sets, facsimile machines, computers, printers, camcorders, machine tools and other successful exports. They are resorting to what is popularly called *original equipment manufacturing* (OEM) contracts with leading local manufacturers or distributors who are incapable of competitively producing comparable products but are interested in marketing under their own brand names the products made in Japan. The models produced under OEM are differentiated from the producers' own export models, hence consumers in Europe are offered a wider lineup of models. Under this arrangement, Chandler-type scale-based scope economies are split up into the scale and the scope components, the former (joint production) being retained by Japanese manufacturers, while the latter (joint distribution) is exploited by European firms.

OEM may be regarded as 'disguised' exports but it can also be considered as an intermediate step between exporting and FDI, just as licensing is. From the point of view of OEM exporters, the OEM contract is an effective way of delegating marketing functions to foreign firms and learning foreign preferences, thereby reducing the marginal cost of a possible entry into local production in the future. OEM importers, on the other hand, may be induced at a later time to set up a joint venture to manufacture the product locally if the OEM arrangement proves successful. OEM is no doubt responsible for a large volume of intracompany trade. (One estimate shows that as much as one-third of Japanese manufactured exports to the US are OEM-created (Morita, 1986), though the proportion for Europe is probably much lower at present.)

The growth of OEM contracts reflects not only the importance of scale-based scope economies but also learning-based scope economies. The more rapid the pace of technological progress and innovation (hence, the shorter the product cycle) and the more locationally clustered the incidence of innovation (hence, the greater the possibility of trade conflict), the more frequent the occurrence of OEM agreements. Learning-based scope economies are often responsible for the willingness of innovators to accept OEM contracts for the sake of securing scale-satisfying output and delegating marketing functions to local distributors. This willingness is perhaps much stronger for small-scale manufacturers. OEM can be construed as an international division of corporate value-adding functions between production and marketing, a sharing scheme designed to exploit the scope economies of both the scale-based and the learning-based types.

The importance of local preferences for product development is well reflected in the recent growth of FDI in R&D/design/engineering ventures. Both Japanese and European multinationals are now eagerly setting up these ventures either as auxiliary corporate units or as separate independent units in each other's markets. These facilities are intended to respond to local customers' changing needs and tastes as well as to capture the locality-specific innovation-conducive assets that can be capitalized upon in developing new products and varieties. Japanese multinationals in particular are interested in letting local talent develop new products or varieties that can also be exported back to Japan – and elsewhere. This import-back scheme may be called a 'develop and manufacture locally and then import back' arrangement. Japanese firms are increasingly eager to employ this approach to internalize access to their rapidly growing home markets.

As for flexible-manufacturing-linked scope economies, it remains to be seen what forms of multinationalism will emerge. No doubt, the adoption of flexible manufacturing will facilitate Japan's efforts to upgrade its industry by discarding limited-variety, large-lot mass manufacturing. Flexible manufacturing is a necessity for the survival of Japanese industry, which has been transferring mass production of standardized, low-end manufactures overseas. For example, Hitachi Ltd has increased refrigerator imports from its subsidiary in Thailand. Initially it shipped back home annually 10,000 small refrigerators with 120-litre capacity, but now plans to import 20,000 medium-sized ones annually in addition to the small model. In the meantime, at Hitachi's home plants in Japan, computer-integrated manufacturing systems are being introduced to make higher-value-added, large refrigerators by responding more effectively to changes in users' needs.[7]

At the moment, in fact, Japanese multinationals have no intention to transplant CIM systems to their European operations – perhaps not only because such systems are still in the developmental stage and need to be perfected, but also because Europe has promising vast markets for standardized manufactures. They are concentrating on transplanting overseas the large-scale mass production of standardized products or models such as semiconductors, medium-end VCRs, cordless telephones, printers, photocopiers and the popular low-end models of automobiles in a trickle-down fashion, while developing and retaining higher-end products at home. This approach still represents ethno-centrically orientated multinationalism whose major function is to use overseas investments as a means of industrial shedding and as catalysts for industrial upgrading at home.

Yet there are some Japanese multinationals who are fast becoming less ethnocentric and more geocentric in orientation, to use Perlmutter's (1969) terminology. For example, Honda's motorcycle manufacturing overseas provides a new paradigm of how a multinational may be able to capture both scale *and* scope economies as strategic advantages by operating in a geocentric manner.

Honda has so far established four manufacturing subsidiaries, one each in Italy (100 per cent-owned Honda Italia Industriale SpA), Belgium (100 per cent-owned Honda Belgium NV), France (equity-acquired Honda France Industries SA) and Spain (87 per cent-owned Montesa Honda SA). Each produces Honda's motorcycles in various models that are separately designed and developed to suit locality-specific tastes (the most marketable combination of attributes) in each host economy and imports each other's models to complement their product lineups for consumers. In addition, they also import high-end American-made Honda motorcycles (large GL–1500 Grand Touring models), as well as those manufactured in Brazil (smaller low-end models).

Each location thus specializes in a given set of unique models ('lead' models) for which the local demand is most strong and which can best be designed, engineered and manufactured by local technical staff and workers. The result is that each manufacturing subsidiary produces the lead model not only for the major segment of its own local market but also for other countries' otherwise-untapped markets through intracompany exports, complementing and supporting each other's marketing efforts (economies of joint distribution) as a totality. Each is thus able to exploit both scale economies in manufacturing and scope economies in marketing, the best of both worlds. This is a fully multinationalized version of Chandler-type scope economies. Honda is also moving to capture Casson-type scope economies by promoting the interchangeability of basic parts and components and their production in the most cost-effective locations.

It should be noted that Honda can pursue this geocentric strategy, since it dominates the world market for motorcycles. It is trying to replicate the same approach in automobiles (its American-designed Accord Coupé is presently exported to Canada, Japan, Taiwan, Australia and New Zealand) – but so far its attempt is still undeveloped and may meet some difficulty because of its much-smaller global market share.

This 'localized-manufacturing-cum-global-marketing' approach can be schematically summarized in terms of the modified neo-Hotelling-Lancasterian 'taste spectrum' lines (Hotelling, 1929; Lancaster, 1966, 1984; Lyons, 1984), as shown in Figure 2.5. The taste spectrum ranks the intensity of a particular attribute preferred by consumers relative to another attribute both embodied in a given model. For example, attribute 1 may represent a high-end characteristic and attribute n a low-end characteristic. A dot indicates the production of a lead model most popularly demanded in that locality (hence at the top of a bell-shaped distribution curve), and an arrow indicates the direction of exports from each location. A set of brackets shows a range of preferences that are satisfied by a given model with a particular combination of attributes, though the model becomes less and less ideal for consumers as their tastes move further away from the dot. In short, under this geocentric strategy, scale-based scope economies are fully multinationalized and appropriated through the medium of optimally localized manufacturing and intracompany trade. This is perhaps the most rationalized and integrated mode of multinational operations that Japanese corporations are striving to achieve by way of restructuring their existing investments in post–1992 Europe where large-scale markets are in the making for locally differentiated and locally produced products. For this 'ideal' form of multinational manufacturing and marketing to occur, the firm involved first needs to possess some dominant technological and marketing prowess (such as a strong brand attraction).

In the light of all this flurry of strategic behaviours on the part of Japanese multinationals in Europe, one may wonder how European multinationals in Japan are reacting to the new age of multivariety manufacturing. Are they too adopting the new approaches? Interestingly enough, they are likewise restructuring their business activities, now that the Japanese market has become equally as important a regional core market in the Pacific Rim as is America's.

First of all, European multinationals are doubling their efforts to expand market share in the growing Japanese markets by cancelling sales-agency agreements with local distributors and setting up their own subsidiaries for distribution. For example, the pharmaceutical companies Bayer AG of Germany and Sandoz AG of Switzerland have taken this approach. Many European firms are also moving into local production by discarding licensing agreements. These moves are intended to *recapture* the economies of joint distribution and joint

Figure 2.5   Honda's multinational 'interleaving' of the 'split' taste spectrums

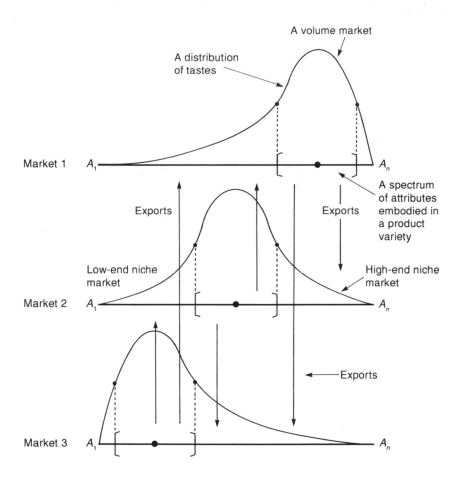

A taste (attribute) spectrum = $A_1, A_2, A_3, \ldots, + A_n$

production (scale-based scope economies) which used to be given to their Japanese partners, since the European multinationals are now able to market a larger variety of products in the increasingly affluent Japanese markets – large enough to justify investments in their own facilities (scale); previously only limited lines of products were sold, hence the European firms were willing to consign marketing and production functions to Japanese firms. They are presently consolidating their business activities by pursuing an increased internalization of corporate value-adding operations.

As briefly mentioned earlier, European multinationals are also active in establishing R&D/design/engineering centres in Japan. They are aiming to develop product varieties that appeal specifically to local needs and preferences. For example, Unilever NV of Holland has developed a locally popular shampoo which now ranks number three among the leading brands in Japan. Other European multinationals such as Tetra Pak of Sweden, ICI of England, Ciba-Geigy of Switzerland and Hoechst of Germany opened new research centres to develop products for the local markets.

Another notable move is the investment made by a group of German companies in Hiroyama High-Tech Industrial Park (Yokohama). Many are medium-sized firms which have been exporting to Japan but which are now more interested in locally manufacturing such technology-intensive, specialty products as electric connectors and laser-cutting machines. They are led by a German real-estate firm which has built plant and office facilities for the purpose of leasing them to the German firms. So far, more than 20 German firms have reportedly signed up to participate in this group-based investment project (JETRO, 1988). Some European multinationals are even resorting to outright acquisition of Japanese firms. Boehringer Mannheim of Germany, Cookson of UK and Adolt Welt of Germany all purchased medium-sized Japanese firms to secure direct local manufacturing and distribution.

Although the value of European investment in Japan is about one-tenth of Japanese corporations' investment in Europe, European multinationals are increasingly attracted to the growth of Japanese markets and technological capacity. They recognize the necessity of locating product development and manufacturing in close proximity to Japanese customers – as Japanese multinationals are to European customers. In short, then, both Japanese and European investments are 'customer-pulled' and 'technology-interactive' in each other's market.

2.7 CONCLUSIONS

Japanese industry is at present interacting with its European counterparts on the newly emerged bases of comparable tastes, technological congruity and industrial sophistication, now that it has succeeded in catching up and closing the gaps in technology and *per capita* income.

In this current phase of economic interchange, manufacturers' ability to respond in a timely manner to the changing needs and tastes of local customers in terms of providing those models and varieties that offer the locally most-demanded combinations of particular product attributes (the 'lead' volume models that can cater to the modal portion of the bell-shaped distribution of preferences) has emerged as the critical determinant of competitiveness. In this 'customer-pulled' and 'technology-interactive' phase of multinationalism, allied with the new era of regionalism (intra-bloc trade liberalization with barriers against outsiders), localized product development and manufacturing is the *sine qua non* for corporate survival. Furthermore, the nature of modern industry and of international business have both evolved in such a direction that the opportunities for scope economies can be capitalized on through multinational business activities more easily than before without being much constrained by the requirements for scale economies.

This chapter has explored the evolutionary configurations of scope economies. The explicit recognition and conceptualization of the role of product variation and scope economies in motivating overseas business presented above can shed light on the recent rush of Japanese multinationals to Europe – and, in turn, European multinationals' to Japan; and they can also help us to understand why lately there have appeared such diverse strategic forms of business interaction as consignment production (sometimes accompanied by cross-shareholding), OEM and the 'production-sharing, separately branded marketing' joint ventures, final-assembly operations ('screwdriver' plants), R&D/design/engineering ventures, and the 'develop and manufacture locally, then import back' arrangements. These 'new' forms are reflective of local preferences ('customer-pulled'), focused on local technological resources ('technology-interactive') variety-expanding, and scope-economies-driven in motivation – in contrast to the 'old' form of FDI which is supply-sided, 'excess-capacity-pushed' but scale-economies-constrained and standardization-driven in motivation.

The former have emerged from the necessity to balance the need to offer local-preference-specific products against the constraint of minimum-scale requirements. Some of these forms may be only the transient phenomena we can observe before multi-variety, small-lot flexible manufacturing itself is globally adopted.

Indeed, modern manufacturing technology is in the transitional phase from mass production to lean or flexible production. We are, in a sense, returning to the era of multi-variety, custom-tailored production once pioneered by craft production – but this time at much lower per-unit costs. Concomitant with the changes in production technology have evolved the nature and extent of scope economies – and of international production. Craft production entails scope diseconomies, mass production exploits scale economies, and flexible production thrives on scope economies. These are the qualitatively demarcating changes of technological accumulation in modern capitalism. In the new era of flexible production both supply- and demand-side factors are unitized into an integrated value-added operation. This represents the trajectory convergence and intersection of the paths of technological progress and taste diversification.

In a recent survey of theories of FDI and multinational corporations, John Cantwell (1991b, p. 41) observes:

> Macroeconomic development approaches relate the investment position of firms to the industrial progression of their home country. They may be demand-side or supply-side driven; in the PCM [product cycle model] the growth of demand leads the relocation of production, while in the arguments of Kojima and Ozawa or Cantwell and Tolentino the emphasis is on supply-side opportunities and constraints in the course of industrial restructuring. However, in each case the underlying development process has both demand-side and supply-side aspects to it.

It is hoped that the analysis presented here fills some of the lacunae in the much-needed demand-side analysis of the evolutionary development of multinational corporations' activities, an analysis that can dovetail with the supply-sided focus of technological trajectory – especially in terms of the recently emerged form of time-based, variety-oriented product development and flexible manufacturing.

NOTES

1. Statistics on manufacturing investments reported by the Japanese Ministry of Finance (MOF) on an approval basis, as reproduced in JETRO (1990, p. 2).
2. Statistics in this section are based on those from MOF as reported in MITI (1990, p. 181).
3. Real incomes are computed in terms of the indices prepared by OECD (Emmott, 1989).
4. 'CIM – the Manufacturing/Information Wave of the Future', *Tokyo Business Today*, **58**, (8), August 1990.
5. 'Now Software isn't Safe from Japan', *Business Week*, 11 Feb., 1991, p. 84.
6. 'Mitsubishi is Taking a Back Road into Europe', *Business Week*, 19 Nov., 1990, p. 64; *Wall Street Journal*, 6 May, 1991, p. A11.
7. *Nihon Keizai Shimbun*, 30 Oct., 1990, p. 13.

REFERENCES

Baumol, William J. (1967), 'Calculations of Optimal Product and Retailer Characteristics: the Abstract Product Approach', *Journal of Political Economy*, **75**, October.

Cantwell, John A. (1989), *Technological Innovation and Multinational Corporations*, Oxford: Basil Blackwell.

Cantwell, John A. (1990), 'The Technological Competence Theory of International Production and its Implications', *University of Reading Discussion Papers in International Investment and Business Studies*, No. 149.

Cantwell, John A. (1991a), 'The Technological Competence Theory of International Production and its Implications', in Don McFetridge (ed.), *Foreign Investment, Technology and Economic Growth*, Calgary: University of Calgary Press.

Cantwell, John A. (1991b), 'A Survey of Theories of International Production,' in C.N. Pitelies and R. Sugden (eds), *The Nature of the Transnational Firm*, London: Routledge.

Casson, Mark C. (1990), *Enterprise and Competitiveness: A Systems View of International Business*, Oxford: Clarendon Press.

Caves, Richard E. (1971), 'International Corporations: the Industrial Economics of Foreign Investment', *Economica*, **38**, February.

Chandler, Alfred D. Jr. (1990), *Scale and Scope: The Dynamics of Industrial Capitalism*, Cambridge, Mass.: Harvard University Press.

DeBresson, Chris (1989), 'Breeding Innovation Clusters: a Source of Dynamic Development', *World Development*, **17**.

Dunning, John H. (1988), *Multinationals, Technology and Competitiveness*, London: Unwin Hyman.

Economist (1991), 'What Makes Yoshio Invent', 21 January.

Emmott, Bill (1989), *The Sun Also Sets: The Limits of Japan's Economic Power*, New York: Simon & Schuster.

Hessel, Mark P., Mooney, Marta and Zeleny, Milan (1988), 'Integrated Process Management: a Management Technology for the New Competitive Era', in Martink Starr (ed.), *Global Competitiveness: Getting the U.S. Back on Track*, New York: Norton.

Hotelling, H. (1929), 'Stability in Competition', *Economic Journal*, **34**, January.

JETRO (1988), *Sekaito Nihon no Kaigai Chokusetsutoshi* [Japanese and Global Foreign Direct Investment], Tokyo: JETRO.

JETRO (Japan External Trade Organization) (1990), *Zaiou Seigogyo Keiei no Jittai* [Business Conditions of Japanese Manufacturing in Europe], Report No. 6, Tokyo: JETRO.

Kogut, Bruce (1988), 'Country Patterns in International Competition: Appropriability and Oligopolistic Agreement,' in N. Hood and J.E. Vahlne (eds), *Strategies in Global Competition*, London: Croom Helm.

Kojima, Kiyoshi (1978), *Direct Foreign Investment: A Japanese Model of Multinational Business Operations*, New York: Praeger.

Lancaster, Kelvin (1966), 'A New Approach to Consumer Theory', *Journal of Political Economy*, **74**, April.

Lancaster, Kelvin (1984), 'Protection and Product Differentiation', in Henryk

Kierzkowski (ed.), *Monopolistic Competition and International Trade*, Oxford: Clarendon Press.

Linder, Stephan B. (1961), *An Essay on Trade and Transformation*, New York: John Wiley.

Lyons, Bruce R. (1984), 'The Pattern of International Trade in Differentiated Products: an Incentive for the Existence of Multinational Firms', in Henryk Kierzkowski (ed.), *Monopolistic Competition and International Trade*, Oxford: Clarendon Press.

Malmgren, Harald B. (1990), 'Technology and the Economy', in W. Brock and R. Hormats (eds), *The Global Economy: America's Role in the Decade Ahead*, New York: W.W. Norton.

MITI (Japanese Ministry of Trade and Industry) (1990), *Gaishikei Kigyo no Doko* [Trends of Foreign-affiliated Firms in Japan], Tokyo: Government Printing Office.

Morita, Akio (1986), *Made in Japan*, New York: New American Library.

Ozawa, Terutomo (1979), *Multinationalism, Japanese Style: The Political Economy of Outward Dependency*, Princeton, N.J.: Princeton University Press.

Ozawa, Terutomo (1991a), 'Europe 1992 and Japanese Multinationals: Transplanting a Subcontracting System in the Expanded Market', in B. Burgenmeier and J.L. Mucchielli (eds), *Multinationals and Europe 1992*, London: Routledge.

Ozawa, Terutomo (1991b), 'The Dynamics of Pacific Rim Industrialism: How Mexico Can Join the Asian Flock of Flying Geese', in Riordan Roett (ed.), *Mexico's External Relations in the 1990s*, Boulder, Col.: Lynne Rienner.

Ozawa, Terutomo (1991c), 'Japan in a New Phase of Multinationalism and Industrial Upgrading: Functional Integration of Trade, Growth, and FDI', *Journal of World Trade*, **25**, February.

Panzar, John C. and Willig, Robert D. (1981), 'Economies of Scope', *American Economic Review*, **71**, May.

Penrose, Edith T. (1959), *The Theory of the Growth of the Firm*, Oxford: Basil Blackwell.

Perlmutter, Howard V. (1969), 'The Tortuous Evolution of the Multinational Corporation', *Columbia Journal of World Business*, **4**, January–February.

Saito, A. (1990), 'Gijitsu Kakushin to Sekai Keizai [Innovations and the World Economy]', in M. Ikema and K. Ikemoto (eds), *Kokusai Boeki to Seisanron no shintenkan* [New Developments in International Trade and Production Theory], Tokyo: Bunshindo.

Stalk, George Jr and Hout, Thomas M. (1990), *Competing Against Time: How Time-based Competition is Reshaping Global Markets*, New York: Free Press.

Teece, David (1980), 'Economies of Scope and the Scope of the Enterprise', *Journal of Economic Behavior and Organization*, **1**, September.

Toyo Keizai (1989), *Gaishikei Kigyo Soran* [Data Book on Foreign-affiliated Firms in Japan], Tokyo: Toyo Keizai.

Womack, James P., Jones, Daniel T. and Roos, Daniel (1990), *The Machine that Changed the World*, New York: Maxwell Macmillan.

3. Direct Investment between the United States and the European Community Post-1986 and Pre-1992

Edward M. Graham

3.1 INTRODUCTION

During the late 1980s foreign direct investment (FDI) flowed among developed countries at rates unprecedented in history. The majority of the flows were among the three major developed regions of the world: Europe, North America and Japan. The flows between Europe and North America were roughly symmetric, in the sense that substantial FDI flowed both directions. But between Japan and both Europe and North America the flows were highly asymmetric: substantial FDI flowed out of Japan into both these regions, but relatively little FDI flowed from Europe or North America into Japan. However, an earlier asymmetry was broken: since the Second World War the United States had been predominantly a source of FDI rather than a host to it, but during the second half of the 1980s massive amounts of FDI flowed into the United States, making it the world's largest host nation by the end of the decade. During the second half of the 1980s the book value of the stock of FDI in the United States more than doubled, from $184.6 billion at the end of 1985 to $403.7 billion at the end of 1990.

The majority (almost 64 per cent) of the stock of FDI (measured on the basis of historic cost) in the United States in 1990 was from Europe. Similarly, almost half the stock of US outward investment (again measured on the basis of historic cost) was located in Europe, and in most member states of the European Community US direct investment exceeded that from any other single nation.

1990 saw a sharp downturn in the rate of foreign direct investment in the United States. More is said about this later in the chapter.

This chapter surveys direct investment flows between the United

States and Europe. First, recent direct investment in Europe from the United States is examined. The original intent of the author was to provide a detailed analysis of this investment and of European direct investment in the United States. The level of detail the author hoped to achieve cannot be done at the time of this writing, however, because the Bureau of Economic Analysis (BEA), the division of the US Department of Commerce that collects and compiles the relevant data, had not yet released the results of its 1988 'benchmark' survey of US outward investment upon which the analysis would depend. The main focus of the chapter, therefore, is on European direct investment in the United States. In particular, efforts are made to sort out some of the main differences between investment from the different European nations, and to compare European direct investment with that from Japan.

3.2   US DIRECT INVESTMENT IN EUROPE: SOME HIGHLIGHTS

Previously published work by this author has examined US-controlled firms' strategies in Europe in light of the 'Europe 1992' programme and related exercises to integrate more completely the economies of the European Community nations (Graham, 1991; the reader might also wish to read Yannopoulos, 1991). What is attempted in this section is a brief update of this previous paper. Highlights of the previous paper are: (a) relatively low measured flows of FDI to Europe from the United States were recorded in the years 1986–8, but these were rather poor indicators of adjustments being made by European affiliates of US firms to a more fully integrated Europe. In general, US firms were adjusting their strategies in Europe by means of rationalizing and integrating their European operations across national boundaries, but these strategic moves did not show up as significant changes in recorded flows of FDI; (b) a better indicator of the rate of strategic adjustment than FDI flow was the rate of new capital expenditures of European affiliates of US firms; these expenditures accelerated significantly following 1986; (c) the reaction of these affiliates to moves towards greater European integration was not uniform across industries or even across firms within one particular industry. In some industries, certain US-controlled firms were developing expansionary pan-European strategies, although these strategies typically were subject to local variation to meet specific differences that exist among national and subnational market segments within Europe. In other industries, US-controlled firms were in a process of retrenchment (and in some cases abandonment) of their European operations.

Table 3.1 indicates that new capital expenditures by (majority-owned) European affiliates of US firms have continued to grow very rapidly since 1989 (the latest year for which data were reported in Graham, 1991). Some fall-off in the rate of growth of these expenditures was forecast for 1991, but even so the forecast was for 11 per cent growth, a rather robust figure in the light of the recession in much of Europe. The United Kingdom remained the most important locus for new capital expenditure. Whereas in the earlier paper only modest growth in these expenditures was reported in Germany, the figures reported in Table 3.1 indicate quite substantial increases there.

Table 3.1   Capital expenditures by majority-owned affiliates in Europe of US firms

	1987a	1988a	1989a	1990b	1991b
European Community					
$ billions	16.1	19.8	22.7	29.0	32.1
% change from previous year	13	23	15	28	11
France					
$ billions	2.3	2.4	2.7	3.5	3.9
% change from previous year	15	2	12	31	10
Germany					
$ billions	3.3	3.9	4.5	5.7	6.7
% change from previous year	− 3	19	14	28	20
United Kingdom					
$ billions	6.2	8.6	9.8	11.8	13.4
% change from previous year	25	39	13	21	13

a = actual expenditures
b = planned expenditures
Source: US Department of Commerce, *Survey of Current Business*, March 1991.

Table 3.2 indicates these capital expenditures for 1989 (the latest year for which data on actual, rather than planned, expenditures are available), broken down by major industry and by country. Overall, as reported in the earlier paper, the majority (almost 60 per cent) of the expenditures took place in the manufacturing industries. The distribution of expenditures by industry varied considerably by country. Over 80 per cent of the expenditure in the petroleum industry was located in the United Kingdom, reflecting presumably the importance of North Sea oil. A higher percentage of manufacturing investment was located in the United Kingdom than in any other EC nation as well, with Germany a not-too-distant second. (Interestingly, the United Kingdom has been the most important locus within Europe for Japanese direct investment as well, both in the aggregate and in the manufacturing sector. See, for example, Thomsen and Nicolaides, 1991. The preference of both US- and Japan-based firms for UK locations stands in some contradiction to an hypothesis introduced later in this chapter, that *outward* direct investment from the United Kingdom is attributable in part to the loss of location advantages by the United Kingdom.)

Table 3.2   1989 capital expenditures by majority-owned European affiliates of US firms, by country and by industry ($ billions)

Country/Industry	EC	France	Germany	UK
All industries	22.7	2.7	4.5	9.8
Petroleum	4.6	0.2	0.2	3.7
Manufacturing (total)	13.1	1.6	3.3	4.1
Food, etc.	1.1	0.1	0.1	0.4
Chemicals, etc	3.1	0.4	0.5	0.7
Non-electrical machinery	2.2	0.5	0.7	0.5
Transportation equipment	2.7	0.1	1.1	1.1
Other mfg	3.9	0.5	0.9	1.3
Wholesale trade, finance, services	5.0	0.9	0.6	1.7
All other	1.0	0.2	0.3	0.4

Source: US Department of Commerce, *Survey of Current Business*, March 1991.

Germany and the United Kingdom together accounted for over 80 per cent of all expenditure in the transportation equipment industry; presumably most of this was concentrated in the automotive industry. Capital expenditures in the chemical and non-electrical machinery industries were fairly evenly spread among all European Community nations. As might be expected, expenditures in the financial sector were concentrated in the United Kingdom; otherwise, service sector expenditures were quite evenly spread through the Community.

As was reported in the earlier paper, flows of new direct investment from the United States to Europe were not very robust from 1986 to 1988, and this situation continued into 1989. Incomplete data suggest that the pattern broke in 1990, and that significant new direct investment did flow from the United States to Europe. The full story must await the release of the US Commerce Department's detailed data on US direct investment in 1990; these data were not available at the time of writing. It appears that the new flows are largely accounted for by shifts in patterns of financing capital investment. Reduced interest rates in the United States (relative to elsewhere) coupled (perhaps) with expectations of future dollar depreciation have made the United States an attractive location for borrowing, and this shows up as changes in patterns of intrafirm borrowing and lending. In 1990 US parent firms lent significant sums to their overseas affiliates, whereas in immediately prior years these sums were either much smaller or, in some years, positive (indicating net borrowing from overseas affiliates by the parents). As is explained later in this chapter, the same changes in intrafirm borrowing and lending behaviour are apparent with respect to US affiliates of non-US firms and the relevant parent organizations.

The picture in Europe thus is one of robust activity by European affiliates of US firms. As noted in Graham (1991) rates of increase of capital expenditure of these affiliates following 1986 (the year in which the 'Europe 1992' programme entered into public consciousness) have been significantly higher than rates of increase of domestic capital formation in Europe. One cannot help but conclude that in net US-based firms are expanding their presence in Europe, in spite of moves towards retrenchment by some such firms. But, as is detailed in the following sections, European-based firms have also greatly expanded their presence in the United States. Thus, overall any expansion of US control of the European economy is one of increased globalization of business activities irrespective of the 'home' nation of the relevant firms, rather than, say, some renewal of *'le défi americain'*, as described in Servan-Schreiber (1967).

3.3 EUROPEAN DIRECT INVESTMENT IN THE UNITED STATES

The really exciting story regarding FDI flows between Europe and the United States during the late 1980s was not US direct investment in Europe but European direct investment in the United States. This is the exact opposite of the situation of 20 years ago. In this section we examine FDI in the United States and the large role in it of European firms. In doing so, we should keep in mind that European FDI in the United States should not be seen as an isolated phenomenon but rather as a part of a bigger picture to which we shall have occasion to refer.

Trying to get a grasp on the effects of European direct investment in the United States is, alas, hampered by two difficulties that must be understood at the outset. The first is that the data publicly available bearing on recent direct investment activity in the United States are neither as comprehensive nor as complete as one would need to do a definitive analysis. But one does what one can with the data that are available.

The second difficulty is the more important. It arises because much of the most recent direct investment in the United States has taken place via acquisition and takeover of existing US firms by foreign ones. The usual intent of the investor (parent) firm is to transform the firm taken over to make it part of a larger global strategy being pursued by the parent organization. Because in many cases insufficient time has elapsed for the transformation to be complete, it is premature to make strong judgements as to the consequences of recent direct investment in the United States. As is argued later in this chapter, this difficulty particularly affects any effort to evaluate recent direct investment in the United States from the United Kingdom. Indeed, a definitive evaluation of European direct investment in the United States must await the passage of time, to allow transitional effects of changes of ownership to work themselves through.

Table 3.3 provides some relevant data regarding the composition of FDI in the United States by source (home) nation for the more-important investing countries. Several points stand out from this table. First, although the book value of direct investment in the United States from Europe grew at the rather phenomenal compound rate of 14.5 per cent per annum during the years 1983–90, this rate was considerably below that for Japanese direct investors: the compound rate of growth of the stock of Japanese direct investment in the United States exceeded 28 per cent per annum over the same period.

Secondly, the rates of growth of the stock of direct investment from individual countries varied greatly. This rate for the United Kingdom was over 17 per cent, highest among the European nations, a rather remarkable fact given that at the beginning of the period the United Kingdom held the largest stock of any source nation and this stock was well over twice the beginning-of-period stock of Japanese firms.

Table 3.3   Characteristics of FDI by major host nation

FDI characteristic/ nation	FDI stock Year end 1990 ($ billions)	Compound growth rate of FDI stock (% per annum)	FDI stock (Mfg only) Year end 1990 ($ billions)	Mfg FDI as % of total (1990)
	(a)	(b)		
United Kingdom	108.1	17.3	53.0	49.0
Netherlands	64.3	11.3	24.4	37.9
Germany	27.8	13.4	15.2	54.8
Switzerland	17.5	13.2	9.1	52.0
France	19.6	12.2	14.7	75.2
Sweden	5.5	13.5	4.9	90.6
All Europe	256.5	14.5	125.6	49.0
Japan	83.5	28.5	15.2	18.2
Canada	27.7	12.7	9.3	33.6
All nations	403.7	15.4	160.0	39.6

(a)   At historic cost, 1987 benchmark basis.
(b)   Base year: 1983.
Source: US Department of Commerce, Bureau of Economic Analysis, various publications.

By contrast, the compound rate of growth of FDI from The Netherlands, the source nation holding the second largest stock at the beginning of the period, was the least among major source nations. This rate was not even two-thirds that of the United Kingdom and not 40 per cent that of Japan. The Dutch rate was indeed not even as high as that of Canada, the rate for which was reduced considerably because of difficulties experienced by just one firm, the Campeau organization. By the end of the period The Netherlands had fallen into third place on the basis of the book value of its stock of direct investment in the United States. Other European nations experienced compound rates of growth in their holdings of direct investment over this period that fell between those of the United Kingdom and The Netherlands, but most of these nations experienced rates closer to that of the latter than the former. The stock of all European direct investment in the United States grew at the relatively high compound rate of 14.5 per cent over the period, reflecting the high base level and high rate of growth of the stock held by the United Kingdom.

Why the stock of Japanese FDI in the United States grew so quickly is probably no mystery. To start, Japan's initial stock was quite low. If firm-specific advantages (here counting both 'O' and 'I' type advantages, following John Dunning's taxonomy; see Dunning, 1988a and 1988b) play a major role in determining the nature of firms' involvements in overseas markets, it is by now common wisdom that Japanese firms possess such advantages by the ream. These would include 'intangible' ownership advantages, such as ability to innovate new products quickly (these abilities seem to be a necessity in the Japanese home market), as well as other intangible advantages such as effective management techniques born of the Japanese culture (see, for example, Casson, 1990 and 1991).

Also, the technological prowess of Japan is known to be somewhat 'spotty'; that is, while this prowess is generally high and is expanding rapidly, there are significant voids in it, that is, specialized domains where Japanese prowess is not up to world standards. Thus, expansion in the United States by Japanese firms can be seen as consistent with John Cantwell's 'technological accumulation' approach, wherein firms expand in order to fill voids in their technological capabilities (see Cantwell, 1987 and 1989). Cantwell's approach also helps to explain the often-observed fact that Japanese firms pay premium prices (relative to those offered by potential domestic or European buyers) for acquisitions in the United States of on-going firms engaged in technology-intensive activities: the specific technologies possessed by the US acquisitions fit into the technological topography of the successful acquiring firm better than into the topography of competing firms.

It is somewhat more mysterious why many European firms (and why British firms in particular) should hold significant advantages over their US rivals. One possibility, of course, is that the Dunning OLI framework is not wholly adequate to explain European direct investment in the United States and some supplementary paradigm is needed (for example, oligopoly reaction, a paradigm that this author long ago advanced as an explanation of European direct investment in the

United States following the lead of Hymer and Rowthorne; see Hymer and Rowthorne, 1970; Graham, 1978). Additional comment on this latter possibility is offered later in this chapter.

Some clues to this and other issues are to be found in the sectoral distribution of the investment. Table 3.4 provides information on this distribution. Unfortunately, this table pertains to 1987, the year of the Bureau of Economic Analysis's periodic detailed 'benchmark' survey, and not to a more recent year, but the data provided in this table are the best currently available. The data also suffer somewhat from the fact that they are based on the primary industry of each reporting enterprise, that is, entire firms and not organizational subentities of firms. Although many multinational firms are diversified across several industries, the data for such firms are reported by BEA as though all activities were concentrated in what is determined to be the primary industry of that firm. In one known case where this leads to a well-known major distortion, this author has taken the liberty of rearranging the data: all Japanese data pertaining to motor vehicles are presented under 'transportation equipment' (a manufacturing category) rather than 'wholesale trade'. This rearrangement doubtlessly exaggerates the Japanese presence in the manufacture of motor vehicles in the United States, but because all of the activities of at least two of the three largest Japanese automotive firms are widely believed to be reported in the 1987 benchmark data under 'wholesale trade' (but for reasons of confidentiality, the BEA does not say for sure), the original classification enormously understates this presence.

When one looks at the industry distribution of European and Japanese direct investment in the United States, the OLI framework does seem to make some sense. The case can be advanced that European investment has taken place most heavily in industries where it has long been conceded that European firms hold ownership advantages relative to US rivals. Direct investment from the United Kingdom, for example, is relatively concentrated in petroleum, insurance, other manufacturing (where more detailed figures show heavy concentration in the stone, glass and clay and the instrument categories), chemicals (where more detailed figures show heavy concentration in industrial chemicals and pharmaceutical products), and services (where more detailed figures show heavy concentration in business services). None of this is inconsistent with one's conceptions of what are the ownership advantages of certain firms based in the UK; for example, Shell and BP are known to be strong players in the petroleum industry, Pilkington in the flat glass industry, ICI, Glaxo and Burroughs Wellcome in chemicals and pharmaceutical products, and so on.

Table 3.4   Distribution of owners' equity of US affiliates of foreign firms, by sector and by nation of ultimate beneficial ownership

Nation/sector	Japan	Europe	United Kingdom	Nether- lands	Germany	France
Petroleum	0.00	0.18	0.14	NA	0.02	0.13
Manufacturing	0.45	0.41	0.42	0.19	0.50	0.63
Food	0.01	0.03	0.04	NA	0.00	0.04
Chemicals	0.03	NA	0.09	NA	0.24	0.16
Metals	0.03	0.02	0.02	NA	0.03	0.02
Non-electric machinery	0.04	0.02	0.02	NA	NA	NA
Electrical machinery	0.01	0.06	0.03	NA	NA	NA
Transport equipment	0.29	0.01	0.01	0.00	0.00	0.08
Other mfg	0.03	NA	0.20	NA	0.10	0.20
Wholesale trade	0.17	0.10	0.08	0.01	0.18	0.12
Retail trade	0.01	0.04	0.03	0.05	0.07	0.01
Finance (excl. banking)	0.22	0.07	0.09	0.00	0.07	0.02
Insurance	0.01	0.10	0.12	0.11	0.07	0.01
Real estate	0.09	0.05	0.06	0.04	0.05	0.00
Services	0.03	0.03	0.05	0.01	0.02	0.03
Other	0.02	0.03	0.02	NA	0.04	0.06
Total	1.00	1.00	1.00	1.00	1.00	1.00

Source: US Department of Commerce, Bureau of Economic Analysis, *Foreign Direct Investment in the United States: 1987 Benchmark Results*.

An alternative explanation for outward direct investment from the United Kingdom, again consistent with OLI theory, is that this investment is driven less by ownership advantages than by location advantages (or, more precisely in this case, location disadvantages). The essential idea is that the United Kingdom itself is losing locational advantages in many industries, especially manufacturing. (One reason advanced for the loss is a running-down of human capital in the United Kingdom, including the base of trained scientists and engineers. On this, the reader is referred to the article by Cantwell and Sanna

Randaccio in this volume as well as Cantwell, 1991. We shall come back to this shortly.)

Germany's direct investment is heavily concentrated in manufacturing and in the chemical industries and machinery industries in particular, again consistent with one's preconceptions of ownership advantages held by German firms. Data suppression plagues the German data due to the BEA's diligence to prevent the release of data that might be attributable to a specific firm. Thus, while figures for Germany's direct investment in the non-electrical and electrical machinery categories are not separately revealed, the combined total of these two categories is equal to about 13 per cent of Germany's total investment.

Data suppression also blocks most of the detail of the distribution of direct investment in the United States from The Netherlands, but it is clear that the percentage of this investment in the manufacturing sector is quite low. It is quite likely that a very large percentage of Dutch direct investment in the United States would be classified as 'petroleum' if the data weren't suppressed, because one firm, the Royal Dutch Petroleum Company (the 'Dutch side' of the Shell Group) almost surely accounts all by itself for a very large percentage of total FDI in the United States from The Netherlands. Again, common perception is that this firm is one that possesses significant ownership advantages. The fact that this and other large Dutch firms have long been established in the United States and did not greatly expand their operations there during the 1980s probably also helps to account for the fact that direct investment from The Netherlands into the United States grew less quickly than that of any other major nation during this decade.

Direct investment from France, more than from any other large home nation, was concentrated in manufacturing. Quite a lot of this was in the chemicals industry, where French firms are known to hold some valuable proprietary technologies, and in the 'other manufacturing' category, where it is known that the Michelin and Saint Gobain firms, both of which possess formidable ownership advantages, figure heavily.

In addition to the industry distribution of FDI in the United States by home country, explanation is needed as to why the growth of FDI in the United States grew from the various countries at such disparate rates. The United Kingdom is the big mystery. While numerous UK-based firms doubtlessly do possess significant ownership advantages, it is not clear that these firms have overwhelming advantages relative to, say, German firms. Further, it is not clear that even if UK-based firms typically were significantly more adept than their German rivals the former would have expanded their activities in the United States so much more rapidly than the latter during the 1986–9 period, because the base levels of US operations of the former at the beginning of the period were much higher than those of the latter. As is noted in the article by Cantwell and Sanna Randaccio in this volume, rapid rates of direct investment by British firms were not limited to the United States during the 1980s; these firms were also active in continental Europe and elsewhere. Is there an explanation for the rapidity of growth of British FDI other than via appeal to overactive British thyroid glands during the late Thatcher period?

Although ownership advantages alone seem inadequate to explain British FDI, declining locational advantages in the United Kingdom, coupled with a retaining of certain ownership advantages by UK-based firms, does offer a possible explanation. The reader again is referred to the article by Cantwell and Sanna Randaccio in this volume for a detailed explanation. One should note, however, one inconsistency in the Cantwell/Sanna Randaccio reasoning on this matter. They attribute at least part of the loss of locational advantage by the United Kingdom to 'hierarchical management styles' of British firms that have the effect of degrading the value of human skills at lower levels of the organization. But if these management styles fare poorly in the UK home market, how can they succeed abroad? Do these styles fare better in the United States than in the United Kingdom, for instance? One thinks not; indeed, one of the common reasons given for the success of the Japanese auto manufacturers in the United States rests on the notion that these firms bring highly non-hierarchical management styles developed originally in Japan to the United States and successfully apply them in the US context.

It is possible that in response to differing conditions outside the United Kingdom, UK-based firms alter their management styles effectively. But then, why aren't the new styles exported back to operations in the UK home market so as to reverse the demise of UK locational advantages? To explain why not, appeals can be made to poor conditions in the UK environment (for example, government policies that have de-emphasized worker training and education in general and have supported institutional financial interests over those of the manufacturing sector). But, as was noted earlier, this runs counter to the fact that non-British (mostly US- and Japan-based) firms have tended to favour the United Kingdom over other European nations as a locus for new FDI activities. If overall the policy environment in the United Kingdom created highly unfavourable conditions for the location of manufacturing operations there, would not one expect US- and Japan-based firms to shun the United Kingdom rather than to aggregate there?

How do hypotheses other than OLI fare? Hypotheses based on oligopoly reaction first come to mind. On the face of it, a case could be made for the 'exchange of threat' variant on oligopoly reaction: the United Kingdom remains for US-based firms the 'nation of choice' for location of their European operations and, given the large *ex ante* presence of US firms in the United Kingdom, the push into the United States by UK-based firms might be a reaction to this presence. Alas, problems with this hypothesis emerge when one examines some of the specific large acquisitions made in the United States by UK-based direct investors. What US-based firm, for example, was 'threatening' Maxwell at the time of the takeover of the (US) Macmillan Group? Likewise, what US-based firm was threatening Grand Metropolitan when it took over Pillsbury? Doubtless some direct investments in the United States by UK-based firms were motivated by oligopoly reaction, but it seems to this author that 'exchange of threat' cannot account for more than some subset of these investments.[1]

A variation on oligopolistic reaction offered by Francesca Sanna Randaccio (1990) might, however, be more promising. In this model the logic follows Edith Penrose (1959): large firms in oligopoly industries equate growth with long-term profit maximization, but growth possibilities within established markets are held in check by rival firms (for example, these firms will not allow rivals to gain market share at their expense). Thus, firms must seek growth opportunities outside their established markets, for example, via horizontal diversification into new product lines or new geographical markets. Subject to some necessary cost conditions, firms might find international diversification the path of least resistance even if foreign markets themselves are characterized by the presence of large, oligopolistic firms. This is because the foreign oligopolists find it less costly simply to accommodate the new entrant than to take steps to counter its entry. The fear of these oligopolists is that any such steps would be perceived by domestic rivals as a threat to the established equilibrium (for example, should an established firm attempt to counter the entry via price cutting, rivals might see this more as a threat to their own market shares than as a legitimate step against the new entrant). For this to be so, of course, the new entrant, though a large player in the home market, must remain something of a fringe player in the foreign market.

But does Sanna Randaccio's hypothesis help to explain the hyperactivity of the British direct investors in the United States compared to the relatively sedate pace of continental investors? Possibly it could be a powerful explanation if one makes some additional (and not too far-fetched) assumptions. Assume for example that under the sway of the ideology of the Thatcher administration, British investors talked themselves into believing that under a like-minded US President the future of the US economy would be more robust than that of continental Europe, whereas European investors took relatively more seriously the potential impact of the Europe 1992 programme. British and continental investors alike would seek opportunities for growth outside their home markets, but the British would tend to focus their attention on North America whereas continental Europeans would tend to concentrate their efforts on opportunities within Europe (including the UK market itself). Neither set of investors would necessarily focus on one area to the exclusion of the other, but the British would give more weight to North America as the most opportune place to achieve growth targets whereas the continental Europeans would give more weight to Europe. The same logic would suggest that US-based firms would concentrate their direct investment activities in the United Kingdom.

The logic of this hypothesis is impeccable, but alas it does not pass empirical tests with high marks. UK-based firms were active as direct investors not only in the United States during the 1980s; they also were very active in continental Europe. At the same time, US-based firms were not by any means the only direct investors in the United Kingdom during the same period. Firms based on the European continent collectively placed more direct investment in the United Kingdom than did US-based firms, albeit that the latter remained in first place when measured against any single other country. And while US firms in the aggregate themselves placed more direct investment in the United Kingdom than in any other single European country, the United Kingdom was by no means an overwhelmingly predominant location for this investment, as is recounted in the second section of this chapter.

What about yet other hypotheses? Cantwell's technological accumulation theory, as previously suggested, is powerful in explaining Japanese FDI in the United States in technology-intensive industries, and it goes a long way towards explaining some European FDI as well. For example, it goes quite far in explaining certain French acquisitions (for example, the motivations for Groupe Schneider's proposed hostile acquisition of the US Square D firm, as reported in the press, are quite consistent with technological accumulation, as were the motivations for the creation of ALCATEL via the merging of ITT's telecommunication equipment activities in both Europe and North America into those of Thomsen-CSF). However, Cantwell's theory seems more able to explain certain investments than to explain the overall pattern of European FDI in the United States during 1986–9; technological accumulation by itself would, for example, have difficulty in explaining the preponderant British role.

One explanation of this role that has been advanced in the financial press lies largely outside the economic literature on FDI and multi-national enterprise and yet is one that really has to be considered. This is that much of British FDI in the United States might in fact defy any truly rational explanation whatsoever. The middle to late 1980s saw a boom in mergers and acquisitions in the United States that was virtually without precedent in terms of the numbers and sizes of the transactions. (There were smaller booms during the late 1960s and the 1920s.) Many of the transactions seemed to be motivated by little more than opportunities to transfer wealth from shareholders and bondholders of the affected firms to investment bankers, lawyers, accountants and in some cases the officers of the firms themselves – in a word, to the persons who put the deals together. Obviously, this implies some breakdown of the system whereby the shareholders and bondholders of the firms are either not informed of where their interests lie or are inadequately represented in the process by which decisions affecting their interests are made. Early in this boom, British investors became involved in the mergers and acquisition 'game', and the case has been advanced that much of British direct investment in the United States simply resulted from such participation by British high rollers.

It would surely be wrong to dismiss all FDI in the United States of United Kingdom origin during the period as simply the result of the successful efforts of a handful of British takeover 'buccaneers' to make themselves fabulously wealthy at the expense of society at large. But it is probably also wrong to dismiss this explanation altogether: some portion of British FDI in the United States during the middle to late 1980s was almost surely more the result of financial engineering than anything else.

This 'buccaneer' hypothesis does help to explain the predominant role of the British investor. The London financial markets during the period in question were much more open to merger and acquisition activities by non-traditional investors than were any continental financial markets, and British investors (or at least some subset of them) understood the mentality of the US financial markets that prevailed in the middle 1980s, which seems to have been pretty much 'anything goes'. Hostile takeovers, leveraged buyouts and other such activities by contrast were almost unknown in continental European financial markets, and continental European investors by and large probably simply did not understand the whole phenomenon that was going on in the United States – or if they did understand it, the understanding came too late for them to cash in. How much of the FDI activity by British investors came down to 'buccaneering' only time will tell; the failure of the worst acquisitions will be one telling indication. An early indicator is that in its June 1991 revision of the FDI positions of various nations in the United States, the BEA revised significantly downward the UK position for 1990. This was because numerous acquisitions in the United States by British investors were subsequently in part or in whole sold off or shut down, and the sell-offs and shut-downs were not reflected in earlier estimates of the UK position.

The 'buccaneer' hypothesis, one should note, is not necessarily inconsistent with OLI theory. One need only hypothesize that an ownership advantage held by at least certain British investors is the ability to turn around faltering firms, and that much of the takeover activity in the United States by British investors involved faltering firms or faltering operations of US-owned firms that were sold to UK firms. As is detailed shortly, certain evidence can be brought forth to support this hypothesis.

A variation on the 'buccaneer' hypothesis, also consistent with OLI theory, is that there exists a class of European firms that are going through a process of consolidation within the European market which is simultaneously enabling them to expand outside this market. These firms did not enjoy the firm-specific ownership advantages necessary to become global: they were too small, or too far behind relevant technological frontiers, or simply too inexperienced to take a major leap into operations outside of their home markets. However, changes occurring within Europe, for instance, the move towards completion of the single market in 1992 and the recent surge in cross-border merger and acquisition activity within Europe, forced these firms to acquire new capabilities and/or new attitudes with respect to external markets. Of course, there is another class of European firm already possessing the skills and outlook necessary to be 'global', but these firms would have established themselves in the United States well before the 1986–9 surge in FDI there.

If this variant has any validity at all, why would British investors be in the lead? The answer would have mostly to do with timing: the consolidation process seems to have begun in the United Kingdom earlier than in the continental European nations, at least if merger and acquisition activity is any indicator. If the hypothesis is correct, then the large amount of British foreign direct investment that has already come into the United States really represents the leading edge of a phenomenon that is likely to continue and in which the British will over time play a relatively diminishing role. Whether or not this actually comes to pass, of course, only time will tell. But the really eager reader might wish at this point to skip to section 3.4.

And so, what exactly caused the massive inflows of FDI from Europe into the United States during the late 1980s? As is suggested above, all the major hypotheses regarding the determinants of foreign direct investment probably have some role in explaining these inflows. The explanation is thus likely to be truly 'eclectic', in the spirit of John Dunning's thinking about the causes of FDI. The problem is that even the combined force of all these hypotheses somehow does not add up to a coherent whole. Such phenomena as the preponderant role of British investors, the mode of the investment (that is, through acquisitions rather than greenfields investment), the timing of the investment (that is, its coincidence with an unprecedented wave of domestic mergers and acquisitions and possibly its rather sudden collapse, discussed later in this chapter), to the mind of this author at least, are not wholly explained by the existing hypotheses.

3.4   WHAT ARE THE CONSEQUENCES OF EUROPEAN FDI IN THE UNITED STATES?

Table 3.5 looks at three measures of economic performance for US manufacturing affiliates of non-US firms by country of origin of parent: value added per worker (a measure of labour productivity); compensation per worker; and research and development expenditures per worker. The figures in the table and any conclusions drawn from them are subject to all the qualifications enumerated in the opening paragraphs of the previous section (for example, the data are less complete than one would desire for comparative analysis; the data include information pertaining to recent acquisitions for which the effects of change in ownership are not yet apparent; and the data are subject to misclassification) as well as a few more that will be noted in this section. None the less, the data do give some indication of the comparative performance of these affiliates.

Table 3.5   Measures of Performance of Manufacturing Subsidiaries of Non-US Parent Firms, by Country of Origin of Parent and of all US Manufacturing Industry 1987 ($ thousands)

Measure/Country of Origin	value added per worker	compensation per worker	research and development per worker
United Kingdom	44.5	28.5	1.72
Germany	49.2	36.5	5.23
Netherlands	43.7	34.7	NA
France	47.5	35.5	3.16
All Europe	45.9	32.0	3.17
Japan	49.8	35.1	2.88
All nations	48.6	32.9	3.61
All US manufacturing	46.0	31.1	2.87

Source: From Bureau of Economic Analysis base data.

What perhaps stands out most from these data is that by all measures the US manufacturing affiliates of British firms look rather bad. That is to say, on average they are less productive (in terms of average product of labour), less well-paying, and perform less research and development than subsidiaries from other countries. Indeed, on all three measures they fare less well than all US manufacturing and on two of the three they fare less well than any other home nation listed. By contrast, by all three measures affiliates of German and French companies really do quite well. In terms of value added and compensation per worker the US manufacturing affiliates of Japanese firms do very well (among these home nations they are in first place), and it must be noted that these data do not include the very productive US manufacturing operations of the big three Japanese carmakers. The US affiliates of Japanese firms do not look as good as those from Germany and France on the R&D per worker measure, but preliminary data for 1988 show that there occurred a major jump in R&D activity by Japanese firms in that year.

It is a rather intriguing issue whether the comparatively poor performance of US manufacturing affiliates of British firms is in any way related to the 'buccaneer' hypothesis offered earlier. This author simply refuses to speculate on this issue at this time, however, because other explanations of the low performance can be offered, namely: (a) there is significant selection bias in the numbers (for example, Germany looks good partly because a large amount of German direct investment in the United States is in the chemicals industry, a sector innately characterized by high average worker productivity and pay and one that tends to be very R&D-intensive; the true test would be to compare US affiliates of German firms with comparable domestic firms operating in this industry, but data are not available to make this sort of comparison) and British investors might simply have the misfortune, in terms of this sort of comparison, to be stuck in low worker-productivity, low-paying, technologically non-dynamic industries; (b) what really matters are not the static comparisons, but dynamic comparisons; that is, a fairer test of whether the British direct investors are underachievers would be whether their recent acquisitions do better under current ownership than under previous ownership than is shown by the average figures; and (c) there is no way to gain from the figures separate data for British acquisitions resulting from financial engineering and for other British direct investment. This last statement of course assumes both that there is something to the 'buccaneer' hypothesis and that those specific British investments that can be explained by it are likely to do less well on aggregate than those that are better explained by more traditional hypotheses regarding FDI.

Indeed, if one ownership advantage held by British firms (or some subset of them) is, as suggested in the previous section, the ability to turn around low-performing operations, then one might actually expect US affiliates of these British firms to show poorly on the basis of all these measures. To put it another way, the relatively poor performance of the US affiliates of British firms to date could be seen as one level of empirical verification of the existence of such ownership advantages. However, full verification of this existence would entail demonstrating that the poor performance was in fact rectified with the passage of time.

These considerations notwithstanding, the data on the performance of US affiliates of foreign firms by nationality are not likely to be comforting to the vociferous faction of American analysts that holds to the position that FDI in the United States from Japan is unhealthy for the US economy whereas that from Europe, especially the United Kingdom, is good. For whatever reason, the fact is that in the aggregate US affiliates of British firms are underperformers.

Not included in the data of this table is information on the performance of non-manufacturing US affiliates of non-US firms. Performance information for the non-manufacturing sectors is even more suspect than that for the manufacturing sector, to the extent that this author feels that it cannot be used in an analytically useful manner.

Indeed, all analysis presented in this section must be treated with caution. The effects of the recent surge of FDI into the United States upon the US economy will become clear only with the passage of time, and analysis based on current data cannot be expected to yield anything like the last word on these effects. To get at these effects, case studies as well as analysis of aggregated data will be needed. None the less, it can be said on the basis of current evidence that the overall initial effect of this FDI on the economy is positive. Furthermore, it seems unlikely that the performance of US affiliates of foreign firms will in the aggregate deteriorate over time. Thus, it is probably safe to claim that the FDI has brought lasting benefits to the United States. This is a result that should come as no surprise to those who are familiar with the current literature on FDI and multinational enterprise.

3.5   WHAT HAPPENED TO FOREIGN DIRECT INVESTMENT INTO THE UNITED STATES DURING 1990?[2]

After five years of rapid and uninterrupted growth, the flow of foreign direct investment into the United States fell off sharply in 1990, from about $70.6 billion in 1989 to about $37.2 billion. It is entirely reasonable on the basis of these numbers to conclude that a 'sea change' has occurred and that the great FDI surge of the 1980s has come to an end.

In fact, the picture is somewhat more complicated than this. To see it in its ambiguous entirety, one must know that, as measured by the Bureau of Economic Analysis, FDI is the sum of three flows: (a) net changes in equity in US affiliates by foreign direct investors; (b) retained earnings of these affiliates; and (c) net intrafirm loans from the foreign investors to the US affiliates. An examination of the first of these shows that there was some fall in 1990 equity flows from those of 1989 ($51.9 billion in 1989 versus $47.0 billion in 1990), but the fall was much less than for total FDI flows. Most of the drop occurred during the last half of the year and this continued into the first quarter of 1991, the latest period for which figures were available at the time of writing. The average equity flows for the first three quarters of 1990 were higher than the average for the period 1987–9.

FDI equity flows show substantial variation from quarter to quarter, and low figures for two or three quarters in succession do not necessarily signal a 'sea change' in foreign direct investment flows. Determination of whether a 'sea change' has in fact occurred will have to await the future release of data for subsequent quarters.

With respect to the second two flows (retained earnings and net intrafirm borrowing), combining them into one category that we shall term 'intrafirm FDI flows' and examining these also on a quarter-by-quarter basis, another complicated pattern emerges. Throughout the 1980s these flows were positive in almost all quarters (with considerable quarter-by-quarter fluctuation and some trend upward), indicating a net flow of funds from parents to US subsidiaries. But the upward trend seems to have broken following the first quarter of 1989, and these flows rapidly dropped in the following quarter and actually became negative in the third quarter of 1989. They became positive again in the fourth quarter of 1989 and the first quarter of 1990, but subsequently they turned negative in all quarters including the first quarter of 1991.

Thus, the 1990 fall-off in overall FDI flows as measured by the BEA resulted more from a major change in the intrafirm flows than from a fall-off of net equity flows. But the latter is in many ways a better measure of investor activity than is the overall FDI flow, because changes in equity reflect the extent to which direct investors are increasing (or decreasing) their control of US economic activities, whereas intrafirm flows reflect changes in the financial situation of these activities. The intrafirm flows are functions of (among other things) the profitability of the underlying activities, relative costs of borrowing in the United States versus abroad, and expectations regarding future movements of the value of the dollar. In a word, intrafirm flows are sensitive to macroeconomic factors, whereas overall FDI activity is more motivated by strategic or industrial organizational factors than by macroeconomic ones. In 1990 the onset of recession reduced the earnings of US affiliates of foreign firms and relative costs of borrowing in the United States came down, both of which *ceteris paribus* could be expected to motivate foreign direct investors to transfer funds from their US affiliates to activities overseas. The propensity of these investors to do this might have also been reinforced by expectations of future dollar depreciation, although such expectations are hard to measure.

It would be of great interest to know the changes in direct investment, broken down by net equity flows and intracompany flows, that occurred between 1989 and 1990 by country of origin. Alas, the

Bureau of Economic Analysis does not publish enough detail to enable such figures to be constructed. Table 3.6 below summarizes changes in the net FDI flows into the United States from the United Kingdom, The Netherlands, Germany, France, Canada and Japan.

Table 3.6   FDI into the United States by source area, 1989 and 1990 ($ billions)

Year/country	1989	1990	1990 flow/ 1989 flow
United Kingdom	18.87	3.67	0.19
Netherlands	7.34	7.08	0.96
Germany	3.84	−0.95	−0.25
France	3.57	4.36	1.22
Canada	3.21	0.01	0.00
Japan	17.43	17.34	0.99

Source: Bureau of Economic Analysis, *Survey of Current Business*, March 1991, pp. 62–4.

As the table indicates, the change in flows varied greatly from source country to source country. FDI flows from France actually increased, and the drop in thcse flows from both Japan and The Netherlands was very small. But FDI flows from Britain were in 1990 less than one-fifth 1989 levels. Flows from Germany in 1990 were actually negative. Were it not for this last point, the pattern of flow changes would be consistent with the 'leading edge' hypothesis offered earlier, whereby firms from the UK would be the first nation from Europe to invest directly and massively in the United States but would be followed by firms from other nations. But as matters stand it is difficult to determine any pattern in the 1989 to 1990 FDI flow changes.

Indeed, what exactly happened to foreign direct investment into the United States in 1990 remains largely a mystery. There may have been a 'sea change' in this investment, but then again there may not; the evidence is not conclusive. The recorded drop in FDI can be largely (but not entirely) explained by changes in the nation's macroeconomic situation. Whether the residual – the portion of the change not accounted for by macroeconomic factors – is indicative of a major trend break or is simply a downtick in a random walk, only time will tell.

3.6 CONCLUSIONS

The transformation of the United States from a net creditor nation on direct investment account to a net debtor is an event of major importance with significant policy implications. The event signals in many ways the coming of age of the multinational enterprise. No longer is this enterprise a largely American institution. To be sure, this enterprise never was exclusively an American institution, but less than a quarter of a century ago the proportion of multinational enterprises that were American in origin was overwhelming and the growth of overseas subsidiaries of these organizations was rapid enough to make serious analysts wonder if the world would not come to be dominated by them. Today, multinational enterprises of American origin remain important fixtures in the world economy, but the fast track has been increasingly occupied by firms of European and Asian origin.

However, US-based firms are hardly out of the picture. The evidence presented in this chapter suggests that, possibly in response to prospects of a more integrated European market, there is in fact a net increase in their presence in Europe, albeit that the increases are modest compared to those they registered during the 1950s and 1960s and are significantly overshadowed by the rapid increase in the presence of non-US firms in the United States.

The policy implications are of significance. For instance, will the international investment policy of the United States go the way of its trade policy? Increasingly, US trade policy can be characterized as 'free trade' in rhetoric but nationalistic and protectionist in actual content. US international investment policy to date has remained open-market orientated in fact and practice (the Exon-Florio provision of US law notwithstanding), but pressures have mounted from both the right and the left in the United States for more restrictive policies regarding inward investment. It would be ironic if the United States were to move towards more-restrictive policies at the same time that many developing countries, especially the more dynamic Latin American ones, restructure their policies towards greater openness.

One point to be had from this chapter is that the great surge of foreign direct investment that took place during the 1980s in both Europe and the United States simply is not completely understood, either in terms of why it occurred or what its effects are likely to be. Theories of the determinants of FDI help to explain the surge, but they leave holes. The large role of British direct investors in the United States is especially difficult to explain, particularly in the light

of evidence that US affiliates of British firms are relative underperformers in the US economy. Likewise, the timing of the FDI boom
is difficult to explain: why did it surge during the late 1980s after a
period of quiescence, and why might it be tapering off, as at the time
of writing? Was the surge causally related to the tumultuous behaviour
of the financial markets during the same period, and in particular to
the merger and acquisition activity in these markets that virtually went
berserk in both the United States and the United Kingdom? Is the
whole phenomenon a candidate for eventual treatment in *The Journal
of Anomalous Behavior*?

These are questions that we hope will fruitfully fill the time of
researchers in coming years. No pretence of definitive answers is made
here. At the end of the day, or at least at the end of the chapter, the
major task accomplished, this author hopes, is to have asked some of
the right questions.

NOTES

1. This conclusion is also supported by Francesca Sanna Randaccio (1990); in criti-
   cizing the 'exchange of threat' hypothesis as an explanation of European direct
   investment in the United States in manufacturing in the 1970s, she notes the often-
   massive nature of this investment and the inconsistency between the scale of actual
   entry and the scale needed to sustain an 'exchange of threat'. While I believe that
   her arguments can be rebutted, to the extent that they are valid they certainly
   apply much more strongly to the even more massive investments of the 1980s than
   to those of the 1970s.
2. This section is adapted from a comparable section appearing in Edward M. Graham
   and Paul R. Krugman, *Foreign Direct Investment in the United States*, 2nd edition,
   Washington, DC: Institute for International Economics, 1991. Data published after
   completion of this chapter indicate that new equity FDI flow into the United States
   continued to fall throughout the remainder of 1991.

REFERENCES

Cantwell, J.A. (1987), 'Technological Competition and Intra-industry Pro-
    duction in the Industrialised World', *University of Reading Discussion
    Papers in International Investment and Business Studies*, no. 106.
Cantwell, J.A. (1989), *Technological Innovation and Multinational Cor-
    porations*, Oxford: Basil Blackwell.
Cantwell, J.A. (1992), 'The Effects of Integration on the Structure of MNC
    Activity in the EC', in M. Klein and P.J.J. Welfens, *Multinationals in the
    New Europe and Global Trade*, Berlin: Springer Verlag.
Cantwell, J.A. and Sanna Randaccio, F. (1992), 'Intra-industry direct invest-
    ment in the European Community: Oligopolistic Rivalry and Technological
    Competition', Chapter 4 in this volume.

Casson, M.C. (1990), 'Moral Constraints on Strategic Behaviour', *University of Reading Discussion Papers in Economics*, series A, volume III, no. 236.

Casson, M.C. (1991), 'Corporate Culture and the Agency Problem', *University of Reading Discussion Papers in Economics*, series A, volume IV, no. 238.

Dunning, J.H. (1988a), 'The Eclectic Paradigm of International Production: an Update and Some Possible Extensions', *Journal of International Business Studies*, **19**, 1.

Dunning, J.H. (1988b), 'The Theory of International Production', *International Trade Journal*, **3**, no. 1.

Graham, E.M. (1978), 'Transatlantic Investment by Multinational Firms: a Rivalistic Phenomenon', *Journal of Post Keynesian Economics*, **1**, 1.

Graham, E.M. (1991), 'Strategies of US Multinational Firms to the Emerging Internal Market of the EC', in G. Yannopoulos (ed.), *Europe and America, 1992: US–EC Relations and the Single European Market*, Manchester: Manchester University Press.

Hymer, S. and Rowthorne, R. (1970), 'Multinational Corporations and International Oligopoly: the Non-American Challenge', in C.P. Kindleberger (ed.), *The International Corporation: A Symposium*, Cambridge, Mass: MIT Press.

Penrose, E. (1959), *The Theory of the Growth of the Firm*, Oxford: Basil Blackwell.

Sanna Randaccio, F. (1990), *European Direct Investment in US Manufacturing*, Rome: Edizioni Kappa.

Servan-Schreiber, J.J. (1967), *Le Défi americain*, Paris: Éditions Nöel.

Thomsen, S. and Nicolaides, P. (1991), *The Evolution of Japanese Direct Investment in Europe*, New York: Harvester-Wheatsheaf.

Yannopoulos, G.N. (1991), 'The European Single Market and Foreign Direct Investment', *University of Reading Graduate School of European and International Studies Discussion Papers in European and International Social Science Research*, no. 41.

4. Intra-Industry Direct Investment in the European Community: Oligopolistic Rivalry and Technological Competition

John Cantwell and Francesca Sanna Randaccio*

4.1 INTRODUCTION

It is well known that foreign direct investment finances a range of different types of international production by multinational corporations (MNCs). It is customary to distinguish between import-substituting investments, in which the objective is to serve local host country markets (local production costs permitting); and resource-based, export-platform and rationalized or internationally integrated investments, which rely essentially on the specific attractions of local production conditions and play little or no role in serving local markets. Resource-based affiliates are often engaged principally in intra-firm exports (as the first stage of a vertically integrated process), while export-platform affiliates aim to serve home and third-country markets. The internationally integrated affiliate is either involved in the import and export of components and sometimes the export of final products (in the case of vertical integration), or is concerned with serving the world or regional market for a specialized product range (where there is a system of horizontal integration).

Strange though it may seem, much of the established literature on intra-industry direct investment (or cross-investments between coun-

*Both authors wish to thank Terutomo Ozawa for helpful comments on an earlier draft, and the referees of the EIBA Conference in Copenhagen where a shorter version was presented.

Francesca Sanna Randaccio gratefully acknowledges financial support from the University of Rome 'La Sapienza' (Ricera di Ateneo). She would like to thank Mr Dandorfer and Ms Schramm of the Deutsche Bundesbank for the help offered with the German direct investment statistics.

tries in the same industry) and strategic interaction between MNCs has disregarded these standard distinctions or assumed them away for analytical purposes. The typical approach has been to treat investments as being purely import-substituting, as a means of focusing attention on the state of competition in final product markets in the home and host country. This has some justification when discussing cross-investment flows between the major industrialized regions, Europe, North America and Japan. In these cases resource-based and export-platform investments are of limited significance, while the growth of integrated affiliate networks have generally been regional rather than 'global' in character. Indeed, for US MNCs in the EC an increased regional integration has been partly at the expense of inter-regional integration (Cantwell, 1992).

Hence, although there has been a trend away from import-substituting and towards internationally integrated investments from the perspective of individual European countries, these affiliate networks have typically aimed at serving the EC market as a whole. So at the level of inter-regional investment flows it is still reasonable to think of investments as being largely of an import-substituting kind, treating regional markets as integrated units. Even at this level, though, some qualification is required. Cross-investments between the major industralized regions have also been motivated by their contribution to the international networks of MNCs. One such motive is the need to tap into local technological expertise in the home regions of important competitors, which is especially noticeable in industries in which localized user-producer interaction in innovation is significant (Cantwell, 1989).

When turning to intra-industry direct investment within the EC, import-substituting models simply cannot be presented as general explanations of the phenomenon. They can only be part of a wider picture. To the extent that the EC market is integrated, MNCs operating within the Community are likely to increase their intra-EC trade, and less and less to invest with the principal objective of serving a local or national market. In most industries there are gains from the international integration of affiliate networks, and so a more integrated system of investments is likely to replace the local-market-serving kind. Indeed, where intra-industry direct investments had been local-market driven at an earlier stage, it is possible that as trade becomes freer and relative transport costs fall, such investments may be cut back and replaced by intra-industry trade. It is only in industries in which a need to be nationally responsive dominates company strategies, such as in defence-related sectors (Doz, 1986), that import-substituting investments will continue to lead the way.

This suggests that intra-industry direct investment and strategic interaction between MNCs within the EC have to be distinguished from the equivalent processes between regions. In the intra-EC case they are becoming bound up with the restructuring of affiliate networks and the refinement of the intra-firm division of labour. Each affiliate becomes specialized in accordance with local production conditions and not simply (or not at all) as a result of the requirements of local markets. An exchange of investments between major rivals within the EC is not so much a matter of trading market shares as of geographically dispersing the production of each company to strengthen their overall European operations. In the first instance this may be a matter of an affiliate engaging in complementary technological and productive activities to support the parent company's servicing of the EC market as a whole, rather than an attempt to increase market share in the host country.

This chapter aims to bring together the treatment of the import-substituting and network restructuring aspects of intra-industry direct investment within the EC. Most existing studies of oligopolistic rivalry and intra-industry investment concentrate on the idea of an interpenetration of markets or trading of market shares by major rivals. Following a survey of the evidence on intra-industry direct investment in the EC in the next section, an adaptation of such import-substituting models of oligopolistic interaction is suggested in section 4.3, to allow for the effect of reducing non-tariff barriers as well as tariffs, as befits the recent EC case. One element in the restructuring of corporate networks that has influenced the observed pattern of intra-industry investment in the EC is then discussed in sections 4.4 and 4.5. Each leading firm must invest in the major centres for technological development in its industry, given that innovative activity is locationally differentiated across countries. Thus we examine the proposition that cross-investments in research tend to be greater where intra-industry direct investment is higher. A major question then becomes whether the degree and the composition of specialization in technological activity in affiliates in foreign centres is similar or dissimilar to that in their parent companies.

The industry-based approach taken here is consistent with other attempts to reconcile the demand-orientated and supply-orientated aspects of intra-industry direct investment from a macroeconomic perspective. In investigations at a macroeconomic level cross-investments are a consequence of the complementary evolution of industries and markets across countries or regions. Where investments are driven by the path of domestic and foreign industrial development the focus tends to be on the supply-side characteristics of industrial evolution at home and abroad, even if the investments may be of an import-substituting kind (see, for example, Ozawa, 1991). In Chapter 2 an effort was made to bring the contribution of locationally differentiated demand into this story, once investments become more internationally integrated. In this respect the macroeconomic and industrial economics approaches to intra-industry direct investment are brought closer together. In studies of the evolution of corporate networks in international industries affiliates specialize in accordance with the differentiated characteristics of local production conditions (supply) and markets (demand).

The conjunction between these approaches can be illustrated in the case of regionally integrated investments in the EC undertaken by MNCs from different EC countries. Suppose further that these are horizontally integrated, so each affiliate serves the entire EC market for its specialized product range. Intra-industry trade rises as intra-industry direct investment becomes more internationally integrated through a process of industrial restructuring within the leading firms. From a macroeconomic viewpoint national industries within the EC evolve in a more specialized direction, each having its own distinct path for a consolidated comparative advantage suited to the development of its own production conditions(supply), and perhaps also to the product varieties which are relatively most favoured in their own country (demand). At a more microeconomic level the process is sustained through strategic interaction between companies. As there are advantages to international integration, each firm must follow its rivals in establishing a suitable geographical dispersal of production in the EC, to exploit the locational differentiation of supply and demand, and in so doing to reinforce it.

4.2   INTRA-INDUSTRY DIRECT INVESTMENT IN THE EUROPEAN COMMUNITY IN THE 1980s

As information on foreign production or sales is not available, data on direct investment (DI) will be used to evaluate trends in the growth of international production within the EC, and the balance between its inter-industry and intra-industry components. Following a well established tradition (Dunning and Norman, 1986; Cantwell, 1989; Clegg, 1990), the index here adopted is that introduced by Grubel and Lloyd (1971) to measure intra-industry trade. The index of intra-industry direct investment (*IIDI*) is given by:

$$IIDI_i = [(O_i + I_i) - |O_i - I_i|]/(O_i + I_i)$$

where O_i = outward DI stock in industry i
$\quad$ I_i = inward DI stock in industry i.

The characteristics of the index have been extensively discussed in the above-mentioned studies; here we would like to draw attention to just certain features. The index varies between zero and one. When $IIDI_i = 0$ there is no intra-industry *DI*, while $IIDI_i = 1$ means that all *DI* is defined as being of an intra-industry kind. The index may be high either because both outward and inward *DI* are high or because both are low. Similarly, the value of this indicator increases as a previous imbalance between O_i and I_i is reduced, and depending on whether a country begins as a net inward or outward investor, this may be due either to a rise or a fall in the value of O_i (or I_i). As the interpretation of the *IIDI* index depends upon the context of each country's investment position, the index will be discussed here with reference to a more comprehensive analysis of the evolution of international production within the EC.

Trends in the Growth of Intra-EC DI

The dynamism of intra-EC DI in recent years has been stressed in a variety of sources (UN, 1991; Eurostat, 1990; Commission of the European Communities, 1990a). However, these studies do not analyse the geographical and sectoral dispersion of this increased investment. In order to cast some light on this aspect, it is necessary to refer to the individual national statistics provided by the major EC investing countries. Here we devote particular attention to the cases of the UK, the major world investor during 1985–9, and Germany, the largest EC economy. The data provided by these two countries on their outward and inward investment stock[1] positions permit a greater degree of sectoral and geographical disaggregation than in other countries. Our attention is confined to the manufacturing sector.

Several national differences persist between the patterns of outward manufacturing DI of the major EC investors. In particular, the Community has a more important role as both a recipient and a source of DI for continental European countries than it does for the UK. British producers show a greater propensity to invest in the USA. In 1987 the stock of manufacturing DI in the EC accounted for a share of total outward investment equal to 27 per cent for the UK; 34.5 per cent for Germany; 43 per cent for France; and 45 per cent for the Netherlands;[2] while the US share was respectively 38 per cent, 32 per cent, 33 per cent and 24 per cent.

However, a gradual convergence in investment patterns can be observed in the EC during the 1980s. Intra-EC DI began to rise in 1984–5, which suggests that the recovery in Europe was an important factor in promoting such investments. On the other hand, the acceleration recorded in the latter part of the 1980s suggests that the application of the internal market programme has also contributed to this process.

Table 4.1 shows that between the end of 1984 and the end of 1987 the rise in manufacturing DI in the EC by UK firms was remarkable (growing at 24 per cent per annum). This upsurge, which partly reflects the depreciation of the pound sterling *vis-à-vis* other European currencies, followed a phase of slow growth during the late 1970s and the early 1980s, when all the major EC countries were affected by stagnation and decline in their industrial production. During those years most of the outward expansion of UK and other EC firms was directed to increasing their presence in the USA. In contrast, though,

Table 4.1   Average annual growth rate of UK manufacturing direct investment stock

	1978–81	Outward 1981–4	1984–7
EC–12	3.2	7.1	23.7
USA	21.6	17.5	10.2
Japan	3.9	79.2	22.2
World	8.2	14.3	17.4

	1978–81	Inward 1981–4	1984–7
EC–12	5.7	14.4	4.0
USA	14.3	7.3	6.3
Japan	na	32.7	42.0
World	14.5	8.8	8.0

Source: Central Statistical Office, *Business Monitor, MO4 (ex MA4), Census of Overseas Assets*, various issues.

multinationals based in the other EC states increased their investment in the UK at an earlier stage (in 1981–4), and between 1984 and 1987 the stock of EC manufacturing DI in Britain rose only at a modest pace (4.0 per cent per annum). The pattern of growth of German investment is similar to that of the UK (Table 4.2), although the acceleration in outward investment recorded after 1983 is less remarkable than in the British case (10.2 per cent per annum up to 1987). French DI also rose quickly in the Community after 1984 (Banque de France, 1990).[3]

Table 4.2 *Average annual growth rate of German manufacturing direct investment stock*

	Outward		
	1980–3	1983–7	1987–9
EC–12	6.2	10.2	14.2
USA	15.4	5.5	11.2
Japan	6.1	31.9	15.9
World	10.2	6.3	11.9

	Inward		
	1980–3	1983–7	1987–9
EC–12	− 2.1	10.1	2.5
USA	4.7	− 2.1	− 2.5
Japan	37.7	31.9	27.7
World	1.8	2.0	0.5

Source: Deutsche Bundesbank, *Appendix to the Statistical Supplement to the Monthly Report of the Deutsche Bundesbank*, various issues.

After 1987, EC firms' foreign operations grew rapidly both in the EC and in the USA. However, German and French stock data show that the acceleration was greater in the EC area. In 1987–9 the stock of German manufacturing DI grew by 14.2 per cent per annum in the EC and 11.2 per cent in the USA. Similarly, in 1988 the stock of French outward manufacturing DI rose by 18.8 per cent in the EC and 11.3 per cent in the USA. No data on the outward and inward investment stock position of the UK are available yet for the period since 1987.

In recent years intra-EC investments have been directed more than in the past towards the most-developed parts of the region. Although it is too early to discern any clear pattern, there does seem to have been a shift away from the trend which had prevailed from 1980 to 1987. A major feature of that period was the attempt by EC MNCs to spread their interests within the Community towards the Mediterranean area. Investments in Spain and Portugal were especially strong, a fact that can be explained as a result of these countries joining the Community in 1986. None the less, a rapid growth in inward investment was also recorded by Italy, a country in which for numerous reasons – from the uncertainty of the political and legal system to the lack of efficient infrastructures – the presence of foreign MNCs has been traditionally low by comparison with the size of the country.

One aspect of the new tendency for investment to concentrate in the larger countries is that, during the final years of the 1980s, the role of the UK as a recipient country became increasingly important. German and French statistics show that the UK share of their manufacturing DI increased after 1987. This finding is confirmed by figures on mergers and acquisitions which show that in 1989 the UK was the most important EC target location for new acquisitions undertaken by firms based in other member states (KPMG, 1990). By contrast, the pace of the increase in EC DI in Germany after 1987 seems to have been less buoyant, although it is difficult to be sure because special factors heavily influence the figure calculated in Table 4.2 for 1987–9.[4] In any case, it has been argued that other EC producers face serious difficulties when attempting to enter the German market. The Banque of France, for instance, emphasises that the share of French DI located in Germany towards the end of the 1980s is rather small when compared to the size of that country. This finding is explained by features of the structure of German business such as the links between large banks and the industrial sector and the role of family ownership (Banque de France, 1990).

Industrial Patterns of Intra-EC DI

The industry breakdown of the total EC stock of manufacturing DI controlled by firms originating from the three major EC countries is presented in Table 4.3. It must be viewed with some caution as the sectoral disaggregation is not fully comparable across countries. Certain national patterns of specialization are evident. Paper and publishing, for instance, accounts for 14 per cent of the stock of UK firms' manufacturing investment in the EC in 1987, but is of rather limited importance for French and German producers. Non-metallic mineral products, by comparison, represent an area of investment which is considerably more relevant for French firms than for other EC producers (accounting for 13 per cent of total French DI in 1988).

Table 4.3   *The sectoral distribution of UK, German and French manu-*
facturing direct investment stock in the EC–12 (%)

	UK (1987)	Germany (1989)	France (1988)
Food, drink and tobacco	26.1	1.7[1]	17.4
Chemicals and allied	22.6	35.0	13.5
Metals	3.5	1.5	7.5
Mechanical engineering	3.0[2]	9.4	1.1
Electrical equipment	9.5	16.0	19.3
Office equipment	n.a.	0.6	1.3[2]
Transport equipment	4.1	12.2[3]	21.3
Paper and allied	13.8	n.a.	1.2
Rubber	n.a.	4.1	1.5
Non-metallic products	n.a.	4.0	13.2
Coal and petroleum products	n.a.	0.2	n.a.
Precision instruments	n.a.	3.1	n.a.
Textiles and clothing	n.a.	n.a.	1.6
Other manufacturing	17.4	12.2	1.1
Total	100.0	100.0	100.0
Total (m.)	$8,146	DM30,916	FF70,702
Total (ECUm.)	11,690	15,274	9,961

n.a. = not available
[1]Excluding tobacco
[2]Including precision instruments
[3]Excluding other transport.
Source: Central Statistical Office, *Business Monitor, MO4, Census of Overseas Assets*, 1987; Deutsche Bundesbank, *Appendix to the Statistical Supplement to the Monthly Report of the Deutsche Bundesbank*, April 1991; data provided directly by the Deutsche Bundesbank; Banque de France, *Note d'information*, no. 89, July 1990.

Other branches of manufacturing, however, have been important areas of expansion across national borders for producers based in several EC member states. This is true for industries like chemicals, electrical engineering, food and transport equipment. Even so, some differences remain in the main locations of origin of DI across these sectors. The chemical industry is a traditional area of investment in the Community for both German and UK firms, and it has recently also become important for French producers. It accounts for a share of the stock of manufacturing DI in the EC equal to 35 per cent (1989) for Germany, to 23 per cent (1987) for the UK and 13 per cent (1988) for France. German companies, which have been highly competitive in this industry since the beginning of the century, are the largest investors. Most of their foreign operations are located in other developed areas in Europe. This is also the case for the British and the French producers. Electrical engineering represents another branch of manufacturing in which extensive foreign operations have been established across the EC by German, British and French firms. In this case as well, production is located largely in the most developed parts of the EC.

In the food and beverage industry, UK producers are the largest investors. This sector ranks first for British manufacturing DI in the EC (26 per cent). This focus is not surprising, given the well-established multinational tradition of UK companies in food and drink. In the last part of the decade French companies have also started to invest heavily in food production elsewhere in the EC, so that in 1988 this sector accounted for 17 per cent of the stock of French manufacturing investment in the EC. The foreign operations undertaken by producers based in these two countries equally tend to be located in the largest countries of the Community. German companies, however, are little-represented in this area, which comprises only 1.7 per cent of their total manufacturing DI. This, of course, reflects the fairly fragmented nature of the German food industry.

In the transport equipment sector a high level of investment in other EC states has been undertaken by German and French producers. Yet here, unlike in the other sectors with substantial intra-EC investment, most activities have been located in southern Europe, mainly in Spain. In 1988 Spain accounted for 56 per cent of the German-owned stock of investment in the EC transport equipment industry and 70 per cent in the case of France.

Intra-Industry Direct Investments

The indices of intra-industry DI for the UK and Germany[5] calculated in turn between each of these countries and the remainder of the EC are shown in Table 4.4. The IIDI indicator is not available for France as this country has not published data on the stock of inward DI. The results must be treated with a good deal of caution due to the differences in sectoral disaggregation between Britain and Germany. Furthermore, the German inward investment data consider only primary DI, thus underestimating the real value of foreign-owned manufacturing activities in Germany.[6]

Table 4.4   The index of intra-industry direct investment between the UK and the EC and Germany and the EC

	UK		Germany	
	1981	1987	1980	1987
Food, drink and tobacco	0.38	0.31	0.66[1]	0.92[1]
Chemicals and allied	0.46	0.57	0.51	0.48
Metals	0.55	0.16	0.39	0.77
Mechanical engineering	0.84[2]	0.92[2]	0.81	0.60
Electrical equipment	0.74	0.83	0.52	0.83
Office equipment	n.a.	n.a.	0.57	0.47
Transport equipment	0.22	0.87	0.25[3]	0.33[3]
Paper and allied	0.65	0.12	n.a.	n.a.
Rubber	n.a.	n.a.	0.90	0.78
Non-metallic mineral products	n.a.	n.a.	0.49	0.65
Coal and petroleum products	n.a.	n.a.	0.14	0.03
Precision instruments	n.a.	n.a.	0.60	0.62
Textiles and clothing	n.a.	n.a.	n.a.	n.a.
Other manufacturing	0.37	0.33	0.85	0.49
Total	0.59	0.47	0.88	0.74
Mean	0.49[4]	0.47[4]	0.51[5]	0.53[5]

[1]   Excluding tobacco
[2]   Including precision instruments
[3]   Excluding other transport
[4]   Mean of 8-industry index
[5]   Mean of 12-industry index.
Source: Central Statistical Office, *Business Monitor, MO4, Census of Overseas Assets*, various issues; Deutsche Bundesbank, *Appendix to the Statistical Supplement to the Monthly Report of the Deutsche Bundesbank*, various issues; data provided directly by the Deutsche Bundesbank.

In electrical engineering there seems to have been an oligopolistic rivalry between EC firms associated with a cross-penetration of investments between the major producers. This industry, which was shown to account for a large share of the investment in both countries, is characterized by a high (and rising) value of the index for both the UK (0.83) and Germany (0.83). Furthermore, the IIDI index continues to have a high value even when calculated on a bilateral basis between individual EC countries.

The chemical industry is another area of substantial investment in which the cross-penetration of production has been fairly important, although we find some differences when examining the relationship between individual countries. German firms have a leading position in this sector and that helps to explain the relatively low value of the indicator calculated between Germany and the EC as a whole (0.48). However, the bilateral index rises when calculated between Germany and the UK (0.87), and falls *vis-à-vis* France (0.33). The latter figure reflects not only the smaller size of French chemical investment in the EC but also the fact that production in Germany plays a less important role for French chemical firms (in 1988 Germany accounted for 17 per cent of the stock of French chemical investment in the EC) than does production in France for German producers (22 per cent of their EC investment total). This probably reflects the greater competitive strength of the leading German chemical firms compared to their French counterparts. This is not the case for the UK producers, which tend to occupy a position midway between their stronger German and weaker French rivals. The UK bilateral index calculated between the UK and Germany (0.68) and the UK and France (0.73) shows a higher value than between the UK and the EC as a whole (0.57).

An interpenetration of investments between the major producers also seems to have taken place in mechanical engineering, although this is a less important area of investment. The IIDI indicator calculated with respect to the EC as a whole is equal to 0.92 for the UK and 0.60 for Germany. Here too it is useful to consider the data in a disaggregated fashion. The bilateral index suggests that integration is more advanced between the German and the UK industries (for the UK–Germany combination it scores 0.89) than between either of these two countries and France (UK–France 0.51; Germany–France 0.28).[7] However, outside the electrical and chemical sectors the results are often difficult to interpret. For instance, the surprisingly high value of the IIDI index for the German food and beverage industry is probably due to the undervaluation of the stock of British DI in this German sector.[8]

Finally, we note that the mean value of the index[9] is lower for the UK than for Germany. This partly reflects the greater imbalance between the outward and inward position *vis-à-vis* the EC for the UK than for Germany, as we can see from the value of the indicator calculated for total manufacturing (0.47 for the UK as against 0.74 for Germany). We saw previously that a rapid growth in DI in the UK has been recorded by other major EC countries in the final years of the 1980s. This development may be expected to create an increase in the IIDI indicators for Britain.

4.3 OLIGOPOLISTIC RIVALRY AND INTRA-INDUSTRY DIRECT INVESTMENT

In this section we analyse – using models of imperfect competition – some of the factors behind the recent rise in intra-EC DI. Attention is focused on the different effects on DI of various categories of non-tariff barriers (NTBs). Other major factors influencing intra-industry DI are then discussed in order to explain the sectoral characteristics of the phenomenon previously highlighted. The role of one of these factors – technological rivalry – which emerges as a particularly important element in the intra-EC experience, is further investigated in the following two sections.

NTBs and Intra-Industry DI

The empirical evidence reviewed in the previous section shows that in the final years of the 1980s a rapid increase in intra-EC DI was recorded. The most developed EC economies have been the major source and recipient countries of this recent upsurge. The information available does not allow us to calculate reliable IIDI indicators for the period since 1987 in the largest EC countries, for reasons explained earlier. Nevertheless, data on mergers and acquisitions seem to suggest that an increase in intra-industry DI has taken place in at least some industries. These recent developments sit in contrast to the scenarios suggested as likely by several analysts of the international direct investment effects of the single market. Itaki and Waterson (1990), for instance, expected 'a relative shrinkage of multinationality particularly among EC MNCs'.

Two features of these models analysing oligopolistic rivalry within the EC help to explain why they fail to account for the rise in intra-EC DI that has occurred. First, they focus on oligopolistic interaction between single product firms. Such models are able to explain import-substituting DI (that is, the relocation of production designed to serve each market for the product concerned), but – as we shall see later – cannot account for other forms of MNC activity. Secondly, these models contemplate only one kind of NTB. This is unsatisfactory as, even if one restricts the analysis to import-substituting investments, the impact of the single market on MNC operations will vary according to the nature of the NTB.

The impact of NTBs on MNC activity has generally been analysed by considering them to be the equivalent of a unit tariff. By way of a simple illustration, let us consider the interaction between international oligopolists as a game in which two firms compete in a Cournot setting (that is, every firm maximizes profits, assuming that the output of the other firm remains the same in each market; see Smith, 1987; Dei, 1990; Graham, 1990). Each player is based in a different country – the two countries are assumed to be identical – and chooses between two separate strategies: exporting and DI.[10] The payoff associated with a strategy is given by the sum of profits in the home and foreign markets.

The usual tariff-jumping analysis may then be applied. As DI involves the additional fixed costs of establishing a new plant but lower variable costs in serving a market from a lesser distance through local production, there is a trade-off between exporting and DI. By producing in the foreign country the firm must incur new plant costs, but by exporting it has to face the extra variable costs of transport over a greater distance, and then additionally those associated with the NTB. The trade barrier thereby alters the trade-off between exporting and DI in favour of DI. The choice depends upon the size of the foreign market and hence the scale of production required to satisfy its demand (which determines the relative significance of fixed and variable costs). Assume that the values of the parameters are such that DI is the dominant strategy (that is, represents the firm's best response, no matter what the other player does). Given the symmetrical nature of the model we will have a Cournot–Nash equilibrium with intra-industry DI. Within this simplified framework, if the NTB is eliminated the new equilibrium may entail the replacement of IIDI by intra-industry trade. However, such a switch also depends upon the magnitude of transport costs and location-specific advantages. In other words, the effect of eliminating the NTB will be sector-specific. Even so, DI is more likely to be the dominant strategy in the presence of NTBs, as they can be jumped via local production.

Yet NTBs consist of a variety of forms of protection and it is therefore impossible to analyse the effect of different types of restrictions within a unified model (Emerson *et al.*, 1988). As Yannopoulos (1990) suggests, 'each NTB must be examined individually as to its impact on DI flows'. Here, in order to analyse their effect on DI, we identify three broad categories of NTB: cost-disadvantage generating barriers type 1 (CDB1); cost-disadvantage generating barriers type 2 (CDB2); and market entry barriers. The CDB1 includes measures, such as customs procedures and some kinds of technical regulations, which impose an extra cost on the foreign exporter. Therefore, this first type of barrier has a similar effect to tariffs and may correctly be analysed within the framework previously discussed.

The CDB2 include measures which represent a cost disadvantage not only for the foreign exporter but also for a foreign owned subsidiary operating in the domestic market. Some technical barriers, for instance, require additional costs of research and development which must be incurred by the foreign firm whether it decides to export or to produce *in loco*. Furthermore, when different technical specifications are requested by each host country, and firms may improve production techniques through experience, we may expect the foreign producer to face higher unit costs than the local firm. These additional costs must be incurred by the foreign firm irrespective of where it sites production. Public aid to industry may exercise a similar effect as such funds are usually directed to selected home-based companies and therefore represent a cost disadvantage for a local foreign-owned affiliate.[11]

The impact on DI of CDB2 is rather different from that of CDB1. Assume as before that the domestic and the foreign producer compete as Cournot duopolists and each decides whether to export to or invest in the rival's home country. If there are no transport costs or location advantages the equilibrium outcome will consist of cross-hauling via exports. The two firms will not invest in each other's domestic market as such a strategy would entail additional fixed plant costs but would not eliminate CDB2. In other words, CDB2 is not DI-promoting as it cannot be jumped. Once transport costs and location advantages are taken into account, it is clear that the equilibrium also depends on the structural characteristics of the sector and the countries (the values of the parameters). Nevertheless, the removal of CDB2 is likely to lead to an increase in intra-industry DI (and not to a decrease as follows from the dismantling of CDB1). The elimination of CDB2 increases the market of the foreign producer.[12] When there are transport costs, the extra profits associated with DI – due to the saving on the cost of transport – increase with the volume of sales. The removal of this type of NTB, by allowing the foreign producer larger sales, increases the profits associated with producing *in loco* and thus stimulates DI. It becomes more likely that the minimum market size that is necessary for DI to take place can be achieved. We can term these investments 'offensive' import-substituting investments as they are prompted by an increase in the size of the market and not by the appearance of impediments to export.

Market entry restrictions (the third category of NTB) include public procurement policies. Such measures have been systematically used to establish and favour the so-called 'national champion': home-based firms selected by a national government to play the role of leader in its domestic market. Large firms also sometimes gain advantages in their home countries in various other ways through industrial policy and through the ties between large national industrial groups on the one hand and the local banking system on the other. Close links between manufacturing firms and local financial interests seem to have been of particular importance in the German case.

When NTBs create such differences in 'status' between local and foreign producers, they may be better described as conferring a first-mover advantage rather than a cost advantage. In this case oligopolistic rivalry may be depicted as a Stackelberg game in which each national champion acts as a leader in its domestic market but as a follower in the foreign market. In each market the leader moves first. It sets its output anticipating that the follower will take the leader's quantity as given and react accordingly. The follower instead makes the Cournot conjecture that the output of the leader is fixed, and determines its own output accordingly. As before, we consider two strategies, exporting and DI, for each of the two players. Intra-industry DI is more likely to occur after the removal of this NTB, following reasoning similar to that for CDB2. So long as the foreign firm remains a follower it cannot overcome its inferior local status by investing abroad, but the removal of the barrier increases the market share of the foreign firm and obliges the domestic producer to become just another Cournot player.

The findings of studies on the costs of non-Europe suggest that these latter two categories of NTB have had a significant influence on the pattern of location within the Community. A recent EC report indicated that 'in the majority of sectors, even those traditionally open, one finds enterprises that enjoy a substantial market share in their Member State of origin and more or less marginal market shares in other Member States' (CEC, 1990b). This result is what we would expect if CDB2 and market entry restrictions are at work. In the presence of CDB1 one would instead anticipate a more symmetrical geographical distribution of sales as most large firms would be able to eliminate the disadvantage created by this NTB through investing abroad.

It is also worth noting that there are some important effects on MNC activities of the implementation of the single market that cannot be analysed using models based on single-product firms. Such models may help to account for import-substituting DI but not for other forms of MNC expansion. In the case of multiproduct firms, the removal of NTBs by favouring greater trade is likely to lead to a shift from systems of independent locally orientated affiliates towards regionally integrated networks. Within sectors formerly protected by CDB1 the reorganization is likely to result in a net increase in intra-industry trade, but not necessarily intra-industry DI. The production of some affiliates may rise, but those created essentially to jump the previous trade barriers may instead close.

In contrast, when the other two categories of NTB are lifted a net expansion of foreign production activities is likely to occur. Accelerations in intra-industry DI and trade become complementary to one another. The bulk of restructuring falls instead on the domestic production activities of firms and not on their foreign operations. The CDB2 and market entry restrictions allow the domestic producer – even when faced by a local subsidiary controlled by a foreign competitor – to enjoy a larger share of the domestic market than it would hold in the absence of protection.

Major Determinants of Intra-Industry DI

The discussion so far of the major factors influencing intra-industry DI can now be summarized. First, for the IIDI index to be high where investment is high the industry must be an international oligopoly: this is a precondition for substantial cross-investment flows. Furthermore, the value of the IIDI indicator rises – *ceteris paribus* – when the oligopoly is symmetrical and countries are similar in size. It is therefore hardly surprising that we found a low value of the indicator for industries such as paper and non-metallic mineral products that tend to be dominated by firms based in one country. Secondly, the size of the market also plays an important role. An increase in the size of two identical domestic markets leads to a rise in the volume of intra-industry DI. This follows provided that the unit variable costs of local production are lower than those associated with exporting. Thirdly, different types of NTB have different effects on the choice between DI and exporting.

A fourth point is that economies of scale (with fixed plant costs) discourage intra-industry DI. However, the effect of scale economies may well be offset by other considerations. The cross-penetration of

markets among EC producers during the 1980s was particularly important in industries characterized by significant economies of scale, such
as electrical engineering and chemicals. Finally, location-specific
advantages need to be taken into account. The major EC economies
are quite similar in their market size and costs of production. Within
this area, therefore, location-specific advantages are likely to be mainly
connected with local technological conditions, or in other words, with
the ability to gain access, via local production, to technological and
organizational abilities specific to the host country. These considerations are of particular importance in industries characterized by
intense technological rivalry such as electrical engineering and chemicals. In the next section it will be shown that location-specific advantages of a technological nature have played a major role in promoting
intra-industry DI within the EC.

4.4   INTRA-INDUSTRY DIRECT INVESTMENT AND TECHNOLOGICAL COMPETITION

Apart from an institutional environment that favours locally owned
firms, another reason why intra-industry direct investment is lower
within the EC than between EC countries and the USA is that there is
less incentive for import-substituting investments within an integrated
region, as argued earlier in the introduction. Affiliates located in other
EC countries are more likely to continue in operation only where, at
least in part, they satisfy the broader motives of an integrated corporate network, taking advantage of variations in the conditions of production across member states. One example of this happening is where
technologically sophisticated production is located in the largest EC
countries, and standardized production is located in Southern Europe
(the Iberian Peninsula).

   However, it is the largest EC countries that are the major sources
and recipients of direct investment. In this case, cross-investments may
result from a process of technological competition between leading
MNCs based in different EC centres. Each aims to gain access to a
stream of technological innovations which are characteristic of the
specific skills and scientific expertise of the host country. These can
then be integrated at a corporate level with the complementary technology of the parent company, which reflects the distinctive elements
of the national traditions of its home country.

   Where this happens between European centres of excellence in an
industry, intra-industry direct investment is likely to be associated with

intra-industry technological activity. In other words, foreign-owned affiliates in each host country engage in local technological development in a form which draws heavily on local expertise and know-how. In this section we present some evidence on intra-industry technological activity in the EC, as a means of better understanding one aspect of the general investment evidence reviewed in section 4.2.

The source of this evidence is a database developed at the University of Reading on the US patenting activity of the world's largest 792 firms and their affiliates. Of these companies, 729 were recorded as patenting in the USA over the period 1969–86, of which 181 had headquarters in the five largest EC countries (77 in the UK, 49 in Germany, 35 in France, 11 in Italy and 9 in the Netherlands). Each of these 181 firms represents consolidated corporate groups, counting together patents assigned either to the parent company or its affiliates, taking the structure of ownership links as of 1984. Relying on information provided in the patent application, each patent can be attributed to an original location of invention (irrespective of the location of the part of the company or the agent which takes out the application), and to a specific type of technological activity (derived from the classification scheme used by the US Patent Office). The database thereby provides an indicator of the combined geographical and sectoral spread of the technological activity of 181 of the largest industrial firms originating in the EC.

By analogy with the index of intra-industry direct investment, the index of intra-industry technological activity is defined in the following way:

$$IITA_i = [(OP_i + IP_i) - |OP_i - IP_i|]/(OP_i + IP_i)$$

where OP refers to outward patenting by firms originating from the country in question, and IP refers to inward patenting by foreign owned firms. Outward patenting covers US patents granted for inventions stemming from research in foreign affiliates; it involves patents which are assigned to domestically owned MNCs or their affiliates, but which derive from technological activity in affiliates abroad; conversely, inward patenting comprises patents controlled by foreign firms, but which are due to inventions in domestically located research facilities. So in this context outward and inward patenting does not refer to the country in which patents were granted – they were all granted in the US – but rather to the home country of the MNCs that ultimately own the patents by comparison with the location of the research facilities responsible. The industry subscript i is defined with reference to the primary sector of output of each corporate group, as with the IIDI indicator above. In view of the need to compare major competitors in an industry, OP and IP for (say) the chemical industry include all the patents of those chemical firms which are involved in the country. For the purpose of the calculation of the IITA index the distinction between different types of technological activity within any firm or industry is not relevant, although this other way of classifying the data is needed when developing the argument further, as will become clear in section 4.5 below.

In the first instance, the IITA index was calculated for patenting by firms originating from the 12 EC countries due to their technological activity in other EC member states, for the 1969–86 period as a whole. This involved a total of 188 companies, adding a further seven firms

Table 4.5 *The sectoral distribution of outward patenting of the largest German, British, Italian, French and Dutch industrial firms, based on their research facilities in other EC countries, 1969–86 (%)*

Food products	5.8
Drink	0.1
Tobacco	0.9
Chemicals	39.9
Pharmaceuticals	1.0
Metals	2.2
Mechanical engineering	2.4
Electrical equipment	9.1
Office equipment	0.1
Motor vehicles	10.8
Aircraft	0.6
Textiles	0.5
Paper products	0.1
Rubber products	1.0
Non-metallic mineral products	4.3
Coal and petroleum products	21.0
Professional instruments	0.1
Other manufacturing	0.1
Total manufacturing	100.0

Source: US patent database developed at the University of Reading, covering the patenting of 729 of the world's largest 792 industrial firms and their affiliates (see section 4.4).

to the 181 mentioned above. In this form IITA corresponds to the IIDI between individual countries and the EC region discussed earlier. To interpret the IITA index it is also necessary to consider the absolute significance of international research activity, since, as with IIDI, a high value of the IITA index only indicates an important interpenetration of facilities where the absolute level of activity is also high. To this end the sectoral distribution of outward patenting for the 181 firms based in the five largest EC countries is reported in Table 4.5.

The results of the estimation of the intra-EC IITA index for the five largest EC countries across a spectrum of 18 manufacturing industries are set out in Tables 4.6 and 4.7. Not surprisingly, in view of the fact that a wide range of industries is considered relative to a limited number of firms, the mean value of the index is low by comparison with IIDI. It is especially low for Italy and the Netherlands, each of which has fewer domestically owned firms in this large class than there are industries and so must have a substantial number of industries with an IITA index of zero by definition. However, it is useful to adopt a reasonably detailed degree of disaggregation if the purpose is to examine the fruits of technological competition between the largest firms in areas in which they clearly sell a similar range of products and must therefore interact with one another. In fact, intra-industry technological activity appears to be significant even for Italy in motor vehicles, chemicals and coal and petroleum products; and for the Netherlands in metals.

Considering the average for the five countries (the mean value across countries, sector by sector), the IITA index is high in metals, chemicals and pharmaceuticals, electrical equipment, motor vehicles and coal and petroleum products. In most of these industries the leading EC companies are involved in an exchange of activities to promote international technological development with their major EC based competitors; but in metals and pharmaceuticals the scale of activity is too low to justify this conclusion (Table 4.5). The remaining industrial pattern is consistent with the findings on IIDI set out in section 4.2, as it is clearly in the chemicals and electrical equipment industries that we observe high values of IIDI and IITA in association with substantial levels of investment and technological activity. It is also useful to know whether countries are net sources or receivers of foreign-owned research. For manufacturing industry as a whole, in Germany there is a rough balance between outward and inward technological activity. In the UK there is a substantial net outward activity, and in France there is only a slightly less impressive net inward research involvement.

Table 4.6 An index of intra-industry technological activity among the largest industrial firms for the five largest EC countries, 1969–86

	Germany	UK	Italy	France	Netherlands	Five-country Average
Food products	0.00	0.00	0.00	0.93	0.00	0.19
Drink	0.00	0.00	0.00	0.00	0.00	0.00
Tobacco	0.00	0.00	0.00	0.00	0.00	0.00
Chemicals	0.50	0.51	0.38	0.26	0.08	0.35
Pharmaceuticals	0.86	0.53	0.00	0.47	0.00	0.37
Metals	0.66	0.89	0.12	0.98	0.94	0.72
Mechanical engineering	0.44	0.10	0.00	0.21	0.00	0.15
Electrical equipment	0.41	0.47	0.00	0.45	0.06	0.28
Office equipment	0.00	0.00	0.00	0.25	0.00	0.05
Motor vehicles	0.39	0.03	0.85	0.17	0.00	0.29
Aircraft	0.50	0.38	0.00	0.18	0.00	0.21
Textiles	0.33	0.34	0.00	0.11	0.00	0.16
Paper products	0.00	0.00	0.00	0.00	0.00	0.00
Rubber products	0.15	0.64	0.00	0.00	0.00	0.16
Non-metallic	0.00	0.06	0.00	0.18	0.00	0.05
Coal and petroleum	0.00	0.07	0.49	0.74	0.00	0.26
Professional instruments	0.00	0.00	0.00	0.00	0.00	0.00
Other manufacturing	0.00	0.00	0.00	0.00	0.00	0.00
Total (national balance)	0.96	0.34	0.92	0.55	0.92	0.74
Mean (of 18 industries)	0.24	0.22	0.10	0.27	0.06	0.18

Source: As for Table 4.5.

The IITA index can be compared with the evidence on IIDI presented earlier for the UK and Germany. In the UK case, a consistently high level of intra-industry direct investment with other EC countries is associated with a strong presence of intra-industry technological activity in chemicals, pharmaceuticals and electrical equipment (comparing Tables 4.4 and 4.6). Just as with the investment picture, IITA is high in these industries due to the importance of foreign-owned technological activity in the UK, given that overall the UK has a positive net outward involvement. Intra-industry technological activity has also been notable for the UK in metals (in which outward investment to the EC has been rising but inward investment falling), and in rubber products and textiles (in which sectors the lack of evidence on the investment position prevents a proper comparison); but in these cases and in pharmaceuticals the level of cross-border technological activity is weaker than in chemicals and electrical equipment, as suggested by Table 4.5.

For Germany, IITA with EC partner countries is high in line with IIDI in metals, mechanical engineering and electrical equipment (looking at Tables 4.4 and 4.6). In chemicals and pharmaceuticals IITA is also high, but intra-industry direct investment is average, owing to strong German outward investment in this sector. A significant exchange of corporate technological activity is also observed in the motor vehicle and textile industries, in which areas the investment data are insufficiently disaggregated to make a meaningful comparison. On the whole, allowing for gaps in the data, it does seem that intra-industry direct investment within the EC tends to be associated with intra-industry technological activity, especially in the chemical and electrical fields in which both corporate research efforts and direct investments are substantial.

It is also interesting to examine the IITA index drawn up on a bilateral basis between particular EC countries. Table 4.7 shows the results for the calculation of intra-industry technological activity between the three largest countries, Germany, the UK and France. In electrical equipment the IITA index is high in all three cases, but in chemicals and pharmaceuticals it is highest between Germany and the UK (the major centres), high between the UK and France, but negligible between Germany and France. While German chemical firms have a significant level of technological activity in France, French firms appear to have little involvement in Germany. This may reflect the very strength of the German chemical sector, making it difficult for outsiders to break in and attract local skilled labour, a feat that

so far only the most capable British and US firms have managed
(Cantwell and Hodson, 1991).

Table 4.7 *The index of intra-industry technological activity in three*
bilateral cases for the three largest EC countries, 1969–86

	Germany/ UK	Germany/ France	UK/ France
Food products	0.00	0.00	0.00
Drink	0.00	0.00	0.00
Tobacco	0.00	0.00	0.00
Chemicals	0.51	0.02	0.37
Pharmaceuticals	0.72	0.00	0.55
Metals	0.88	0.59	0.55
Mechanical engineering	0.12	0.00	0.00
Electrical equipment	0.59	0.89	1.00
Office equipment	0.00	0.00	0.00
Motor vehicles	0.04	0.13	0.00
Aircraft	0.00	0.00	0.14
Textiles	0.33	0.00	0.00
Paper products	0.00	0.00	0.00
Rubber products	0.00	0.00	0.00
Non-metallic	0.00	0.00	0.33
Coal and petroleum	0.00	0.00	0.07
Professional instruments	0.00	0.00	0.00
Other manufacturing	0.00	0.00	0.00
Total (national balance)	0.32	0.39	0.48
Mean (of 18 industries)	0.18	0.09	0.17

Source: As for Table 4.5.

In other cases of high IITA values the absolute level of activity is
not substantial. The IITA index is high for all three bilateral combinations in the metals sector, although the investment data suggest a
recent switching away from the UK as a centre by the firms of other
EC countries in this case. In mechanical engineering the high value
of the IITA index between Germany and the rest of the EC as a
whole (Table 4.6) does not carry through to bilateral comparisons
(Table 4.7). In this industry the bulk of foreign-owned technological
activity in Germany is carried out by British firms, but German com-

panies spread their foreign research among a wider range of other EC centres. By comparison, for the textiles sector high values of IITA for Germany and the UK respectively and the remainder of the EC, and a low value for France, are reflected in a significant bilateral IITA between Germany and the UK but the absence of intra-industry technological activity between these countries and France. Not surprisingly, the textiles industry is a sector in which German and British firms are technologically advantaged, but French firms are not (Cantwell, 1989).

To summarize: in most industries where a relatively strong intra-industry direct investment within the EC can be identified, a system of intra-industry technological activity has grown up to accompany it. The industries in question are chemicals and allied products, metal products, mechanical engineering and electrical equipment. Of these, the scale of activity is greatest in chemicals and electrical equipment. Using the German and UK evidence, the qualifications both apply to the UK case. For the UK, IIDI has recently slipped back in the metals sector and IITA is weak in mechanical engineering, in both cases due to a relative lack of interest by foreign firms in the UK. In any event, intra-industry technological activity seems to run primarily between the major EC centres of excellence for the industry concerned. Between Germany and the UK the IITA index is especially prominent in the chemicals, pharmaceuticals and textiles sectors, in which both German and British companies hold a comparatively strong technological position. This suggests that in these cases cross-investments are motivated more by the requirements of corporate networks than local market servicing; but it is only in chemicals that these networks linking Germany and Britain as centres have exerted an important impact in the organization of European industry.

4.5   INTRA-INDUSTRY DIRECT INVESTMENT AND PATTERNS OF SPECIALIZATION IN TECHNOLOGICAL ACTIVITY

The evidence just discussed suggests that intra-industry direct investment in the EC is typically associated with an exchange of research facilities as well as production. In other words, in the other major EC centres the largest firms carry out innovative development which is complementary to their domestic technological activity. The question which then arises concerns the form that this complementarity takes.

There are two obvious possibilities. The first is that technological activity in the foreign centre is directly supportive of domestic research or a direct extension of it. That is, the types of technological activity which firms concentrate on at home are also to the fore in their innovative efforts in other centres. The second alternative is that in foreign locations firms undertake related diversification, principally engaging in technological activities other than those which lie at the heart of their domestic operations. In this case firms may gear their technological activity towards the comparative strengths of the location in question, to take advantage of locally specific skills and experience. If so, the types of technological activity emphasized in the foreign location will be more similar to those of the domestic operations of indigenous firms than to their own domestic research.

These are issues of the pattern of intra-industry technological specialization of the largest firms across different locations or major centres within the EC. It is in this context that the distinction between different types of technological activity within an industry becomes relevant. The starting point is the distribution of technological activity across various kinds of innovation in the core domestic research of the largest industrial firms originating from a given EC country.

To illustrate the argument, consider the chemicals and pharmaceuticals industry, in which it has been shown that intra-industry direct investment and technological activity is significant within the EC, especially between Germany and the UK. The distribution of technological activity in the domestic research of the largest German and British firms can be measured using the patent database previously described. To do so, we refer to the total number of US patents granted to the largest non-US chemical firms in the period 1969–86 which are attributable to their domestic research (but not to their foreign research facilities). This involves the patents of German firms due to inventions in Germany, those of UK firms due to their UK research, and so forth. The share of German and British firms in the total can then be calculated for each branch of technological activity.

The results of this exercise are set out in Table 4.8. The great strength of German companies in the chemicals sector can be seen from this table, accounting on average for three to four times the number of US patents granted to UK firms. In total, the largest German chemical and pharmaceutical firms were granted 25,332 US patents between 1969 and 1986, by comparison with 6,879 granted to the equivalent UK companies. The 17 varieties of technological activity listed in the table are not comprehensive, but they are those which are most important for firms in the chemicals industry. The criterion for inclusion of such fields is that non-US firms in the chemicals sector were granted a total of at least 440 US patents with the relevant technological classification during the period in question. This is an admittedly arbitary cut-off point, but the findings of the analysis that follows are not very sensitive to the choice of threshold.

Table 4.8   *The share of German and British firms in US patents attributable to the domestic research of the largest non-US chemical and pharmaceutical companies, by type of technological activity, 1969–86 (%)*

	Germany	UK
Inorganical chemicals	46.3	10.1
Agricultural chemicals	46.3	7.9
Chemical processes	46.4	11.0
Bleaching and dyeing	57.3	6.3
Organic chemicals	45.9	8.9
Pharmaceuticals	36.9	16.3
Metal products	40.9	17.2
Chemical equipment	39.5	10.7
Assembly equipment	51.5	7.6
Specialized mechanical equipment	36.8	22.8
General industrial equipment	39.2	22.4
General electrical equipment	39.7	19.3
Rubber products	36.7	20.1
Non-metallic mineral products	33.8	13.8
Coal and petroleum products	36.2	19.2
Photographic instruments	36.1	0.8
Other instruments	26.7	7.2

Source: As for Table 4.5.

Table 4.8 also permits an assessment of the relative technological strengths of different national groups of firms in their domestic base. German firms are strongest in mainstream chemicals research, especially in their traditional core activities of dyeing and bleaching. By comparison, UK firms in this industry are comparatively advantaged in pharmaceuticals and in technological activities less related to basic chemistry, such as metal products, mechanical and electrical equipment, rubber products, and coal and petroleum products. Of course, British firms also had most of their patents in the chemical and pharmaceutical fields, but these are relative measures of their activity in each sector in turn.

It now remains to describe the measurement of the distribution of technological activities which a national group of firms in the chemicals and pharmaceuticals industry is inclined to carry out in a particular foreign centre. This can be achieved in one of two ways. First, it can be measured with reference to the overall foreign research of that group of firms. This entails, for example, the share of US patents granted to German firms for inventions originating outside Germany which is attributable to research in the UK. This is a measure of the relative attractiveness of the UK as a research centre for German chemical firms, by comparison with other foreign centres, across the range of possible types of technological activity.

The second alternative measure brings in an additional element of comparison between firms of the chosen nationality and other companies in the composition of their foreign-located research. Here the point of reference is the patenting of the largest non-US firms which is due to foreign research facilities outside their home country. What is calculated is then, for instance, the share of all US patents granted to the largest non-US chemical firms and due to foreign research facilities which is accounted for by German-owned research in the UK. This involves the strength of German firms' technological activity in the UK by comparison with the foreign-located research of all the largest non-US chemical companies, across the various kinds of activity. Each of these measures can then be related to the pattern of comparative advantage in their domestic research held by the largest German and British firms. To this end four cross-section regressions were run as follows:

$$SGFPGUK_i = \alpha_1 + \beta_1\ SADPGDP_i + \gamma_1\ SADPUKDP_i + \epsilon_{1i} \qquad (1)$$

$$SAFPGUK_i = \alpha_2 + \beta_2\ SADPGDPi + \gamma_2\ SADPUKDP_i + \epsilon_{2i} \qquad (2)$$

$$SUKFPUKG_i = \alpha_3 + \beta_3\ SADPGDP_i + \gamma_3\ SADPUKDP_i + \epsilon_{3i} \qquad (3)$$

$$SAFPUKG_i = \alpha_4 + \beta_4\ SADPGDP_i + \gamma_4\ SADPUKDP_i + \epsilon_{4i} \qquad (4)$$

where the variables are defined in the following way:

$SADPGDP_i$: The share of all the largest non-US firms' patents granted in the US from 1969–86 for their domestic inventions accounted for by German companies in technological activity i.

SADPUKDP$_i$: The share of all the largest non-US firms' patents granted in the US from 1969–86 for their domestic inventions accounted for by UK companies in technological activity i.

SGFPGUK$_i$: The share of the largest German firms' patents granted in the US from 1969–86 from their foreign research accounted for by facilities located in the UK in technological activity i.

SAFPGUK$_i$: The share of all the largest non-US firms' patents granted in the US from 1969–86 from their foreign research accounted for by German-owned facilities in the UK in technological activity i.

SUKFPUKG$_i$: The share of the largest UK firms' patents granted in the US from 1969–86 from their foreign research accounted for by facilities located in Germany in technological activity i.

SAFPUKG$_i$: The share of the largest non-US firms' patents granted in the US from 1969–86 from their foreign research accounted for by UK-owned facilities in Germany in technological activity i.

The results of these regressions are reported in Table 4.9. They demonstrate the differences between the sectoral structure of British and German firms in their intra-industry technological activity in the chemicals and pharmaceutical industry. The distribution of technological activity carried out by German firms in the UK is significantly and positively related to the equivalent distribution in the domestic operations of indigenous UK firms (though only weakly so), but bears little relationship to the pattern of their own domestic activity. By contrast, what UK chemical and pharmaceutical companies do in their German research is significantly and positively linked to the distribution of their own domestic UK operations (even if not strongly so), but not to the comparative strengths of local German firms. This difference perhaps reflects the fact that Germany is a more important centre than the UK in chemicals as a whole, which British companies treat as a general reservoir of scientific experience that can be used to extend their own major lines of core technological activity. German firms, though, use the UK as a site for more specialized research purposes stemming from the relative strengths of the UK as a location, thereby giving access to local expertise, for example in pharmaceuticals.

Table 4.9   Results of the regressions relating the intra-industry techno-logical activity of German and British chemical firms to their own strengths and those of the foreign location

| | Dependent variable | | | |
	SGFPGUK	SAFPGUK	SUKFPUKG	SAFPUKG
Intercept	1.77	0.64	0.06	0.03
	(0.41)	(0.45)	(0.01)	(0.02)
SADPGDP	−0.05	−0.01	−0.03	−0.01
	(−0.50)	(−0.47)	(−0.16)	(−0.25)
SADPUKDP	0.18	0.05	0.38	0.07
	(1.80)*	(1.39)	(1.63)	(1.92)*

Notes
Number of observations = 17
Figures in brackets are t-statistics
*denotes coefficient significantly different from zero at the 10 per cent level.

Apart from the pharmaceuticals case a number of other sectors of technological activity stand out for their contribution to the regression results. Both British firms in Germany and German firms in the UK have little work in the fields of agricultural chemicals, bleaching and dyeing and photographic instruments, but both are significantly involved in research in the area of mechanical equipment. As was noted from Table 4.8, in their domestic innovation British companies are relatively weak in the first three activities, but strong in the fourth, helping to explain the two positive and significant coefficients shown in Table 4.9. Another interpretation from this evidence would be that in their foreign research the leading chemical firms are reluctant to concentrate on mainstream chemistry which they concentrate at home, but instead they emphasize research in supporting areas such as mechanical technologies.

However, the difference between Germany and the UK in their importance as major centres in the chemicals industry seems to play a greater role, as is revealed by extending the exercise above to Italy. The relationship between German and Italian firms in their intra-industry technological activity in chemical and pharmaceuticals is essentially the same as that between German and British firms. German firms gear their Italian research towards the comparative strengths of Italian firms rather than their own, but Italian firms carry out research in Germany in essentially the same lines of technological activity as at home. The interesting finding, though, is that UK chemi-cal and pharmaceutical companies in Italy behave more like the German firms in that country, having a pattern of technological activity which is closely related to the composition of the domestic research of indigenous Italian firms and not correlated with their own domestic strengths. All these results hold in an even stronger form than for the German–UK analysis, in that the relevant coefficients are all significant at the 1 per cent rather than the 10 per cent level. They are consistent with the German–UK results, as in this case both Germany and the UK are more important centres for the chemicals and pharmaceutical industry than is Italy. The fact that Germany is a still stronger location than the UK is perhaps further illustrated by the absence of Italian-owned research in the UK, while it can be found in Germany.

Such relationships between EC centres in the chemicals industry are weaker in the case of France. This can be partly attributed to French government policy. The research of German and British firms in France leans towards pharmaceuticals, in which local companies are only moderately advantaged. This is because of the regulations imposed by the French pharmaceutical purchasing authorities, which require a local research content. The weakening of non-tariff barriers of this kind after 1992 may be expected to reduce these distortions. However, together with the other evidence this suggests that cross-technological development within the EC is still at an early stage, just as is wider intra-industry direct investment.

It is worth exploring further, however, the role played by the rela-tive significance of locational centres in each industry in explaining the observed pattern of intra-industry technological activity. Looking beyond the chemical and pharmaceutical industry, in each sector the degree of locational concentration of technological activity within the EC can be estimated, as a means of measuring the relative strengths of the leading centres in each case. This involves calculating the vari-ance in national shares of US patenting among EC countries. In this context the national share derives from patents due to inventions originating in the country in question, whether assigned to indigenous or to foreign-owned firms. The patenting of all the world's largest 792 firms was considered for this purpose, even though the 188 EC-based companies mentioned earlier make the strongest contribution to EC located research. As all 12 EC countries are included for every indus-try, the average national share is 8.33 per cent, around which the variance is estimated.

The results of estimating this measure of the locational concentration of technological activity in the EC are recorded in Table 4.10 for the same set of industries for which the IITA index was calculated in Table 4.6. Roughly speaking, an inverted U-shaped relationship can be established between locational concentration (the variance of patent shares across countries) and the extent of intra-industry technological activity in the EC. Where innovative efforts are quite widely dispersed (a variance of less than 2.25) the IITA for the five leading EC centres considered together tends to be below the average value of 0.18. This holds for the office equipment, rubber products, non-metallic mineral products and other manufacturing industries. The one exception is the coal and petroleum products industry in which technological activity is spread across the EC most evenly of all, but in which Italy and especially France have a substantial IITA. However, this is not sustained at a bilateral level (see Table 4.7).

Table 4.10   *The variance in the cross-EC country percentage share of the US patenting of the world's largest firms in each industry, 1969–86*

Food products	2.59
Drink	4.94
Tobacco products	5.38
Chemicals	3.34
Pharmaceuticals	2.78
Metal products	3.46
Mechanical engineering	3.53
Electrical equipment	2.81
Office equipment	1.36
Motor vehicles	2.94
Aircraft	2.45
Textiles	3.13
Paper products	2.58
Rubber products	1.82
Non-metallic mineral products	1.71
Coal and petroleum products	1.04
Professional instruments	4.17
Other manufacturing	2.22
Total manufacturing	2.51

Source: As for Table 4.5.

Conversely, where technological activity is highly locationally concentrated (a variance greater than 4), the average IITA reported in Table 4.6 is even lower, namely zero. This happens in the drink, tobacco and professional and scientific instruments sectors. In the case of the first two of these it might be claimed that a low absolute level of technological development is responsible for both the high degree of concentration of activity in a single EC centre (the UK) and a lack of intra-industry technological activity. However, this is not true of the professional instruments industry in which technological activity takes place on a significant scale, and it does seem reasonable to hypothesize that IITA will rise as a smaller group of centres become established as regional leaders, but then fall as a single centre becomes dominant, eventually falling to zero as in the three industries mentioned. Germany is the dominant centre in the development of technology by instrument producers.

In the five industries in which the average IITA of the five leading centres is greater than 0.27, the variance of patent shares is just above average. This applies to the chemicals, pharmaceuticals, metal products, electrical equipment and motor vehicles industries, in which there is some degree of balance between centres and a significant level of intra-industry technological activity. Germany leads the way in all five cases, though it is equally matched with the UK in pharmaceuticals. It is also in these sectors that intra-industry direct investment is most notable, once again supporting the view that IIDI is associated with supply-orientated considerations of extended technological development in foreign centres with complementary capabilities, especially within the EC.

It seems that such intra-industry technological activity is at its strongest where a hierarchy of centres has emerged, but without the leading country being completely dominant. The evidence of the chemicals and pharmaceuticals industry suggests that where this happens the composition of technological activity that the firms of a higher-order centre locate in a lower-order one tends to follow a different pattern than that associated with investments running in the other direction. The firms of the most-important centres are more likely to adopt a strategy of related technological diversification abroad, and thereby are more likely to develop a more complex network of intra-firm cross-country specialization in innovative activity.

However, as MNCs continue to develop internationally integrated technological development further, and as corporate restructuring within the EC proceeds in the aftermath of 1992, it may be that a wider spectrum of firms in each industry will come to resemble this pattern. It is by this means that MNCs operating in the EC would be able to take full advantage of their multinationality.

For now, our results on technological competition in Europe can be summarized as follows. Within the EC, intra-industry technological activity tends to be high in sectors where intra-industry direct investment is high. This suggests that cross-investments are in part motivated by the desire of MNCs to establish EC-wide networks of technological activity. The structure of these networks depends upon the form of locational hierarchy that is implied by the ranking of different EC research centres in a particular industry. Intra-industry technological activity is greatest where the locational hierarchy is neither very weak (all centres are of similar strength) nor very pronounced (one centre alone is dominant). Firms from a lower-order centre when investing in a high-order centre are prone to try and extend their research in their own fields of technological strength, but firms from a high-ranked centre of excellence are more likely to attempt to tap into areas of local strength in lower-order centres.

NOTES

1. Stock data were preferred to flow figures as flows are not collected to analyse MNC activities *per se* but for balance of payments purposes, and are often subject to substantial year-to-year fluctuations.
2. The chemical industry is excluded for The Netherlands, as in the Dutch statistics this sector is grouped with oil and other extractive industries.
3. As data on the outward stock of French DI are not available before 1987, this contention relies upon flow figures.
4. In 1988 and 1989 several large foreign investors set up holding companies in Germany to which they assigned enterprises previously directly owned by them (Deutsche Bundesbank, 1991). This change has resulted in an undervaluation of the German inward stock of manufacturing DI. Furthermore, it has become more difficult than in the past to assess which branches of German industry are of particular interest to foreign investors.
5. We report the 1987 index because the major organizational changes which took place in 1988 and 1989, as previously described, made it more difficult to evaluate correctly the sectoral composition of the stock of inward DI in Germany.
6. In 1988 total (primary and secondary) world DI in German manufacturing was DM69,398m. of which secondary DI accounted for 31.8 per cent.
7. The bilateral index between Germany and the UK calculated with the German data is equal to 0.54 which remains considerably higher than that between Germany and France.
8. The stock of UK DI in the German food industry in 1987 is estimated to be £553m. by the British source and DM73m. (or about £216m.) from German data.
9. This is the weighted average of the indices calculated for the individual industries. See Grubel and Lloyd (1971).
10. We are assuming that each producer has a non-negative profit in the home market. In other words, the issue of exit is ruled out.
11. Subsidies to indigenous firms and cost-disadvantage generating barriers influence

the DI-export choice examined here in a similar way, although they are rather different in certain respects, such as in their welfare effects. Although a subsidy to indigenous firms discourages DI less than CDB2, as it lowers the equilibrium price of the good, and so increases global output (while CDB2 by raising the unit variable cost of the foreign firm has the opposite effect), its removal is equally DI-promoting.

12. In the case of a production subsidy to indigenous firms, the elimination of the NTB also increases the market served by either a local foreign-owned affiliate or a foreign-located exporter.

REFERENCES

Banque de France (1990), *Note d'information*, no. 89, July.

Cantwell, J.A. (1989), *Technological Innovation and Multinational Corporations*, Oxford: Basil Blackwell.

Cantwell, J.A. (1992), 'The Effects of Integration on the Structure of MNC Activity in the EC', in M. Klein and P.J.J. Welfens (eds), *Multinationals in the New Europe and Global Trade in the 1990s*, Berlin: Springer Verlag, pp. 193–233.

Cantwell, J.A. and Hodson, C. (1991), 'Global R and D and UK Competitiveness', in Casson, M.C. (ed.), *Global Research Strategy and International Competitiveness*, Oxford: Basil Blackwell.

Clegg, L.J. (1990), 'Intra-industry Foreign Direct Investment: a Study of Recent Evidence', in A. Webster and J.H. Dunning (eds), *Structural Change in the World Economy*, London: Routledge.

Commission of the European Communities (1990a), *Panorama of EC Industry, 1990*, Brussels: European Communities.

Commission of the European Communities (1990b), *European Economy: Social Europe*, Brussels: European Communities.

Dei, F. (1990), 'A Note on Multinational Corporations in a Model of Reciprocal Dumping', *Journal of International Economics*, **29**, 161–71.

Deutsche Bundesbank (1991), *Monthly Report of the Deutsche Bundesbank*, April.

Doz, Y. (1986), *Strategic Management in Multinational Companies*, Oxford: Pergamon Press.

Dunning, J.H. and Norman, G. (1986), 'Intra-industry Investment', in H.P. Gray (ed.), *Uncle Sam as Host*, Greenwich, Conn.: JAI Press.

Emerson, M., Aujean, M., Catinat, M., Goybet, P. and Jacquemin, A. (1988), *The Economics of 1992*, Oxford: Oxford University Press.

Eurostat (1990), *Les Investissements directs de la Communauté Européenne – Années 1984 à 1988*, Brussels: Eurostat.

Graham, E.M. (1990), 'Exchange of Threat between Multinational Firms as an Infinitely Repeated Noncooperative Game', *International Trade Journal*, **4** (3), 259–77.

Grubel, H.G. and Lloyd, P.J. (1971), 'The Empirical Measurement of Intra-industry Trade', *Economic Record*, **47** (120), 494–517.

Itaki, M. and Waterson, M. (1990), 'European Multinationals and 1992', *University of Reading Discussion Papers in International Investment and Business Studies*, no. 141.

KPMG (1990), *Deal Watch, International Mergers and Acquisitions*, March.

Ozawa, T. (1991), 'Japanese Multinationals and 1992', in B. Bürgenmeier and J.L. Mucchielli (eds), *Multinationals and Europe 1992: Strategies for the Future*, London: Routledge.

Smith, A. (1987), 'Strategic Investment, Multinational Corporations and Trade Policy', *European Economic Review*, no. 31, pp. 89–96.

UN Commission on Transnational Corporations (1991), *Recent Developments Related to Transnational Corporations and International Economic Relations*, New York: United Nations.

Yannopoulos, G.N. (1990), 'Foreign Direct Investments and European Integration: the Evidence from the Formative Years of the European Community', *Journal of Common Market Studies*, **28** (3), 235–59.

5. The Belgian Metalworking Industries and the Large European Internal Market: The Role of Multinational Investment

D. Van Den Bulcke and Ph. De Lombaerde

5.1 INTRODUCTION

Belgium has played an important role in the formative years of the European Community (EC) and is one of the most enthusiastic advocates of closer economic integration among the member countries. It has also been very open towards Foreign Direct Investment (FDI). At the end of the 1950s, when the EC was still in its start-up phase and not yet concerned about FDI as such, the Belgian 'expansion laws' already provided generous incentives to foreign-owned firms that located in Belgium. Together with its central location within the Community and the availability of qualified labour, these government incentives succeeded in attracting a large share of foreign, mainly American, investment. The openness of its economy is often regarded as one of Belgium's main assets.

According to *The Financial Times*, Belgium combines a vision of a united Europe with internal fragmentation (Gardner, 1991). The dismantling of Belgium's unitary state probably reflects the belief of its inhabitants that part of their problems and tensions can be solved in a 'Europe of regions', which can only be achieved within an integrated EC. The devolution of Belgian political decision-making towards the regions of Flanders, Wallonia and Brussels is indirectly one of the reasons why this chapter focuses on the Belgian metalworking industries (MWI). Since the beginning of the 1980s national data on FDI in Belgium are to all intents no longer available. The Belgian MWI are about the only sectors about which systematic information is regularly published and for which some indication of both the inward and outward activities of companies is provided. This is primarily due to the efforts of Fabrimetal, the employers' federation of the Belgian metalworking industries, which in principle carries out a survey on foreign-owned enterprises every three years and a study on Belgian MWI investment abroad every four years. The latest available data on inward investment refer to 1988, while for outward investment the year of reference is 1989. To concentrate on the MWI is also justified because it is the most important sector in Belgian industry. Besides, the MWI cover some very diversified sectors and therefore allow for comparisons among different branches. In addition they are some of the most multinationalized sectors in a country where the degree of foreign participation is generally very high.

In the rest of this introductory section more information is presented about the Belgian MWI. The second section confronts the Belgian MWI with the large European internal market (LEIM) and analyses its strengths and weaknesses as compared with European MWI in general. Section 5.3 illustrates the dominating role of FDI and multinational corporations (MNCs) in the Belgian economy, while Section 5.4 shows the significance of outward investment for the Belgian MWI. Section 5.5 discusses Belgium as a cross-investment country, in particular for the metalworking sectors, and elaborates the strategic role of multinational investment. Section 5.6 seeks to draw some general policy conclusions.

The Belgian Metalworking Industries

The concept of the Belgian MWI as used in this study is somewhat peculiar as it consists of those industrial branches which belong to the employer's federation Fabrimetal. As such the Belgian metalworking industries are not completely comparable to the metal sector as defined in national statistics. One of the characteristics of the MWI is that they also include firms which are in plastics conversion. The subsectors which are part of Fabrimetal's MWI are: preliminary processing; metal products and plastics; metal construction, shipbuilding and rail; mechanical engineering, arms and aeronautics; electrical engineering; automobiles, cycles and allied industries.

The Belgian MWI employs almost a quarter of a million (about 245,000) people and represents 25 per cent of total employment in Belgian industry and 34 per cent of the manufacturing sector. Fabrimetal is dominated by small and medium-sized enterprises, as 80 per cent of them provide fewer than 100 jobs. Although the available jobs have been decreasing for many years, the downward employment trend in the small and medium metalworking companies (with 17 per cent of total employment in the Belgian MWI) has stopped since about

1985, while the larger enterprises continued to shed jobs. However, it should be realized that the growth of the smaller firms is to some extent due to the 'filialization' of larger groups and that the small and medium firms have both a high death and birth rate.

Fabrimetal groups the Belgian industries with the highest export intensity in a country which ranks among the ten largest exporting nations (ninth position in 1989) and has the highest level of exports *per capita* in the world. From 1960 to 1986 the percentage of sales of the MWI which were exported doubled from 38 to 73 per cent. From 1960 to 1970 the annual growth rate for metalworking exports was 1.7 per cent as compared with 1 per cent after 1970. The export share in the automobile sector almost quadrupled from 26 per cent in 1960 to 91 per cent in 1986. The major expansion in the automotive sector took place in the first decade of economic integration in Europe and exports as a percentage of sales tripled from 26 per cent in 1960 to 74 per cent in 1970. With an export share as high as 50 per cent in 1986, the subsector of metal manufactures scored lowest among the major branches in the Belgian MWI (Boelaert, 1989).

The export explosion of the Belgian MWI is strongly linked to the Europeanization of Belgian industry. The fact that the export share of Europe in the MWI increased from 69 per cent in 1960 to 87 per cent in 1986 is especially due to foreign – especially American – firms, which increasingly used their Belgian subsidiaries as an export base to the other EC countries. Intra-group trade expanded quite strongly and was also to some extent responsible for an increase in the import share of the Belgian MWI from 48 per cent in 1960 to 79 per cent in 1986. The MWI activities which were directed towards the local Belgian market tended to be the most regressive ones. MWI firms were therefore urged further into export markets.

Belgium and the Large European Internal Market

Belgium, as one of the pioneering countries in the European integration process, had high expectations of the beneficial effects of the 1992 internal market. In 1988 the Belgian government even created a ministerial position of 'Secretary of State Europe 1992' whose task it was to inform, explain and prepare the Belgian public and business communities about the European single market. In the following review of possible macroeconomic and industrial effects of 1992 for the Belgian economy, attention is also drawn to the interrelationship with investment flows.

Already in the early stages of European integration (Dunning,

1970), a link was established between economic integration and (mainly US) inward direct investment, and its positive impact on European growth. To measure the causal relationship between integration measures and investment decisions and to estimate the growth effects of these investments proved to be more difficult, however.

Estimates of the 'potential' macroeconomic effects of the completion of the single market were presented in the Cecchini Report (Catinat, Donni and Italianer, 1988). Results for individual countries are only available for France, the FRG, Italy and the UK. McDonald (1989, p. 69) argues that the EC study is basically over-optimistic, an opinion which is shared by the Dutch Central Planning Bureau (CPB). Winters (1989, pp. 15, 17) assumes that the projected growth gains can be achieved, but situates them on the upper side of the fork of possible outcomes. Van Sebroeck (1988) and Italianer and Vanheukelen (1989) used partial results for Belgium and added average results from the 'big four' countries to cope with supply effects in order to calculate the potential impact. Belgium would obtain average growth effects (4.5 per cent of GDP after six years), although the expected labour productivity growth rate would be below the EC average (+ 2.1 per cent compared to + 3.0 per cent). This results in a more-than-average employment effect (2 per cent compared to 1.5 per cent after six years). According to Italianer (1990, p. 10), this is due to the openness of the Belgian economy. The positive impact on the current account would also be significantly superior to the corresponding impact on the EC current account after six years (+ 2.4 per cent of GDP as compared with + 1 per cent). On the basis of the Dulbea DRY Model, Guillaume, Meulders & Plasman (1989) demonstrated for Belgium that simulations which rely on the same assumptions as the EC Commission's study produce significantly different (that is to say, less optimistic) results. For instance, depending on the model used, the medium-term GDP effect is practically halved. Independent calculations for The Netherlands (Zalm, 1989; Bakhoven, 1989) confirm that small open economies with a strong orientation towards the European market could possibly gain relatively more than other countries from 1992. A sort of 'small-country effect' can be expected[1] (Cuyvers and De Lombaerde, 1990).

The completion of the single market is generally expected to lead to an increase in inward direct investment, especially from Japanese firms which want to be present in the European market and produce 'European' products. During the last few years there has been an acceleration in the share of Japan in FDI in general. However, Japanese FDI in Europe and the internationalization process of many

Japanese enterprises is still in its early stages (Dunning, 1989). The economic effects for the EC will consist of volume and distribution effects. The establishment of production units by outsiders affects growth, employment, trade levels and trade balances (cf. production, import substitution and export development). In addition to this, investments are likely to affect regional growth and intra-European trade balances.

The Dutch Central Planning Bureau (Zalm, 1989) estimated the importance and impact of integration induced foreign direct investments at 0.3 per cent of the EC's GNP. The expected economic mechanisms which would result from this shift in production include a short-run import stimulus followed by an increase in European production and intra-European trade, which replaces imports from the investor's country outside the EC and which, in turn, has a positive effect on Europe's trade balance. Six years' effects (as cumulative percentage changes) of this flow of inward direct investments would represent: 0.6 per cent on the volume of GNP; 0.4 per cent on exports of goods and services; −0.1 per cent on imports; and 0.5 per cent on employment. The current account of the balance of payments would improve (in absolute terms) with 0.3 per cent of GNP. For Belgium no (quantitative) forecast of the effect of 1992 on the volume of foreign direct investment is available, however.

5.2 THE BELGIAN METALWORKING INDUSTRIES AND THE LARGE EUROPEAN INTERNAL MARKET

Industries Sensitive to the Internal Market

An interesting study which links company strategies and the situation of industrial sectors has been carried out by Buiguesand Ilzkovitz (1988). These authors have presented a list of sectors which were considered to be most sensitive to the effects of the LEIM. The sectors were identified on the basis of a number of characteristics of which price differentials as an indication of non-tariff barriers (NTBs) and the degree of intra-EC trade were the main aspects (see Table 5.1).

Table 5.1   Typology of sensitive industries with special indication of metalworking industries (1985)

| | *Intra-EC trade intensity* | |
	High	Low
Not important	**Characteristics:** - fast growth of world demand - advanced technology - high government intervention (procurement, subsidies, R&D standards) - presence of large MNCs - global industries - potential economies of scale - domination of US & Japan - takeovers & alliances - share of VA: 6.1% in EC, 4.0% in Belgium	**Characteristics:** - important extra-EC impacts (NIC competition) - increases in rationalization and restructuring - share of VA: 5.6% in EC, 4.3% in Belgium
Price differentials within EC	**Industries:** - *Computers* - *Burotics* - *Telecommunication* - *Medical equipment*	**Industries:** - *Shipbuilding* - *Electrical equipment* - Food industry
	Characteristics: - NTBs of medium importance - relatively more distribution than production effects - trend towards more co-operation - share of VA: 30.8% in EC, 33.2% in Belgium	**Characteristics:** - traditional industries - high government spending - 'national champions' - important rationalization expected - share of VA: 6.4% in EC, 7.3% in Belgium

Table 5.1 continued

	Industries:	**Industries**:
	- Basic chemistry	- Pharmaceuticals
	- *Machine construction*	- *Railway equipment*
Important	- *Electrical & electronic consumer products*	- *Boilers*
	- Glass	
	- *Automobile industry*	
	- *Aeronautics*	
	- Textiles & clothing	

Notes
MWI industries are in italics.
VA = Value added.
Source: Sleuwaegen and Van Den Bulcke (1990, pp. 34, 35); based on Buigues, Ilzkovitz and Lebrun (1990, Figure 2.1).

These criteria allow for the distinction among four different categories of sensitivity to the realization of the large European internal market (Buigues, Ilzkovitz and Lebrun, 1990; Sleuwaegen and van den Bulcke, 1990). The first group typically has a high intra-EC trade intensity and relatively low price differentials. The sectors which belong to this group are relatively more important in the total value added of the EC than in Belgium and include information industries and medical equipment. In the second group intra-community trade is low and price differentials are more important. In these more traditional sectors, such as railway equipment and boiler construction, the Belgian relative share is somewhat higher than in the EC as a whole. The third group has low intra-EC trade and low price differentials and includes electrical equipment and shipbuilding. The industries in the fourth category, with high intra-EC trade and important price differences, take up about 33 per cent of value added in Belgium (as compared with 30 per cent in the EC) and include several MWI sectors. Table 5.2 summarizes the relative strength of Belgian companies in these sensitive industries. In 16 out of the 28 industrial branches Belgian companies are relatively strong. Among the MWI sectors which appear in this category are motor vehicles, lighting equipment and radio and TV equipment.

Table 5.2   Relative strength of Belgian companies in sensitive industries

Indication of competi- tiveness	Number of indus- tries	% of industrial value added	% of industrial employ- ment	MWI sectors (examples)
Weak*	7	13.3	17.1	Machines Railway equipment Shipbuilding Electrical equipment Telecommunications, etc.
Average*	5	11.6	8.7	Aeronautical equipment
Strong*	16	23.9	24.4	Motor vehicles Lighting equipment Radio & TV equipment

*Based on competitiveness indicators reflecting trade performance within the EC, price competitiveness and flexibility of response to changes in demand.
Source: Buigues, Ilzkovitz and Lebrun (1990); Sleuwaegen and Van Den Bulcke (1990, pp. 36, 37).

Impact of Non-Tariff and Other Barriers on the Belgian Metalworking Industries

From the point of view of industry the non-tariff barriers (NTBs) which seriously hindered economic integration, even after the realization of the Common Market, and which are clearly identified in the Cecchini Report, are:

(a)   formalities and procedures in relation to export activities, especially customs systems;
(b)   national systems of public procurement;
(c)   different national standards and certification procedures.

For the MWI, Houard (1991, p. 17) mentions specifically:

(a)   the tendency to harmonize and in the longer term to eliminate national support schemes and incentives which interfere with the transparency of the market;

(b) the intention to reinforce the European research and development agreements.

Out of 37 three-digit NACE sectors Houard's analysis shows that the harmonization of technical norms and certification procedures will have a strong impact on 21 and a medium impact on 13 sectors, leaving only four sectors which have little to worry about (Table 5.3). The simplification and harmonization of customs procedures affect mostly those sectors which are backward-linked with metal and chemical products and operate mainly via subcontracting. A study by Nerb (1988), which analysed data for 11,000 companies in 18 industrial sectors in the EC, ranked motor vehicles as the sector that would be most affected by technical standards. Electrical and electronic products were ranked second, and machines third, in the list of the most-affected sectors. Office machines and computers and motor vehicles were ranked first and third in the list of all industries according to all NTBs taken together.

Table 5.3 Theoretical impact of non-tariff barriers in the Belgian metalworking industries: 37 NACE sectors (3 digit)

Type of barriers	Number of affected sectors (total = 37)			
	Strong	Medium	Weak	Total
Non-tariff barriers (total)	12	19	4	35
Customs	6	–	1	7
Public markets	7	5	–	12
Norms	21	13	–	34
Complementary elements of sensibility				
Incentives	3	4	1	8
R&D programmes	8	2	1	11

Source: Houard (1991, p. 18, summary of Table 1).

The opening-up of public procurement will have a strong and medium effect on one-third of the 37 NACE sectors, that is, mainly on plate and boilerworks, electric wires and cables, telecommunications, rail and tramway equipment and shipbuilding. For Belgium a positive impact is expected as the Belgian public markets are already more open than those in the other EC countries. The larger size of the other EC countries' markets means that Belgian firms have more to gain from the liberalization of those markets than to lose from the increased competition on their home turf.

The fact that many Belgian firms are subsidiaries of multinational groups may have a special implication in the case of procurement, however. It is to be expected that in the near future multinational groups will bid for large projects in a more centralized way and parcel out different tasks or assignments to their subsidiaries. A survey carried out by the Central Economic Council (CRB, 1989, p. 15) showed that for 119 firms in the Belgian MWI public procurement represented a large part of their total activity. Although government purchases have strongly diminished, especially by the Belgian Railways, they are still of substantial importance to the electrotechnical sector (42 billion BEF in 1987), machine construction, arms and aeronautics (10 billion BEF) and metal construction, shipbuilding and railway equipment (7 billion BEF). In these three sectors government purchases represented as much as 42, 54 and 53 per cent respectively of total domestic sales. Although government purchases are not all that substantial for the Belgian MWI as a whole, they are most important to the above-mentioned sectors and to a number of particular companies. This significance can also be illustrated in terms of employment. While total MWI employment, which is connected with government purchasing, decreased from about 14,500 jobs in 1984 to 11,700 in 1987, the relative share of workers and employees was 23 per cent for the electrotechnical sector, 12 per cent for machine construction, arms and aeronautics, and 24 per cent for metalworks, shipbuilding and railway equipment.

Public incentive programmes affect eight out of the 37 sectors. A strong impact occurs in electrical wires and cables, telecommunications and shipbuilding, while medium effects take place in informatics, electric capital equipment, rail and aeronautical equipment. The decision of the EC Commission to eliminate cost distortions among the member countries and harmonize government subsidies, obliged the Belgian regional governments in August 1991 to do away with the aid which was given to large enterprises outside of the so-called development regions on the basis of the expansion laws of 1959. An exception has temporarily been granted for smaller enterprises with not more than 150 employees, when the aid programme represents less than 7.5 per cent. Aid may be continued in special cases after the explicit authorization of the EC Commission has been obtained, however. The new expansion laws will have to be more selective and conditional than the previous ones, and will take into account the strategic and ecological importance of the new investments as well as their employment impact.

The reinforcement of R&D programmes is likely to have a positive impact on 11 sectors of which eight will register a strong effect, such as medical and hospital equipment, aeronautics, precision equipment, telecommunications, electrical equipment, wires and cables and informatics equipment.

In total these various measures which are linked to the formation of the LEIM could have a strong impact on 32 per cent of the employment in the Belgian MWI. For those employed in the Belgian MWI 53 per cent would be moderately affected, while 15 per cent would register only a weak effect. This is a theoretical impact and will depend on the degree of integration that has already been reached before the LEIM was instituted (Houard, 1991, p. 20).

Two factors of great importance for the LEIM are, on the one hand, the existing degree of concentration of supply and, on the other hand, the existence of potential economies of scale. Houard (1991, pp. 32–7) uses six different criteria to measure this:

(a) the average size of companies with more than 20 employees;
(b) the proportion of the number of companies with 10 to 20 employees in the total number of companies and the value added of those firms as a proportion of the total sectoral value added;
(c) the percentage of exports in total sales;
(d) the export proportions to the total industrial exports to the sectoral sales proportion in the total industrial sales;
(e) the proportion of sectoral added value of companies with 20 to 100 employees in all EC countries;
(f) the existence of non-exploited economies of scale.

It is on the basis of these structural criteria that three major groups of MWI industries are distinguished:

(a) Activities which have mainly backward linkages with the '*filières*' of metal and plastic products, that is, foundries (NACE 311, 312), second transformation (313), metal manufactures (314), plate and boiler works (315), plastics conversion (483). Characteristic of this group is that it is dominated by subsidiaries of groups; that the export intensity and specialization is relatively weak; and that there are opportunities for reaping technical economies of scale.

(b)   Subsectors of the mechanical engineering sector (NACE 32), where the firms are medium-sized compared with the rest of the MWI; the export rate and export specialization are high and non-technical economies of scale can be carried out.

(c)   The third group, that is, equipment for information technology, electric and electronic consumer goods, motor vehicles, and construction of other transport equipment (shipbuilding, rail, aeronautics) (NACE 33, 34, 35, 36) is made up of large enterprises, with high export specialization and potential economies of scale which are non-technical.

The conclusion to be drawn from Table 5.4 and its four 'strategic' groups is that, on the one hand, the sectors with a domination of SME (Group I) and non-integrated large enterprises (Group II) are relatively more important in Belgium than in the European Community as a whole, while on the other hand, the subsidiaries of international groups and large integrated enterprises on a European or world level are under-represented. The implication from Table 5.4 is that the Belgian MWI should be more concerned about financial

Table 5.4   Structure of supply and mobilization strategies of Belgian metalworking industries for the advantages of the large European internal market

I	Small and medium enterprises (SME)	II	Large non-integrated enterprises
312	Forgings	341	Wires and electric cables (8%)
313	Second transformation	342	*Electrical capital equipment (47%)*
314	Metal manufacturers	352	Car bodies, trailers and containers
315	Plate and boilerworks (26%)*	361	Shipbuilding (0%)
319	Mechanical engineering	362	Rail- and tramway construction (4%)
348	Technical engineering		
483	Plastics conversion		
Pct	*Employment EEC: 19.3*	*Pct*	*Employment EEC: 14.3*
Pct	*Employment Belgium: 23.3*	*Pct*	*Employment Belgium: 17.8*

Table 5.4 continued

III	International groups	IV	Large integrated enterprises
316	Transmission equipment	*330*	*Information technology equipment (92%)*
321	*Agricultural machinery and equipment (89%)*	343	Electrical installation equipment
		344	*Telecommunications (94%)*
322	*Metalworking machine tools (63%)*	*345*	*Electrical-acoustic equipment (88%)*
323	Textile machines (2%)	*346*	*Electrical and electronic consumer goods (92%)*
324	*Food and chemical machines (59%)*		
325	*Hoisting, handling, weighing and construction equipment (79%)*	*347*	*Lamps and lighting equipment (41%)*
		351	*Automobile construction (99%)*
327	Other specific equipment (2%)	351	Automobile equipment and accessories
371	Precision and control instruments		
372	*Medical and hospital instruments (41%)*	364	Acronautical industry
373	Optical and photographic instruments		
Pct	*Employment EEC: 21.1*	*Pct*	*Employment EEC: 45.3*
Pct	*Employment Belgium: 16.8*	*Pct*	*Employment Belgium: 42.1*

*Figures in brackets show the degree of foreign participation on the basis of sales in 1985. The sectors where the percentage for foreign-owned firms is known and higher than 40 per cent are in italics.
Source: Houard (1991, p. 45); Vanden Houte and Veugelers (1989).

integration strategies and exploitation of the advantages of the LEIM in terms of product value (added value) than by strategies about technical economies of scale and price competition (Houard, 1991, p. 46).

A comparison of the different branches of the Belgian MWI with other EC countries shows that five out of 35 subsectors take up more than 5 per cent of total employment in Fabrimetal. They represent almost half of the MWI employment. With, respectively, 15.9 per cent for automobiles (NACE 351), 9.2 per cent for metalworking machine tools (316), 6.3 per cent for radio and TV (345) and 5.2 per cent for wire-drawing and allied products, four sectors are relatively more important in Belgium than in the European Community. Telecommunications (344), with 9.1 per cent of total MWI employment, is as important in Belgium as in the EC. The only other sectors which are more important in Belgium than in the Community as a whole are: metal manufacturers (4.4 per cent) (314), car bodies (3.5 per cent) (352), agricultural machinery (2.4 per cent) (321), electrical equipment (1.8 per cent) (343), textile machines (1.8 per cent) (323) and rail equipment (1.1 per cent) (362).

Between 1979 and 1989 employment in the Belgian industry diminished by almost 20 per cent, that is, by 100,000 jobs (from 526,400 to 424,500). The decline in the automobile sector (the only MWI sector which can be considered expansionary in terms of the average growth-rate of value added) was limited to 7 per cent as the level of employment came down from 79,600 to 74,000. Without domestic automobile companies, Belgium succeeds in producing the highest number of cars *per capita* in the world (Generale Bank, 1991a). When the Belgian automobile sector reacted to the technological and Japanese challenge by restructuring programmes based on automation and robotization at the beginning of the 1980s, it carried out 45 per cent of all investment in the Belgian MWI.

The barriers in the automobile market which will have to disappear are: the incomplete harmonization of technical requirements for initially bringing vehicles into service; delays at customs control posts and the administrative cost of processing customs documents; different VAT rates; and the selective distribution systems with networks of exclusive dealers (authorized by the Commission until 1995) (Emerson *et al.*, 1988, pp. 76, 77). In addition, national import quotas for Japanese exporters exist in France, Italy, Spain and the UK. These formal barriers to trade within the Community are expected to have a 'relatively marginal' impact as 1992 to a large extent stimulates the restructuring processes and technical developments which are already underway. The completion of the single market is expected to stress further the role of 'platforms' in car manufacturing processes. These platforms permit flexible manufacturing of differentiated products while allowing the efficiency levels of the mass-production lines to be maintained. Widespread introduction of these 'platforms', co-operation between different manufacturers for joint use of these platforms, and greater specialization in specific car types could bring about significant economies of scale (Emerson *et al.* 1988, pp. 76–9). The further development of these platform types of organization implies that fewer production lines are required for the production of differentiated products and consequently that Belgian production lines are *a priori* candidate-victims of such restructuring processes. That these assembly lines are foreign-owned could mean that they are politically less-protected than their counterparts in their parent countries. This process of restructuring and technical change in the car industry will in principle result in static and dynamic competitiveness effects, higher sales and a greater demand for components. The car components industry will also be exposed to these competitive pressures, which will lead to more concentration, more just-in-time deliveries (and therefore reduction of stocks), and more co-operation with car manu-facturers (Emerson *et al.*, 1988, p. 79).

Although machine construction is not important overall, Belgian firms continue to play a dominant role in niches such as textile machines. During the 1980s textile machines were one of the most expansive subsectors. Although there is still a relatively high number of domestic firms in machine construction, an increasing number are coming under foreign control. One of the most important became part of the Asea Brown Boveri (ABB) group in 1989. Radio and TV production is dominated by the Dutch Philips-MBLE group which probably takes up 80 per cent of this subsector, while in wire-drawing and allied products the major producer is the Belgian multinational, Bekaert. This latter firm has been restructuring its activities quite extensively since the mid-1980s.

The strong points of the Belgian telecommunications industry, which have been mentioned by the Ministry of Economic Affairs (MAE, 1988), are its high development potential, its export capacity, its con-ception and production of know-how for components and systems, its ability to master integration problems of complete systems, its great flexibility because of its relatively moderate scale, and the existence of strong and performing competence centres which are parts of the largest foreign MNCs.

The European telecommunications equipment market is still very fragmented as a result of the monopsonistic character of national markets where local telecommunications authorities hold monopolies for telecommunications network services. Different technical stan-dards, selective procurement policies, control by certification of prod-ucts, and input specificity for new equipment are the main barriers to intra-EC trade (Emerson *et al.*, 1988, p. 86). This results in very low levels of intra-community trade and relatively low economies of scale. White Paper proposals for the telecommunications equipment market include: liberalization of public procurement; opening of the markets for customer premises equipment and core equipment; and the setting up of a European Telecommunications Standards Institute (ETSI). These measures should result in a more open and competitive market with higher degrees of specialization and higher investment levels in new technologies.

5.3   FOREIGN MULTINATIONAL INVESTMENT IN BELGIUM AND THE BELGIAN METALWORKING INDUSTRIES

Ownership of Belgian Industry

With 80 per cent of its companies being Belgian-owned, less than half of Belgium's industrial sales in 1985 were carried out by these local firms (Table 5.5). With less than 4 per cent of the total number of enterprises, Belgian MNCs took up about 14 per cent of the sales in Belgian industry. The foreign-owned firms realized 40 per cent of Belgian industrial sales with only 17 per cent of the total number. Within this group of foreign MNCs, US firms represent almost one-third of the total number and almost half of total sales (Vanden Houte and Veugelers, 1989). In 1990 one-third of the largest 3 100 Belgian companies – which represented 88 per cent of value added in Belgium – were controlled from abroad. The United States was, with 25 per cent, the principal investor country. Together the four major EC partners were in control of 57 per cent of the larger foreign firms in Belgium, with the Netherlands and France, having respectively 17 and 16 per cent, and Germany and the UK each 12 per cent (Daems and Van De Weyer, 1991). In 1975 one-third of Belgium's industrial employment occurred in foreign-owned firms as compared with 18 per cent in 1968. In the metalworking sector (inclusive of steel and non-ferrous metals and exclusive of plastics) these proportions were respectively 40 per cent in 1975 and 23 per cent in 1968 (Van Den Bulcke, 1985).

Foreign-owned enterprises represented 28 per cent of Fabrimetal's members in 1988 and employed more than 130,000 people. This amounted to almost two-thirds of the jobs provided by the companies which belong to Fabrimetal and 54 per cent of the Belgian MWI. On the basis of sales, foreign-owned multinationals take up, mainly because of the automobile sector, as much as 76 per cent of the companies that are included (Fabrimetal, 1990a).

Table 5.6 shows that the number of foreign-controlled firms in the Belgian MWI has increased from 304 to 349 between 1980 and 1989,

Table 5.5   Ownership structure in the Belgian industrial sector: percentage distribution of total sales and number of companies (1985)

Nationality	Number of companies (%)		Sales (%)	
Belgian enterprises	79.3		46.6	
Belgian multinational enterprises	3.4		13.6	
Foreign-owned enterprises	17.3		39.8	
Japan		2.1		2.0
Luxembourg		1.2		2.9
Switzerland		4.3		3.3
Sweden		3.7		5.4
UK		11.4		6.1
France		12.7		8.0
Netherlands		19.9		9.0
Germany		9.3		15.2
USA		31.0		46.6
Rest		2.5		–
Total Belgian industry	100.0	100.0	100.0	100.0

Source: Vanden Houte and Veugelers (1989).

while employment declined from 149,000 to 134,000. The involvement of Belgium's EC partners in the metalworking sectors went up in terms of both numbers and jobs, mainly because of the increased French presence as a result of acquisitions. Yet the German companies in the Belgian MWI are still the largest employers. Dutch firms rank second of the European employers in the Belgian MWI. While North American companies still contribute in a substantial way, their relative importance has fallen in terms of both numbers (from 36 to 27 per cent) and employment (from 41 to 29 per cent). In some instances, firms switched nationalities when American subsidiaries were taken over by European groups; for example, Bell, which left American ITT for the French Alcatel group. Although the number of Asian (that is, Japanese) companies in the Belgian MWI doubled, employment barely exceeds 1 per cent of the total foreign jobs in the Belgian MWI.

Table 5.6   Foreign companies in the Belgian metalworking industries according to country of origin (1989)

Country of origin	Number of companies		Employment ('000s)	
	1980	1989	1980	1989
European Community	143	201	70.6	81.6
France	33	62	9.7	19.9
The Netherlands	47	45	21.9	22.7
Germany	26	42	24.5	27.8
UK	21	35	9.6	9.4
Rest of Europe	28	41	10.8	11.0
Sweden	14	19	7.8	7.8
Switzerland	10	22	2.1	1.7
US and Canada	108	95	61.3	38.9
Asia	4	9	1.2	1.5
Mixed*	21	–	6.1	–
Total	304	349	149.9	134.0

*The comparison between 1980 and 1989 is somewhat artificial as the mixed companies (i.e. owned by at least two different nationalities) of 1989 have been put in separate national categories while those for 1980 have not been classified as such.
Source: Fabrimetal (1990a).

Employment Contribution of Foreign-Owned Enterprises in the Metalworking Industries

It is quite striking that 82 per cent of the total employment in foreign enterprises in the Belgian MWI is the result of investment decisions by firms which were established in Belgium before 1973, that is, before the first petroleum crisis (Table 5.7). More than one-third of all jobs are provided by companies which located in Belgium before 1960. At that time the Dutch and American firms were the largest employers and are retrospectively responsible for two-thirds of all jobs. Germany, together with the US, became – each with one-third of the total – the most important investors in Belgium during the period 1960–73, to which almost half of today's employment in the foreign firms of the Belgian MWI traces its origin. The employment contribution during the post-crisis period was very bleak, as the lack of new investment initiatives on the one hand and disinvestment decisions on the other caused important job losses. At a much lower absolute level than in the previous periods, France became the dominant investing country

Table 5.7 Foreign-owned enterprises in the Belgian metalworking industries according to country of origin and period of establishment (1989)

Region and country	Before 1960		1960–73		1974–85		After 1985	
	Number	Employment	Number	Employment	Number	Employment	Number	Employment
European Community	55	29,000	64	35,700	37	4,900	45	12,100
France	17	6,300	13	6,300	12	2,500	20	4,900
The Netherlands	19	18,200	14	3,800	7	300	5	300
Germany	5	3,000	22	20,800	9	1,100	6	2,900
UK	7	400	14	4,800	5	600	9	3,700
Rest of Europe	11	3,800	10	3,600	10	2,700	10	900
Sweden	4	2,600	5	3,400	5	1,400	5	400
Switzerland	5	1,100	1	50	2	300	4	200
US and Canada	15	15,500	61	20,300	11	800	8	2,000
Asia	-	-	3	500	4	700	2	300
Total	82	48,400	142	60,800	72	9,500	66	15,300

Source: Fabrimetal (1990a).

and started more than one-quarter of almost 10,000 jobs during the period 1974–85. France even increased its relative position in the period since 1985, during which about one-third of the 15,000 jobs are associated with companies that came under French control. While American metalworking firms showed a renewed interest in the prospects of the Belgian MWI, after the 1992 deadline had been set in the Cockfield Report, the US employment contribution fell short of that of the three individual EC countries, France, UK and Germany.

With 34,000 employees, foreign enterprises in the Belgian MWI were responsible for 17 per cent of all jobs in 1953 (Table 5.8). In preliminary processing this proportion was only 8 per cent, while it was almost five times as high (37 per cent) in electrical engineering. In 1965 foreign participation in the automobile sector had, with 64 per cent, surpassed electrical engineering, which itself had almost reached the 50 per cent mark. In 1974 and 1980 these two subsectors reached a level of foreign ownership in terms of employment of more than 80 and 90 per cent. Although the figures for 1988 are not completely comparable with previous years, it would seem that foreign involvement in the Belgian MWI is declining. Many jobs have been shed since 1974, especially in electrical engineering.

Table 5.8   Foreign-owned companies in the Belgian metalworking industries: employment per sector (in thousands) (1953–88)

Sector	1953		1965		1974		1980		1988*	
	Abs.	%	Abs.	%	Abs.	%	Abs.	%	Abs.	%
Preliminary processing	2.7	8	2.9	8	6.2	24	5.1	23	n.a.	n.a.
Light metal construction	3.3	11	5.8	23	9.0	47	8.0	44	16.8	27
Heavy metal construction	1.8	10	1.4	8	2.3	7	2.5	10		
Mechanical engineering	5.8	12	13.5	21	34.7	47	29.9	46	26.9	40
Electrical engineering	15.3	37	32.3	49	73.6	83	58.6	83	44.4	72
Automobiles	5.1	31	13.9	64	38.8	90	47.4	92	42.9	82
Total	34.1	17	69.8	30	164.6	59	151.5	60	131.1	54

*1988 is not completely comparable with the previous years because of some changes in the classification system.
Source: Boelaert (1989, Table 2).

Performance of Foreign-Owned Enterprises in the Belgian Metalworking Industries

In general, the foreign multinational firms in the Belgian MWI have a fairly good record, especially in comparison with Belgian holding companies. During 1980–7 foreign multinationals operating in Belgium realized a higher growth rate of total sales (4.6 per cent per year) than the Belgian MWI (2.9 per cent). The differences between the growth performance of American and EC firms (5.9 and 4.8 per cent) were small, while the other countries did less well (2.8 per cent) because of some firms in machine construction and electrotechnics. While the expansion of total sales in the Belgian holding companies was negative (−5.9 per cent per annum) the Belgian independent firms succeeded in maintaining a positive level (+0.6 per cent). Although sectoral differences to some extent explained the poor results of the Belgian firms, it should be stressed that in practically all subsectors foreign firms did better than Belgian ones.

In view of these trends it is not surprising that during this same period of 1980–7 the employment retrenchment was less pronounced in foreign-owned companies (−2.6 per cent per year) than in the Belgian firms (−4.8 per cent). It has been established before that, during the crisis of the 1970s, the employment loss in foreign companies was less important in relative terms than for local firms (Van Den Bulcke, 1985).

The better performance of foreign enterprises in the Belgian MWI stands out even more when one uses the difference between the percentage increase of production and employment as a measure for productivity growth. On the basis of this criterion, Boelaert (1989) concluded that productivity in foreign multinationals expanded three times as fast as for Belgian companies (7.2 per cent as compared with 2.4 per cent). The lower rates of productivity growth applied to the independent firms as well as to the holdings.

Foreign-owned firms are also relatively more export orientated. While they exported 86 per cent of their production, all Belgian MWI firms only reached 73 per cent. Their sales abroad increased with 11.7 per cent per year during 1980–7 compared with 4.6 per cent for Belgian firms. Although the differences among EC, US and other foreign multinationals were negligible, the discrepancy between Belgian holding companies and independent firms (respectively 0.4 and 7.2 per cent) was quite impressive.

The analysis of the financial results indicates that from 1982 to 1986 solvency – that is the ratio between capital and reserves and total liabilities – was higher for foreign subsidiaries (on average 35.5 against 24.6 per cent). As the difference from the independent Belgian firms was negligible (34.8 per cent) the lower ratio was entirely due to the financial situation of the holding companies. The differences are also small for gross profitability, that is, before taxes, while net profitability shows more variation, with the foreign-owned firms again doing better than their Belgian counterparts, especially the holding companies. The independent Belgian firms actually outperformed the foreign ones in net profitability. American subsidiaries generally scored best on these financial ratios.

5.4 OUTWARD DIRECT INVESTMENT OF BELGIAN MULTINATIONALS FROM METALWORKING INDUSTRIES

Belgian Outward Investment

In 1975 96 Belgian industrial MNCs employed about 182,500 people outside Belgium, that is to say, about 16.5 per cent of the Belgian industrial employment at that time. The ratio between the employment provided by Belgian MNCs outside and within Belgium in 1975 amounted to 1.1 as compared with 2.79 for the Netherlands and 2.14 for Switzerland. The difference between Belgium and the other smaller industrial countries is to some extent explained by the domination in the other countries of a relatively small number of large multinationals. While the six largest Belgian MNCs were responsible for 114,000 jobs abroad, this represented only 13 per cent of the employment provided by the six largest Dutch MNCs outside of the Netherlands (Van Den Bulcke, 1986a, p. 112). The metal sector with 58,000 jobs abroad was the second most important outward sector, trailing behind only the chemical industry with about 91,500 foreign jobs. While 34 parent companies in the metalworking sector had established 153 subsidiaries abroad, the average number of subsidiaries per parent company of 4.5 was lower than for all Belgian MNCs (6.3) and much lower than in the chemical industry (24.3 units). About two-thirds of both the Belgian and metal sector subsidiaries were located in the European Community, which in 1975 consisted of only nine countries, as compared with about three-quarters in what is now the EC of 12 countries (Haex and Van Den Bulcke, 1979, pp. 36, 39).

Belgian Metalworking Industries Abroad

According to Fabrimetal's most recent survey, 74 Belgian MWI companies controlled 209 subsidiaries abroad, of which 92 were engaged in industrial activities and 117 were commercially orientated. The Belgian parent companies were responsible for about 30 per cent of the total MWI sales and exports in Belgium and provided 21.5 per cent of the employment in their sectors. These proportions are highest in metal products (especially preliminary processing) and electrical engineering.

The ratio between the employment of these Belgian MNCs in the MWI outside and inside Belgium amounts to 0.50 in 1974 and 0.60

Table 5.9   Belgian metalworking industries abroad: Fabrimetal's surveys (1974–88)

Characteristics	1974	1978	1982	1986	1988
1. Number of surveyed parent companies	81	79	63	56	74
2. Number of foreign subsidiaries	229	188	207	220	209
3. Number of foreign plants	123	122*	88	100	92
4. Employment in Belgium**	78.6	64.8	49.9	50.1	40.9
5. Employment abroad**	39.5	39.0	30.6	25.8	24.2
6. Foreign/Belgian employment ratio (5):(4)	0.50	0.60	0.61	0.51	0.59
7. Sales in Belgium***	61.2	96.2	106.7	147.3	286.1
8. Sales by foreign subsidiaries***	48.1	31.0	81.6	112.4	108.5
9. Foreign/Belgian sales ratio (8):(7)	79	32	76	76	38
10. Export ratio of parent companies	50	62	69	–	82

*   Of which 37 assembly plants
**   in thousands
***   in billion BEF.
Source: Fabrimetal (1974, 1979, 1981, 1990a); Boelaert (1989).

in 1978 (Table 5.9). Since then this ratio has remained at more or less the same level, meaning that the outward orientation of Belgian metalworking firms, expressed in terms of employment, has not changed much. It should be stressed here that the Fabrimetal surveys carried out over the years do not always include all companies, even though representation is generally very high. Although Fabrimetal states that the margin of error is quite low, one should not exaggerate the comparability from one survey to another.

Within the MWI metal construction is the only sector which had a ratio higher than one (1.16 in 1978) and still has the highest outward orientation of the subsectors, even though the different split-up of recent years does not allow for a detailed comparison. For mechanical engineering the ratio increased from 0.32 in 1978 to 0.58 in 1988, while electrical engineering during the same period declined systematically from 0.60 to 0.35, even though the number of subsidiaries increased after 1986. The more traditional branches of metal and machine construction are the subsectors which are internationalizing most. In the automobile sector there is little or no investment abroad as most firms belong to large foreign multinational groups.

While the 209 MWI subsidiaries abroad in 1988 employed 24,200 people outside Belgium, it is surprising that in 1974 Fabrimetal already registered 81 parent companies with 229 subsidiaries and 39,500 employees outside Belgium. Over the years the number of manufacturing plants has declined together with employment abroad. The economic crisis of the 1970s clearly had not spared Belgian subsidiaries abroad. In 1982 ten metalworking enterprises reported that they no longer had any foreign subsidiaries. In total these firms had owned 35 foreign industrial and commercial affiliates before 1974. While the sales abroad, as a proportion of sales from Belgium, do not show a clear trend, the export ratio for the parent companies has gone up steadily from 50 per cent in 1974 to 82 per cent in 1988.

Geographical Shifts in Belgian Metalworking Investment Abroad

Again taking into account the limitations of the data provided by Fabrimetal's surveys, Table 5.10 indicates that although fewer Belgian metalworking affiliates were located in the European Community and Europe in 1988 than in the previous years, the relative change was much less pronounced. The loss of employment of 17,000 units from 1974 to 1988 in the 12 countries of the EC and of 20,000 in Europe as a whole, amounts to a relative decline of 60 per cent. In 1988 only about half of the total employment of Belgian MWI affiliates abroad took place in the EC, as compared to 72 per cent in 1974. Europe's relative share in the Belgian foreign industrial employment went down from 87 to 60 per cent during the same period. The sales to the EC and Europe as a proportion of total sales confirm that Belgian FDI in the metalworking sector was turning away from Europe, at least before the 1992 programme became a reality.

Within the EC France is the country with the highest number of Belgian MWI subsidiaries. In 1988 there were 49 affiliates in France, of which 23 were manufacturing plants, and 2,700 employees. Germany and the Netherlands ranked second and third in terms of number of establishments (respectively 19 and 17). The United Kingdom, which took fourth position in the ranking by number, was the largest employer with 4,600 employees, mainly because of the important presence of Bekaert. Most of the subsidiaries in Germany were of a commercial nature, however.

Table 5.11 illustrates the relative decline of the European Community in a different way and also shows that the Common Market regained importance in the last period. The table indicates that of the existing MWI subsidiaries abroad in 1988 about 15 per cent were established before 1960. Of the affiliates that survived until 1988, nearly three out of four located within the EC, while also about 75 per cent of the employment was created in the countries which now form the European Community. In the periods 1961–74 and 1974–85 the number of EC subsidiaries within the total that was established overall fell to about half and even to 40 and 17 per cent of total foreign employment during these same periods. The EC seems to have caught on again in the most recent period, however. Although almost one-third of all MWI subsidiaries abroad were set up as recently as 1986, three out of four were established in the EC, while half of the employment creation was also situated in the LEIM.

The shift of Belgian affiliates abroad towards developing countries is documented in Table 5.12. Although the proportion of foreign subsidiaries located within the developing countries only increased from 15 per cent in 1974 to 21 per cent in 1988, the number of jobs that were created during these years in the developing areas went up from 4 100 to about 6 600, after having peaked at 7 400 in 1982. In relative employment shares, the drift towards developing countries almost tripled from 10 per cent in 1974 to 28 per cent in 1988. Again, this trend is confirmed for sales, most of which were for the local markets.

Table 5.10 Belgian metalworking subsidiaries in the European Economic Community* and Europe: numbers, employment and sales (1974–88)

	1974		1978		1982		1986		1988	
	EC	Europe	EC	Europe	EC	Europe	EC	Europe	EC	Europe
Number of subsidiaries	155	170	136	145	137	152	126	139	130	150
% of total	68	74	72	77	67	73	57	63	62	72
Number of industrial subsidiaries	–	–	60	87	59	65	49	56	50	57
% of total	–	–	49	71	61	67	49	56	54	62
Employment**	28.3	34.6	22.5	29.9	19.9	20.4	14.8	17.8	11.3	14.5
% of total	72	87	58	77	65	67	57	67	47	60
Sales***	39.8	42.1	18.0	20.3	50.8	53.9	60.5	61.9	55.0	62.6
% of total	83	87	58	65	62	66	60	60	51	58

* For comparative reasons Greece, Portugal and Spain are included in the EC total even before they became members.
** in thousands.
*** in million BEF.
Source: As for Table 5.9.

Table 5.11 Belgian metalworking subsidiaries abroad according to the period of establishment (1989)

Regions	Before 1960		1961–74		1975–85		1986–9	
	Number	Employment*	Number	Employment	Number	Employment	Number	Employment
EC	23	5.7	23	2.5	36	1.0	48	2.1
Rest of Europe	4	0.1	8	0.3	4	2.7	4	0.2
North America	2	1.2	1	0.2	9	0.8	1	0.7
Latin America	–	0.7	4	2.0	9	0.5	2	0.6
Asia	–	–	3	0.9	7	1.0	6	0.3
Africa	–	–	5	0.5	3	0.1	3	–
Oceania	1	–	–	–	–	–	1	0.1
Total	32	7.7	44	6.4	68	6.1	65	4.0

*in thousands
Source: Fabrimetal (1990a).

133

Table 5.12   Belgian metalworking subsidiaries in developing countries*: numbers and employment (1973–88)

	1974	1978	1982	1986	1988
Number of subsidiaries	35	33	41	54	44
% of total	15	19	20	25	21
Number of industrial subsidiaries	–	–	–	30	26
% of total	–	–	–	30	28.2
Employment	4,123	3,973	3,376	6,071	6,589
% of total	10.4	10	24	24	28
Sales (in million BEF)	3,058	2,949	14,034	21,191	23,621
% of total	6	10	17	19	22

*Japan is included as it could not be separated from Asia's total.
Source: As for Table 5.9.

5.5   MULTINATIONAL CORPORATIONS IN BELGIAN INDUSTRY: TOWARDS CROSS-INVESTMENT?

From Host to Crossroads Investment Country

In terms of FDI Belgium is a net receiver. According to Mucchielli (1982, pp. 17–22), who applied a Balassa indicator[2] (Balassa, 1966) to long-term direct investment flows in industrialized countries, Belgium was a 'host country' with an average value of −0.58 for the whole period 1967–75, together with Spain, Australia, Norway, Austria, Denmark and Italy (Balassa indicators between −0.33 and −1). Belgium,[3] together with Spain, Denmark and Austria, were considered 'transforming countries':[4] that is, small countries which benefit (permanently or otherwise) from comparative advantages on the basis of either their lower wages, their geographical position or MNC-friendly economic policies. In the case of Belgium it is obvious that the latter two reasons apply rather more than the cheap-labour argument. As Belgium, Denmark, Spain, Norway and Australia were close to the −0.33 threshold[5] for the Balassa indicators during this period, they were already tending towards the situation of 'crossroads countries'.

Belgium's direct investment is still mainly orientated towards and interwoven with the other EC countries. In 1970 Belgium already had the highest 'coefficient of interpenetration' in the EC[6] and the second lowest 'b coefficient of cross establishments'.[7] Of all major industrial-

ized countries Belgium also had the highest share of production subsidiaries abroad which were located in neighbouring countries (43 per
cent in 1971) (Mucchielli, 1982, p. 67). This is probably linked to the
absence of large Belgian MNCs. Small and medium-sized enterprises
in particular generally invest close to the home market when they
venture abroad. This is consistent with the results of Ammeux's (1989)
econometric evidence for France, that there is a negative relationship
between the importance attached to distance, both physical and psychic, and firm scale for doing business abroad, and even more specifically for the choice of export markets.

Molle and Morsink (1991) presented new data on investment flows
among EC countries for the period 1975–83 (see Table 5.13). Calculating Balassa indicators and considering similar categories as in the
Mucchielli study, one finds that Belgium – with a ratio of −0.23 – has
indeed evolved into a crossroads country, both in relation to the world
and to the EC.[8] However, it has the lowest coefficient in this group
(compared with 0.23 for the UK, 0.16 for France, 0.10 for Denmark
and −0.12 for Italy) and the overall cross-investment balance is still
negative. The investment balances in relation to the EC on the one

Table 5.13 *Direct investment flows between the BLEU and EC
member states (1975–83) (billions of ECU)*

EC countries	From BLEU	To BLEU	Balance
Denmark	0.0	0.0	0.0
FRG	0.6	1.8	−1.2
France	1.0	0.9	+0.1
Greece	0.0	0.0	0.0
Italy	0.5	0.1	+0.4
Ireland	0.0	0.0	0.0
Netherlands	0.4	1.1	−0.7
Portugal	0.0	0.0	0.0
Spain	0.3	0.0	+0.3
UK	0.2	0.6	−0.4
EC 12	3.0	4.5	−1.5
Other	2.3	4.0	−1.7
Total	5.3	8.5	−3.2

Source: Molle and Morsink (1991, p. 86, Table 5.1).

hand and in relation to the rest of the world on the other hand, are more or less comparable in size (−1.5 billion ECU and −1.7 billion ECU). The Balassa indices for the investing countries, Germany and the Netherlands, are 0.46 and 0.39.

The share of the BLEU in total inward investment flows in the USA rose gradually from 2.9 per cent in 1965 to 4.6 per cent in 1979, which in relation to other European countries and to the scale of the Belgian economy is an intermediate result. Apart from Italy, Belgium had the lowest share of its stock of direct investments in the USA invested in manufacturing industry (only 1.4 per cent at the end of 1979) (Thuillier, 1982, pp. 106–7). However, within manufacturing industry Belgium had, after France, the highest share of investments in the metal and mechanical industries (36.8 per cent).

Indications of Belgium's Crossroads Investment Position

The significance of Belgium as a crossroads country in general and in the metalworking industries in particular can also be documented by a number of other elements. First of all Belgium is endowed with the advantage of its geographically central location within Europe. In a survey in the mid-1980s, 92 per cent of the foreign firms sampled quoted Belgium's geographical location as a positive investment factor. Transport infrastructure as an engineered advantage was ranked in second position with 73 per cent, closely followed by the positive attitude of employees towards work (70 per cent). Access to other markets scored seventh, with 68 per cent with regard to the investment decision as seen in 1984. This moved up to fourth place from the perspective of the post–1984 period, thereby anticipating the single market proposals even before 1985 (Beernaert, 1984, p. 69; Van Den Bulcke, 1986b). Communication infrastructure was evaluated less positively in a later survey. Although the impact of the presence of the EC Commission and the EC Council in Brussels should not be exaggerated, it is likely that the formation of the single market will move the lobbying activities of MNCs away from national capitals. As long as unanimous decisions were required for a number of issues, each country could veto a particular decision and it was often sufficient for interest groups to lobby their national minister to achieve this. Now they may need to stretch their influence over many countries and centralize it in Brussels (Tyszkiewicz, 1991, p. 101).

It is likely that locational factors may become even more important with an increase in integrated and controlled activities. Reduction of transport and assimilated costs, the expansion of production per unit and the centralization of product and marketing management on a European scale are likely to enhance the need for a central location. Roodenburg (1989) calculated for all EC subregions their 'distance' to the European market and their ensuing degree of suitability for location (Table 5.14). While the hypothesis that, on average, demand is distributed like value added seems acceptable for industrial goods, factor income imbalances could slightly distort this picture for consumption goods. Distance (the inverse of central-locatedness) is then computed as the weighted arithmetic average of geometrical distances to all EC subregions (with gross value added as weights). Geometrical distances can then be interpreted as proxies for transportation costs. Obviously, the importance of centrality in the locational decision-making process is positively related to the importance of transportation in the cost structure of products and industries.

Table 5.14   Market distance and wage levels of EC countries (indices) (1985)

Countries	Weighted average of distance	Minimum[1]	Maximum[1]	Wage level[2] (1984)
Luxembourg	100	100	100	479
Belgium	*104*	*101*	*107*	*572*
Netherlands	113	103	125	593
France	114	100	153	531
Germany	118	101	152	617
UK	140	119	204	386
Italy	156	115	240	454
Denmark	175	161	178	520
Ireland	185	185	185	384
Spain	204	162	447	231
Portugal	260	232	465	100
Greece	289	266	360	173

Notes
EC minimum = 100
[1] of regional figures per country
[2] hourly wages in marketing industries (1984).
Source: Roodenburg (1989, pp. 4 and 7).

Belgium's central position in an EC context is clearly indicated by

Table 5.14. However, from the investor's point of view there will be a trade-off between centrality and wage levels. In relation to wage levels Belgium occupies a middle position compared with its neighbouring countries. As current European integration goes hand in hand with the opening up of Central and Eastern Europe one might expect the centre of gravity to shift to the East, however.

Secondly, data on the MWI sector illustrate Belgium's particular intermediate (or secondary) position in the international investment context, resulting in a particular block-wise cross-investment structure (Table 5.15). On the one hand, Belgium plays an intermediary role for investment flows from North to South, while on the other, Belgium developed its own outward investment activities relatively late. It was not until 1975–88 that there was a positive balance for outward investment. If we consider stocks of MWI investments in 1988 of foreign companies in Belgium and Belgian companies abroad, balances are systematically negative in relation to the Northern regions in the world and systematically positive in relation with the Southern (LDC) blocks.

Table 5.15   Balance of new inward (−) and outward (+) foreign direct investment in the Belgian metalworking industries according to period of establishment

	Before 1960	1961–1974	1975–1988
Number of companies	−46	−109	+56
	(=32−84[1])	(=44−153)	(=133[2]−77)
Employment	−47,499	−53,327	−6,046
	(=7,692−55,191)	(=5,363−59,690)	(=10,134[2]−16,180)

[1]Of which 43 investments dated from before 1946.
[2]Figures for 1975–89; 65 establishments between 1986 and 1989.
Source: Boelaert (1989, Tables 4 and 7); Fabrimetal (1990a).

Another and third indication of Belgium's crossroads position is the number of 'mixed' enterprises, that is, companies where ownership is shared among two or more parent countries. In the MWI Fabrimetal noticed that 29, or 10 per cent, of all foreign-owned firms had multiple foreign parent companies, possibly in addition to a Belgian holding company. These firms employed more than 16,000 people, about 12 per cent of total employment in foreign-owned metalworking firms (Boelaert, 1989, p. 76).

Fourthly, the role of crossroads country is illustrated by the large number of foreign-owned firms which have set up and/or control foreign operations from Belgium. No fewer than 44 out of 74 (59 per cent) Belgian MWI parent companies with subsidiaries in other countries in 1988 are actually themselves controlled from abroad. In 1978 the proportion of foreign-owned firms in the Belgian MWI with foreign affiliates was 37 per cent. Although in a number of cases this is the result of Belgian MWI multinational enterprises which have been taken over by foreign multinationals, in many other instances the foreign subsidiary in Belgium was allowed to set up manufacturing and sales subsidiaries in the rest of Europe and elsewhere.

Fifthly, inward investors which are at the same time outward investors not only show the importance of Belgium as a crossroads country but also indicate that there is a certain degree of autonomy in decision-making. A crossroads function implies a relatively higher degree of the autonomy of decision-making in foreign multinational subsidiaries. About half the MWI subsidiaries which participated in a recent survey by Fabrimetal (Boelaert 1989, p. 92) claimed that they had a world product mandate in their group (for example, Philips-Hasselt for compact discs). This surprisingly high and probably exaggerated proportion of world product mandates was highest in the more technological branches (68 per cent in electronics as compared with 37 per cent in metal manufactures). The same enquiry indicated that a number of functions which were carried out by the Belgian subsidiary were also applicable to other firms which belonged to the same multinational group. Marketing and applied research and development were extended to other subsidiaries abroad in respectively 38 and 34 per cent of the responding firms. Decisions in the field of financing, purchasing, engineering, informatics and fundamental research and development applied across borders in about one out of five cases.

Last but not least, Belgium plays an intermediate role in international investment for those MNCs which have chosen to locate their regional headquarters in the country. On behalf of the parent companies, regional headquarters co-ordinate and control activities of affiliates in several countries and pass on information from the regional centre to the subsidiaries and vice versa. A special fiscal and social regime for so-called Co-ordination Centres (CCs) was established in 1982 by Royal Decree 187 in order to attract MNCs which wanted to centralize and rationalize certain operations and activities in Belgium. The criteria for qualifying as a CC include the provision that its co-ordinating activities should be of an auxiliary nature and *intra muros*, that is, only for the benefit of the member companies. It should also be part of an international group which has a specified minimum equity capital and turnover; have subsidiaries in at least four countries besides the parent company; a certain percentage of its activities must be realized outside the parent firm; it must only engage in the activities mentioned in the Royal Decree, such as financial management, R&D, information collection and dissemination, marketing, advertising and so on; and it must employ at least 10 people two years after start-up. The benefits of the status of a CC are that corporate taxation is on a cost-plus basis, and that withholding tax on sums placed or paid out by a CC and registration duties on capital contributions and real-estate tax are exempted.

According to Forum 187, the employer's federation of those companies which have set up a CC in Belgium, 225 CCs employed about 4 000 people in Belgium. As 47 per cent of these employees had been transferred from other entities of the group, the net employment creation was considered to be 2 100 jobs, that is, an average size of 16.4 jobs (Hoge Raad voor Financiën, 1991). In 1987 23 per cent of the 126 CCs which were surveyed (Van Den Bulcke and Van Wymeersch, 1988) belonged to the metalworking companies. The chemical firms were the first to take advantage of CC status as they took up 42 per cent of the total in the first period 1982–5 compared with 12 per cent in metals and electronics.

One-third of the 29 CCs in the metalworking sector in 1987 were Belgian-owned companies. Although originally intended to attract foreign-owned enterprises to Belgium, the broad formulation of the Royal Decree also allowed Belgian firms to apply for CC status and to use it as a co-ordinating centre for their multinationalization efforts. While American firms represented 44 per cent of all CCs in 1987, their share in metals and electronics was only 21 per cent. Average employment in 1987 for the MWI CCs was 23.2 as compared with an average size of 18.9 for all CCs. Co-ordination Centres are mainly engaged in financial activities. The five most-frequently performed operations are all of a financial nature: funding of investment in Belgium; cash management; foreign exchange management; funding of working capital; and credit management. Accounting and factoring, as service activities, take up sixth and seventh positions. The functions of centralized general management, marketing and purchasing, which are normally part of the activities of full-fledged regional headquarters, are performed less-frequently. Distribution Centres, which have certain similarities with CCs and have been authorized since 1989 for physical merchandise transactions, have not had much success, however.

5.6 CONCLUSIONS

Europeanization of Belgian Industry

Especially since the founding of the European Community, Belgium has attracted foreign enterprises which have used its open economy as an export platform for the European market. At the beginning of the 1990s the Belgian metalworking industries sold 86 per cent of their output to other European countries. The 'Europeanization' of the export activities of the Belgian MWI is quite remarkable, especially in those sectors where the foreign presence is relatively high. Of course, as MNCs have been more export-orientated than their local counterparts from the beginning, their export share expanded with the growth of their production. Yet the spectacular expansion in the automobile sector points to a substantial intensification of the degree of integration of the affiliates located in Belgium and the rest of the multinational group.

These developments also indicate that the large integrated internal market of the EC is not an isolated phenomenon and that other factors such as globalization and technological change have already left their mark on the Belgian economy, mainly in those sectors where large integrated groups dominate. The single unified market will have an accelerating effect, however. Small and medium-sized enterprises (SMEs) will have to cope with the pressures towards more technical and financial integration and explore new forms of economic co-operation with other firms in the fields of research, purchasing, production and servicing, in order to strengthen their competitive position. As SMEs and large non-integrated firms take up a larger share of total employment in the Belgian MWI than in the EC, the success of these restructuring efforts is highly important.

The 'Europeanization' of the Belgian MWI is also apparent from the changing composition of inward FDI. The relative share of American firms in Belgium continued to decline even after the heavy disinvestment of the second half of the 1970s and the early 1980s. While in 1980 40 per cent of employment in the Belgian MWI was in American subsidiaries in Belgium, this proportion dropped to 29 per cent by 1989. The share of EC-owned affiliates in the Belgian MWI went up from 47 per cent in 1980 to 61 per cent in 1989. From 1980 to 1989 the absolute number of employees in American affiliates declined by more than 20,000, while employment in EC MWI firms in Belgium increased by about 10,000 to a level of more than 80,000 jobs. The so-called American challenge of the 1960s has become very remote.

At the same time as Belgian MWI trade and inward investment is becoming more and more interlocked with the European Community and Europe, Belgian outward investment in the metalworking sectors seems to be moving further away from the 'old' continent and extending its presence in North America and the developing countries. Since the mid–1970s the decline in the number of subsidiaries abroad and the fall in jobs created by Belgian metalworking firms in foreign countries has continued steadily until recently. The hesitant outward expansion of Belgian firms is partly due to their limited size compared with other small European countries. Belgium counts only eight companies in the list of the largest 500 European enterprises, compared with 18 for Finland, 23 for The Netherlands, 31 for Switzerland and 34 for Sweden (Daems and Van de Weyer, 1991). It has been claimed that cultural factors and the fact that Belgium had been occupied by most other European countries before its independence in 1830 explain the lack of Belgian outward entrepreneurship (Generale Bank, 1991b, p. 10). The shortlived participation of Belgian industrialists in Russia, China and Latin America during the end of the nineteenth and the beginning of the twentieth centuries usually ended in nationalizations. The repetition of the nationalization experience in Zaire in the 1960s certainly did not reassure Belgian entrepreneurs as far as foreign ventures were concerned (Van Den Bulcke, 1986b, pp. 107–9).

Belgium's Crossroads Investment Position

The combination of a relatively low level of outgoing FDI and a high volume of incoming foreign investment had made Belgium into a 'host' country. Even though Belgium became a 'crossroads' country, according to some calculations, and the size of Belgian FDI abroad increased from 221 billion BEF during the period 1983–7 to 624 billion BEF in 1988–90, inward FDI still topped this with an amount of 721 billion BEF during the latter period. There are, however, more convincing indications of the crossroads nature of Belgium's investment position which go beyond its traditional advantage of being in a central geographical location. Typical of Belgium are, on the one hand, the high number of mixed enterprises, which are controlled by multiple parent companies from different countries, and on the other hand, an increasing number of foreign MNCs which own and control commercial and manufacturing activities through their Belgian subsidiaries. About three out of five foreign firms in the Belgian MWI control foreign subsidiaries from their Belgian location. By establishing a special fiscal regime for co-ordinating intra-group activities (Co-ordination Centres), Belgium has banked on the increasing role for MNCs of centralized activities in a European context.

When the special tax regime for Co-ordination Centres was set up in 1982 one major objective was to re-establish confidence in Belgium as an attractive location for FDI. Belgium's reputation had been badly tarnished by an alarming balance of payments deficit and unparalleled budget deficits, declining investments and decreasing industrial production. Instead of confining itself to encouraging industrial investment, the new policy was also intended to stimulate the development of Belgium as an international service centre. The overall cost to the Belgian taxpayer of this regime, though difficult to assess, was not considered too high compared to the total economic activity that it generated, especially if one takes into account the total amount of government aid to private business in Belgium in general. The hypothetical total cost was estimated at 8.9 billion BEF, that is, on average less than 3 billion BEF per year, and compared quite favourably with the average investment of 35 million BEF per year for 1985–7. This represented 6.3 per cent of the total yearly business investment and 15.1 per cent of the total investment in manufacturing industry in Belgium (Van Den Bulcke and Van Wymeersch, 1988). Co-ordination Centres have become the major conduits for new investment in Belgium and were responsible in 1989 for 44 per cent of total new investment. The success of the Co-ordination Centres has increased the gross budgetary cost to 16.6 billion BEF in 1989 (Hoge Raad voor Financiën, 1991, p. 23). While the cost to the government of maintaining Belgium's status as a Co-ordination Centre has somewhat decreased by the lowering of tax concessions, it would be awkward in any case to dismantle further an incentive system which is regarded by MNCs as a symbol for the political credibility of the Belgian government.

A Belgian 'Anchor' For Foreign-Owned Companies?

The limits of Belgium as a cross-investment country are also documented by the systematic survey of takeover activity as reported in a major Belgian financial paper from July 1985 to July 1990. Out of a total of 392 takeovers in Belgian industry, 57 per cent were initiated by foreign-owned firms (45 per cent concerned Belgian firms taken over by foreign companies and 12 per cent changed one foreign nationality for another). Only 4 per cent of all these acquisitions resulted in a return to Belgian ownership, while 39 per cent of the reported acquisitions replaced one Belgian owner by another. During the same period Belgian firms acquired only 97 firms abroad, less than half the number of Belgian companies which became foreign-owned through acquisition (Daems and Van de Weyer, 1991).

It is surprising that after so many years of an extensive foreign presence in Belgian industry, the acquisition by the French group Suez in 1988 of Belgium's largest industrial holding company, the Société Générale de Belgique, has launched a debate about the necessity for a Belgian 'anchor' to assure autonomy of decision-making in foreign-owned groups. It is not clear what the reasons are for this belated nationalistic reaction. Of course, the Société Générale represented a large slice of the Belgian economy extending to a great many sectors. Also other large companies in sensitive sectors such as energy, banking and insurance became increasingly foreign-owned, while the proportion of acquisitions as a mode of entry increasingly replaced the more-favoured green-field investments. Perhaps Belgium's new federalist structure led to more adverse reactions towards the so-called French takeover of the Belgian economy. The contested disinvestment decisions by Citroën and Michelin in previous years and the fact that many French groups are still partly government-owned certainly did not allay exaggerated fears about the loss of Belgian sovereignty.

Apart from the general motives underlying an expansion of mergers and acquisitions, a specific factor for Belgium may be the relative importance of traditional industries which are more prone to takeovers, as it is often the only way for strong groups to extend market share and diminish competition. However, there is an increasing feeling that the high frequency of acquisitions of Belgian firms is somehow linked to the Belgian industrial structure and the institutional and legal system which is less protective than in most other European countries. Wilmes (1991, p. 21), president of the National Investment Company, a state holding company, mentioned that the shareholders of many Belgian firms, family-owned and others, are very dispersed and therefore more vulnerable to friendly or hostile takeover raids. As there are no legal structures such as trusts, as there are in the US, Germany and the Netherlands, family companies with succession problems seem to have little choice but to sell out to (mostly foreign) firms (Generale Bank, 1991b, p. 12). Wilmes (1991) also blames the weak strategic entrepreneurial options of the larger Belgian groups and the absence of an industrial policy which is needed in the case of restructuring activities. Finally, preventive and defensive arrangements to safeguard against takeovers are less well-developed than in other EC countries.

Since the Société Générale episode certain measures have been taken to improve the situation of Belgian firms on the European battlefield of mergers and acquisitions (Wilmes, 1991, pp. 11–13; Martens, 1991, pp. 11–17). The law of 21 March 1988 obliges firms to announce important participations in companies which are listed on the stock exchange, while the Royal Decree of 8 November 1989 regulates public takeover bids. There also is a proposal to adapt existing company law so as to give some legal basis to the concept of a Belgian 'anchor'.

It is doubtful whether these new legal instruments are the right way to allow Belgium to develop its competitive advantages so that it can continue to attract the foreign firms that have become essential to its development. Protectionist moves and artificial interventions to 'Belgianize' its economy will undermine its attractiveness to multinational subsidiaries as a location in which to engage in manufacturing and service activities as well as for their administrative and co-ordinating operations. A more appropriate action would be to continue to work for the elimination of the national anchors of the other EC countries and to improve Belgium's engineered comparative advantage in human resources.

NOTES

1. There are some methodological problems in testing this small-country effect assumption for other countries. Relative results can neither be derived from a study about Denmark (Italianer, 1990) (which also calculated 'realistic' instead of 'potential' effects like the Dutch study) because appropriate figures for the EC are lacking, nor from a study for Ireland (O'Sullivan, 1989). Obviously, the Danish and Irish economies are not only small and open but also peripheral.
2. Defined as $(X - M)/(X + M)$, with X = capital exports and M = capital imports. Mucchielli (1982) based his calculations on three-year averages.
3. Investment and trade figures are actually for the Belgian-Luxembourg Economic Union (BLEU) as a whole. As a financial centre Luxembourg occupies a special place for investments, however.
4. Mucchielli stresses the difference with the so-called *'filiales-ateliers'* notion of Delapierre and Michalet (1978); 'transforming country' is a macroeconomic notion (with an explicit role for the government to pursue transformation strategies) where the link between specialization and internationalization of the economy is established.
5. Countries with scores between +0.33 and −0.33 are labelled 'crossroads countries' while countries with scores between +0.33 and + 1 are called 'investing countries' (Mucchielli, 1982, pp. 17–23).
6. EC = EC + UK. Score for the BLEU was 149, the coefficient was calculated as $C = (F_{i.EC} / F_{i.m})/(F_{EC.EC} / F_{EC.m})*100$, where $F_{i.EC}$ = subsidiaries of country i in the EC, $F_{i.m}$ = subsidiaries of country i in the world (Mucchielli, 1982, p. 29).
7. Score for the BLEU: −0.06; the b coefficient is a Balassa-type index where X = number of subsidiaries in other EC countries, M = number of European (EC) subsidiaries in own country (Mucchielli, 1982, p. 28). These statistics are based on

the numbers of establishments and do not provide information on the amount of investment.
8. Only the peripheral EC members – Spain, Ireland, Greece and Portugal – are considered 'recipient countries', with coefficients of respectively −0.7, −0.9, −1, −1.

REFERENCES

Ammeux, J.P. (1989), 'The Role of the Size of Firms in the Selection Process of Foreign Markets', in R. Luostarinen (ed.), *Dynamics of International Business: Proceedings of the Annual Conference of the European International Business Association*, vol. II, Helsinki: Helsinki School of Economics and Business Administration, pp. 850–67.

Bakhoven, A.F. (1989), 'The Completion of the Common Market in 1992: Macroeconomic Consequences for the European Community', *Research Memoranda, 55*, The Hague: Central Planning Bureau.

Balassa, B. (1966), 'Tariff Reductions and Trade in Manufactures among the Industrial Countries', *American Economic Review*, **56**, June, 466–473.

Beernaert, L. (1984), *Enquête Buitenlandse Vestigingen*, Antwerp: Vlaams Economisch Verbond.

Boelaert, R. (1989), 'Transnationale vervlechting van de industriële produktie. De metaalverwerkende en electrotcchnische nijverheid', in *Mundialisering van de Economie: De uitdaging van de jaren '90*, 19th Flemish Economic Scientific Congress, Leuven: V.V.E., 67–96.

Buigues, P. and Ilzkovitz, F. (1988), *The Sectoral Impact of the Internal Market*, Brussels: Commission of the EC (II/335/99EN).

Buigues, P., Ilzkovitz, F. and Lebrun, J.F. (1990), *Les États membres face aux enjeux sectoriels du marché intérieur*, Brussels: Commission of the EC (II/364/89-FR).

Bureau du Plan (1988), *Les Aspects macroéconomiques du marché 1992*, Dossier 1992, (RM/4193/al/5451), Brussels: Bureau du Plan.

Catinat, M., Donni, E. and Italianer, A. (1988), 'Macroeconomic Consequences of the Completion of the Internal Market: the Modelling Evidence', in *Research on the Cost of Non-Europe, Studies on the Economics of Integration, Basic Findings*, vol. II, Brussels: Commission of the European Communities, 559–627.

CRB (Conseil Central de l'Economie – Centrale Raad voor het Bedrijfsleven) (1989), *Stuurgroep 1992, De markt van de overheidsopdrachten*, Brussels: CRB.

Cuyvers, L. and De Lombaerde, P. (1990), 'Scenarios for Economic Growth after 1992', in F. Cripps and T. Ward (eds), *1992: Problems of External and Internal Balance of Europe in the World Economy*, Paris: Commissariat du Plan.

Daems, H. (1990), 'Nationale verankering en concurrentievermogen', *Tijdschrift voor Economie en Management*, **1**, 73–85.

Daems, H. and Van De Weyer, P. (1991), *Verankering en concurrentievermogen*, Brussels: Koning Boudewijn Stichting, *mimeo*.

Delapierre, M. and Michalet, C.A. (1978), *Les implantations étrangères en France: stratégies et structures*, Paris: Calmann-Levy.

Dunning, J.H. (1970), 'Technology, United States Investment, and European Economic Growth', in C.P. Kindleberger (ed.), *The International Corporation*, Cambridge, Mass.: MIT Press, 141–76.

Dunning, J.H. (1989), 'Foreign Direct Investment in the European Community: a Brief Overview', *Multinational Business*, **4**, 1–9.

Emerson, M., Aujean, M., Catinat, M., Goybet, P. and Jacquemin, A. (1988), *The Economics of 1992: The EC Commission's Assessment of the Effects of Completing the Internal Market*, Oxford: Oxford University Press.

Fabrimetal (1974), 'Investeringen van de Belgische metaalverwerkende nijverheid in het buitenland', *Fabrimetal Maandschrift*, October, 22–4.

Fabrimetal (1979), 'Investeringen van de Belgische metaalverwerkende nijverheid in het buitenland', *Fabrimetal Maandschrift*, January, 9–12.

Fabrimetal (1981), *Enquête relative aux sociétés étrangères dans l'IFME*, Brussels, *mimeo*.

Fabrimetal (1990a), 'Belgische MVEN-Filialen in het Buitenland', *Economische Studies*, **6**, 1–9.

Fabrimetal (1990b), 'Investeringen in de MVEN in 1989 en Prognoses voor 1990', *Economische Studies*, **7**, 1–9.

Gardner, D. (1991), 'Survey: Belgium. Aiming for Federalism', *The Financial Times*, 25 June.

Generale Bank (1991a), 'Sectoriële doorlichting van het Belgisch bedrijfsleven', *Bulletin van de Generale Bank*, **323**, 1–10.

Generale Bank (1991b), 'Internationalisering van de beslissingscentra: een gevaar voor de Belgische welvaart?', *Bulletin van de Generale Bank*, **324**, 10–17.

Guillaume, Y., Meulders, D. and Plasman, R. (1989), 'Simulation des impacts de l'achèvement du marché intérieur. Le cas de la Belgique', *Cahiers Economiques de Bruxelles*, **124**, 449–73.

Haex, F. and Van Den Bulcke, D. (1979), *Belgische Multinationale Ondernemingen – Historische, Bedrijfseconomische en Macroeconomische Aspecten*, Diepenbeek: LEHOC.

Hoge Raad voor Financiën (1991), *Verslag aangaande bepaalde aspecten van de hervorming van de vennootschapsbelasting*, Brussels: Hoge Raad voor Financien.

Houard, J. (1991), *Impact de 1992 sur le secteur belge des fabrications metalelectriques*, Rapport final, Louvain la Neuve: IRES.

Institut Royal des Relations Internationales (1987), 'Les Investissements belges à l'étranger', *Studia Diplomatica*, **1**, 3–24.

Italianer, A. (1990), '1992, Hype or Hope: a Review', *Economic Papers*, 77.

Italianer, A. and Vanheukelen, M. (1989), 'De Voltooiing van de Europese Interne Markt in een Mundiale Context', in *Mundialisering van de Economie: De Uitdaging van de Jaren '90*, 19th Flemisch Economic Scientific Congress, VVE, Leuven, 305–53.

MAE (1988), 'Le Secteur des telecommunications en Belgique face à l'ouverture des marchés et à l'échéance 1992', *Dossier Europe 1992*, Brussels: Ministère des Affaires Economiques, Administration de l'Industrie.

Maldague, R. (1989), *De markt van de overheidsopdrachten*, Brussels: Centrale Raad voor het Bedrijfsleven, Stuurgroep Europa 1992.

Martens, P. (1991), 'Verankering van het bedrijfsleven', Brussels: CEPESS, *mimeo*.

McDonald, F. (1989), 'The Single European Market', *Journal of Economic Studies*, **16** (4), 60–70.

Molle, W. and Morsink, R. (1991), 'Intra-European Direct Investment' in B. Burgenmeier and J.L. Mucchielli, *Multinationals and Europe 1992: Strategies for the Future*, London: Routledge, 81–101.

Mucchielli, J.-L. (1982), 'La Dynamique des investissements internationaux', in J.L. Mucchielli, J.P. Thuillier, C.A. Michalet and B. Lassudrie-Duchene, *Multinationales européennes et investissements croisés*, Paris: Economica, 1–93.

Nerb, G. (1988), 'The Completion of the Internal Market: a Survey of European Industry's Perception of the Likely Effects', in Research on *The Cost of Non-Europe*, vol. I, Brussels: EC Commission.

O'Sullivan, L. (1989), 'Macroeconomic Effects of 1992', in J. Bradley and G. Fitz (eds), *Medium-Term Review: 1989–1994*, Dublin: ESRI.

Puylaert, L. (1981), *Enquête Buitenlandse Vestigingen*, Antwerp: Vlaams Economisch Verbond.

Roodenburg, H.J. (1989), 'Central Locations in the European Common Market', in *Research Memoranda*, The Hague: Central Planning Bureau, 59.

Sleuwaegen, L. and Van Den Bulcke, D. (1990), *1992: Strategie des entreprises et nouvelles formes de coopération*, Brussels: Conseil Central de l'Economie.

Thuillier, J.-P. (1982), 'Investissements croisés entre l'Europe et les Etats-Unis', in J.L. Mucchielli, J.P. Thuillier, C.A. Michalet and B. Lassudrie-Duchene, *Multinationales européennes et investissements croisés*, Paris: Economica, 95–207.

Tyszkiewicz, Z. (1991), 'L'Unice. La voix des entreprises à Bruxelles', *L'Entreprise et l'homme*, **3**, 100–2.

Van Den Bulcke, D. (1985), 'Belgium', in J. Dunning (ed.), *Multinationals, Market Structure and International Competitiveness*, London: John Wiley, 249–80.

Van Den Bulcke, D. (1986a), 'Role and Structure of Belgian Multinationals', in K. Macharzina and W. Staehle (eds), *European Approaches to International Management*, New York: W. De Gruyter, 105–26.

Van Den Bulcke, D. (1986b), *The Role of American Companies in the Belgian Economy*, Brussels: American Chamber of Commerce in Belgium.

Van Den Bulcke, D. and Van Wymeersch, C. (1988), *Coordination Centres of Multinational Companies in Belgium: A Survey Covering Five Years of Royal Decree 187*, Brussels: Forum 187, Federation of the Coordination Centres.

Vanden Houte, P. and Veugelers, R. (1989), 'Buitenlandse Ondernemingen in België', *Tijdschrift voor Economie en Management*, **34** (2), 9–34.

Van Sebroeck, H. (1988), 'De Algemeen Ekonomische Gevolgen voor België van de Europese Eenheidsmarkt', *Dossier Europe 1992*, Brussels: Planbureau.

Vincent, A. (1991), *Les Groupes d'entreprises en Belgique, le domaine des principaux groupes privés*, Brussels: CRISP, 407.

Wilmes, P. (1991), *Controle of Internationalisering van de Belgische Economie?*, Brussels: Nationale Investeringsmaatschappij.

Winters, L.A. (1989), 'Les Effets du grand marché de 1992', *Economie Prospective Internationale*, **40**, 7–18.

Zalm, G. (1989), 'Nederland en Europa '92', *Werkdocument*, 's-Gravenhage: Centraal Planbureau.

6. Cross-Investments between France and Italy and the New European Strategies of Industrial Groups

Julien Savary*

6.1 INTRODUCTION

Of course, we must first answer a preliminary question: what is the purpose of studying cross-direct investments between France and Italy, when this phenomenon clearly appears to be part of the general internationalization of these two economies, which is in turn part of a much wider and world-wide trend throughout Europe and North America? The internationalization of one economy, and the international strategy of one firm, cannot be studied fully through an analysis of investments in just one foreign country. The international opening up of one economy is geographically diversified, just as the international development of one firm is.

However, today the European level has become a major component of the internationalization process of both European economies and European firms. This hypothesis is supported by the empirical evidence: since 1983–5 cross-investments between the European economies have been growing in importance for all countries, and this is particularly true for France and Italy.

6.1.1 French-Italian Cross-Investments and the Increase in Intra-EC Investments

The substantial scale of intra-EC investments is a recent phenomenon. During the period 1975–83 cumulative flows of FDI between the 12 EC countries were often weak and sometimes absent altogether (see

*I am grateful to Nicola Acocella, Francesca Sanna Randaccio and John Cantwell for helpful comments on a first draft of this paper which they gave during the Cargese seminar and later.

Molle and Morsink, 1991). This record was consistent with the analysis of many authors. For them European integration (which is, in the second stage of the completion of the internal market, removing internal non-tariff barriers to trade) can be expected to have a negative effect on intra-EC direct investments. Indeed, the market-orientated foreign investments of European firms in other European countries should become less necessary as European markets become more easily accessible through direct exports. For instance, M. Itaki and M. Waterson (1991) have forecast that European integration will lead to a reduction of intra-EC foreign direct investments and to an increase of intra-EC trade and non-EC foreign direct investments in the EC. Reasoning in a similar fashion, other analysts have argued that European integration should lead to a decrease in intra-European joint ventures, since these joint ventures occur when access to national markets is difficult (see Kay, 1990).

Yet in the most recent period, that is to say, when the second stage of European integration is beginning to come into effect, intra-EC investments have been growing faster. Indeed, recent data compiled by Eurostat have shown that *from 1984 to 1988 intra-EC direct investments grew quickly in both absolute and relative terms*. We define the 'rate of intra-EC FDI flows' as the ratio of direct investment flows to the 12 EC countries relative to direct investment flows to the world as a whole. That rate has grown, for the total of the 12 EC countries, from 24.5 per cent in 1984 to 62 per cent in 1988 (see Table 6.1).

Table 6.1   Average rate of intra-EC FDI flows* in their overall world investment for all 12 EC countries, for France and for Italy, 1975–83 and 1984–8

Country of origin of FDI	1975–83 (%)	1984–8 (%)
Total 12 EC Countries	28.3	47.6
France	32.9	48.5
Italy	19.6	61.7

*Rate of intra-EC FDI flows = FDI flows to 12 EC countries/FDI flows to the world as a whole.
*Source:*For period 1975–83: Molle and Morsink (1991); for period 1984–8: J. Savary, compiled from Eurostat preliminary report, 1990.

The average rate for the total of the 12 EC countries shifted from 28.3 per cent in 1975–83 to 47.6 per cent in 1984–8. The trend is clear and strong: since 1983–4 the 12 EC countries are investing more abroad (their total FDI flows doubled in four years) and, even if they are strongly increasing their investments outside the EC, particularly in the USA where many important European groups are expanding, their intra-EC investments are growing faster.

Intra-EC investments from France and Italy are also increasing faster than their investments outside the EC and, as a consequence, the 'rate of intra-EC FDI flows' is increasing for both these two countries, especially for Italy (see Table 6.1).

Cross-direct investments between France and Italy have also been increasing since 1984. French direct investments (cumulative flows) in Italy have grown from 1 billion Ecus in 1975–83 to 1.46 billion Ecus in 1984–8. During the same period Italian direct investments (cumulative flows) in France have grown much more: from 0.5 to 1.57 billion Ecus.

This growth in intra-EC direct investments has often taken the form of transnational mergers and acquisitions: between 1983 and 1989 the mergers and acquisitions involving firms from different countries of the EC have increased faster (+ 282 per cent) than those involving firms within the same European economy (+ 111 per cent) or those involving an EC firm and one non-EC firm (+ 132 per cent) (source: EC Commission).

These trends justify the study of the cross-investments between these two EC countries. France and Italy are an appropriate choice for such a study as they are two of the four largest EC economies which account for a large share of FDI flows within the Community, and because they show some similarities in their national economic structures. In these two countries state policy and state-owned firms are more important than elsewhere in Europe. Furthermore, their foreign direct investments are more recent and less established than those of the Northern EC countries.

6.1.2   French-Italian Cross-Investments and the Patterns of Internationalization of France and Italy

French-Italian cross-investments are just part of the more general internationalization of France and Italy, in which respect these countries present some similarities and some differences.

The first investments abroad from these two countries were made mainly in less-developed countries: Africa and the Middle East for France, Latin America for Italy, and Spain for both of them. The foreign investments of the two countries then increased during the 1960s, and still more during the 1970s, above all in Europe, and more recently in the USA. French investments abroad have been focused towards other European countries for a longer time than Italian investments, which were more focused towards the LDCs and Southern Europe. French investment in the USA is today much more important than is the Italian equivalent.[1]

Today French industry has a level of internationalization, in terms of both inward and outward FDI, which is clearly higher (about 20 per cent) than that of Italian industry (about 10–12 per cent) (see Table 6.2).

Table 6.2 Internationalization of French and Italian industries

| Country | Level of internationalization (as % of domestic employment) | |
	Inward FDI*	Outward FDI**
France	20.7	20.0
Italy	12.5	9.2

* Employment in foreign owned firms compared to national employment.
**Employment in foreign subsidiaries compared to national employment.
Source: For France: Savary (1984) and Ministry of Industry; for Italy: Cominotti and Mariotti (1991).

The patterns of sectoral specialization of the foreign investments of the two economies are quite similar. This is a result of the existence of major multinational groups with similar profiles of activity in the two countries. However, the French investments abroad are more focused in technology-intensive sectors, such as chemicals and pharmaceuticals, mechanical products, electronic products and so on.

The degree of concentration of outward FDI is very high for both economies. The major industrial groups control the majority of total foreign investments. But the degree of concentration is higher for Italy than for France, as the five top Italian investors abroad account for 77 per cent of total outward Italian FDI (Cominotti and Mariotti, 1991). French outward FDI is more widely spread across a larger number of big investors.

The major multinational groups are more often state-owned in the French case. Elf, Total, Renault, Thomson, Rhône Poulenc (state-owned groups) and CGE and Saint-Gobain (state-owned groups until 1986) all belong to the top 15 French investors abroad. For Italy only ENI and IRI belong to the top 15 Italian investors abroad, in fifth and sixth places only.

Today the internationalization of French industry appears to be more important and more diversified than the internationalization of Italian industry. But Italian investments abroad have grown recently, especially in France.[2] So cross-FDI between France and Italy is a significant phenomenon that warrants further investigation.

6.1.3 From Empirical Evidence to Analytical Assessment

This study begins with some empirical evidence and then provides an interpretation of it. The main features of foreign direct cross-investments are first summarized with reference to the relevant statistics (in section 6.2). The corporate strategies of the major investors are then described through a case study approach (in Section 6.3). The empirical results are then interpreted in a combined way. French-Italian cross-investments are analysed as the outcome of an interactive process, which is explained jointly by industrial, financial and institutional factors (in section 6.4).

6.2 FRENCH-ITALIAN CROSS-INVESTMENTS: THE STATISTICAL EVIDENCE

In this section we analyse the main patterns of cross-investments between France and Italy. We rely on the available aggregate statistical data and on unpublished and original corporate data which have been collected by two research teams, LEREP in Toulouse, and CERIS in Torino (Alzona and Gilly, 1990; Savary, 1990).

6.2.1 The Growing Relative Importance of Cross-Investments between France and Italy

The flows of FDI between France and Italy have been growing since 1980 in all sectors. Yet France is much more important for outward Italian FDI than is Italy for French outward FDI.

France is the first country of destination for Italian outward FDI; at the end of 1989 France received 22.8 per cent of the total stock of Italian FDI in manufacturing (based on the numbers of employees of foreign owned firms) (Cominotti and Mariotti, 1991). In contrast, Italy has always been a country of destination for French outward FDI, but not a major one; at the end of 1988, and for all industrial and non-industrial sectors, Italy received 4.7 per cent of the total stock of

French outward FDI and she appears as the eighth most important country of destination (Banque de France, 1990).

On the other side, from the viewpoint of the country that is host to inward FDI, French firms are also more important in Italy than are Italian firms in France. In Italy, France appears as the second largest country of origin of inward FDI, after the USA, controlling 20.2 per cent of total inward FDI in industry at the end of 1989 (Cominoti and Mariotti, 1991). In France, Italy is only the seventh largest country of origin of inward FDI, controlling 4.1 per cent of total inward FDI in industry at the end of 1988 (Ministry of Industry). Four years ago Italian investments represented just 1.8 per cent of total inward foreign investments. The increase in Italian investment in France is very recent: it began during the years 1987 and 1988.

6.2.2 1900–90: The Gradual Increase of Cross-FDI in Industry

The historic evolution of French FDI in Italy and of Italian FDI in France appears to be quite similar. Data collected by LEREP/CERIS for industry show that more than 60 per cent of total cross-FDI has been set up after 1980, and more than 40 per cent in the last three years (see Table 6.3).

Table 6.3 *Foreign direct investments in industry between France and Italy, from 1900 to 1989 (number of enterprises with foreign participation, by period)*

Period of investment	Italian FDI in France % of total	French FDI in Italy % of total
Before 1950	3.69	2.67
1951–1960	1.58	4.01
1961–1970	5.26	6.69
1971–1980	19.47	26.09
1981–1986	20.52	19.06
1987–1989	47.89	41.47
Total %	100.00	100.00
(number)	(190)	(299)

Source: Alzona and Gilly (1990).

At the very beginning of the twentieth century the earliest cross-investments between France and Italy were made by financial companies (such as the creation of Societa Generale di Credito Mobiliare in Italy, or the creation of Banque Sudameris in Paris by Banca Comerciale Italiana). From 1910 to 1970 the first industrial investments were made by important groups. These firms have continued to invest frequently over a 40-year period, and remain major investors today. In Italy Saint-Gobain created its first industrial subsidiary in 1889; Michelin did so in 1906; and Air Liquide in 1909. Other French groups then invested, such as Total, Elf, Rhône Poulenc, Pechiney, L'Oreal, Thomson and Matra. In France, Martini & Rossi created their first subsidiary in 1925; CEAT did so in 1930, Buitoni in 1934, Pirelli in 1950, while Fiat had a minority participation in Simca (sold in the 1960s) and bought Unic in 1960. Since that time other Italian groups have invested in France, such as SMI (1957), Ferrero (1960), Borletti (1960), SGS (1962), Montefibre (1972) and Fiat in 1970 through a minority participation in Citroën (sold in 1973). Practically all these French and Italian groups have continued to invest in Italy and in France up to 1970 and beyond.

In the more recent period from 1970 to 1990, and especially after 1987, apart from the continued growth of established investors, important new groups have made substantial acquisitions and investments in both countries, and these new and huge investments have boosted the FDI flows. In Italy the most important new French investors were firms such as Crouzet (1968, 1970), Valeo (1981), Peugeot (1981), Perrier (1981), Bull (1981), Merlin Gerin (1981, 1984), Thomson (1970, 1980), CGE (1980, 1987, 1989), BSN (1986, 1987, 1988, 1989), and Générale des Eaux (1988). In France important new investments, mainly through acquisition, were made by Pirelli (1980), Olivetti (1981), Fiat again (1986 acquisition of Solex and of Jaeger), Ferruzi (1986, 1987, 1988 acquisitions of Beghin Say, SPC and Lesieur), CIR-De Benedetti (1986 and 1987 acquisitions of Valeo, Neiman and Chausson Thermique), SMI (1987), Novicelli (1989) and Merloni (1989). (See *Appendix 6.1* for a list of the main Italian investments in France.)

At the same time small or medium-sized companies began to invest across the Alps. In Italy these new French firms included Skis Rossignol (1980), Pernod Ricard (1985), Midial (1987), Pompes Funèbres Générales (1989), Delalande (1990), Strafor (1991) and Pomagalski (1991). In France some of the new Italian investors were Ratti (1976, 1987), Riva (1980, 1988), Benetton (1982), Richetti (1982), Simonazzi (1983), Sandretto (1986), Vamatex (1987), Cantoni (1988), Redaeli (1988), Bassano (1990), Unichips (1990) and Mediolanum (1991).

In 1987 the two state-owned companies SGS-Microelettronica (Italy) and Thomson Semiconducteurs (France) combined their activities in electronic components and created the joint venture SGS-Thomson.

6.2.3   The New Role of Financial Cross-Investments and of International Alliances since 1986

Since 1984–6 two related new trends are the growth of cross-FDI in the financial sector and the growth of investments in minority owned ventures. Cross-FDI between France and Italy has recently been increasing in other service sectors, such as transportation, distribution, hotels, and engineering services to enterprises. According to the LEREP/CERIS database the total number of cross-FDI operations in these sectors has grown from four at the end of 1984 to 48 by the end of 1989 (see Table 6.4).

Table 6.4   Cross-FDI between France and Italy by sectors at the end of 1984 and 1989 (number of enterprises with foreign participation)

Sector	Italian FDI in France		French FDI in Italy	
	1984	1989	1984	1989
Industry	81	173	158	268
Non-financial services	4	17	–	31
Total non-financial sectors	85	190	158	299
Finance	14	46	6	43
Total (all sectors)	99	236	164	342

Source: Provisional data LEREP/CERIS, in Alzona and Gilly (1990).

However, another major trend is the growth of cross-FDI in financial activities such as banking, insurance and financial services. The total number of cross-FDI operations in finance has grown from 20 at the end of 1984 to 89 by the end of 1989. It grew by a factor of 4.5. Over the same period the total number of cross-FDI ventures in the non-financial sectors increased from 243 to 489, or by a factor of 2 (see Table 6.4).

In Italy the French groups Mutuelles du Mans, UAP, Crédit Lyonnais, and Crédit Agricole have bought a stake in Italian firms. In

France São Paulo di Turino took the control of Banque Vernes, and CIR (De Benedetti group) took the control of Banque Dumenil Leblé.

Another observed trend is the growth of minority participations, that is to say, of FDI which does not necessary entail control over the foreign company in which it is made. This phenomenon does exist for industrial cross-FDI but it is stronger for cross-FDI in finance. In financial activities majority participations as a share of the total number of foreign participations have dropped from 86 per cent in 1984 to 59 per cent in 1989 for Italian FDI in France, and at the same time from 100 per cent to 52 per cent for French FDI in Italy (see Table 6.5).

Table 6.5   Majority and minority cross-FDI between France and Italy by sector at the end of 1984 and 1989 (Majority participations as a % of total number of foreign participations in enterprises)

Sector	Italian FDI in France		French FDI in Italy	
	1984	1989	1984	1989
Industry	80.2	82.1	77.2	73.5
Non-financial services	100.0	76.5	–	35.5
Non-financial sectors	81.2	81.6	77.2	69.6
Finance	85.7	58.7	100.0	51.6
Total	81.8	77.1	78.0	65.5

Source: Provisional data LEREP/CERIS, in Alzona and Gilly (1990).

Some examples of minority participations are the 10 per cent interest of Einaudi in Gallimard (1990), and the 4 per cent interest of Rizzoli in TFI (1991). This growth of cross-FDI between France and Italy in services, including finance, is not unique but forms part of a general trend in recent world FDI.

The growth of international alliances between the financial and industrial groups is another new trend, which is specific to cross-French-Italian cross-FDI.[3] During the last ten years some major strategic agreements were signed between French and Italian financial groups, and these agreements have often led to cross-investments in industrial activities controlled by these financial groups (see Figure 6.1).

One important agreement has existed for a long time between CIR (De Benedetti), which controls Olivetti, and the French group Suez. This agreement has led to interlocking capital stock structures. CIR, through its French holding CERUS, today owns a 3.5 per cent participation in Suez capital (since 1988, after the failure of CIR to take over Société Générale de Belgique, which was finally bought by Suez).[4] Many direct investments of CIR in France can be partly explained by its international alliance with Suez. For instance, in 1986 CIR acquired a major participation in the important French group Valeo (in vehicle equipment). Valeo has been influenced by Suez for many years, and Suez controls Ferodo, the main actor in setting up the Valeo group through several acquisitions. In another case in 1988, CIR bought a majority participation in the French bank Banque Dumenil Leblé, in which Suez still holds a minority participation.[5]

Another agreement was reached before 1982 between the Italian family group Ferruzi, a major agro-industrial conglomerate, and the family-owned French bank Banque Vernes. The chairman of Banque Vernes, J.M. Vernes, was also chairman and managing director of the major agro-industrial group Beghin-Say (in which the Suez group also participated). In 1981 J.M. Vernes helped Ferruzi to acquire a significant participation in Beghin-Say, which gave it control of the French group in 1986. Banque Vernes was nationalized in 1982 and bought by the Italian bank São Paulo di Torino in 1988. Today Ferruzi is still co-operating with the new merchant bank of J.M. Vernes, the Société Centrale d'Investissements.

In 1990 CGE and FIAT signed an important agreement which gave them substantial equity stakes in each other's business; Fiat had bought a 6 per cent stake of CGE capital, and CGE a 3 per cent stake of Fiat capital. This agreement also led to cross-investments between their subsidiaries. In telecommunications, Alcatel, the subsidiary of CGE, took control of Telettra, the subsidiary of Fiat with a 7.7 billion francs turnover and a major share of the Italian market. The subsidiaries of the two groups which produce railroad equipment, Ferroviaria (Fiat) and GEC-Alsthom (CGE) have been merged and are now managed by GEC-Alsthom. Magnetti Marelli, another subsidiary of Fiat, took control of CEAC, the French subsidiary of CGE which produces car batteries. It is safe to forecast that this first deal between Fiat and CGE will be followed by further co-operation in the near future.

Since 1987 the Agnelli group, which controls Fiat, has formed

Figure 6.1 International alliances and cross-investments between France and Italy (some major agreements between financial and industrial groups, 1980–1990)

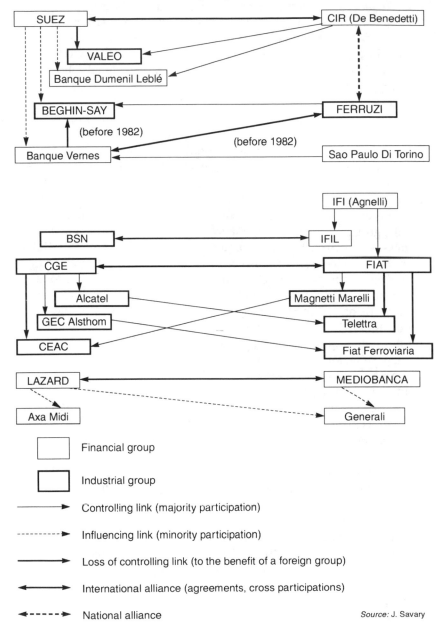

another alliance with the French agro-industrial group BSN to develop joint investments in France and in Italy (see further the BSN case study below).

Besides its numerous direct investments in France and these two agreements with CGE and BSN, the Agnelli group has signed other agreements, often through a minority participation, with many French groups, such as Safic Alcan, Bolloré Technologies, Groupe Rivaud, Club Méditerranée, Pechelbronn, Labinal, TFI, Accor, Exor, Worms et Cie and Saint-Louis.

Another striking example occurs in insurance. The international alliance between the two merchant banks Mediobanca in Italy and Banque Lazard in France played a role in 1988, when Generali, the important Italian insurance group which is influenced by Mediobanca and in which Lazard holds 4.8 per cent of the capital, tried without success to take over Axa Midi, the French private insurance group, which is influenced by Lazard.

The development of these international alliances and interlocking interests between the French and Italian industrial and financial groups appears to be specific to French-Italian cross-investments. These alliances occur mainly between private and family-owned industrial and financial groups.

6.2.4 The Sectoral Specialization of Cross-FDI between France and Italy (in Manufacturing)

The LEREP/CERIS database allows us to study the sectoral spread of industrial cross-FDI between France and Italy at the end of 1984, and the shifts in this sectoral distribution between 1984 and 1991 (see Appendix 6.II and 6.III).

At the end of 1984 Italian FDI in France was concentrated in three main sectors (87 per cent of the total), namely the food industry (42 per cent), industrial equipment – mainly cables – (24 per cent), and motor vehicles and parts (21.6 per cent).

In contrast, French FDI in Italian industry was also concentrated – although to a lesser extent – in four sectors (70 per cent of the total): rubber and plastic products (26.9 per cent), building materials (20.4 per cent), industrial equipment (11.9 per cent) and motor vehicles and parts (11.1 per cent). French FDI in Italy was greater in high-technology sectors (electronics, chemicals and pharmaceuticals), where investments accounted for 11.9 per cent of the total, compared to 2.0 per cent of the total for Italian FDI in France in the equivalent sectors.

During the last five years (from the end of 1984 to June 1991), important investments were made by Italian groups in French industry, mainly through acquisitions. More than 90 French firms have been acquired, with total employment of about 90,000; today Italian FDI in France is greater in absolute value than French FDI in Italy. The new Italian FDI has been focused in the motor vehicles and parts sector (CIR and Agnelli groups) and in the food industry (Ferruzi). But many new Italian investments in France were also made by large or medium-sized groups that were investing for the first time in France, and which belong to sectors in which Italian enterprises are very competitive, such as metal products, specialized machine tools, ceramics, electrodomestic products and apparel.

During the same period French FDI in Italy has also grown, but more slowly. The main French investments in Italy have been in electronics (Bull's take over of Honeywell in 1987), telecommunications (Alcatel's take over of FACE in 1987 and of Telettra in 1990) and electrical equipment (Legrand). Other major investors have been BSN, Saint Gobain, Carnaud, Générale des Eaux, AMP and Fayat.

All these sectoral specializations are due to the huge investments of some important groups, such as the four acquisitions of CIR in France between 1984 and 1991 (involving 32,000 employees), or the ten acquisitions of Ferruzi in France during the same period (involving 20,458 employees). So the sectoral specialization of French-Italian cross-FDI can be analysed as a reflection of the existence in each country of important industrial groups, which are responsible for most investment abroad (see Savary, 1981).

The sectoral specialization of cross-FDI can thus be described in terms of the composition of the multinational groups that belong to one country and invest in the other (see Table 6.6).

This table also helps to illustrate the thin intra-sectoral specialization in terms of products which exists in cross-FDI between France and Italy. Indeed, French and Italian groups which are quoted in the same sector are often making cross-investments in different products. For instance, the two leading tyre manufacturers, Pirelli and Michelin, have cross-investments, but in different activities. Michelin produces all the parts of tyres in Italy. Pirelli, which is a more diversified group, only produces cables in France. In electronic products, Italian groups invest in France mainly in computers (Olivetti), while French groups invest in Italy in computers (Bull), in telecommunications (Alcatel) and in consumer electronics (Thomson). In building materials, Italian groups invest in France in ceramics, while French groups invest in Italy in glass production.

Table 6.6 *Cross-FDI between France and Italy: the main foreign investors in 1991 (ranked by their importance within the total FDI of each industrial sector*)*

Sector	Italian FDI in France	French FDI in Italy
Food industry	1. *Ferruzi* 2. Martini 3. Buitoni (CIR) 4. Unichips 5. Ferrero	1. *BSN* 2. Perrier 3. Roquette frères 4. Pernod Ricard
Energy, water, mining		1. *Air Liquide* 2. Total 3. Elf
Chemicals	1. Montedison 2. Ferruzi 3. Kelemata	1. Rhône Poulenc 2. L'Oréal 3. Atochem
Metal and metal products (incl. cables)	1. *Pirelli* 2. *CEAT* 3. SMI 4. Redaelli	1. Pechiney 2. Imetal 3. Carnaud 4. Cables de Lyon (CGE) 5. Strafor
Industrial, farm, transport equipment	1. CIR 2. Fiat (IFI) 3. Vamatex 4. Bassano	1. *Legrand* 2. *Merlin Gerin* (Schneider) 3. Schlumberger 4. Crouzet 5. C. Fayat
Electronics products (incl computers, telecom.)	1. Olivetti	1. *Alcatel* (CGE) 2. *Bull* 3. *Thomson*
Domestic appliances	1. Novicelli 2. Candy 3. Merloni	
Motors vehicles and parts	1. *CIR (De Benedetti)* 2. *IFI (Agnelli)*	1. Peugeot 2. Matra

Table 6.6 continued

Rubber, plastic		1. *Michelin* 2. Sommer Allibert
Pharmaceuticals		1. Sanofi (ELF) 2. Rhône Poulenc
Textiles, apparel	1. Zucchi Bassetti 2. Marzotto 3. Cantoni	
Furniture, toys, shoes, other consumer products	1. Galeppio	1. Skis Rossignol
Building materials	1. P.A.F. 2. Fidenza Vetraria 3. Fin Riwal	1. *Saint-Gobain*

*Restricted to sectors with major FDI, and to groups which control affiliates with more than 200 employees in Italy or France. The groups controlling affiliates with more than 2,000 employees are in italics.
Source: Savary; LEREP/CERIS database.

In conclusion, these cross-investments show the cross-industrial specializations of the two economies, and the cross-industrial strengths in terms of the existence of their most competitive and most multinational groups.

6.2.5 The Major Role of Some Industrial Groups

Cross-FDI often takes the form of multiple foreign investments controlled by the same industrial groups. At the end of 1989, in industry and non-financial services, the 208 Italian enterprises which were owned by French firms were in fact controlled by only 91 independent decision centres or groups. The 155 Italian-owned French enterprises were controlled by only 63 Italian groups (Alzona and Gilly, 1990).

The investments of the major industrial groups represent the majority of cross-FDI between France and Italy. In both directions the concentration of foreign investment is very high, but the concentration of Italian FDI in France is higher than that of French FDI in Italy. At the end of 1991 the ten major investors, in terms of groups, accounted for about 76 per cent of total FDI for Italian investments

Table 6.7 *The top ten Italian investors in France in 1991 (industrial groups ranked by total employees of their French subsidiaries)**

Group	Total employees of French affiliates
1. CIR (CIR international, Olivetti, IPB)	39,700
2. Ferruzi Agricola Finanziaria	20,498
3. IFI (Fiat Iveco, Fiat Auto, Magnetti Marelli)	17,950
4. SMI	3,854
5. CEAT	3,680
6. Pirelli	3,000
7. Novicelli	1,500
8. Fumagali	1,261
9. Martini et Rossi	950
10. PAF	900

*SGS-Thomson excluded
Source: J. Savary; LEREP/CERIS provisional data.

Table 6.8 *The top ten French investors in Italy in 1991 (industrial groups ranked by total employees of their Italian subsidiaries)**

Group	Total employees of Italian affiliates
1. CGE	11,600
2. Michelin	10,084
3. BSN	7,200
4. Saint-Gobain	5,871
5. Bull	4,600
6. Legrand	3,800
7. Air Liquide	2,500
8. Schneider	2,200
9. Thomson	2,200
10. Rhône Poulenc	1,600

*SGS-Thomson and JV of Peugeot in Italy excluded.
Source: Cominotti and Mariotti, 1991; J. Savary; LEREP/CERIS provisional data.

in France (ranked by size in France: CIR, Ferruzi, IFI (Agnelli), SMI, CEAT, Pirelli, Novicelli, Fumagali, Martini and PAF), and about 66 per cent of total FDI for French investments in Italy (ranked by size in Italy: CGE, Michelin, BSN, Saint-Gobain, Bull, Legrand, Air Liquide, Schneider, Thomson and Rhône Poulenc) (see Tables 6.7 and 6.8).

The recent and important acquisitions in France by the CIR De Benedetti group (five acquisitions in five years of affiliates with a total of 32,000 employees, including Valeo), and by Ferruzi group (ten acquisitions involving 20,458 employees, including Beghin-Say and Lesieur) explain why the concentration of FDI is higher for Italian FDI in France than for the reverse.

Further tables (Tables 6.7, 6.8) describing the main foreign investors in France and Italy at the end of 1991 show the differences between the patterns of investment in each direction. The degree of concentration of Italian FDI in France is higher mainly because the three largest Italian investors have a very important weight: they represent nearly two-thirds of the total Italian FDI in France (see Table 6.9). These three private and family-owned groups – CIR (De Benedetti family), Ferruzi (Ferruzi family) and IFI (Agnelli family) – are the dominant players in France.

Table 6.9   *The concentration of cross-investments between France and Italy in 1991 (total employees in foreign controlled enterprises for the major investors abroad, in number and %, in manufacturing)*

Foreign investors	Italian FDI in France		French FDI in Italy	
	Employees	%	Employees	%
Top 3 groups	78,148	64	28,884	37
Top 10 groups	93,293	76	51,655	66
Total FDI (estimate)	122,000	100	78,999	100

Source: J. Savary; Tables 6.7 and 6.8.

In conclusion, the descriptive statistics set out above have shown some important features of French-Italian cross-investment which will be analysed further below. The corporate strategies of the firms which undertake and manage these cross-investments will be described first.

This case-study approach will illustrate some other features of French-Italian cross-investments.

6.3   FRENCH INVESTMENTS IN ITALY: SOME CASE STUDIES OF CORPORATE STRATEGIES

What is the place of Italy within the international strategies of French groups? What are the functions given to Italian plants within the international production networks of these groups? What are the main factors promoting investments in Italy? Are these factors changing over time, particularly in the 1980s with the European integration process? In this section we try to answer these questions by studying the corporate strategies of some French industrial groups which are major investors in Italy: Saint-Gobain, Thomson and BSN.

6.3.1   Saint-Gobain in Italy: From a Market-orientated Strategy to a European Integrated Strategy

Since 1872 Saint-Gobain has had a genuine European strategy, the objective of which was to establish favourable market shares in Europe, particularly in Italy. However, more recently the method of reaching these national markets has shifted from a country-by-country to an integrated approach. This change has been apparent in the glass products divisions, on which we focus our attention.

From 1853 to 1975: Italy as one national market in a 'country-centred' European strategy
From its origin in the seventeenth century, the Compagnie Saint-Gobain focused on glass production, and from an early stage it was very multinational; from 1872 outwards foreign production in Germany accounted for 30 per cent of total world production and Saint-Gobain exported to other countries.

In 1888 the group, facing a growing European demand, established its third foreign plant in Italy. It was located in Pisa, at the 'barycentre' of the Italian market, in order to sell to that growing market.

In 1913, with eight plants in seven European countries, Saint-Gobain was a highly multinationalized company: foreign production accounted for 70 per cent of the firm's total world production. It was also a leading group, controlling 36 per cent of the European market and

60 per cent of the Italian market. All the Italian production was sold within the peninsula. (For Saint-Gobain's history see Daviet, 1988.)

Until 1975–80, even though the group had diversified into new activities besides glass products, it had always had a European strategy of both selling and producing in all important markets. This international strategy can be described as 'multidomestic'. The plants operating in each national market produced the full range of products and sold them mainly in the same national market. The main reasons for this system of international organization were: (a) the partition of national markets by customs and regulations barriers; (b) the low value-to-weight ratios of glass products and hence high transportation costs; and (c) the mode of entering national markets through acquisitions.[6]

Today Saint-Gobain is a more diversified group: the four glass-related divisions represented 53 per cent of its total sales in 1989. And it remains a very multinationalized group which produces and sells abroad over 65 per cent of its total production, mainly in Europe where it enjoys sizeable market shares. In Italy it produces the whole range of glass products and owns over eight subsidiaries and 21 plants, with about 4,000 employees (see Table 6.10).

From 1975 to 1992: Italy becomes an element in an integrated European and global strategy
In recent years Saint-Gobain has continued to invest heavily in Italy, including in 1981 the acquisition of Vetrotex Italia (reinforcement fibres for plastic), in 1986 the acquisition of Vitrofil Spa (reinforcement fibres), and in 1989 the launching of a new float-glass project and the acquisition of Vetri (bottles). However, these new investments are more specialized than before, and the group is restructuring its existing plants in order to manage more large-scale but specialized facilities. In 1987 in southern Italy it closed a small-capacity float-glass plant in order to make better use of the new central and northern plants.

This restructuring of the Italian plants is one part of a broader process of integrating European production. The process of globalization within Europe, or 'Europeanization', has led to greater plant-level specialization, with each plant producing large volumes of a narrow range of products in order to benefit from economies of scale. These plants are therefore serving a wider regional market and not just individual national markets (see Savary, 1991). This has resulted in a growth in intra-European trade between the national subsidiaries of Saint-Gobain, which is more important for the divisions which are

Table 6.10 Plants and subsidiaries of St Gobain in Italy in 1990 (glass products only)

Division	Subsidiary	First year of invest.	Number of plants	Locations of main plants	Share of exports %	Employees (1990)
1.	Fabrica Pisana	1889	2	Pisa, Turin	10	452
	SGIA		1	Savigliano		401
	Toscana Glas	1984	1	Pisa		334
	Luigi Fontana	1951	7	Pari, Cagliari, Casserte, Messine, Milan, Padoue, Rome		285
2.	Vetrotex Italia	1981	1	Besana Briança	42	496
	Vitrofil	1986	1	Vado Ligure	52	441
3.	Balzaretti	1926	3	Chieti, Crespiatica, Vidalengo		458
4.	Vetri	1989	5	Dego, Gazzo Veronese, Longo, Pescia, Villa Poma	15	1,124
Total			21			3,991

Divisions: 1. Glass panes division; 2. Reinforcement fibres division; 3. Insulating products division; 4. Hollow glass products division.
Source: J. Savary, compiled from annual reports and *Dun's Europe.*

more internationally integrated, such as the glass panes and reinforcement fibres divisions (see Table 6.11).

Table 6.11   *Intra-European trade between Saint-Gobain plants in 1989*
            (as % of total sales of the division)

	Glass panes division	Reinforcement fibres division
Share of intra-European trade	12%	32%

Source: Saint-Gobain.

In the reinforcement fibres division Saint-Gobain modernized each
of its European plants, and each plant was assigned a specialization
in one type of production: textile fibres, fibres for plastic products,
glass veils and so on (five plants in France, Germany, Italy and Spain).
It also set up the company Vetrotex International SA to manage all
the R&D and marketing operations of the division on a world-wide
level. The aim is to 'Europeanize the marketing of the products of
Saint-Gobain, and to create "Vetrotex" as a genuine European brand'.
As a result of this process of Europeanization, the two Italian plants,
Vetrotex Italia and Vitrofil, are today exporting more than 40 per
cent of their total production (see Table 6.10).

In the glass panes division, which operates 17 companies and many
more plants in Europe, the integration of European production is also
proceeding. For instance, the production of specialized products for
motor vehicles (heated windscreens, reflecting roofs) has been concentrated in only three plants (in France, Germany and The Netherlands)
which serve the entire European market. The production of specialized
glass panes for the construction industry has also been concentrated
in two European plants for low-emitting panes, in four European
plants for reflecting panes, and in six plants for glass mirrors. The
locational specialization of plants within Europe is more noticeable in
specialized products, because their volumes of production are lower
and their value-to-weight ratios are higher than for the other bulk
products of the division. Yet today the 'Europeanization' of production
extends to one heavier and more standardized product. In 1989 Saint-
Gobain opened an important plant called 'Eurofloat', which is located
near Lyons in France and which produces ordinary dish glass panes

for construction. With only 120 employees, this highly automated factory will eventually produce 120,000 tons of glass panes a year, which will be sold in southern France, northern Italy, southern Germany, Switzerland and Austria.

Four main reasons explain the company's shift from a multidomestic strategy towards a global strategy: (a) the increasing competition, particularly from low cost products made in the US; (b) the high level of scale economies in this capital intensive production, which allows important cost reductions through the specialization of plants in high volumes products;[7] (c) the growing specialization and differentiation of products which reduce production volumes and encourages their sales abroad again to reach the minimum efficient scale; (d) the European integration process, which tends to homogenize international demand and facilitates international trade and the international integration of management.

6.3.2 Thomson Consumer Electronics in Italy: One Workshop Plant Within an Integrated European System

Since 1987, when Thomson[8] sold its subsidiary Compagnie Générale de Radiologie (which owned a plant in Monza) to General Electric, the only important Thomson plant in Italy[9] is the TV tubes plant at Agnani, near Rome, which is managed by the Consumer Electronics division of the group. We shall focus on the activities in Europe of Thomson Consumer Electronics in order to explain its reasons for investing in Italy and the role of the Italian plant.

Towards an integrated system in Europe
Thomson Consumer Electronics (TCE) is the main subsidiary that manages all the consumer electronics activities of Thomson. It is ranked fourth on a world-wide level (no. 1: Matsushita: no. 2: Sony; no. 3: Philips; no. 4: TCE), and second on a European level (after Philips). It produces a full range of products: TVs, VCRs, cameras, hi-fis and so on, and it manages international operations employing 53,295 people in 1989.

TCE grew through numerous important acquisitions in Europe and in the USA (for instance, Normende, Saba and Dual in Germany, and the Consumer Electronics activities of General Electric in the USA, Europe and Asia).

Today TCE manages an international system, based on two types of integrated production network: in North America and Europe it produces and sells high-value products. East Asia is the major site for the sourcing of low-cost products that are sold in Europe and North America. So the international production network is a bi-continental integrated system, spanning North America and Europe, with low-cost products sourced from Asia.

Following numerous acquisitions, a major restructuring and rationalization of its operations have now been conducted by TCE, both in North America and in Europe, to increase the competitiveness of the company and build an integrated production system. In Europe many plants were closed down in France, Germany and Great Britain. Production was shifted between European plants in order to increase specialization. Much low-cost production, such as that of audio products and small TVs, was moved to Asian countries like Singapore, Thailand or Malaysia. In Europe TCE produces only medium and large TVs and videotape recorders. All other products sold in Europe are produced outside the EC, mainly in Asia and mainly in TCE's East Asian plants. This rapid growth and the subsequent restructuring were intended to help the firm to face the competitive challenge of American and especially Japanese and Southern Asia competitors.

The growing specialization of the Italian plant within the European network for the production of colour TVs

The Agnani plant is large (with 2,000 employees) and has become specialized since it was set up in the production of colour TV tubes, that is to say, the more technological and valuable part of a colour TV. It was initially set up by the American group RCA in 1970 as one part of Videocolor in Europe.

The location in Agnani, 30 kilometres south of Rome, was chosen because the Italian government provided substantial grants and incentives for creating jobs in this area of southern Italy. The relatively low level of wages in that region may also have played a role.

In 1979 Thomson-Brandt and AEG-Telefunken jointly acquired 58 per cent of Videocolor's capital stock. In 1981 Thomson became the sole owner of Videocolor, which had three plants producing TV tubes in France (in Lyons, with about 1,000 employees), Germany (in Ulm, where 1,600 employees produced 600,000 tubes in 1981, in a plant with a production capacity of 1,200,000 tubes) and Italy (in Agnani 2,000 employees produced over 1,000,000 tubes, and the plant had a production capacity of 1,500,000 tubes in 1981), but which at that time had a total production volume of only 2,500,000 tubes per year.

Thomson then invested heavily in the Agnani plant, in order to increase the volume of its production to 3,000,000 TV tubes a year. This production volume today corresponds to the minimum technical efficient scale in this activity. At the same time the two other European plants producing TV tubes were closed down.[10]

The Agnani plant is one part of TCE's system of integrated European production. This system implies both a specialization of plants by products, with one plant making VCRs (Berlin), two plants producing TVs (Angers and Celle, Tarancon producing only for Spanish market), and a specialization along the value chain, by components, just one European plant making TV tubes and seven manufacturing TV components. Of course, the Angers and Celle plants do not produce the same TV: each plant specializes in certain sizes and brands of TV (TCE is responsible for six brands in Europe) (see Figure 6.2).

In conclusion, the Italian plant of TCE is only one element in an integrated European network of specialized plants. The Italian location was first chosen by RCA to take advantage of government incentives. Thomson then concentrated its European productions in that site for the same reason (the high level of Italian incentives), and because this plant already produced the greatest volume of any of the three European plants and was thus closest to the optimal size. From a geographical point of view the German or French plants would have been better located, near the final assembly plants of Celle and Angers. The specialization of the Agnani plant has recently deepened further with the opening of a new TCE plant in Poland.[11]

6.3.3   BSN: From International Growth in Specific Segments to a Focus on Italy

BSN is today a leading group in agro-industry and is very European. Its international strategy has been focused on Italy since 1985 and is partly explained by its alliance with an Italian group.

From 1966 to 1985: national and international growth in specific segments

At the end of 1989 BSN, which was created in 1966 and grew quickly, was the largest French agro-industrial group and the sixth biggest in Europe. It had consolidated total sales of 48.7 billion francs, but influence over total sales (including minority-owned firms) of 72.0 billion francs. It managed one glass division (packaging, 11 per cent of total sales), and five agro-industry divisions, three of which accounted for 67.7 per cent of total sales, that is to say, fresh products, biscuits and grocery products. It controlled important market shares in Europe. It was also a multinational group, mainly developed in

Figure 6.2   Manufacturing network of Thomson Consumer Electronics in Europe (1990)

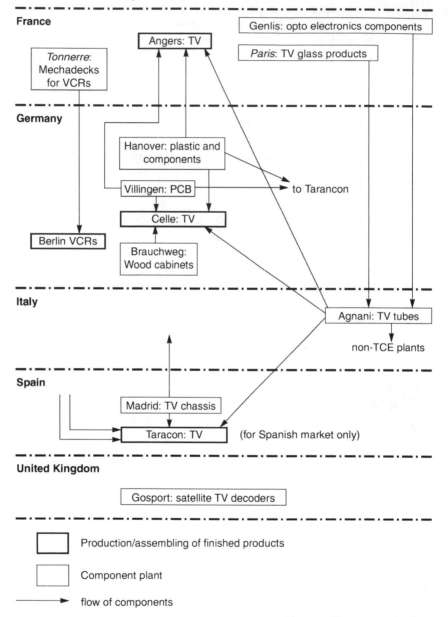

Source: J. Savary (based on annual reports, newspaper information, Eurostat report).

Europe, with foreign employment accounting for more than 40 per cent of its total workforce.

In 25 years BSN strategy has always been voluntarist and the company has chosen quick growth through acquisitions. The main strategic objective has changed, from being a leading glass producer until 1980 to being a leading food industry producer after 1980. Even if this quick change in sectoral specialization and the use of financial instruments of growth (acquisitions) corresponded to conglomerate behaviour, all these strategic choices of BSN were directed towards an industrial strategy: to become a leading group in the food industry (see Martinet, 1988). This aim required the company to grow faster than its slow-growing markets, and so implied the use of acquisitions (see Perez, 1988).[12]

During the early years of its development, internationalization was only one avenue for its strategy of growth in the food industry. In each new industry segment that it entered, BSN has always given priority to the creation of a strong national base in France, in order to become quickly a dominant player at home. From 1980 to 1989 foreign growth has assumed increasing significance within the overall strategy of the group. This multinationalization has been achieved mainly through acquisitions.[13]

Until 1985 Italy did not have a specific place in the strategy of BSN. Indeed, its first investments in Italy happened indirectly when BSN acquired companies that already controlled a subsidiary in Italy: Gervais Danone in 1973 and the European activities of Liebig in 1980. As Italy was a fast-growing market BSN wanted to invest there, and this was facilitated by the opportunities for acquisitions which existed in the weakly concentrated Italian industry. BSN bought Wueher (beer) in 1980. In 1981 it tried to acquire Buitoni, but CIR De Benedetti took over that enterprise and then sold it to Nestlé. That failure may have pushed BSN into an alliance with an Italian financial group, because Antoine Riboud, chairman and managing director of BSN, believed that such an alliance was necessary to be able to succeed in its acquisitions in Italy.

Since 1985: the focus on Italy and the alliance with the Agnelli group
Since 1985 BSN has boosted the number of its acquisitions and agreements in Italy. Some acquisitions have been made directly by BSN (Ponte in 1985, Angelo Ghigi and Mantovano in 1987), while others came about indirectly (the control of Saiwa through the acquisition of some Nabisco concerns in 1989).

However, the main acquisitions were made jointly with the private

Italian group Agnelli, either directly or through jointly owned holding companies: IFIL Partecipazioni and SIFIT (see Figure 6.3). Between 1986 and 1990 five important Italian enterprises were brought under joint control in this way: *Agnesi*, the largest third Italian producer of pasta, *Sangemini*, the biggest Italian mineral water producer, *Birra Peroni*, the largest Italian beer producer, *Star*, a grocery producer, and *Galbani*, the major Italian producer of fresh cheese.

These joint acquisitions are the outcome of an international alliance set up between BSN and the Agnelli group in 1986. This alliance also took the form of cross-participations between BSN and a subsidiary of the Agnelli group, IFIL Partecipazioni. In 1987 BSN bought 20 per cent of the capital of the Italian holding company IFIL Partecipazioni, which is controlled by Agnelli group, and IFIL acquired 4 per cent of the capital of BSN. These cross-participations have since been extended and restructured. It was planned that IFIL Partecipazioni would control all the future joint investments of the two groups in the food industry.[14]

That international alliance also had an important financial side for BSN. The 5.12 per cent Agnelli participation in BSN capital is a means of protecting BSN, whose capital is very diluted, from a takeover. The Agnelli family today belongs to the 'hard nucleus' of BSN capital, that is to say, to its friendly shareholders, who hold 25 per cent of the BSN shares.[15]

At the same time BSN has grown internationally in other European countries, but with less intensity than in Italy. It has made acquisitions in Germany, Spain, Great Britain and Greece.

Growth in Europe and Italy and its alliance with the Agnelli group show that BSN is entering a second stage of its internationalization. International growth in Europe is now a priority. Indeed the group has already established strong market shares in its French markets, and so its growth here is now limited. Therefore BSN has to grow through expansion in European markets, where its market shares are as yet still low. In this context growth in the Italian market has become a central objective, and is facilitated by BSN's financial and industrial alliance with the Agnelli group. This French-Italian alliance has facilitated development both in Italy and elsewhere in Europe; for example, some Spanish firms have been jointly acquired by BSN and Agnelli group. Today BSN is moving towards the creation of a genuine European group, with bi-national financial control and a European strategy.[16]

At the same time BSN is restructuring its European operations for the same reasons as Saint-Gobain: to avoid duplications, to promote

Figure 6.3 *The alliance between BSN and the Agnelli group in Italy as of 1989 (Financial participations with % of total capital stock of each company)*

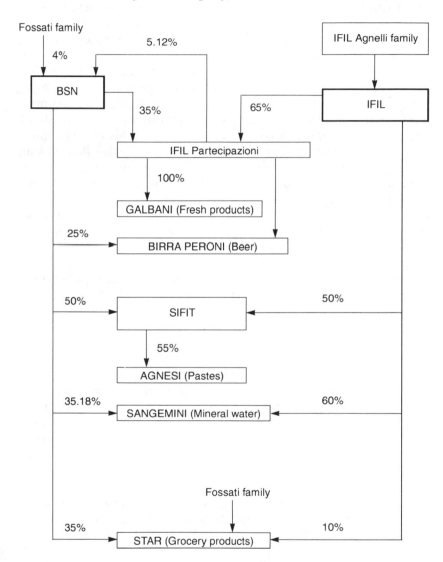

Source: J. Savary (based on annual reports and newspaper information).

European specialization and to achieve economies of scale. In its beer
division BSN has for ten years developed its brand Kronenbourg in
Italy, Belgium and Spain. In Italy it has merged its subsidiary Wueher
with Birra Peroni (1988), and it has closed down its Brescia brewery.
In the biscuits division the group has reduced its workforce by 2,000
workers in two years and is rationalizing its operations in Italy: it is
closing down the Genova plant in southern Italy, whose production
will be shifted to the modern plant of Saiwa in Capriano d'Orba.[17] In
the production of pastas the two German subsidiaries are merging
(Birkel and Sonnen-Basserman). In Italy as well there are too many
plants (four) and this will lead to restructuring in the years ahead.
The group is planning to merge all its Italian brands of pasta into a
single company before 1992 bringing together Panzani-Ponte-Liebig
and Agnesi.[18] In the fresh products division, the European specialization of plants is already very important. For instance, the Belgian
plant is producing 'Dan Up' for several countries. In 1987 BSN built
a huge plant near Lyons for milk products, producing 3,000,000
yoghurts a day (10,000 tons a year), with sales in several countries.

In conclusion these three cases emphasize the main pull-factors[19]
behind French investments in Italy. Two main pull-factors can be
distinguished: market and cost.

Market-orientated investments
The early investments of Saint-Gobain and BSN in Italy were clearly
market-orientated, and they are representative of many other similar
French investments in Italy. For these investments the aim of producing in Italy was to gain access to the important and fast-growing Italian
market which, at the time the direct investment occurred, was difficult
to reach through direct exports (due to customs and non-tariff barriers,
the specificity of national demand, transportation costs and so on).
This kind of investment seems to have been the most frequent. Since
the years 1980–5 Italian subsidiaries and plants of French groups which
were set up to reach the local market, such as those controlled by
Saint-Gobain and BSN, have often been restructured and have become
specialized in products sold in Italy and in Europe.

Cost-orientated investments
The Italian plant of Thomson (formerly owned by RCA) was from
the outset integrated into its European production network, linking
plants which were specialized along the value chain. The location in

southern Italy was determined by cost considerations: high government incentives and relatively low labour costs. Indeed, in the 1970s other French investments in Italy were attracted by similar cost considerations, as the wages in many Italian regions were lower than those prevailing in central Europe (as in the case of the investment of Crouzet).

6.4   AN INTERPRETATION: FRENCH-ITALIAN CROSS-INVESTMENTS AS AN INTERACTIVE PROCESS

Cross-investments between two economies are difficult to analyse because they are a narrow part of the broader internationalization of the economies concerned. Nevertheless, this concluding part tries to bring together into a general framework the empirical results discussed above. The basis for our reasoning derives from an examination of the differences and similarities between French investments in Italy and Italian investments in France.

The statistical approach has shown many similarities in the patterns of French investments in Italy and of Italian investments in France: the recent growth after 1970 and especially after 1984, the leading role of the major industrial groups, and the new investments of small and medium-sized firms in recent years.

But France has many more highly multinational groups with investments in Italy than docs Italy in France. This imbalance is related to a more open and voluntarist industrial policy in France, and in particular to the French government's policy towards state-owned industrial groups which has allowed them to invest heavily abroad. Differences in the local government requirements that firms must meet for production and employment in their country of origin may also have played a role: official restrictions seem to be more onerous in Italy and so they may have limited Italian FDI.

Another significant difference is that France is much more important for Italian FDI abroad than is Italy for French FDI abroad.[20] That result cannot be explained by differences in the size of the two markets (larger markets attract more market-orientated investments), because France and Italy are similar from this point of view.[21] This difference must instead be related to the different degrees of multinationalization of French and Italian industries. Italian industry is less multinationalized, and in their first stage of multinationalization Italian groups have often chosen to invest in France for a number of reasons: the cultural

and political proximities, which also explain the international alliances
between French and Italian private groups, and the geographical
location of the French market, being close to Italy and central within
Europe.

These similarities and differences between French and Italian cross-
investments are mainly related to the general patterns of internationalization of the two economies. We now outline five other results which
correspond to three types of interaction between the investments of
each country.

6.4.1   Cross-FDI and Cross-National Specialization and Competitiveness

Intra-industry evidence on cross-FDI between France and Italy shows
that the main investors were competitive important national groups,
and that the sectoral specializations of FDI often correspond to the
sectoral specializations of the respective national industries. These
specializations are, for the French FDI in Italy: glass, tyres, industrial
equipment, motor vehicles and parts and agro-industry. For the Italian
FDI in France they are: food, industrial equipment (cables), and
motor vehicles and parts. The most-recent Italian FDI in France has
occurred in competitive Italian sectors such as metal products, specialized machine tools, ceramics, electrodomestic products and clothing.

FDI specialization and industrial specialization[22] do not match one
another exactly. Cross-FDI is sometimes absent:

(a)   in sectors where national firms are competitive and invest heavily
       abroad (for example, in the cement industry the French groups
       Lafarge and Ciments Français, which are highly multinationalized
       groups, do not invest in Italy);
(b)   in sectors where national firms are competitive but are not invest-
       ing abroad (for example, in France in armaments and aerospace;
       although if we take into account the numerous co-operative
       agreements which French and Italian groups are developing in
       these sectors, there is already mutual penetration of a kind).

Cross-FDI between France and Italy reveals the cross-industrial
specialization of these economies, which also applies to the trade-
related specialization of France and Italy (see our earlier suggestions,
in Savary, 1981).

6.4.2   Cross-FDI and Cross-National Industrial and Market Structures

Firm surveys and case studies have shown that the main French and Italian cross-investors have often been big companies controlling large market shares in their national market. These firms have first grown within their own national markets and in a second stage have invested abroad. (This is true of Saint-Gobain, BSN, Fiat in components, Ferruzi and many others.) Some investors are smaller than these leaders, but they also generally hold a dominant position in their national market for some specific products.

These results verify explanations of FDI based upon market structures and on the competitive advantages of firms. Recent analysis based upon oligopoly rivalry also seems to be relevant to some French-Italian cross-FDI.[23]

6.4.3   European Integration and the Growth of Cross-FDI

Aggregate data (in sections 6.1 and 6.2) as well as microeconomic data (in Section 6.3) show that the intra-EC investments of France and Italy have increased faster than their investments outside the EC. Italian FDI in France and French FDI in Italy have also increased since the creation of the European Community. Now they are growing even faster since the Single European Act (1987). The European integration process is clearly a major cause of the growth in cross-FDI within Europe, mainly because it is spurring competition and therefore encouraging the leading firms to speed up their growth through acquisitions. (Acquisitions are the major entry-mode for cross-FDI today.)

Intra-European cross-FDI is increasing even if European integration has weakened the necessity to produce within each national EC market in order to reach it. However, that need has been weakened but not erased. Competitive new European firms that want to grow in European markets still need to control national subsidiaries and plants inside each important EC economy, partly in order to gain better access to the market concerned. Segmentation of national markets does exist, even if it is less pronounced, in several sectors and products, due to differences in customers' tastes and needs, specific state-related markets, specialized distribution networks and nationalistic opinions.

6.4.4   European Integration and the Restructuring of European FDI

The case studies of Saint-Gobain and BSN revealed one recent trend. Today the industrial groups that have many subsidiaries and plants in Europe are restructuring them. They aim to create a more-integrated system, based on more-specialized plants, with increasing intra-firm trade between them.[24] This globalization of strategies and structures is clearly a result of the second stage of the European integration, due to its effects in spurring competition and facilitating the cost-saving Europeanization of strategies.[25] This trend has also affected new multinational groups which have recently created subsidiaries in European countries and are now restructuring them.

6.4.5   Cross-FDI and Financial Alliances

Since 1985 cross-FDI between France and Italy has often taken the form of international agreements and alliances between French and Italian financial groups. These financial alliances have been playing an important role in the growth of French-Italian cross-FDI in manufacturing. The BSN alliance with the Agnelli group is a striking example of such alliances which are based on private and family-owned groups. These French-Italian alliances between important family-controlled groups are today a primary characteristic of cross-direct investments between France and Italy, and they help to explain a good part of its recent growth.

This phenomenon illustrates the direction of internationalization of what C. Dupuy and F. Morin (1991) call the 'financial hearts'[26] of the European economies. These networks of strategic alliances between financial groups are created within each economy in order to finance mergers and acquisitions in industrial sectors. Today, similar international networks of financial alliances are also increasingly linking national financial groups between European countries. Such cross-border alliances orientate and finance cross-border acquisitions in Europe. French-Italian cross-FDI provides an example of this growing influence of financial interests in the industrial sphere.

6.4.6   An Interactive Process

The results just outlined can be summarized as the outcome of three general effects which explain French-Italian cross-FDI: an industrial factor, a financial factor and an institutional factor.

The first industrial factor corresponds to the first result above: the importance in cross-FDI of, on the one hand, industrial structures and, on the other hand, the competitiveness of firms. So the combined French and Italian growth in industrial concentration and in the size and capabilities of firms helps to explain the growth of French-Italian cross-FDI.

The second factor is a financial factor which relates to the fifth result outlined above: the key role played by the cross-investments of financial groups in industrial cross-FDI: they have increased the volume of industrial FDI (and particularly of Italian FDI in France), and explain the geographical composition of investment as a result of the particular alliances that have been formed.

The third issue is an institutional factor which corresponds to the third and fourth results outlined above: the effect of European integration on the extent and form of cross-FDI within Europe. As European integration is above all a political process, which is promoted by the 12 national governments, it can be said to constitute an institutional factor.[27] Thus institutional factor helps to explain cross-FDI, together with industrial and financial factors.

The cultural, social and political proximity of France and Italy may explain some of the increase in cross-FDI between these two Latin and Southern European countries. In particular they play a role in the development of international alliances across the Alps. A more behavioural approach in the case studies, including interviews with the managers, would have been likely to confirm this. The 'cultural factor' could then be added to the economic analysis provided above.

NOTES

1. For a study of Italian investments in the USA see F. Sanna Randaccio in N. Acocella and R. Schiattarella (1989, pp. 337–72). For a comparative study of European investments in the USA see F. Sanna Randaccio (1990, pp. 342, 363), which shows that French FDI in the USA represents more than six times Italian FDI.
2. On French FDI see J. Savary (1984); on the recent growth of Italian FDI see N. Acocella (1985); N. Acocella and R. Schiattarella (1989, pp. 263–96); and R. Cominotti and S. Mariotti (1991).
3. The increase in the international agreements of industrial Italian groups is described by G. Viesti in Acocella and Schiattarella (1990, pp. 375–93). F. Brioschi, L. Buzzachi and M.G. Colombo have also emphasized that most of the great private Italian groups have recently set up financial and industrial agreements with French groups (see Brioschi, Buzzachi and Colombo, 1990, pp. 148–50). They explain how at the same time these Italian groups are developing between us a network of financial links, through participations, in Italy (see pp. 144, 145).
4. The group Suez was also in 1987 – through its 10 per cent stake – the third

shareholder of COFIDE, the chief holding of the CIR group (Brioschi, Buzzachi and Colombo, 1990, p. 149).

5. The CIR De Benedetti group has other links with Paribas, which is a shareholder of Valeo, and with UAP, which is a shareholder of Cerus and Valeo.
6. For instance, during the year 1987 Saint-Gobain acquired seven companies in Europe in the glass panes division (annual report).
7. For a 'typical product of Saint Gobain' the cost of production decreases from 6.5F per kilo to 5.0F per kilo when the annual production volume increases from 30,000 to 80,000 tons (*Lettre d'information de la Compagnie Saint-Gobain*, Juin 1988).
8. Thomson has total sales of 76.7 billion francs (1989) and employs about 100,000 people. It is very multinational: 72 per cent of total sales are produced abroad. It focuses mainly on two activities, and its four divisions are: (a) Defence and Electronic systems (with Thomson-CSF), 42 per cent of the total group sales; (b) Consumer Electronics (with Thomson Consumer Electronics), 47 per cent of the total group sales; (c) Home Appliance, 7 per cent of the total group sales; (d) Other activities, 4 per cent of the total group sales.
9. This excludes the activities of SGS-Thomson. In 1987 the two companies Thomson Semi-conducteurs and SGS-Microelettronica were merged to form SGS-Thomson which is owned by Thomson (49 per cent) and SGS (51 per cent). SGS-Thomson manages all the former activities in electronic components of SGS in Italy and in France (where it had created a subsidiary in 1962 with 500 employees), and of Thomson in France. It is trying to improve its competitiveness, but it ranks as only the eleventh world group.
10. In 1982 the Ulm plant was shut down and the Lyons plant became a subcontractor for Agnani, where investment was concentrated. In 1988 the assembling of TV tubes was also stopped in the Lyons plant.
11. In July 1991 TCE created a joint venture in Poland with the Polish firm Polkolor to manage a plant producing colour TV tubes (35–55 cm). It will produce 2,000,000 tubes a year, which will be sold in Eastern and Western Europe. TCE is planning to shift some production of medium-sized TV tubes from Agnani to Poland. The Agnani plant will then become more specialized in large TV tubes.
12. The power of the concentrated retail sector in food products also led BSN to increase its size (for negotiating power), and to manage a marketing policy based upon innovation, brand portfolio and advertising (see Perez, 1988).
13. BSN also used agreements with foreign groups, such as Ajimoto in Japan, Carruzo in Spain and local investors in Nigeria.
14. The financial structure of the Agnelli group and its international financial alliances in December 1987 are analysed in Brioschi, Buzzachi and Colombo (1990, pp. 66–76 and 148–50).
15. The Fossati family, the former owners of the Italian group Star now controlled by BSN, and the Carasso family (Spain) also belong to that 'hard nucleus'. (BSN has often bought companies which were controlled by these families by paying them with lots of BSN capital shares.)

Main shareholders of BSN (at the end of 1989)	% of total capital stock
Family groups**	10.00
Lazard group*	6.00
Agnelli group	5.12
Saint Louis group	2.71
UAP*	2.80

* Over 5% of voting rights
**Fossati family (Italy) 4%, Carasso family (Spain) 4%, A. Riboud 0.2%, BSN employees 1%
Source: Eurostat BSN exercise 1988.

16. Since 1988 international growth has been progressively extended to non-European countries, such as the United States, India and the Eastern European countries.
17. In France it has closed down two plants in Normandy and in Château Thierry.
18. 'With three plants in Europe, one in Germany and two in Italy, we could provide all our European customers but today we are managing five plants of pasta products . . .' (BSN interview in *Les Echos*, 21 March 1991).
19. We call 'pull-factors' those which are related to the host country of the foreign direct investment, in this case Italy. On the other side, 'push-factors' relate to the country of origin of the investor (such as market structures) and to the firm (competitive advantages).
20. Although Italian investments in France have increased recently.
21. In 1987 GNP in France was 854 and in Italy 859 millions Ecus SPA; population in France was 55.6 and in Italy 57.2 millions (Eurostat).
22. In some sectors the intensity of cross-FDI does not correspond to the reciprocal competitive positions of the two economies. For instance in the car industry, Fiat and CIR De Benedetti are investing heavily in France, but the French groups are quite absent from Italy.
23. For instance, CIR De Benedetti and Fiat, which compete in the oligopolized Italian market (they are the leaders of their respective industries) are both investing heavily in France. In some other sectors this does not apply. For instance in fresh milk products BSN is the only oligopolistic leader in France to invest in Italy. The co-operation between SGS (Italy) and Thomson (France) in electronic components may also be viewed as the result of oligopolistic competition, but in the world-wide market.
24. These strategies of Europeanization imply the specialization of plants and an increase in intra-firm trade. On the recent increase of intra-firm trade in Italy see L. Birindelli and R. Schittarella in Acocella and Schiattarella (1989, pp. 313–28).
25. See Savary (1991).
26. For Dupuy and Morin (1991) the 'financial heart' of an economy is made up of a network of strategic (and polarizing) alliances between financial groups, which are durable alliances and which act to finance mergers and acquisitions.
27. The institutional factor also covers national government requirements which exist currently and which will remain even after 1993.

APPENDIX 6.I   THE MAJOR ITALIAN INVESTMENTS IN FRENCH INDUSTRY (CURRENT EMPLOYMENT IN THE FRENCH COMPANY >500 PERSONS)

Year	Italian company	Type*	French company	Activity (of French company)	Employees (of French company)
1934	Buitoni	C	Buitoni S.A.	Food industry	810
1951	Piaggio	C	Piaggio (1)	Motorcycles	600
1960	Ferrero	C	Ferrero France	Food industry	530
1960	Fiat	A	Unic	Trucks	3,500
1960	Borletti (Fiat)	C	Veglia	Auto equipment	2,000
1962	SGS Microelettronica	C	SGS Atès France	Electronic components	560
1964	Chatillon	C	Polyfibres (2)	Synthetic fibres	1,260
1968	CEAT	A	C.G.Fab. Cables	Electric cables	780
1969	CEAT	A	Cordons Equip.	Cables	591
1973	CEAT	A	Cemrep	Mechanical prod.	500
1974	Galeppio	A	Ampa France (3)	Toys, baby prod.	780
1977	Laverda (Fiat)	A	Hesston	Agricult. equip.	720
1980	Pirelli	A	Trefimetaux	Cables	3,400
1981	Olivetti	A	Logabax	Computer prod.	1,500
1981	Olivetti	A	Jappy Hermès Precisa.	Office equip.	820
1986	Magnetti Marelli (Fiat)	A	Solex	Auto equipment	1,780
1986	UFIMA (Fiat)	A	Jaeger	Auto equipment	5,400
1986	Ferruzi	A	Beghin Say	Sugar	9,600
1986	CIR (De Benedetti)	A	Valeo (4)	Auto equipment	26,000
1986	Buitoni	A	Davigel (5)	Food ind. distrib.	1,300

Year	Acquirer	Company	Type*	Product	
1987	PAF	Ceraver	A	Glass products	900
1987	CIR (De Benedetti)	Neiman	A	Auto equipment	4,100
1987	CIR (De Benedetti)	Chausson thermique	A	Auto equipment	2,000
1987	Candy	Rosières	A	Home ovens	700
1987	Ferruzi	Produits du Maïs	A	Glucose, starch	2,370
1988	Ferruzi	Lesieur	A	Oil food products	7,800
1988	Redaelli	Sodetal	A	Metal cables	500
1989	CIR (De Benedetti)	Cartier Système	A	Auto equipment	730
1989	Novicelli	Chaffoteaux et Maury	A	Gas boilers	1,500
1989	Merloni	Scholtes	A	Cooking ovens	600
1990	Montedison	Orkem Polyéthylènes	A	Plastic products	800
1990	Zucchi Bassetti	Jalla	A	House linen	700
1990	CIR (De Benedetti)	Ets Rosi	A	Auto equipment	570
1990	Unichips	Flodor	A	Food products	700
1991	Magnetti Marelli (Fiat)	CEAC	A	Auto batteries	2,400

*Type of investment: A = acquisition; C = Creation
(1) Closed in 1958; (2) Closed in 1981 by Montedison; (3) Sold in 1985; (4) 26,000 employees in France in 1986; (5) Sold to Nestlé in 1988.
Source: Savary, 1990.

APPENDIX 6.II   CROSS-FDI BETWEEN FRANCE AND ITALY BY INDUSTRIAL SECTOR AT THE END OF 1984 (NUMBER OF AFFILIATES AND EMPLOYMENT IN AFFILIATES)

Sector	Italian FDI in France			French FDI in Italy		
	n*	Employees	%	n*	Employees	%
Food industry	15	12,102	42.4	9	2,713	5.5
Energy, water, mining	1	5		8	2,012	4.1
Metals	–	–	–	3	859	1.7
Metal products	3	247	0.9	14	2,622	5.3
Chemicals	2	61		1	1,150	2.3
Industrial, farm, transportation equipment	17	6,880	24.1	29	5,853	11.9
Electronic products (inc. computers office equip.)	4	1,780	6.2	4	2,612	5.3
Motor vehicles and parts	5	6,173	21.6	9	5,455	11.1
Paper, printing	1	180	0.6	5	627	1.3
Rubber and plastic products	3	295	1.0	9	13,237	26.9
Pharmaceuticals	–	–	–	7	1,192	2.4
Textiles, apparel	2	196	0.7	1	336	0.7
Furniture, toys, shoes, other consumer prod.	1	20		4	441	0.9
Building materials	6	627	2.2	33	10,035	20.4
Total	60	28,566	100.0	136	49,144	100.0

*n = number of enterprises
Source: Provisional data LEREP/CERIS, in Steve (1988, Table 3.1/1–2).

APPENDIX 6.III NEW ITALIAN FDI IN FRENCH INDUSTRY BY SECTOR FROM END–1984 TO MID–1991 (FRENCH FIRMS NEWLY ACQUIRED OR CREATED BY ITALIAN INVESTORS)

Sector	Number of firms	Number of employees	% of total employees
Food industry	20	23,715	26.4
Energy, water, mining	–	–	–
Metals	3	1,014	1.1
Metal products	5	3,657	4.1
Chemicals	6	1,335	1.5
Industrial, farm, transportation equipment	11	7,203	8.0
Electronic products (inc. computers, office equip.)	3	4,891	5.4
Motor vehicles and parts	20	42,876	47.6
Paper, printing, publishing	1	109	0.1
Rubber and plastic products	2	148	0.2
Pharmaceuticals	1	150	0.2
Textiles, apparel	11	1,981	2.2
Furniture, toys, shoes, other consumer products	3	950	1.1
Building materials	6	1,960	2.2
Total	92	89,989	100.0

Source: Savary (1990).

REFERENCES

Acocella, N. (ed.) (1985), *Le Multinazionali Italiane*, Bologna: Collana del IRM, Societa Editrice Il Mulino.

Acocella, N. and Schiattarella, R. (eds) (1989), *Theoria della internazionalizzazione e realta italiana*, Naples: Liguori Editore.

Alzona, G. and Gilly, J.P. (1990), 'L'internazionalizzazione produttiva incrociata Italia-Francia: un quadro di riferimento', *Quaderno del CERIS* (CNR), no. 4.

Banque de France (1990), *Balance des Paiements de la France, Rapport Annuel*, Annexes, Paris: Banque de France.

Brioschi, F., Buzzachi, L. and Colombo, M.G. (1990), *Gruppi di imprese e mercato finanziario, la struttura di potere nell'industria italiana*, Rome: Ed. La Nuova Italia Scientifica.

Cantwell, J.A. (1988), *The Reorganisation of European Industries after Integra-*

tion: Selected Evidence on the Role of Multinationals' Enterprise Activities, in Dunning and Robson (1988).

Cominotti, R. and Mariotti, S. (eds) (1991), *Italia multinazionale 1990*, Rome: Franco Angeli.

Daviet, J.P. (1988), *Un destin international: la Compagnie de Saint-Gobain de 1830 à 1939*, Paris: Ed. Les Archives Contemporaines.

Doz, Y.L. (1986), *Strategic Management in Multinational Companies*, Oxford: Pergamon Press.

Dunning, J.H. and Robson, P. (eds) (1988), *Multinationals and the European Community*, Oxford: Basil Blackwell.

Dupuy, C., Milelli, C. and Savary, J. (1992), *Stratégies des multinationales*, volume of *Atlas mondial des multinationales*, vol. 2, Paris: Ed. Reclus/La Documentation Française.

Dupuy, C. and Morin, F. (1991), 'Le coeur financier allemand', *Revue d'economie financière*, September, 83–106.

EEC (1988), '1992, the new European economy', *Revue Economie Européenne*, (35), 109.

Eurostat (1990), *Les Investissements directs de la Communauté Européenne, Années 1984 à 1988*, Rapport provisoire de C. Spanneut, Brussels: Commission of the European Communities.

Hood, N. and Vahlne, J.E. (eds) (1988), *Strategies in Global Competition*, London: Routledge.

Itaki, M. and Waterson, M. (1991), *European Multinationals and 1992, University of Reading Working Papers in International Investment and Business Studies*, Series B, vol. iii, no. 141.

Kay, N.M. (1990), 'Multinational Enterprise as Strategic Choice: Some Transaction Cost Perspective', in C.N. Pitelis and R. Sugden (eds), *The Nature of the Transnational Firm*, London: Routledge.

Martinet, A.C. (1988), 'Un "Euro-groupe français": BSN', in P. Joffre and G. Koenig (eds), *L'Euro-entreprise*, Paris: Editions Economica.

Molle, W. and Morsink, R. (1991), 'Intra-European Direct Investment', in B. Burgenmeyer and J.L. Mucchielli (eds), *Multinationals and Europe, 1992*, London: Routledge.

Onida, F. and Viesti, G. (eds) (1988), *The Italian Multinationals*, London: Croom-Helm.

Perez, R. (1988), 'Les Stratégies d'internationalisation des groupes agro-alimentaires, l'exemple de BSN', *Travaux et documents de recherche de l'ERFI*, WP no. 88–9.

Sanna Randaccio, F. (1990), *European Direct Investments in US Manufacturing*, Rome: Edizioni Kappa.

Savary, J. (1981), 'La France dans la division internationale du travail, une approche par l'investissement direct international', *Revue Economique*, **32**, (4).

Savary, J. (1984), *French Multinationals*, London: Frances Pinter.

Savary, J. (1990), 'Les Investissements italiens en France de 1984 à 1989: premiers résultats de la base de données du LEREP', Toulouse: LEREP, *unpublished document*.

Savary, J. (1991), 'Des stratégies multinationales aux stratégies globales des groupes en Europe', paper given at LEREP's conference September 1989, in J.P. Gilly (ed.), *L'Europe industrielle: horizon 93*, Paris: Editions La Documentation Française coll. Notes et Etudes Documentaires.

SESSI, *L'Implantation étrangère dans l'industrie au 1/1/19..*, annual reports, Paris: Ministry of Industry.

Steve, E. (1988), *Il fenomeno dell'internazionalizzazione incrociata dei sistemi produttivi: il caso Italia-Francia*, thesis, Universita Degli Studi di Torino.

7. Trade and Direct Investment within the EC: The Impact of Strategic Considerations

Nicola Acocella*

7.1 INTRODUCTION

The economic literature on the likely effects of '1992' has largely predicted the same kinds of consequences as from the first stage of the European integration process begun in 1957, namely, a further increase in the role of trade in so far as the operations of firms already established in the Community are concerned.

The literature has two main shortcomings. First, it implicitly assumes substitutability between foreign trade and investment, thereby referring to a specific kind of direct investment (DI), namely the market-orientated one. Secondly, it has focused on efficiency considerations and disregarded strategic ones, that is, those pertaining to the likely reactions of competitors and the resulting market structure.

This chapter follows a tradition dating back to Hymer that has been largely neglected for a long time. However, in recent years models have been presented which consider both the cases for a 'follow-the-leader' and for an 'exchange-of-threats' kind of direct investment.

The model presented here analyses the case of an 'absorb-the-rival' and 'rent-seeking' kind of direct investment and intends to explain some aspects of the international operations that have taken place within the EC in recent years, that is, the marked increase in the number of Community (and international) mergers and acquisitions experienced in the last three to four years,[1] a period when at least

* The author would like to thank L. Campiglio, J. Cantwell, G. Ciccarone, M. Franzini, M. Graham, M. Motta, P. Ramazzotti, F. Sanna Randaccio, R. Schiattarella, F. Silva and the participants to seminars held at Louvain-la-Neuve, Naples and Cargèse for their comments on earlier versions of the paper. The usual disclaimer applies. Funding from the Italian Council for National Research (CNR) and from the European Community is gratefully acknowledged.

medium and large firms have incorporated the formation of the single market in their strategies.[2]

Section 7.2 gives a very brief presentation of the usual argument on the effects of the single market on trade and investment within the European Community as well as of its main shortcomings. Section 7.3 depicts the possibility of interpenetration of markets by exports ensuing upon the removal of non-tariff barriers as a classic example of the prisoner's dilemma. Section 7.4 examines the conditions favouring an interpenetration of markets by exports *vis-à-vis* green-field direct investment. Sections 7.5 and 7.6 consider the possibility of takeovers in symmetric and asymmetric conditions of demand and costs, respectively.

7.2 THE EFFECTS OF THE SINGLE MARKET ON INTRA-EC TRADE AND DIRECT INVESTMENT

As we mentioned in the Introduction, there are many aspects involved in the question under examination. Attention will be focused, therefore, on trade and investment within the EC, disregarding international operations outside the Community by EC firms and those within the Community by non-member countries.

The consequences of Mark II Community integration have been envisaged by economists more or less in the same way as those of Mark I: a process of trade creation and trade diversion should take place, leading to a rise in intra-EC trade – at the expense of intra-EC investment – and in import-substituting DI from non-member countries.[3]

Itaki and Waterson (1990) is a good example of this position. Their argument is as follows: the existence of firm-specific fixed costs gives rise to economies of multiplant operation. Establishment of plants abroad involves additional fixed costs, whereas exports from one country involve only variable costs. The completion of the internal market will lower the level of variable costs of exports, thus leading to a preference for exports rather than the establishing of plants abroad (that is, carrying out DI).[4]

This literature has two main shortcomings. The first one is dealt with by Yannopoulos (1990) and Cantwell (1991) and refers to the assumption of substitutability between trade and investment. This assumption has largely been used during debates over both the effects of the formation of the EC and the consequences of 1992. The conclusion is drawn – based on that assumption – that trade is the preferred kind of international operation when tariff or non-tariff barriers are removed, in so far as the activity of EC firms in the EC is concerned. On the contrary, the erection of some kind of protection from foreign goods induces a rise in FDI. However, as we know, foreign trade and direct investment are not always substitutes. They may be complements for all kinds of FDI other than market-orientated FDI in a specific line of product.

The second kind of shortcoming in the relevant literature relates to strategic considerations. In order to overcome the first kind of difficulty we shall henceforth restrict our analysis to market-orientated DI in a specific line of product and disregard questions connected to vertical integration.

With very few exceptions, the theoretical and empirical literature has focused on efficiency considerations when considering the choice between DI and trade, usually disregarding the likely reactions of competitors and the resulting structure of the market. Elsewhere (Acocella, 1988, 1989, 1992), it has been argued that this is at odds both with the very foundations of the theory of DI and with some rather recent developments in the field of industrial organization.

The analysis of the sections that follow will be carried out in terms of strategic considerations, following a tradition dating back to Hymer (1960)[5] that had been lost for a long time (see Acocella, 1992; Yamin, 1991). This line of analysis, in showing dissatisfaction with the now dominant theories of DI – that is to say, with the eclectic paradigm and the internalization theory – mainly based on efficiency considerations, has enriched our understanding of the determinants of foreign DI: Knickerbocker (1973) presented the case for a 'follow-the-leader' kind of DI; Graham (1978, 1990a, 1990b) dealt with models of 'exchange-of-threats' DI; Casson (1987, ch. 3) further developed this case; Smith (1987), Horstmann and Markusen (1987) and Jacquemin (1989) analysed cases of 'market pre-emption' by DI. The models we present in sections 7.5 and 7.6 analyse the case of a 'rent-seeking' kind of DI accomplished by 'absorbing the rival'.

The strategic approach to international operations can explain some aspects of the international operations that have recently taken place within the EC, namely, the marked increase in the number of Community (and international) mergers and acquisitions experienced in recent years: this has caused the Community mergers to outnumber national ones, for the first time in 1989–90, whereas in the past the latter had been largely predominant (see Commission of the European Community, various years).

This increase needs an explanation that cannot be given only in terms of the factors underlying the wave of such operations at a purely national level. In our opinion, it is also *the prospect of increased competition* in view of the completion of the internal market and the ensuing possibility of reduced profits that makes mergers and acquisitions so attractive at a Community or an international level. Abolishing non-tariff barriers in an industry raises serious problems for the existing firms in that industry. Let us first consider these problems.

7.3   INTERPENETRATION OF MARKETS BY EXPORTS

One can imagine each of the firms operating in the European Community as earning monopoly profits in a sub-market, which for convenience's sake may be thought of as being a national market, before the abolition of non-tariff barriers. Once these are dropped, the possibility arises that each firm may penetrate other firms' markets by exports. If there are two firms producing the same good, firm A, operating in country a, and firm B, established in country b, the former can penetrate the latter's market and raise its profits if the latter continues to stay in its own market. The same is true for firm B. However, if both A and B follow this course of action, they will earn a profit that is lower than in the case of segmentation of markets and also lower than in the case where only one of them penetrates the foreign market.

The situation can be represented as in payoff Matrix 1 (Model 1). P stands for the payoff to the firm indicated by the subscript, A or B. The superscript xa or xb indicates exports to a or b by the firm established in the other market, B or A, respectively. So $P_A^{xb,xa}$ indicates the pay-off accruing to firm A, staying in market a, which exports to b, when market a is also penetrated by exports from b.

It is self evident that $P_A^{xb, xa} > P_A^{xa}$ and $P_A^{xb} > P_A$. In addition, one can assume that $P_A^{xb,xa} < P_A$[6] since: (a) there exist economies of scale; (b) sharing markets depresses profits as firms do not collude and adopt Cournot strategies when coexisting in the same market. (A symmetrical set of inequalities holds for B.)

Thus the situation is one typical of the prisoner's dilemma. Exports are a dominant strategy for both firms.

In conclusion, in a static game[7] such as the one presented in this section, the equilibrium solution[8] is interpenetration of markets by

Matrix 1

B

	Exports	Stays in its own market
Exports	$P_A^{xb,\,xa},\,P_B^{xa,\,xb}$	$P_A^{xb},\,P_B^{xb}$
Stays in its own market	$P_A^{xa},\,P_B^{xa}$	$P_A,\,P_B$

A

exports, even if this gives a less-profitable solution than that of isolation of the markets (*A* stays in *a*, *B* in *b*) for both firms.

7.4 INTERPENETRATION BY EXPORTS AND GREEN-FIELD DIRECT INVESTMENT

Let us now consider the possibility of interpenetration of markets not only by exports but also by 'green-field' direct investment.

The situation can be represented by pay-off Matrix 2 (Model 2), where the superscript *DIa* indicates *DI* carried out in country *a* and similarly for *DIb*.

We can make the following assumptions:

(1) $P_A^{xb,\,DIa} > P_A^{DIa}$
(2) $P_A^{xb,\,xa} > P_A^{xa}$
(3) $P_A^{xb} > P_A$, and similarly for firm *B*.

These assumptions simply state that, for each firm, exports are a dominant strategy over staying in its own market.

If one assumes, in addition, that there are plant economies of scale, so that exports have a lower unit cost than foreign production,[9] exports are a dominant strategy over green-field DI as well, and the solution to this game is the same as in Model 1.

As a way of illustration of this issue, let us suppose that $p^a = D^a - q^a$, $p^b = D^b - q^b$, where p and q are, respectively, prices and

Matrix 2

B

	Invests in *a*	Exports to *a*	Stays in *b*
Invests in *b*	$P_A^{Dlb,Dla}$, $P_B^{Dla,Dlb}$	$P_A^{Dlb,xa}$, $P_B^{xa,Dlb}$	P_A^{Dlb}, P_B^{Dlb}
Exports to *b*	$P_A^{xb,Dla}$, $P_B^{Dla,xb}$	$P_A^{xb,xa}$, $P_B^{xa,xb}$	P_A^{xb}, P_B^{xb}
Stays in *a*	P_A^{Dla}, P_B^{Dla}	P_A^{xa}, P_B^{xa}	P_A, P_B

A

quantities, and D^a and D^b are constants. Let us also assume that there are fixed production costs, C_0, that unit variable costs of production for the home market are C_1 and that unit export costs are $e \geqslant C_1$. In other words, production for foreign markets implies only additional variable costs, that is, transport and selling costs, tariffs and so on, equal to $e - C_1 \geqslant 0$. Since there are unlimited economies of scale, exports imply only variable costs.[10] One can easily show that sufficient conditions for exports to be a dominant strategy are: (a) symmetry of variable costs in *b* (or in *a*) as between *A* and *B*; (b) export costs equal to variable production costs (see Appendix 7.I.)

These conditions ensure that profits from exports are larger than profits from *DI* by exactly the amount of fixed production costs abroad. *DI* is no longer an inferior strategy to the extent that economies of scale are limited and/or export costs are significantly higher than variable costs of producing abroad.

In general terms, exports are more likely to be a dominant strategy for firm *A* the higher are the variable costs of *A* in *b*, the lower the export costs, the lower the size of market *b* and the higher the variable and fixed costs of *B* in *b* (in the last two cases, if export costs are higher than the direct costs of *A* in *b*). Similarly, one can state analogous conditions favouring exports to the detriment of *DI* for firm *B*.

This means that only conditions of asymmetry between the costs of *A* and *B* and/or the existence of limited scale economies and supplementary costs of exports (over those of selling in the same market where production takes place) may induce a superiority of green-field market-orientated *DI* over exports, for a homogeneous product.

7.5 INTERPENETRATION BY EXPORTS AND TAKEOVERS: THE SYMMETRIC CASE

Let us suppose that conditions ensuring that exports are a dominant strategy over both green-field investment and staying in the home market are satisfied. For simplicity's sake we could then limit our strategies to exports and takeovers.[11] However, consideration of the strategy that consists in staying in the home market could be useful. The situation can be represented by pay-off Matrix 3 (Model 3). The first row and column need explanation. If only one of the two firms plays the strategy of buying the other, the latter gains the price paid for the takeover – *whatever its strategy*[12] – while the former gains monopoly profits from staying both in *a* and *b* and serving each of these markets by local production. These monopoly profits are, obviously, reduced by the price paid to buy the other firms, TOB.

If both firms play the strategy of buying the other – and do not co-operate, for example, by merging – they stand as monopolists, each in its own market, but suffer a loss, L, to be deducted from their profits in isolation. One can think of this loss as being determined by legal expenses and/or by premiums paid to minority shareholders in order to resist the opponent's takeover. With reference to strategies followed by *A*, let us consider the following three conditions:

$$P_A - L_A > TOB_B \tag{1}$$

$$P_A{}^{a,b} - TOB_A > P_A{}^{xb,\ xa} \tag{2}$$

$$P_A{}^{a,b} - TOB_A < P_A{}^{xb} \tag{3}$$

We can think of similar conditions (1′), (2′), (3′) referring to B's strategies. In this model symmetry is assumed, which implies that satisfaction of condition (i) implies satisfaction of condition (i′), for i = 1, 2, 3.

If condition (2) is not satisfied ($\sim$(2)), interpenetration by exports

Matrix 3

	B		
	Buys *A*	Exports to *a*	Stays in its own market
Buys *B*	$P_A - L_A, P_B - L_B$	$P_A^{a.b} - TOB_A, TOB_A$	$P_A^{a.b} - TOB_A, TOB_A$
A Exports to *b*	$TOB_B, P_B^{a.b} - TOB_B$	$P_A^{xb,xa}, P_B^{xa,xb}$	P_A^{xb}, P_B^{xb}
Stays in its own market	$TOB_B, P_B^{a.b} - TOB_B$	P_A^{xa}, P_B^{xa}	P_A, P_B

is still a solution (either unique, if ~(1) and (3) are satisfied, or multiple, together with other solutions, all implying takeovers). In all the other cases the solution always implies a takeover by one and/or the other firm.

Condition (2), then, is crucial to the existence of DI by a takeover. In other words, it is only if condition (2) is not satisfied that a takeover can be avoided.

Condition (2) can be restated as follows:

$$P_A^{a, b} - P_A^{xb, xa} - TOB_A > 0 \qquad (4)$$

The price that *A* has to pay in order to take over *B* depends on a number of factors. However, we can imagine that it cannot be, under ordinary circumstances, lower than the profit that *B* can earn in the alternative equilibrium position (interpenetration by exports).

If $TOB_A = P_B^{xa, xb}$, (4) amounts to the following:

$$P_A^{a, b} - P_A^{xb, xa} - P_B^{xa, xb} > 0 \qquad (5)$$

Let us assume that $P_A{}^{a,b} = P_A + P_B$.[13] Then (5) turns into the following:

$$(P_A - P_A{}^{xb,\ xa}) + (P_B - P_B{}^{xa,\ xb}) > 0 \tag{6}$$

This inequality certainly holds under the assumptions of section 7.3: the existence of economies of scale and the adoption of Cournot strategies by both players ensure that each expression in parentheses is positive.

In the specific case when the assumptions about demand and costs of Model 2 hold and, in addition, it is assumed that $D^a = D^b = D$ and $C^b{}_{OA} = C^a{}_{OA} = K$ we have from (6):

$$P_A{}^{ab} - 2P_A{}^{xb,\ xa} = 1/18\ (D - C)^2 > 0 \tag{7}$$

where C is the common value of variable costs (in a and b by A and B) and export costs.

This means that under such assumptions about demand and costs – in a situation of symmetry – condition (2) is always satisfied, which, as we know, implies the choice of a takeover strategy. We can then say that, under plausible conditions, DI by takeover can ensure a larger pay-off than interpenetration of markets by exports. This result can be attributed largely to the advantages gained by the firm when taking over its opponent: it can eliminate its competitor and monopolize both markets,[14] thus avoiding a solution of interpenetration of markets by exports which would depress its prospective profits. Monopoly extra-profits could even be shared in some way with the opponent by inflating the price offered for the takeover.

The stimulus for A to monopolize the markets is higher the lower is the profit it can earn in a situation of interpenetration of markets by exports. With reference to the problems deriving from the single European market, we can say that the larger the reduction in export costs (hence, the more profitable are exports vis-à-vis greenfield DI) the higher the stimulus for one firm or the other to monopolize the markets. By keeping strictly to the symmetry assumption of this model, however, each firm would find it profitable to take over its opponent, which leads to an indeterminate solution. Section 7.6 will investigate asymmetric conditions, which can ensure a unique and determinate solution, thus showing the likely characteristics of acquisitive firms and of those which are candidates to be taken over. But adding such elements must not lead us to forget that it is strategic considerations and the related possibility of gaining monopoly profits that are at the very basis of takeovers in the situations we are considering.

7.6 INTERPENETRATION BY EXPORTS AND TAKEOVERS. ASYMMETRIC CONDITIONS

The pay-off matrix is the same as in Model 3, but equality of demands, costs and so on between the two firms is no longer assumed. Matrix 3 is then asymmetric.

There may be two kinds of asymmetry. First, conditions of demand and cost may not be too dissimilar so that a 'soft' asymmetry comes out: even if the values of the pay-offs for the two firms in similar conditions differ, when condition (i) is satisfied condition (i') also holds, for i = 1,2,3. In other words, the conditions in which the two firms operate are not so different to make, for example, condition (i) satisfied for firm *A* whereas ~(i) holds for firm *B*. In this case, the eight possible outcomes are those listed in Table 7.1 and the considerations made in the previous section as to the solution still apply.

Alternatively, the conditions between the two firms may be so different that if (i) holds, (i') no longer holds or vice versa, for i = 1,2,3. The number of possible outcomes is now 8^2.

Let us now discuss the solution(s) in this alternative, 'harder' case of asymmetry. After examining all the possible cases, we can conclude as follows:

(1)   Interpenetration of markets by exports takes place if and only if both ~(2) and ~(2') hold.

The possibility of condition (2) not being satisfied has been negatively assessed in the previous section. The same considerations apply to condition (2'). This outcome can then be ruled out as unlikely.

(2)   A *simultaneous* attempt at takeover by both firms (that is, the playing of S1 and S1') can take place only if both (1) and (1') hold.

If this is not the case, either *A* will take over *B* – if (1) holds while (1') does not – or *B* will take over *A*, if (1') holds while (1) does not.

The likelihood of this outcome depends on the three kinds of vari-

Table 7.1 *Interpenetration by exports and takeovers: the symmetric case*

S1: Investing abroad;
S2: exporting;
S3: staying in the home market.

Conditions (1), (2), (3)

	S1'	S2'	S3'
S1	X X	X	
S2	X		X
S3		X	

Conditions (1), (2), ~(3)

	S1'	S2'	S3'
S1	X X	X	X
S2	X		
S3	X		

If (1) and (2), then always takeover by both.

Conditions (1), ~(2), (3)

	S1'	S2'	S3'
S1	X X		
S2		X X	X
S3		X	

Conditions (1), ~(2), ~(3)

	S1'	S2'	S3'
S1	X X		X
S2		X X	
S3	X		

If (1) and ~(2), then either takeover or export.

Conditions ~(1), ~(2), (3)

	S1'	S2'	S3'
S1		X	X
S2	X	X X	X
S3	X	X	

Conditions ~(1), ~(2), ~(3)

	S1'	S2'	S3'
S1		X	X X
S2	X	X X	
S3	X X		

If ~(1) and ~(2), then export if (3) and either takeover or export if ~(3).

Conditions ~(1), (2), (3)

	S1'	S2'	S3'
S1		X X	X
S2	X X		X
S3	X	X	

Conditions ~(1), (2), ~(3)

	S1'	S2'	S3'
S1		X X	X X
S2	X X		
S3	X X		

If ~(1) and (2), then always takeover.

ables involved in conditions (1) and (1'): P_A and P_B, L_A and L_B, TOB_B and TOB_A.

The larger the difference between the two firms as to: (a) the profitability of each firm in its home market; (b) the costs of resisting the opponent's takeover while playing the same strategy; (c) the price paid by the opponent for the take-over; the higher is the prospect of condition (1) being satisfied while condition (1') is not (and thus of A taking over B) or vice versa (and thus of B taking over A).

Factors underlying (a) and (b) can be easily understood. Let us concentrate instead on (c), that is, on factors on which TOB_B and TOB_A depend.

As we said before, there is a lower limit to the price each firm has to pay in order to take-over its opponent:

$$TOB_A \geqslant P_B^{xa,\ xb}; \ TOB_B \quad P_A^{xb,\ xa} \tag{8}$$

However, there is an upper limit too. We can imagine that A would not be willing to give up its differential gain, that is, the difference between the monopoly profits gained in the two markets and the profits that could be gained in the alternative equilibrium position, that of interpenetration by exports. Indeed, A would not pay more than that difference. It should be then:

$$TOB_A \leqslant P_A^{ab} - P_A^{xb,\ xa}; \ TOB_B \leqslant P_B^{ab} - P_B^{xa,\ xb} \tag{9}$$

Ceteris paribus, the likelihood of condition (1) being satisfied while (1') is not, or vice versa, depends on the difference between the two prices, TOB_A and TOB_B: the higher the difference, the higher the probability of such an outcome.

If we consider the maximum values of TOB, that means that this outcome depends on how large is:

$$P_A^{ab} - P_A^{xb,\ xa} - (P_B^{ab} - P_B^{xa,\ xb}) = (P_A^{ab} - P_B^{ab}) + (P_B^{xa,\ xb} - P_A^{xb,\ xa}) \tag{10}$$

If we take the minimum values of TOB, the outcome depends on how large is:

$$P_B^{xa,xb} - P_B^{xb,xa} \tag{11}$$

which is a component of (10).

The value of (10) (and (11)) is then crucial to the possibility of A

taking over its rival. The greater the value of (10) (and (11)), the higher is the probability of such a result.

Let us now concentrate on the conditions that lead to the fulfilment of (10). Generally speaking, the firm having higher costs in its home market or higher export costs or a smaller domestic market will have a stronger incentive to resort to takeovers instead of choosing a strategy of penetrating its opponent's market through exports (see Appendix 7.III). This result looks a bit surprising,[15] particularly with reference to costs in the home market. However, the surprise diminishes if one considers that:

(a) we are speaking of the *incentive* to choose a strategy of takeovers as opposed to one of exports, not of the *strength* of firms, particularly on the financial side;

(b) higher costs at home, let us say for firm A, mean *both* that A can derive higher profits from a monopoly position (that would result from taking over its opponent) than it could derive from interpenetration of markets by exports *and*, *in addition*, a reduction of the excess monopoly profits of its opponent (firm B) over the profits that B can derive from interpenetration of markets by exports.

7.7 SUMMARY AND CONCLUSIONS

In this chapter we have examined some games related to firms established in different countries which show that: (a) expansion abroad through exports is a dominant strategy over staying in the market of origin; (b) exports are also a dominant strategy over expansion abroad through 'green-field' direct investment, under certain conditions (relevance of scale economies, low transport costs); (c) penetration of foreign markets by takeover of local firms is a strategy that can be preferred to exports since it allows the exploitation of monopoly extra-profits; (d) the incentive for a firm to eliminate its opponents is higher the higher is the gap between monopoly profits and the profits that can be earned in a situation of interpenetration of markets by trade and, given the amount of monopoly profits, the incentive is higher the higher is the competitive effect of removing tariff and non-tariff barriers, which tend to reduce the profits related to trade; in other words, the lowering of barriers threatens the monopoly positions of firms in the various markets and each one of them, then, has an incentive to remove the danger by eliminating competition; and (e) in the race to buy their opponents, a stronger incentive is held by those firms which have higher production costs at home and/or originate from smaller countries.

These models stress some strategic elements which should be considered when analysing international operations. They are highly stylized and thus have a number of limitations, the most important being the assumption of only two firms and two markets. However, they may shed some light on the consequences of the completion of the internal market. Economic literature, by focusing on the efficiency aspects of the problem, tends to stress the importance, in view of 1992, of trade as opposed to foreign direct investment by EC firms as an instrument of integration. As a matter of fact, we are also observing a sharp rise in the number of Community (and international) takeovers and mergers, which could mean, on the contrary, that direct investment is indeed playing a larger role than expected, at least on a provisional basis, that is, on the transition path to a new equilibrium position.

There are many more strategic elements to be considered in the realm of international operations, which can be dealt with appropriately in terms of game theory. From this point of view the present chapter only touches the surface of an important field of analysis that will hopefully develop in the future.

NOTES

1. See Commission of the European Community (various years); CNEL (1991).
2. See Tsoukalis (1990).
3. The effects on trade and direct investment of Mark I have been examined, among others, by Scaperlanda and Mauer (1969); Goldberg (1972); Lunn (1980). Those of Mark II by Buigues and Jacquemin (1989); Cantwell (1991); Dunning and Robson (1987); Economists Advisory Group (1990); Garella (1989); Geroski and Vlassopoulos (1990); Itaki and Waterson (1990); Kay (1990a); Kay (1990b); Yannopoulos (1990). Data on trade and investment within the European Community are given by Molle and Morsink (1991) and Schiattarella (1990).
4. It is true that fixed costs of establishing plants abroad can be reduced also as a consequence of the harmonization of national regulations and/or of the decrease of the 'economic' distance between the home and host countries. However, one can assume that these reductions are of a lower order of magnitude as compared to the reduction of variable costs of exports.
5. Antecessors can be found to Hymer pointing out some of the concepts later developed and stated in a clearer framework by this author. These include Lewis (1938); Penrose (1956); and Dunning (1958). Kindleberger (1973) claims that Lamfalussy's concept of 'defensive' investment is the same as defensive motives discussed later by other authors in the literature on foreign DI, even if Lamfalussy used the concept with reference to domestic investment (see Lamfalussy, 1961, drawn from his thesis of 1958).

M. Graham has also called to my attention Hendrick W.A. Deterding's description of the motivation of Royal Dutch Shell in entering the US market via DI that is contained in the 1911 Annual Report of this firm: the logic of Royal Dutch Shell is almost exactly that of Graham's 'exchange-of-threats' model.

6. There may be other factors that can temper the validity of these considerations, but they are not important in the context of our models.

7. All the games we present are of a one-shot type. This seems to be the simplest way to emphasize the case for a 'rent-seeking' kind of direct investment. In this context we need not adopt an extensive form. There is at least one implication of this very simple and general way of approaching our problem which should be pointed out: the pay-offs have to be thought of as the discounted sum of all future profits accruing to each firm.

8. Equilibrium does not involve price equalization either in this model or in those that follow. Such a situation is sustainable in the long run if arbitrage by consumers or other agents is prevented by information and other kinds of barriers.

9. One can assume, for example, that exports imply only direct costs of the same order of magnitude as direct costs for domestic production and sales and these, in turn, are equal to direct costs of overseas production.

10. This is a very strong assumption, introduced only to stress the case for exports against direct investment.

11. We will disregard mixed strategies.

12. When a firm plays the strategy of acquisition, the distinction between playing 'exports' or 'staying in its own market' becomes meaningless for the other firm, which is indeed taking a passive attitude thus losing the power to choose. The only way the latter can survive is to respond by playing the same strategy as the former firm, i.e. the strategy of acquisition.

13. This is not always the case. There are reasons why it could be $P_A{}^{a,\ b} < P_A + P_B$: there are costs of integrating two different organizational apparatuses, for example, costs of operating at a distance. In fact, the possibility that horizontal mergers may result in private losses for the merging firms has been demonstrated, with no specific reference to multinational enterprises, by Salant, Switzer and Reynolds (1983); for the evidence on loss-producing mergers, see Scherer (1980).

However, there are also reasons why the opposite may be true, namely, the possibility of playing off one against another various operators acting in the two countries, such as trade unions and governments.

14. This is a rather straightforward result within the assumptions of the model, namely, the existence of only two firms.

15. If we combined this result with Krugman and Venables (1990) we would have not only a concentration of production in large markets but a concentration of ownership in the hands of high-cost firms from small countries.

APPENDIX 7.I

With reference to Model 2, we show sufficient conditions for exports to be a dominant strategy.

Let us assume that the conditions stated in section 7.4 as to demand, production and export costs are satisfied.

The profits that A can earn when it plays the strategy of investing in b while B invests in a are:

$$P_A^{DIb,DI} = (D^a - q^a_A - q^a_B) q^a_A - C^a_{OA} - C^a_{1A} q^a_A + \tag{7.I.1}$$
$$+ (D^b - q^b_A - q^b_B) q^b_A - C^b_{OA} - C^b_{1A} q^b_A$$

A similar expression holds for $P_B^{DIa,DIb}$.

By differentiating A's profits with respect to q^a_A and q^b_A and B's profits with respect to q^b_B and q^a_B, we can derive the values of q^a_A, q^b_A, q^b_B, q^a_B, and substitute them into (7.I.1) so as to have:

$$P_A^{DIb,DIa} = [1/3 (D^a - 2C^a_{1A} + C^a_{1B})]^2 + \tag{7.I.2}$$
$$- C^a_{OA} + [1/3 (D^b - 2C^b_{1A} + C^b_{1B})]^2 - C^b_{OA}$$

The profits that A can earn when it exports to b while B invests in a are:

$$P_A^{xb,DIa} = (D^a - q^a_A - q^a_B - C^a_{1A}) q^a_A - C^a_{OA} + \tag{7.I.3}$$
$$+ (D^b - q^b_B - q^b_A - e_A) q^b_A$$

The profits that B can earn in the same situation are:

$$P_B^{DIa,xb} = (D^b - q^b_B - q^b_A - C^b_{1B}) q^b_B - C^b_{OB} + (D^a - q^a_B + $$
$$- q^a_A - C^a_{1B}) q^a_B - C^a_{OB} \tag{7.I.4}$$

By making the above-mentioned operations of differentiation we can obtain the values of q^a_A, q^b_A, q^b_B, q^a_B and substitute them into (7.I.3) so to have:

$$P_A^{xb,DIa} = [1/3 (D^a - 2C^a_{1A} + C^a_{1B})]^2 - C^a_{OA} + [1/3 (D^b + \tag{7.I.5}$$
$$- 2e_A + C^b_{1B})]^2$$

By subtracting (7.I.5) from (7.I.2), we have:

$$S \equiv P_A^{DIb,DIa} - P_A^{xb,DIa} + 4/9 [(C^b_{1A})^2 - e_A^2 (C^b_{1A} - e_A) \tag{7.I.6}$$
$$(C^b_{1B} + D^b)] - C^b_{OA}$$

The sign of (7.I.6) is indeterminate. If, however, $C^b_{1A} = e_A$ we have:

$$P_A^{DIb,DIa} - P_A^{xb,DIa} = - C^b_{OA} < 0 \tag{7.I.6'}$$

(A similar condition must hold for B: $C^a_{1B} = e_B$. Taking the two conditions together and recalling that we are in a symmetric case, we should have: $C^b_{1A} = C^a_{1B} = e_A = e_B$).

More generally, if we differentiate expression (7.I.6) with respect to the relevant independent variables, we have:

$$\delta S/\delta C^b_{1A} = 2C^b_{1A} - C^b_{1B} - D^b \tag{7.I.7}$$

$$\delta S/\delta C^b_{1B} = 4/9 \, (e_A - C^b_{1A}) \tag{7.I.8}$$

$$\delta S/\delta D^b = 4/9 \, (e_A - C^b_{1A}) \tag{7.I.9}$$

$$\delta S/\delta e_A = 4/9 \, (D^b + C^b_{1B} - 2e_A) \tag{7.I.10}$$

Expression (7.I.7) is likely to be negative if market b, which is reflected in parameter D^b, is large enough.

Expression (7.I.8) and (7.I.9) are positive, zero or negative if $e \gtrless C^b_{1A}$ respectively.

Expression (7.I.10) is likely to be positive for the same reason given for (7.I.7).

In a similar way a comparison can be made between $P_A^{DIb,xa}$ and $P_A^{xb,xa}$ which gives the same result as in (7.I.6').

The same result as in (7.I.6') holds for $P_A^{DIb} - P_A^{xb}$.

APPENDIX 7.II

With reference to Model 3, let us consider conditions (1), (2), (3) of section 7.5. Since we are considering a symmetric case, whenever condition (i) holds (does not hold) condition (i′) holds (does not hold), for i = 1, 2, 3.

Table 7.1 reproduces the cells of the matrix of Model 3 in a suggestive way. The solutions in each situation are underlined.

We can easily see that, if conditions (1), (2), (3) are satisfied, the solution consists in strategies (S1, S1′). The solution is the same if conditions (1) and (2) are satisfied but condition (3) is not.

If condition (2) does not hold, there are multiple solutions, consisting in strategies (S1, S1′) and (S2, S2′).

If neither (1) nor (2) holds, but (3) holds, we have the only case of a unique solution not implying a takeover.

If none of the three conditions is satisfied we have multiple solutions: one of them, (S2, S2′), implies interpenetration by exports; the others imply takeovers as well: (S3, S1′), (S1, S3′). If (1) is not satisfied whereas (2) holds, we have multiple solutions all implying takeovers.

A comparison of the various cases can confirm the statement in section 7.5: only when condition (2) does not hold the solution can be 'interpenetration by exports'. When (2) does not hold, if either (1) or (3) holds or if both (1) and (3) hold, solutions implying takeovers can occur in addition to the solution 'interpenetration by exports'. However, if neither (1) nor (2) is satisfied, but (3) is, interpenetration by exports is the unique solution.

The conclusion can be drawn that condition (2) is sufficient for the development of foreign trade.

APPENDIX 7.III

With reference to Model 3 when asymmetry in production and/or export costs and/or in the size of the market is assumed we have:

$$
\begin{aligned}
R \equiv P_A^{a,b} - P_A^{xb,xa} - (P_B^{a,b} - P_B^{xa,xb}) = {} & 1/12\,[(C^b_{1B})^2 + \\
& - (C^a_{1A})^2] + 1/6\,(D^aC^a_{1A} - D^bC^b_{1B}) + 1/2\,(D^aC^a_{1B} - D^bC^b_{1A}) + \\
& + 2/3\,(D^be_A - D^ae_B) + 1/4\,[(C^b_{1A})^2 - (C^a_{1B})^2] + 1/3[(e_B)^2 + \\
& - (e_A)^2] + C^a_{OB} - C^b_{OA}
\end{aligned}
$$

where e_A and e_B are, respectively, export costs met by A established in a and B established in b.

In general $R = 0$ does not hold. This implies that the prices that A and B can offer are different.

By differentiating R with respect to the different variables we have:

$$\delta R/\delta C^a_{1A} = 1/6 \ (D^a - C^a_{1A}) \tag{7.III.1}$$

$$\delta R/\delta C^b_{1B} = 1/6 \ (C^b_{1B} - D^b) \tag{7.III.2}$$

$$\delta R/\delta C^b_{1A} = 1/2 \ D^b < 0 \tag{7.III.3}$$

$$\delta R/\delta C^a_{1B} = 1/2 \ D^a > 0 \tag{7.III.4}$$

$$\delta R/\delta e_A = 2/3 \ (D^b - e_A) \tag{7.III.5}$$

$$\delta R/\delta e_B = 2/3 \ (e_B - D^a) \tag{7.III.6}$$

$$\delta R/\delta D^a = 1/6 \ C^a_{1A} + 1/2 \ C^a_{1B} - 2/3 \ e_B \tag{7.III.7}$$

$$\delta R/\delta D^b = 2/3 \ e_A - 1/6 \ C^b_{1B} - 1/2 \ C^b_{1A} \tag{7.III.8}$$

The meaning of these derivatives can be stated in the following way:

The difference between the price that can be paid by A and the price that can be paid by B is:

(a) smaller the higher the costs A has to meet in b (this derives from (7.III.3) as to variable costs and, by inspection of the expression for R, as far as constant costs are concerned);

(b) greater the higher the costs B has to meet in a (see (7.III.4) and the expression for R);

(c) greater the higher the variable costs A has to meet in a, if the size of a is large enough (see (7.III.1));

(d) smaller the higher the variable costs of B in b, if the size of b is large enough (see (7.III.1));

(e) greater the higher the export costs met by A, if market b is large enough (see (7.III.5));

(f) smaller the higher the export costs met by B, if market a is large enough (see (7.III.6));

(g) smaller the larger market a is, if export costs met by B are higher than the average variable costs met by A in either markets (see (7.III.7));

(h)   greater the larger market b is, if export costs met by A are higher than the average variable costs met by A in both markets (see (7.III.8)).

REFERENCES

Acocella, N. (1988), 'I processi di concentrazione del capitale multinazionale', in N. Acocella *et al.* (eds), *Sindacato e processi di internazionalizzazione*, Rome: Ediesse.

Acocella, N. (1989), 'Efficienza e strategia nel processo di multinazionalizzazione: verso una teoria piu' generale', in N. Acocella and R. Schiattarella (eds), *Teorie dell'internazionalizzazione e realta' italiana*, Naples: Liguori.

Acocella, N. (1992), 'The Multinational Firm and the Theory of Industrial Organization', in A. Del Monte (ed.), *Recent Developments in the Theory of Industrial Organization*, London: Macmillan.

Buigues, P. and Jacquemin, A. (1989), 'Strategies of Firms and Structural Environments in the Large Internal Market', *Journal of Common Market Studies*, **28** (1), 52–67.

Cantwell, J.A. (1987), 'The Reorganization of European Industries after Integration: Selected Evidence on the Role of Multinational Enterprise Activities', *Journal of Common Market Studies*, **26** (2), 127–51.

Cantwell, J.A. (1991), 'The Effects of Integration on the Structure of MNC Activity in the EC', in T.I. Klein and P. Welfens (eds), *Multinationals in the new Europe and Global Trade in the 1990s*, Berlin: Springer Verlag.

Casson, M.C. (1987), *The Firm and the Market: Studies on Multinational Enterprise and the Scope of the Firm*, Oxford: Basil Blackwell.

CNEL (Consiglio Nazionale dell'Economia e del Lavoro) (1991), *Italia multinazionale, 1990*, Milan: Angeli.

Commission of the European Community, various years, *Report on Competition Policy*, Brussels: CEC.

Dunning, J.H. (1958), *American Investment in British Manufacturing Industry*, London: Allen & Unwin.

Dunning, J.H. and Cantwell, J.A. (1991) 'Japanese Direct Investment in Europe', in B. Burgenmeier and J.L. Mucchielli (eds), *Multinationals and Europe 1992*, London: Routledge.

Dunning, J.H. and Robson, P. (1987), 'Multinational Corporate Integration and Regional Economic Integration', *Journal of Common Market Studies*, **26** (2), 103–25.

Economists Advisory Group (1990), *European Economic Integration and TNC Activity, 1958–1988: The Record Assessed. A Study Prepared for the UNCTC*, mimeo.

Garella, P.G. (1989), *European Industry before 1992: Mergers and Acquisitions*, mimeo.

Geroski, P.A. and Vlassopoulos, A. (1990), 'European Merger Activity: a

Response to 1992', in Centre for Business Strategy, *Continental Mergers are Different*, London: London Business School.

Goldberg, M.A. (1972), 'The Determinants of US Direct Investment in the EEC: Comment', *American Economic Review*, **62**, 692–99.

Graham, E.M. (1978), 'Transatlantic Investment by Multinational Firms: a Rivalistic Phenomenon?', *Journal of Post Keynesian Economics*, **1** (1), 82–99.

Graham, E.M. (1990a), 'Exchange of Threat Between Multinational Firms as an Infinitely Repeated Non-cooperative Game', *International Trade Journal*, **4** (3), 259–77.

Graham, E.M. (1990b), 'Strategic Management and Transnational Firm Behavior: a Formal Approach', in C.N. Pitelis and R. Sugden (eds), *The Nature of the Transnational Corporation*, London: Routledge.

Horstmann, I.J. and Markusen, J.R. (1987), 'Strategic Investment and the Development of Multinationals', *International Economic Review*, **28**, 109–21.

Hymer, S. (1960), *The International Operations of National Firms: A Study of Foreign Direct Investment*, Ph.D. dissertation, MIT (published by MIT Press, 1976).

Itaki, M. and Waterson, M. (1990), 'European Multinationals and 1992', University of Reading, Dept. of Economics, D.P. in *International Investment and Business Studies*, Series B, **3**, (141).

Jacquemin, A. (1989), 'International and Multinational Strategic Behaviour', *Kyklos*, **42**, 495–513.

Kay, J.A. (1990a), 'Identifying the Strategic Market', *Business Strategy Review*, **1**, 1–24.

Kay, J.A. (1990b), 'Mergers in the European Community', in Centre for Business Strategy, *Continental Mergers are Different*, London: London Business School.

Kindleberger, C.P. (1973), *International Economics*, 5th edn, New York: Richard D. Irwin.

Knickerbocker, F.T. (1973), *Oligopolistic Reaction and the Multinational Enterprise*, Boston, Mass.: Harvard University Press.

Krugman, P.R. and Venables, A.J. (1990), *Integration and the Competitiveness of Peripherical Industry*, CEPR D.P. (363), January.

Lamfalussy, A. (1961), *Investment and Growth in Mature Economies: The Case of Belgium*, London: Macmillan.

Lewis, C. (1938), *America's Stake in International Investments*, Washington, D.C.: Brookings Institution.

Lunn, J. (1980), 'Determinants of US Direct Investment in the EEC: Further Evidence', *European Economic Review*, **13**, 93–101.

Molle, W. and Morsink, R. (1991), 'Intra-European Direct Investment', in B. Burgenmeier and J.L. Mucchielli (eds), *Multinationals and Europe 1992*, London: Routledge.

Penrose, E.T. (1956), 'Foreign Investment and the Firm', *Economic Journal*, **66**, 220–35.

Salant, S.W., Switzer, S. and Reynolds, R.J. (1983), 'Losses from Horizontal Merger: the Effects of an Exogenuos Change in Industry Structure on Cournot-Nash Equilibrium', *Quarterly Journal of Economics*, **98**, 185–99.

Scaperlanda, A. and Mauer, L.J. (1969), 'The Determinants of U.S. Direct Investment in the EEC, *American Economic Review*, vol. 59, pp. 558–68.

Scherer, F.M. (1980), *Industrial Market Structure and Economic Performance*, Chicago: Rand McNally.

Schiattarella, R. (1990), *Integrazione europea e strategie delle imprese multinazionali*, mimeo.

Smith, A. (1987), 'Strategic Investment, Multinational Corporations and Trade Policy', *European Economic Review*, 31, 89–96.

Tsoukalis, L. (1990), *European Integration and Economic Order*, paper presented at the Conference on 'Changing Economic Order', Antwerp, 12 October.

Yamin, M. (1991), 'A Reassessment of Hymer's Contribution to the Theory of the Transnational Corporation', in N. Pitelis and R. Sugden (eds), *The Nature of the Transnational Firm*, London: Routledge.

Yannopoulos, G.N. (1990), 'Foreign Direct Investment and European Integration: the Evidence from the Formative Years of the European Community', *Journal of Common Market Studies*, 28 (3), 235–59.

8. Cross-Direct Investment and Technological Capability of Spanish Domestic Firms

Juan José Durán Herrera*

8.1 FDI IN THE EUROPEAN SINGLE MARKET PERSPECTIVE

With the approval of the Rome Treaty in 1957, the building of the European Economic Community (EC) formally began. With the reduction of tariff barriers and the creation of a common external tariff, together with the expectations generated by the project itself, significant progress was made in the integration of the member states in the following years, and there was a noticeable increase in foreign trade and direct investment, both within the Community and by third countries. The inward investment from the USA was especially relevant, owing in part to the size of the EC market and its degree of protection (Franko, 1976; Scaperlanda and Balough, 1983). The significant presence and progressive increase of the USA's investment in the EC[1] became noticeable in the first phase (1958–73). Subsequently (1973–85), in addition to American investment, intra-European direct investment (DI) and Europe's DI in the United States became more significant, as did the generalized extension of the multinationalization of services. In this second phase, the presence of Japanese DI in the USA and in Europe is notable (UNCTC, 1988; Dunning and Cantwell, 1990). The increase in technological capacity and in corporate management which occurred in European companies, compared with American companies as a whole, explains the strong presence of European companies in the USA (Graham and Krugman, 1989). This, together with the policy of product differentiation, is the background to intra-industrial foreign direct investment (FDI) and cross-border transactions.

*The author wishes to thank John Cantwell for very helpful comments on an earlier draft of this chapter.

FDI allows the appropriation of income derived from the direct exploitation of the advantages resulting from company ownership, which combines with production factors of the country in which FDI is located (Dunning 1981, 1988). Additionally, the process of internationalization of production generates economies of scale, and FDI also permits the maximization of opportunities deriving from asymmetries of information, as well as allowing a more efficient reaction to the actions (both offensive and defensive) of oligopolistic rivals (Krugman, 1987). At the same time the deeper integration of the Triad, its high potential for economic growth and its role in the international arena, led to a restructuring of international production and corporate strategies. In part, the reorientation of economic activity has been undertaken through mergers and acquisitions and co-operative agreements.

The accumulation of technology and the convergence between countries (equivalent-risk hypothesis) underlies the flow of FDI between geographic areas. The technological capacity of domestic industries determines the impact of FDI, and the degree of technological convergence between countries creates opportunities for co-operation and for international competition (Cantwell, 1990).

Moreover, countries with a pronounced technology lag may fall into a vicious circle where their initial position will be further undermined and they may find themselves expelled from world markets (Cantwell, 1987). However, this possibility, which may be a certainty for the more-protected and less-competitive sectors, may be avoided and a virtuous circle initiated for those companies and sectors possessing a critical mass of accumulated knowledge, within an environment producing an efficient articulation between government policy and company strategy. Thus the analysis of the innovative capacity and competitiveness of a country's economy ought to follow a systems approach.

The approval of the Single Act in 1987 and the subsequent boost given to the creation of a true European single market starting in 1993 was a major consideration in the reformulation of company expectations and strategies. The reordering of economic space and the adaptation of institutions and legal systems went hand in hand with certain strategic actions, both defensive and offensive, undertaken by European and third-country companies. The positive effects to be gained from European integration into a single market were perceived to be real (Cecchini, 1988; Baldwin, 1989). The exchange rate is a factor which may influence FDI to a certain extent (Aliber, 1971), since the value of exposed assets and liabilities, as well as cash-flow amounts, will be conditioned by variations in the exchange rate. The degree of exposure to exchange risk, together with coverage and hedge policies, will determine the effect of exchange rates on FDI. The evaluation of the net effect of these factors on the flow of FDI is not simple (Caves, 1988). In the case of the intra-Community flow, the exchange risk will be reduced as the degree of efficiency of the European Monetary System increases and European financial integration and monetary unity is achieved. In any case, the election of an invoicing and conversion currency (the Ecu, for example) and coverage techniques (leads and lags and financial markets) will minimize the effect of the exchange rates on intra-European FDI.

Thus the absence of tariff and other barriers will automatically cause the disappearance of certain market segmentation criteria, which may result in a reduction in costs due to the creation of economies of scale (Yannopoulos, 1990). In addition, with the disappearance of all barriers to integration and the prioritizing of the market mechanism, FDI will only be adopted according to efficient criteria and its location will be based on comparative 'natural' advantages.

However, in the run-up to 1993, governments have been drawing up economic policies designed to facilitate the competitiveness of companies resident in their country. For this purpose they have created incentives (cash-grants, tax subsidies and so on) in order to attract FDI and in some cases (Spain, for example) to facilitate the multinationalization of domestic firms.

Empirical evidence and the trends we have been seeing guarantee that at the beginning of 1993 the EC will find itself with very high and irreversible levels of integration. Thus the disappearance of tariff, technical and administrative barriers, the harmonization of legal systems and the convergence achieved in systems of production, distribution and purchase processes, together with technological advances, will lead to savings in transaction costs. These costs will be of two types: internal (production costs and operating–co-ordinating costs of hierarchies in organizations) and external or market transaction costs. As the intra-Community barriers disappear, sales points become physically nearer, which in cost terms will encourage trade exchanges; that is to say, there will be a progressive increase in exports. Thus we expect that the absolute cost advantages anticipated (provision and productivity of factors and differentiation and technological capacity) will be taken into account in decisions concerning the redimensioning and relocation of activities.

Corporate restructuring in the EC will show different tendencies for horizontal MNCs, which are market-orientated, and vertical MNCs, whose international diversification depends to a great extent on production. In both cases, transport and communication costs will become a relevant factor in the location of activities. Horizontal MNCs, which carry out similar activities in various countries, may find that with the savings in production costs due to economies of scale, localized economies and external factors of the integration of the single market, there is a tendency to concentrate production. In fact the localization could be satisfied by solving a mathematical programming model with a cost-minimizing function and capacity constraints, where the spatial variables are the localization of plants, warehouses and trade centres. Economic logic leads to the conclusion that location will probably be in those areas which offer greatest absolute advantages in production and distribution costs. In this context, some authors (Itaki and Waterson, 1990) indicate that production plants will be eliminated so as to reduce fixed costs, and export volumes, which depend more on variable costs, will be increased. A tendency towards centralized production will be compatible with decentralized business strategies.

The location of the activities of vertical MNCs will depend on their production function. Thus those production functions which may be broken down into phases with different optimal dimensions may be located in geographically distant places. The productivity of production factors and transport costs will therefore be the considerations which govern the location of activities. Thus, depending on the phase of the production function and its positioning in the value chain, the factor supply centres or the assembly and sales points will take precedence in the choice of most suitable location for the corresponding phase. In this respect, given the increase which will occur in factor mobility, the principle of absolute advantage will predominate over the principle of comparative advantage. Consequently, if technology is the relevant factor, the best locations will be those offering greater externals and productivities.

The co-ordination of activities in sectors whose competitive nuclei of activity in the value chain are internationally integrated will be done by MNCs. As a result, those countries which do not have strategic decision-making centres located in their territory, that is to say, those which do not have their own MNCs, will see that part of their economy which is directly related to global sectors assimilated into the domain of the MNCs. Because of this, the investment–disinvestment process within the scope of the European single market will depend on the competitiveness of the auxiliary or complementary industry of the country in which the absolute advantages become relevant in this context.

A country with a comparatively low technological capacity will have

Figure 8.1   International trade and production matrix

Comparative (locational) advantages/technological capacity
(Country of origin)

		High	Low
	High	– Local production – Export – Outward investment	– Outward investment – Local industrial diversification
Competitive advantages of domestic firms	Low	– Inward investment – Export platform	– Imports – Trade subsidiaries

scant possibilities of reducing the gap separating it from the technologically more advanced EC countries. This is not only because of its existing technological capacity but due to the fact that R&D priorities are established exogenously, and therefore part of the R&D resources will be dedicated to those priorities. In addition, if the large MNCs in global sectors and with a high technological content are located outside the country, only the creation of an efficient critical mass which can effectively compete in the international network of high-technology global sectors, and particularly in the area of the triangle of the developed world (Triad), will prevent a fall into the vicious technology circle.

The evolution of the Spanish balance of payments corresponds to the trends suggested above. The degree of integration has been increasing continuously and significantly since 1986, in terms of both trade and direct investment flows. According to a systems approach, the international competitiveness (or locational attractiveness) of a country is a function of the technological capacity accumulated and the interface between government policies, the strategies of MNCs (and the role played by its affiliates in the corresponding country) and the multi-nationalization of domestic corporations as well as stated-owned companies. In an open economy with efficient government policies international production and trade will follow the pattern shown in Figure 8.1.

The interaction between the country's technological capacity and locational factors with the competitive advantages of domestic firms will determine the flows of direct investment and international trade as well as the strategies of firms. Governments have been increasingly required to be effective in their policies designed to facilitate the competitiveness of domestic firms. A country with inward and outward DI has to adopt a holistic approach in its policy, since both flows are interrelated.[2]

Lastly, we must point out the increased importance of cross-licenses, joint ventures and strategic alliances as mechanisms for minimizing transaction costs. Probably several intra-community strategic alliances will end up as mergers and acquisitions in the future. Meanwhile, they constitute a reversible decision, which gives flexibility to the process of creation of the European single market.

8.2   INDUSTRIAL AND GEOGRAPHICAL DISTRIBUTION OF FDI FLOWS IN SPAIN

Spain has been a net importer of direct investment (DI) without interruption since its economic opening-up to the outside based on the 1959 Stabilization Plan, up to the present moment. Its role in the balance of payments and in the Spanish economy as a whole has been a considerable and determining factor in production specialization and in international trade. With the steady improvement of Spain's country risk profile and the successful completion of its political transition, the presence of foreign direct investment has been noticeably reinforced. It has constituted the most solid foundations for the international integration of Spain's economy during the entire period (1960–91). Over these three decades, foreign direct investment in Spain has increased progressively. Until the beginning of the 1970s, outward investment was of little significance by comparison with inward investment. Since then, it has been around 5 or 6 times lower than inward investment, a proportion which, with a slight decrease, has remained up to the present time. However, from a quantitative point of view, outward investment has been significant since 1977. In both cases, the disinvestment effected was relatively low. If we calculate the indicator used by Mucchielli (1985), which consists of dividing the difference between DI inflow and outflow by the sum of both flows, we obtain values of −0.63 and −0.64 for the entire period 1981–5 and 1986–90. Values less than −0.33 mean that a country is a receiver of DI; Spain is an example of this type of country. If we calculate the ratio only between Spain and the EC, then we notice a small improvement in the Spanish position; since from a figure of −0.78 for the period 1981–5 we obtain a ratio of −0.65 for the 1986–90 period, which implies an increase in integration with the EC.[3]

Table 8.1 *Industrial and geographical distribution of majority owned foreign direct investment in Spain, 1981–90 (percentages and thousands of millions pesetas)*

	Primary sector		Manufacturing		Construction		Trade services	
	1981–5	1986–90	1981–5	1986–90	1981–5	1986–90	1981–5	1986–90
EEC								
France	1.0	27.3	7.9	11.6	0.9	32.8	5.3	10.9
Bel-Lux.	0.6	4.5	1.6	3.3	17.5	1.7	1.1	3.1
Netherlands	0.5	14.3	8.5	10.3	4.9	16.6	8.3	15.2
Germany	4.9	2.1	13.5	12.8	1.3	5.6	7.7	9.6
Italy	0.1	0.8	2.2	3.4	0.5	0.8	1.1	1.2
United Kingdom	1.8	8.1	4.9	4.4	10.3	7.5	9.3	9.2
Ireland	-	-	0.7	0.0	-	0.3	0.4	0.2
Denmark	0.1	0.2	1.1	0.3	-	0.2	0.3	1.8
Greece	-	-	-	-	-	-	-	0.0
Portugal	-	0.2	0.0	0.1	-	-	0.1	1.0
Subtotal	9.0	57.5	40.4	46.2	35.4	65.5	33.6	52.1
Spain*	2.2	25.0	15.2	32.0	0.3	9.2	16.2	20.4
Switzerland	2.8	5.8	6.7	5.8	2.9	5.1	14.2	6.0
USA	3.2	1.5	23.3	4.3	19.9	4.0	12.3	8.2
Japan	-	0.3	9.0	4.4	-	-	1.2	1.7
Latin America	0.4	1.6	0.1	0.2	6.2	1.6	10.0	0.7
Tax havens	77.2	3.0	2.2	1.8	8.2	8.0	2.6	2.5
East Europe and USSR	-	0.0	-	-	-	-	0.0	0.0
Others	5.2	5.3	3.1	5.3	27.1	6.6	9.9	8.3
Total	100	100	100	100	100	100	100	100
Total (Ptas)	48.71	187.71	592.41	2,107.16	10.76	58.31	146.05	656.51

*Most of this investment is made by MNCs from the USA, established in Spain in previous years.
Source: Prepared with data from Dirección General de Transacciones Exteriores (Ministry of Economy and Finance).

Transportation & communication		Finance, insurance and business services		Other services		Total (Th. m. Ptas)				
1981–5	1986–90	1981–5	1986–90	1981–5	1986–90	1981–5[1]	%	1986–90[2]	%	(2):(1)
6.2	7.9	12.9	19.3	6.3	14.8	88.8	9.1	807.7	15.3	9.1
0.8	5.1	1.0	2.3	3.4	3.2	24.2	2.5	155.6	2.9	6.4
-	15.3	3.8	25.7	5.1	7.3	67.9	7.0	916.0	17.5	13.6
1.8	5.8	3.1	2.7	17.9	4.5	102.5	10.6	404.2	7.6	3.9
0.3	2.4	1.0	1.6	8.5	8.9	16.9	1.7	123.7	2.3	7.3
4.4	15.9	13.1	13.4	22.7	12.4	77.4	8.0	484.5	9.2	6.3
-	0.2	0.0	0.0	0.3	0.4	3.1	0.3	3.4	0.0	1.1
12.1	0.6	0.2	0.2	0.4	0.4	5.2	0.5	23.9	0.4	4.6
-	-	-	0.0	-	-	0.1	0.0	0.1	0.0	1.0
-	-	-	0.7	0.1	3.1	0.5	0.1	27.3	0.5	54.6
22.6	53.3	35.2	65.9	64.7	55.0	386.7	39.8	2,946.4	55.7	7.6
55.0	23.5	7.8	11.3	4.8	21.4	120.4	12.4	1,135.2	21.5	9.4
3.0	4.5	11.0	5.9	5.4	6.0	106.2	10.9	309.9	5.9	2.9
3.5	0.5	9.7	2.3	8.8	3.3	167.7	17.3	201.8	3.8	1.2
-	0.2	0.0	3.3	-	6.8	38.2	3.9	182.0	3.4	4.8
8.3	0.9	4.1	1.2	0.7	1.3	18.7	1.9	41.0	0.8	2.2
0.3	12.0	5.6	3.4	8.8	5.8	44.5	4.7	150.0	2.8	3.4
1.5	0.2	-	-	-	0.0	0.1	0.0	0.3	0.0	3.0
6.0	4.9	26.5	6.7	6.8	0.4	88.3	9.1	323.1	6.1	3.7
100	100	100	100	100	100		100		100	
10.88	65.82	152.56	2,140.51	9.66	73.64	970.8		5,289.7		5.9

Table 8.2 *Sectoral and geographical distribution of majority-owned Spanish direct investment abroad (percentages and thousands of millions pesetas)*

	Primary sector		Manufacturing		Construction		Trade services	
	1981–5	1986–90	1981–5	1986–90	1981–5	1986–90	1981–5	1986–90
EEC								
France	1.0	11.5	5.9	5.6	-	2.2	12.2	12.3
Bel-Lux.	-	-	0.0	6.7	-	-	1.1	1.7
Netherlands	0.6	0.1	0.0	0.0	-	-	1.5	0.7
Germany	0.3	0.1	0.9	14.4	-	-	7.4	5.3
Italy	-	0.6	0.6	9.7	-	-	1.1	4.3
United Kingdom	2.5	15.6	5.7	3.0	-	-	7.1	8.0
Ireland	1.0	-	0.7	-	-	-	0.3	0.9
Denmark	-	-	0.3	0.5	-	-	0.7	0.0
Greece	-	-	-	0.0	-	-	-	0.4
Portugal	4.9	2.7	15.4	21.0	2.4	54.1	3.8	14.5
Subtotal	10.3	30.6	29.5	60.9	2.4	56.3	35.2	48.1
Switzerland	-	-	0.9	1.7	1.4	0.6	4.6	2.0
USA	31.0	31.1	7.2	8.3	16.2	2.6	28.8	10.0
Japan	0.3	-	-	0.2	-	-	1.1	0.0
Latin America	23.3	7.9	41.2	15.1	45.4	21.1	12.7	14.9
Tax Havens	10.0	2.0	10.5	2.7	16.1	6.1	10.8	7.4
East Europe and USSR	-	-	-	2.8	-	-	-	0.6
Others	25.1	28.3	9.7	8.3	18.6	13.3	6.7	16.9
Total	100	100	100	100	100	100	100	100
Total (Ptas)	15.21	103.41	44.02	198.59	7.65	8.94	31.06	103.10

Source: Prepared with the data from Dirección General de Transacciones Exteriores (Ministry of Economy and Finance).

Transportation & communication		Finance, insurance and business services		Other services		Total (Th. m. Ptas)				
1981–5	1986–90	1981–5	1986–90	1981–5	1986–90	1981–5[1]	%	1986–90[2]	%	(2):(1)
3.9	21.7	1.2	4.3	-	9.8	8.05	3.6	71.20	6.1	8.8
2.6	3.3	4.6	9.6	0.9	17.8	6.04	2.7	85.02	7.4	14.1
1.3	0.6	0.9	13.8	-	0.8	1.72	0.8	100.79	8.7	58.6
0.7	0.6	1.6	3.1	-	1.0	4.72	2.1	57.26	4.9	12.1
0.3	8.6	1.9	1.5	19.0	1.9	3.09	1.4	36.91	3.2	11.9
45.7	4.1	3.5	15.3	-	1.0	10.48	4.7	141.85	12.2	13.5
-	-	-	0.0	2.9	-	0.62	0.3	1.30	0.1	2.7
-	0.0	-	0.0	-	-	0.37	0.2	1.04	0.1	2.7
-	-	-	0.1	-	-	0.10	0.0	1.15	0.1	11.5
1.0	4.6	2.8	8.4	1.8	17.4	12.69	5.7	126.78	10.9	10.0
55.6	43.4	16.6	56.2	24.7	49.7	47.76	21.4	623.30	53.8	13.1
0.3	0.6	4.2	6.4	-	-	6.98	3.1	51.51	4.4	7.4
1.6	5.4	14.6	6.7	10.5	10.2	35.90	16.0	109.88	9.5	3.1
-	-	0.1	0.6	-	-	0.48	0.2	4.82	0.4	10.0
9.2	1.9	29.0	7.2	48.6	17.6	64.90	29.1	108.44	9.4	1.7
4.6	36.3	19.3	17.1	-	0.7	34.16	15.8	145.13	12.5	4.2
-	0.0	-	0.0	-	7.7	0.50	0.2	6.92	0.6	13.8
28.6	12.4	16.2	5.8	16.2	4.2	32.12	14.1	108.37	9.4	3.3
100	100	100	100	100	100		100		100	
3.04	16.57	120.77	721.04	1.05	6.72	222.80		1,158.37		5.2

223

Until the beginning of the 1980s, three-quarters of foreign direct investment in Spain was in the manufacturing sector and about 15 per cent was in trade. The EEC's FDI amounted to 37 per cent in the period 1960–80, 40 per cent in the period 1981–5, and 50 per cent in the period 1986–90.

These figures would increase if the figures on investment by subsidiaries already resident were calculated, although most of this investment is made by American subsidiaries. These are shown in Table 8.1 in the row corresponding to Spain. This trend towards greater penetration of direct investment by the EEC can be seen in all sectors of activity, especially in primary production, construction, transport and communication, and financial services and trade. The lower relative importance of the United States and the greater Japanese presence is also worth mentioning.

Similarly, Spanish outward investment in the first phase (1960–76) was aimed mainly towards Europe (around 50 per cent) with the creation of trade and financial subsidiaries. In this period, Latin America received approximately one-third of the total, placed in manufacturing and financial sectors. Until the beginning of the 1980s, the geographical and industrial destination was mainly Latin America (almost 70 per cent), with European participation reduced to 20 per cent. Among other reasons, we should point out the international and domestic economic crisis which, together with the Spanish political transition, had as a means of partial solution the redirecting of outward investment towards Latin America, where Spanish technology was positively valuable.

Tables 8.1 and 8.2 show foreign investment in Spain and direct Spanish investment abroad throughout the 1980s (1981–90), divided in two sub-periods. In the first place, we can see the important growth occurring in investment flows in both directions, which demonstrates the greater international economic integration of the Spanish economy. However, the interpenetration with the European Community countries is much greater than that occurring with the rest of the world. Proportionally, investment by Spanish companies in the Community is greater than that received, which represents a certain reduction in the gap which exceeds both flows and shows a certain 'scope' effect in favour of the internationalization of Spanish companies.

Direct investment received from EC countries has increased (more than five times overall) in all countries except Greece and Ireland and very insignificantly in Portugal. Among the main countries of origin are France, the Netherlands, United Kingdom, Germany and Italy within the Community, and Switzerland and the United States outside the EC. However, the relative decline of the United States as an investing country in comparison with other countries should be pointed out, although in terms of accumulated FDI stocks it is still the main investor in Spain. A notable increase by Japan and the 'tax havens' countries, as investors over the period 1986–90, has also been evident. FDI from Latin America is still relatively low, while FDI from other non-Community countries has increased.

Among the fundamental characteristics of outward investment abroad which can be seen in the information in Table 8.1, the following are of interest: in the first place, it is clear that in FDI orientated to the EC, Portugal has always been the primary country of destination for investment. The investments destined for France, United Kingdom, the Netherlands and Benelux are also significant, particularly in the second half of the decade, followed by Italy and Germany, while FDIs located in Denmark, Greece and Ireland are small. The increase of Spanish outward investment towards the Community is notable on an overall level: 45 per cent in 1986–90 in comparison with 21 per cent in 1981–5.

Regarding non-Community countries, we must stress the importance of Spanish investment in the United States, and the level that Puerto Rico has reached on the whole (around 12 per cent of the total in both periods) as an investment-receiver country, as well as the increase in the role of tax havens in the internationalization of Spanish companies. On the other hand, outward investment to Japan is insignificant and, compared to the preceding decade, outward investment destined for Latin America is low (Duran and Sanchez, 1981). In the period 1975–80, 53 per cent of Spanish outward investment was destined for Latin America, while in 1981–5 this figure was 29 per cent, and fell to 9 per cent in 1986–90.

From the Community point of view and comparing both flows, it is evident that Spain is a net capital exporter to Portugal and a net importer from the Netherlands, France, Germany, United Kingdom and, to a lesser degree, from Italy and Benelux. Relations with Greece and Ireland are irrelevant and balanced, and are somewhat greater although quantitatively low with Denmark. In general, a 'natural' extension towards greater integration with Portugal, France, Italy and the United Kingdom can be observed. The complementary nature of their economies, cultural aspects and geographic proximity facilitate the expansion of companies between these countries. In addition, the greater presence of Spanish companies in Belgium and Luxembourg is to a certain extent associated with the creation of economies of agglomeration.

By sectors, and in addition to the information contained in Tables 8.1 and 8.2, the following may be stressed. DI has been distributed more symmetrically among the major sectors, with an emphasis on finance and services due to a twofold phenomenon: the deregulation of the Spanish economy and the dynamics of the internationalization of services worldwide. From the point of view of Spanish outward investment, we must point out the uninterrupted continuity of the financial sector as the main investor, as well as the increase in the manufacturing and trade and distribution sectors. On the whole, greater integration and consistency in the internationalization of Spanish companies is evident. The importance of instrumental companies and tax havens in the internationalizing process is also worth noting.

During the period 1986–90 the merger and acquisition wave in Spain has been very relevant, both in domestic terms and in a cross-border context. As could be expected, the Spanish cross-border sales significantly exceeded the purchase side by more than three-fold in monetary terms and by more than six times in terms of the number of deals (see Table 8.3). There are also some geographical and sectoral differences between the pattern of growth of inward and outward DI. The countries of origin follow the general tendency: principally the EC and USA, and Kuwait, through the Kuwait Investment Office (KIO). The other countries of origin are concentrated in Latin America. From the target industry point of view the main acquisitions of Spanish firms have taken place in the food, wholesale distribution and construction sectors. Spanish acquisitions abroad have also followed the general path of outward DI: banking, finance and insurance as well as the food and chemicals industries being of special interest, together with purchases in the utilities sector. Although the greater part of Spanish international economic activity is internalized within global MNCs there is also some evidence of an offensive–defensive strategy on the part of Spanish firms acquiring foreign firms in the same sectors in which foreign firms have been most active in their acquisitions in Spain. This evidence is also observed in the case of green-field manufacturing investment. The finance sector is the main exception, mainly due to the fact that it was legally protected from inward investment until 1978 and also due to its primary role in the industrialization of the economy through its equity and credit involvement in non-financial firms.

Table 8.3 Spanish international mergers and acquisitions, 1987–90

A. Spanish sales by bidder

	$ million		Number of deals
UK	3,119	UK	105
France	1,827	France	93
Italy	677	Italy	27
Germany	518	Germany	26
Kuwait	216	Netherlands	23
Other	1,203	Other	92
Total	7,560	Total	366

B. Spanish sales by target industry

	$ million		Number of deals
Food, drink & tobacco	1,532	Food, drink & tobacco	36
Chemicals & pharmaceuticals	989	Chemicals & pharmaceuticals	33
Construction & building products	978	Wholesale distribution	32
Insurance	756	Construction & building products	32
Banking	743	Engineered products	25
Other	2,562	Other	208
Total	7,560	Total	366

C. Spanish purchase by source country

	$ million		Number of deals
Argentina	1,415	France	16
Chile	391	Portugal	8

Table 8.3 Continued

Germany	164	Belgium	6
USA	127	Germany	6
Portugal	100	Italy	5
Other	256	Other	16
Total	2,453	Total	57

D. Spanish purchases by target industry

	$ million		Number of deals
Utilities	1,806	Banking & finance	11
Banking & finance	264	Food, drink & tobacco	7
Rubber & plastics products	160	Utilities	5
Oil & gas	82	Chemicals & pharmaceuticals	4
Construction & building products	38	Insurance	4
Other	103	Other	26
Total	2,453	Total	57

Source: KPMG (1990), *Deal Watch*, *International Mergers and Acquisitions*, March.

8.3 DIRECT INVESTMENT AND TRADE

In the case of the Spanish economy, the empirical evidence also confirms the existence of a complementary relation between direct investment flows and foreign trade. In this respect, we may indicate the existence of a certain parallelism between the pronounced deterioration in the Spanish balance of trade since 1986 in general, and particularly with the EC (see Table 8.4) and the strong increase in FDI.[4] However we must point out that the decline of the foreign goods trade, particularly in manufactured goods, has been due not only to integration in the EC but to the considerable economic recuperation of the Spanish economy, which has produced a sharp increase in internal demand simultaneously with the appreciation of the peseta.

Table 8.4   Spanish trade with the EC

	1981	1983	1985	1986	1987	1988	1989	1990
Exports to the EC (percentage of total)	46.0	49.9	52.1	60.2	63.7	65.6	66.8	69.3
Rate of growth of exports	11.3	31.0	12.4	7.4	16.7	14.0	14.9	11.4
Imports from the EC (percentage of total)	29.1	32.9	36.6	50.5	54.5	56.8	57.1	59.5
Rate of growth of imports	12.8	24.3	18.1	33.8	31.9	20.3	21.6	9.8
Trade balance with the EC (bn pts)		2.8	47.6	269.0	−205.7	−619.3	−913.3	−1.318.6	−1.390.3

Source: D.G. de Aduanas y Gabinete del Sector Exterior (Ministry of Economy and Finance).

Overall, there is enough empirical evidence to suggest that during the period 1960–75 MNC subsidiaries exported on average less than Spanish companies, while since the mid–1960s MNC subsidiaries have shown a greater tendency to export.[5] However, in both periods a greater tendency to import can be seen in foreign-owned companies. In the first period the location factor which appeared most important was an internal market in a state of rapid growth and expansion. Indeed, the buoyancy of the local market has helped to attract inward FDI throughout the whole period (1960–90). Given their focus on serving local markets, the Spanish affiliates of foreign firms have imported more than they exported. Although in more recent years some newer affiliates have had a wider regional role in the early stages of development, they have been dependent upon imports and often need more time to build up their export achievement. Meanwhile, some of the older affiliates have used the liberalization of the Spanish economy as an opportunity to import more. Spanish multinational companies have always maintained a stronger export stance and a more favourable trade balance than foreign-owned companies (Duran and Sanchez, 1981; Duran, 1987 and 1990). This conclusion is confirmed by an inspection of the list of the top hundred Spanish exporters and importers. MNC subsidiaries are well-represented among both the top exporters and importers. In this context we should specify that most of these subsidiaries are in global or internationally integrated sectors, such as transport vehicles, electronics, pharmaceuticals, oil and chemicals. As a consequence it is reasonable, just as the theory predicts, to expect this type of intra-company trade.

The top hundred export and import companies, of which more than half are MNC subsidiaries, account for a large proportion of foreign trade, although the degree of concentration has fallen in recent years. Thus in 1984 they accounted for about 48 per cent of exports and 60 per cent of imports, while in 1986 these figures were about 43 per cent and 45 per cent respectively. In 1988 40 per cent of international trade was done by the top hundred exporters and importers and they accounted for 38.5 per cent of the trade deficit. In 1990 the top hundred exporters and importers accounted for about 58 per cent of exports and 62 per cent of imports.

In Table 8.5 we show the companies which are members of both the top hundred exporters and the top hundred importers. There were 30 companies in 1986, of which 13 were in deficit, and 39 companies in 1990, of which 27 were in deficit. The rate of growth of total exports and imports by the largest companies between 1986 and 1990 was about 49 per cent and 82 per cent more respectively. Also in this table we have calculated the international trade integrated ratio (ITIR), measured by the sum of exports and imports divided by domestic sales. This ratio has to be positive in all cases and the greater the ratio the more internationally integrated the company is. Also, it is expected that international integration rises where the trade of the firm grows faster than its domestic sales. In general, the degree of international integration of companies has increased and so has the proportion of companies that during the period showed a ratio greater than one. This trend is a consequence of integration in the sectors they belong to: motor vehicles, oil, steel and chemicals.

Furthermore, in a study by Iranzo (1990) referring to 1989 information in which a sample of 1,000 companies is examined, it is shown that almost a quarter of the Spanish trade deficit was due to the balance of payments of Spanish subsidiaries of foreign MNCs. It was also estimated that MNC subsidiaries contributed around 12 per cent of Spanish GDP, and that almost half of the value of their production was due to exports.

Table 8.6 shows the percentage of exports over sales in certain industrial sectors for three years. In the first place we can see that those sectors with export rates of 30 per cent or more (non-ferrous metals, non-metal minerals, rubber and plastics, leather and footwear, and other manufacturing industries) belong to the segments with the

*Table 8.5A   The largest companies in Spanish international trade, 1986
(thousands of million pesetas)*

Company	X	M	X−M	ITIR
Ford España	132.2	96.8	35.4	2.000001
General Motors	128.3	111.3	17.0	2.686098
SEAT (VW)	99.5	49.7	49.8	0.997326
Empetrol	76.4	367.6	−291.2	1.296728
FASA Renault	75.0	58.8	16.2	0.614325
IBM	69.6	57.7	11.9	1.152036
Petronor	68.9	100.5	−31.6	1.483362
ENSIDESA	54.7	33.8	20.9	0.783185
Citroën	52.0	27.4	24.6	1.017948
CEPSA	44.4	190.4	−146	0.997451
Michelin	39.0	23.3	15.7	1.068610
UERT	34.4	74.0	−39.6	0.712220
Altos Hornos de Vizcaya	27.3	18.6	8.7	0.729729
Cía Acero Inox.	25.2	26.5	−1.3	3.114457
Fab. Esp. Magnetos	25.1	15.6	9.5	1.808888
Talbot	21.9	17.5	4.4	0.461899
Río Tinto Min.	21.1	15.8	5.3	2.396103
Firestone	18.3	8.6	9.7	0.781976
CASA (Constr. Aeronáuticas)	17.5	9.3	8.2	1.102880
Dow Chemical	17.3	27.6	−10.3	1.066508
Petromed	14.5	48.6	−34.1	1.080479
Motor Ibérica (Nissan)	13.5	12.7	0.8	0.396369
ENASA (E.N. Autocamiones)	8.1	6.5	1.6	0.218236
Siderúrgica Med.	7.8	12.1	−4.3	0.904545
Aristrain	7.6	7.4	0.2	1.339285
Com. Ind. Abastec.	6.0	43.4	−37.4	0.721167
Oleaginosas Espa.	4.7	16.5	−11.8	1.472222
Rank Xerox	4.7	8.3	−3.6	0.643564
Hispano Olivetti	4.6	12	−7.4	0.661354
Cía. Continental	3.9	19.1	−15.2	0.603674
All above firms % of total	30	40		
The 100 largest % total	43	45		

ITIR = International Trade Integration Ratio = X+M/domestic sales

Source: Elaborated upon the data drawn from the Secretaría de Estado de Comercio and Fomento de la Producción.

*Table 8.5B   The largest companies in Spanish international trade, 1990
(thousands of million pesetas)*

Company	X	M	X−M	ITIR
SEAT (VW)	214	172.4	41.6	1.620125
General Motors	201	111.3	89.7	1.903107
Ford España	196.2	90.9	105.3	1.701837
FASA Renault	170.8	170.5	0.3	1.317252
Repsol	103.7	380.5	−276.8	1.036165
Citroën Hispania	96.4	84.3	12.1	1.305635
CEPSA	72.9	209.8	−136.9	1.151527
Petronor	63.6	136.4	−72.8	1.503759
Michelin	62.7	50.3	12.4	1.443167
Peugeot-Talbot	50.3	64	−13.7	0.800420
ENSIDESA	50.1	37.6	12.5	0.645802
CASA (Constr. Aeronaut. SA)	49.6	29.8	19.8	1.623721
IBM	47.7	92.5	−44.8	0.819403
Nissan-Motor Ibérica	37.6	37.9	−0.3	0.593553
Fab. Esp. Magnetos	36.4	24.5	11.9	n.a.
Cía Acero Inox.	34.3	30.9	3.4	2.151815
Air España	31.2	42.9	−11.7	10.1506
Dow Chemical	27	50.6	−23.6	1.295492
Mercedes Benz	25	47.4	−22.4	0.923469
Altos Hornos de Vizcaya	20.3	18	2.3	0.500653
Río Tinto Minera	15.4	13.9	1.5	0.839541
Ertoil	14	39.3	−25.3	n.a.
Iberia	12	112.6	−100.6	0.342684
Petromed	11.4	63.4	−52	1.052039
Alcatel	10.7	23.2	−12.5	−0.261574
Sarrió	9.8	10.3	−0.5	0.424947
ENASA (IVECO)	8.7	9.6	−0.9	0.315517
John Deere	8.7	11.3	−2.6	0.869565
Cía Ind. Abast.	8.1	31.6	−23.5	n.a.
Hewlett Packard	7.8	17.7	−9.9	0.951492
Nestlé	7.1	12.2	−5.1	0.193193
Thomson	7	12.5	−5.5	n.a.
Bayer	7	11.2	−4.2	0.159789
Sony	6.4	38.6	−32.2	0.696594
Basf	6.3	32.7	−26.4	0.775347
Roca	6.3	13.8	−7.5	0.323671
Fujitsu	6.2	13	−6.8	0.700729
Cristalería Esp.	5.8	10.3	−4.5	0.351528
National Panasonic	5.6	14.8	−9.2	0.718309
All above firms. % of total	31	27		
The 100 largest. of total	58	62		

ITIR = International Trade Integration Ratio = X+M/domestic sales
Source: As for Table 8.5A.

Table 8.8 Competitiveness of industrial exports

Sectors	1984			1988			1990			Volume of FDI**
	% of industrial exports	Coverage ratio (%)	CRA*	% of industrial exports	Coverage ratio (%)	CRA*	% of industrial exports	Coverage ratio (%)	CRA*	
1. **Strong demand**	*16.6*	*50.0*	*−26.6*	*21.9*	*41.8*	*−41.1*	*21.5*	*40.5*	*−42.3*	
Aircraft	0.9	105.5	6.7	1.8	68.4	−18.8	2.1	49.8	−33.5	M
Office & data-proc. machinery	2.1	18.2	−46.1	2.4	29.1	−54.9	2.1	28.0	−56.2	L
Electrical equipment	3.3	85.1	−3.3	4.0	62.9	−22.8	4.5	57.8	−26.7	H
Electronic equipment	0.5	16.5	−66.9	1.2	13.6	−76.1	1.7	19.3	−67.5	H
Precision instruments	0.4	19.0	−74.0	0.8	15.4	−73.3	0.9	17.0	−71.0	L
Pharmaceuticals	1.0	80.3	−8.8	1.6	82.5	−9.6	1.3	63.9	−22.1	H
Chemicals	8.4	64.4	−16.4	10.1	52.5	−28.7	8.9	50.6	−32.7	
2. **Moderate demand**	*43.4*	*125.4*	*24.2*	*47.9*	*84.3*	*−8.5*	*50.0*	*88.9*	*−5.9*	
Rubber and plastics	2.3	304.0	56.1	3.0	186.7	30.2	2.7	129.0	13.0	M
Motor Vehicles	13.3	243.6	43.9	19.5	105.2	2.5	22.0	124.9	11.0	H
Mechanical equipment	6.0	60.1	−20.4	7.8	36.5	−46.5	8.8	42.2	−40.6	M
Railway equipment	0.1	38.2	26.8	0.1	29.4	−54.5	0.1	60.0	−25.0	M
Food products	8.6	138.7	44.4	8.2	123.0	10.3	7.4	110.4	49.4	H
Oil refining	9.7	111.4	26.4	5.3	146.8	18.9	5.7	158.7	22.7	M
Paper	3.4	149.6	14.9	4.0	83.0	−9.3	3.3	62.1	−23.4	H
3. **Weak demand**	*40.0*	*289.5*	*48.9*	*30.2*	*106.5*	*−3.1*	*28.5*	*82.3*	*−9.7*	
Steel industry	9.6	321.3	58.5	3.9	85.6	−7.8	3.6	82.4	−9.6	L
Non-ferrous metals	3.7	173.3	21.5	2.4	76.9	−13.0	1.8	59.5	−25.3	L
Shipbuilding	2.9	354.2	88.4	1.1	117.0	7.8	1.7	358.8	56.4	L
Metallic products	4.6	389.2	35.1	4.9	109.1	4.3	5.0	62.8	−22.9	M
Non metallic mine. manuf.	4.6	371.3	58.6	4.4	172.1	26.5	4.2	120.4	9.2	M
Wood and cork	2.3	129.7	20.0	2.3	72.4	−16.0	2.2	60.0	−25.0	L
Textiles	2.8	213.0	31.3	2.6	78.8	−11.9	2.5	67.0	−19.7	M
Leather	1.6	299.1	44.2	1.7	145.4	18.5	1.2	99.8	-	'
Footwear & clothing	6.0	584.2	78.4	5.4	190.1	31.1	4.8	112.8	6.0	L
Other	1.9	143.3	32.9	1.5	74.5	−14.6	1.5	60.9	−24.3	L
Total industry	100.0	124.1	−9.4	100.0	63.7	−17.3	100.0	61.6	−23.7	

* Comparative Revealed Advantages: $\dfrac{Xi - Mi}{Xi + Mi}$,

where Xi and Mi reflect Spanish exports and imports in sector i.

**Calculated upon the annual average of FDI in each sector. H = high FDI; M = moderate FDI, L = low FDI.

Source: Elaborated upon the data drawn from the Secretaría General Técnica. Ministerio de Industria, Comercio y Turismo.

233

weakest domestic demand. Those sectors with export rates of between 20 per cent and 30 per cent (machinery, mechanical equipment, iron and steel, vehicles, precision instruments, paper and metal products) are usually classified as medium demand, except for iron and steel (weak demand) and precision instruments (strong demand). These observations suggest that the realization of the export potential of the sectors with strong local demand and with high technological content is relatively low, with the exception of some individual companies. It is also true that these sectors are the most penetrated by foreign direct investment (MINER, 1991). The sectors which have shown a positive evolution are the following: non-metal minerals, non-ferrous metals, chemicals, food, textiles, clothing, rubber and plastics and other manufacturing industries. The rubber and plastics sector is particularly notable. An improvement in the competitiveness of these sectors might be expected, as they have had certain comparative advantages.

Finally, we may expect that as public purchases are liberalized, Spanish imports will increase, particularly in goods with a high technological content (telecommunications and office equipment, certain railway equipments goods and so on).

8.4 THE BALANCE OF PAYMENTS AND TECHNOLOGICAL DEPENDENCE

The Spanish balance of technological payments, which includes receipts and payments for technical assistance and royalties, shows a significant deficit throughout the period 1960–90 (see Table 8.7). The

Table 8.7 Spanish technological balance of payments, 1960–90 (in thousand millions of pesetas)

	Receipts (1)	Payments (2)	Deficit	Coverage (1) : (2) %
1960–75	14.92	121.43	−106.51	12.29
1976–80	32.61	169.48	−136.87	19.24
1981–85	95.98	408.46	−312.48	23.50
1986–90	144.60	796.60	−652.00	18.15

Source: Prepared with balance of payments data from Ministerio de Economía y Hacienda.

best position in the technological balance of payments occurs in 1981–5, while during the period 1986–90 it falls to levels close to those reached in relative terms during the second half of the 1970s.

Both in receipts and payments, a greater weight of flows for technical assistance versus those for royalties is observed. Thus, from the point of view of payments, those corresponding to technical assistance account for around 70 per cent of the total, this figure being greater (close to 90 per cent in the most recent years) for receipts for technology exports. As regards imports, in the first stage and until 1981 the situation may be partially explained by the legal prohibition imposed on royalty payments in the case of companies with foreign capital interest. Until 1987 this restriction still applied to interconnected companies. As for exports, very few Spanish patents appear in foreign industrial property registers,[6] although the propensity to patent has increased recently; we shall comment on this later in the chapter.

Table 8.8 refers to a constant sample of 1,426 manufacturing companies from nine sectors. Given the number of companies and the level of aggregation of the sectors, the conclusions are tentative. Thus, for instance, current expenditures in R&D activities are undervalued compared to other sources, as owing to the formulation of the questions the companies were asked, it is estimated that in several cases the expenses of personnel involved in the research process are not computed as R&D expenditures. However, this chart does provide relevant information on business activity in the Spanish economy and on the role played by multinational companies. The innovation effort is measured by the ratio between R&D expenditures and value added. First, an increase can again be seen in the innovation effort together with significant technological dependence, as well as a relative concentration of R&D in a few sectors (chemicals, metal processing, food, other manufacturing industries and energy). Regarding domestic R&D expenditures, the relative concentration is limited to energy, chemicals and metal processing, which account for 83–4 per cent of total R&D expenditures. Overall, payments for imports of technology based on added value are considerably greater than the domestic R&D effort.

By sectors, we should point out the strong technological dependence of the metal processing industry. This sector has great relative importance in Spanish industrial production, and has considerable indirect effects on the rest of industry. This sector includes, among others, the manufacture of vehicles and transportation items, and is one of the most-penetrated by MNCs. At the same time, it is a sector with a significant domestic research effort in the Spanish context. This effort

Table 8.8 Domestic and imported R&D effort classified by manufacturing sectors (percentages of value added)

Sector	Domestic R&D expenses				Imported technology payments				Total R&D expenses			
	1985	1986	1987	1988	1985	1986	1987	1988	1985	1986	1987	1988
Mining	0.80	1.08	0.06	0.68	0.00	0.00	0.00	0.00	0.80	1.08	0.06	0.68
Energy	0.33	0.82	0.88	0.91	0.04	0.07	0.07	0.07	0.37	0.89	0.96	0.98
Steel	0.19	0.01	0.21	0.57	0.16	0.08	0.02	0.02	0.35	0.09	0.23	0.59
Non-metallic mineral products	0.00	0.78	0.78	0.76	0.08	0.12	0.15	0.14	0.08	0.90	0.92	0.89
Chemicals	1.19	1.41	1.58	1.75	0.60	0.84	0.81	0.62	1.79	2.25	2.39	2.37
Metallic transformation	0.57	0.94	1.24	1.23	0.34	1.72	3.46	3.00	0.92	2.65	4.70	4.23
Food, beverages and tobacco	0.57	0.58	0.59	0.57	1.57	1.50	1.54	1.34	2.15	2.08	2.13	1.91
Other manufacturing	0.08	0.16	0.19	0.23	1.89	1.64	2.02	2.29	1.97	1.79	2.22	2.52
Construction	0.02	0.04	0.02	0.04	0.02	0.00	0.01	0.03	0.04	0.04	0.03	0.07
Total manufacturing	0.42	0.72	0.84	0.89	0.47	0.79	1.25	1.12	0.89	1.51	2.09	2.01

Source: Secretaría General Técnica. Prepared with data of Central de Balances del Banco de España. Sample of 1426 firms for the period 1983–8.

236

is carried out both by subsidiaries of MNCs and by Spanish companies interrelated with these MNCs. The association between the two will determine whether Spain continues to maintain comparative location advantages, so that possible disinvestment of MNCs is avoided and Spanish companies related to this sector become more internationalized. Other manufacturing industries show an imbalance in favour of payments for imported technology.

In the food sector it is also evident that payments for technology exceed the domestic R&D effort. This reflects not only the technological dependence of this sector, since wholly Spanish companies (public and private) pay for imported technology, but also the progressive increase in the presence of MNCs in the sector. This sector is marked by the absence of competitive Spanish companies with state-of-the-art technology that could benefit from the trend towards international integration by becoming more internationalized. On the other hand, this deficiency is an incentive (a location advantage) for foreign direct investment.

In the chemical sector, the domestic research effort exceeds payments for the import of technology. The situation in this sector, which has strong demand and is technology-intensive, reflects certain competitive possibilities for Spanish companies, although it is also an important sector as regards technology imports.

The technological deficit shown by the balance of payments must be put in the context of the Spanish economy as a whole, especially as regards those variables which define the internationalization of companies and the R&D efforts made by corporations. Thus, the relation between payments effected for the import of technology and company R&D expenditures is very symptomatic. This relation is known as the dependence rate. Table 8.9 shows the technological dependence rate of Spanish companies; at first sight, a progressive improvement is noticeable over the years. According to this indicator, the greater the research effort of a country's companies, the greater the capacity for assimilating and developing imported technology, which results in low dependence rate levels. Although Spain has improved considerably,[7] it is still very far from the rates shown by other European countries. Thus, as an example, a decade ago the developed countries for which information was recorded showed a dependence rate of around 0.02 to 0.4, while the average was placed at 0.3 (OECD).

Table 8.9   Technological dependence index of Spanish firms

Year	Technology payments (mill. pesetas) (1)	R&D expenses of firms (mill. pesetas) (2)	Dependence index (1):(2)
1970	9,364	2,369	3.95
1976	31,236	14,538	2.15
1979	34,698	24,308	1.43
1980	44,393	32,129	1.38
1981	52,342	33,121	1.58
1982	78,983	46,862	1.69
1983	88,338	52,143	1.69
1984	84,700	65,411	1.29
1986	107,800	110,338	0.98
1987	114,300	126,707	0.90

Source: Column (1): Balana de Pagos
		Column (2): Instituto Nacional de Estadística (INE).

Spanish technological imbalance also occurs in the area of information technologies. The Spanish economy as a whole clearly reveals
the significance of information technologies (microelectronics, data
processing, telecommunications and derivatives) that constitute an
intermediate product practically throughout the entire range of production activity. The quantitative and qualitative improvement made
by Spain in this sector is truly surprising,[8] although there is also a
certain imbalance between the contribution of MNCs and domestic
companies (basically small and medium-sized companies) to R&D
and production: public initiative has undoubtedly contributed to the
coexistence of an indigenous business interaction with the subsidiaries
of the large MNCs of the sector.

However, the delay in achieving a greater and better harmony in
the relations between producers and users, between basic and applied
research, and between personnel training and demand for jobs leads
to a loss of effectiveness, since the sector's productivity and competitiveness still remain below their potential (Castells, 1990). In this
respect, one may point not only to the lack of follow-up to the
prototypes agreed with the MNCs on technology transfer but also the
failure to create a network of auxiliary companies to facilitate the

dissemination of technological knowledge through industrial training and improvement in the quality of products.

These events show not only the necessity of a holistic approach in government policies and their implementation but also the importance of an effective quality control system.

8.5   TECHNOLOGY TRANSFER AND DOMESTIC TECHNOLOGICAL CAPACITY

Although the balance of payments shows a very important and constant technological dependence, it has also to be said that as measured by the receipts of technological exports, there is some domestic capacity. For this reason, with more disaggregated data some other qualitative conclusions can be drawn. First, it is possible to appreciate (see Table 8.10) that the sectors most penetrated by foreign capital are also the most dynamic in exporting technology. These sectors are: chemicals and pharmaceuticals, office and data processing machinery, and electronic equipment. The other main areas of Spanish exports of technology are: engineering and management services, construction and other manufacturing.

All the sectors mentioned above, together with textiles and motor vehicles, account for most of the contracts of technology transferred and for three-quarters of the total payments (see Table 8.11). At the same time, according to Table 8.12, over 80 per cent of the number of firms and transactions and almost 70 per cent of the payments are in the hands of domestic Spanish firms, with no foreign capital. The majority-owned subsidiaries (12 per cent of the sample) account for 15 per cent of the transactions and 27 per cent of the payments. Only 43 per cent of the firms importing technology are engaged in R&D but they account for more than half the number of transactions. Also almost 20 per cent of the firms that imported technology have some exports of technology. The geographical distribution of Spanish technology trade is very much concentrated on the payment side towards the OECD countries (about 98 per cent, of which the EC takes more than 60 per cent and the USA over 20 per cent). However, the receipt side shows a greater degree of diversification. Spanish exports go mainly to the EC, which tends to receive almost half the receipts, and the USA is also an important purchaser. It is also interesting to observe that the non-OECD countries account for more than 20 per cent, of which the majority goes to the Latin American countries (see Table 8.13).

Table 8.10 *The structure of technological trade*

| | 1988 | | | | | 1989 | | | | | 1990 | | | | |
| | Exports | | Imports | | | Exports | | Imports | | | Exports | | Imports | | |
	%T	%R	%T	%R	Cov.	%T	%R	%T	%R	Cov.	%T	%R	%T	%R	Cov.
Chemicals & pharmaceuticals	4.6	17.1	10.2	15.8	6.1	5.5	21.4	12.3	18.7	8.2	17.0	32.2	11.2	27.3	12.2
Office equipment	6.5	0.1	8.3	9.7	10.6	8.2	0.1	8.3	5.9	18.2	5.5	0.5	7.3	4.7	15.8
Electrical equipment	4.9	1.7	2.7	4.7	24.7	4.2	0.9	2.6	5.0	30.4	4.9	0.3	4.4	5.3	21.7
Electronic equipment	3.6	0.9	4.0	9.6	12.2	3.0	0.2	2.5	2.9	21.4	2.5	0.5	3.5	4.8	13.6
Engineering & management services	24.3	43.8	5.9	3.4	55.8	24.2	33.6	8.4	8.4	53.1	24.1	27.4	7.3	5.7	62.3
Energy	-	-	4.1	0.2	0.3	-	-	2.2	0.1	-	-	-	1.9	0.6	-
Motor vehicles	-	-	29.0	30.9	-	-	-	19.3	27.8	-	-	-	14.5	15.8	-
Other manufacturing	3.9	3.3	-	-	0.24	-	-	4.3	3.5	-	-	-	2.3	1.8	-
Construction	5.2	0.9	-	-	0.7	6.8	9.4	-	-	-	4.8	0.2	-	-	-
Total values*	22,020		162,307			35,466		192,715			43,346		224,854		

%T = percentage of technical assistance
%R = percentage of royalties
Cov. = converage ratio = (Exports/imports) × 100
*million pesetas
Source: Based on data from Secretaria de Estado de Comercio.

Table 8.11   Technology transferred: main areas

	Transactions		Payments
	Number	%	%
Computers	1,219	26.0	16.8
Management	950	20.3	16.6
Motor vehicles	109	2.3	11.6
Telecommunications	44	0.9	5.9
Materials	208	4.4	5.8
Chemicals	124	2.7	5.3
Textiles	492	10.5	2.3
Mechanical	233	5.0	5.8
Construction	196	4.2	1.9
Pharmaceuticals	237	5.1	2.7
Electronic	56	1.2	3.2
Food	36	0.8	2.6
Others	779	16.5	19.4
Total	4,686	100.0	100.0

Source: Ministerio de Industria y Energía.

Table 8.12   Technology transactions by importing firms, 1989

Foreign Capital	Firms		Transactions		Payments (%)
	Number	%	Number	%	
No participation	1,615	82	3,776	81	69
Minority	110	6	198	4	4
Majority	240	12	712	15	27
Total	1,965	100	4,680	100	100

R&D expenditure	Firms		Transactions		Export of technology	
	Number	%	Number	%	Number	%
Yes	837	43	2,636	56	187	19
No	1,128	57	2,050	44	1,778	81
Total	1,965	100	4,686	100	1,965	100

Source: Ministerio de Industria y Energía.

Table 8.13   *The geographical distribution of Spanish technology trade (percentages)*

Country	Payments		Receipts	
	1988	1989	1988	1989
United Kingdom	11.0	10.0	4.1	7.1
France	17.7	20.5	19.1	16.1
Germany	22.8	19.1	8.2	7.9
Italy	3.0	3.7	5.0	2.8
Belgium	2.7	2.4	4.1	6.7
Netherlands	5.3	4.8	1.8	5.6
Other EC	0.7	0.8	2.7	2.8
EC	63.2	61.3	45.0	49.0
USA	20.8	21.6	24.1	19.1
Switzerland	9.4	10.1	7.3	3.7
Japan	2.7	2.0	0.9	2.0
Sweden	1.4	2.0	1.8	2.0
Others	1.4	1.0	0.4	2.2
OECD	98.9	98.0	79.5	78.0
Others	1.1	2.0	20.5	22.0
	100.0	100.0	100.0	100.0
Total value (Th. mill. pesetas)	162.3	192.7	22.0	35.5

Source: Ministerio de Industria y Energía.

8.6 THE TECHNOLOGICAL ACTIVITY OF SPANISH COMPANIES

Although the average Spanish company as a rule does not place much emphasis on R&D, there are obviously exceptions and the situation varies between sectors. Thus, in a sample of Spanish multinational companies, it was observed that the research effort made at the beginning of the last decade accounted for an average of about 1.25 per cent with a tendency to increase (Duran, 1987). We may also mention as an example that Spanish pharmaceutical companies devote approximately 3.4 per cent of their sales to R&D (Spanish subsidiaries of multinational companies devote 0.8 per cent), while the large Spanish-owned multinational companies in the sector have overall levels of between 10 per cent and 13 per cent.

The role of the public company in Spanish technological activity is shown in Table 8.14. In the first place we can see a greater research effort, approximately double the average of private companies. The efforts of the public companies are concentrated on energy, processed metal products and mineral extraction, while in the private sector the focus is on the chemical sector and processed metal products.

Table 8.14   Expenditure on R&D by public and private firms, classified by industrial sectors (percentages)

Sectors	Private firms				Public firms			
	1985	1986	1987	1988	1985	1986	1987	1988
Mining	0.00	0.13	0.07	0.07	3.93	4.03	0.00	2.66
Energy	0.18	0.48	0.52	0.51	0.68	1.54	1.60	1.68
Steel	0.00	0.01	0.38	1.09	0.36	0.01	0.03	0.00
Non-metallic mineral products	0.00	0.80	0.79	0.77	0.00	0.00	0.00	0.00
Chemicals	1.24	1.47	1.60	1.76	0.02	0.05	0.02	1.43
Metals	0.54	0.84	0.99	0.96	0.80	1.91	3.82	3.51
Food, beverages and tobacco	0.62	0.67	0.61	0.60	0.25	0.21	0.51	0.47
Other manufacturing	0.09	0.13	0.17	0.22	0.00	0.44	0.42	0.45
Construction	0.02	0.04	0.02	0.04	0.00	0.00	0.00	0.00
Total manufacturing	0.39	0.62	0.70	0.74	0.59	1.15	1.46	1.50

Source: Secretaría General Técnica del Ministerio de Industria. Prepared with data from Central de Balances del Banco de España. Sample of 1426 firms for the period 1983–8.

The importance of MNCs in technology transfer in Spain is considerable. This means that on occasions MNC subsidiaries have been compared with the public companies and Spanish private companies. Thus, for example, we may mention the study by the Circulo de Empresarios (1988), which estimates the intensity of innovation and technology transfer in these three groups of companies. The indicator of intensity and technology transfer is based on the greater or lesser frequency and distance in the time of introduction of new products or new processes. The results obtained (see Table 8.15) indicate that MNC subsidiaries are on average the most active in the introduction of new products or processes. The imports and exports of technology are concentrated in relatively few firms. Thus the top hundred import companies pay about 70 per cent of the total and about 20 of them are responsible for 50 per cent of total payments.[9] Out of these, three-quarters are subsidiaries of multinational companies. This tendency was already evident in the 1970s. According to the 1977 investment census, somewhat over two-thirds of the imports of technology were made by MNC subsidiaries. More than half the contracts for the transfer of technology registered by the Ministry of Industry occurred in the sphere of Spanish subsidiaries of foreign multinational companies (Buesa and Molero, 1991; Sanchez, 1984). As an example we might also mention that for the period 1979–86, out of the 86 companies which registered the highest number of patents in Spain, 85 were subsidiaries of multinational companies, and the other was the Consejo Superior de Investigaciones Cientificas (Higher Council for Scientific Research) (MINER, 1987). In 1987 the top hundred exporters and importers of technology accounted for about 80 per cent of exports and 77 per cent of imports, while in 1990 the figures were 72 per cent and 68 per cent respectively. In the last few years the top hundred exporters registered approximately three-quarters of the total income obtained, while the 30 biggest companies reached 50 per cent of the total. In general this is a confirmation of the fact that, in quantitative terms, MNC subsidiaries and Spanish public companies are important exporters of technology. Most of the companies exporting technology are wholly Spanish, with a small number of Spanish subsidiaries of foreign MNCs. A large proportion of the exports of Spanish technology is made by small and medium-sized companies and is connected to the exports of capital goods and merchandise. The income from technical assistance is considerably higher (about five times higher) than that from patents. Therefore, the export of technology is largely linked to engineering and market studies, turn-key plants and after-sales servicing. Sanchez's (1988) study of Spanish technology exports shows that 137 Spanish companies have a technological balance coverage rate (exports over imports) of 116.3 per cent while the 32 subsidiaries of multinational companies included in the sample reach a coverage rate of 26.3 per cent (the foreign trade coverage rate is 65.7 per cent). These same indicators for the top 1,000 companies with foreign capital for 1989 show a coverage rate of 118.4 per cent (Iranzo, 1990). The limited export of technology by some MNC subsidiaries can also be demonstrated in the particular case of German companies operating in Spain (Buesa and Molero, 1991). Thus, 14.2 per cent of the subsidiaries of German companies export technology, particularly to Latin America. Moreover, most subsidiaries dedicate somewhat less than 2 per cent of their sales to R&D, and more than half the subsidiaries collaborate with the parent company in product development. The number of companies that are included in both the hundred largest exporters and importers of technology are increasing over time as is shown on Table 8.16. The main sector of these companies (mostly subsidiaries of MNCs) are the electronics and computer business, management consulting and engineering and vehicles. These facts are similar to those described in the sections of trade and investment flows, except that MNC affiliates are even more heavily net importers of technology than they are of goods. In summary, it should be pointed out that MNC subsidiaries export less technology than Spanish companies, which is consistent with the theory of the localization of R&D activities in MNCs and with the theory of the technological cycle.

Table 8.15   Density of companies located in Spain according to their ownership structure

Capital ownership	Sample	Broad criterion (1)		Restricted criterion (2)	
		Innovative companies	Innovative density %	Innovative companies	Innovative density %
Public sector	57	16	28.1	4	7.0
Multinational group	136	86	63.2	34	25.0
Private Spanish	246	102	41.5	33	13.4

(1) Companies which over the last five years have introduced a new product or process.
(2) Companies in which over half the sales correspond to products under five years of age, or over half the processes and products have been introduced during the last five years. Innovative density is defined as the percentage of innovative companies in relation to the total number of companies from the corresponding group which are included in the surveyed sample.

Source: Círculo de Empresarios (1988).

Spanish participation in the new R&D programmes of the European Community also gives us some interesting information. In the first place, there is a relative imbalance between the Spanish contribution to the financing of Community programs (about 8 per cent) and the financing (returns) committed to Spain (approximately 5 per cent). The

Table 8.16   The largest companies in the Spanish technological balance of payments (thousand million pesetas)

1987

Company	X (1)	M (2)	X−M (3=1−2)
Construcciones Aeronáuticas, SA (CASA)	1.0	0.9	0.0
Arthur Andersen y Compañía, SRC	0.5	1.2	−0.7
McKinsey and Company, SL	0.2	0.2	0.0
IBM, SAE	0.2	10.9	−10.7
Ericsson Telecomunicaciones, SA	0.2	0.5	−0.3
SE Automóviles Turismo, SA (SEAT-VW)	0.1	4.2	−4.1
Alcatel Standard Eléctrica, SA	0.1	1.7	−1.6
Pirelli Neumáticos, SA	0.1	0.3	−0.3
NCR España, SA	0.0	0.2	−0.1
All firms: % of total	11	18	
100 largest: % of total	80	77	

1990

Company	X (1)	M (2)	X−M (3=1−2)
Construcciones Aeronáuticas, SA (CASA)	3.9	0.9	3.0
IBM, SAE	2.2	22.9	−20.6
Arthur Andersen y Compañía, SRC	2.0	3.9	−2.0
Alcatel Standard Eléctrica, Sa	0.5	5.8	−5.2
Sener Ingeniería y Sistemas, SA	0.3	0.5	−0.2
E. Nal. Bazán Constrc. Navales M.	0.3	0.6	−0.3
E. Nal. Electrónica y Sistemas, Sa	0.2	0.5	−0.3
E. Nal. Electricidad, Sa	0.2	0.3	−0.2
Philips Informática y Comunic. SA	0.1	0.3	−0.2
Siemens, SA	0.1	0.7	−0.5
AT & T Network Systems España, SA	0.1	1.3	−1.1
Land Rover Santana, SA	0.1	0.5	−0.4
Pirelli Neumáticos SA	0.1	0.4	−0.2
All firms: % of total	23	16	
100 largest: % of total	72	68	

Source: Elaborated upon data drawn from The Secretaría de Estado de Comercio.

financing obtained is equivalent in relative terms to the importance of Spanish scientists and technicians within the Community (Buesa and Molero, 1991), while the Spanish contributions correspond to the country's relative economic weight. This imbalance is reflected in the fact that in several cases the contributions by Spanish research institutions do not go hand in hand with the active presence of Spanish companies. As a consequence, Spain in net terms contributes scientific resources, the results of which will be 'appropriated' by companies located in other countries. Moreover, some of the projects led by Spanish companies are in fact led by MNC subsidiaries. All this demonstrates once again the lack of technological capacity of Spanish companies. However, this conclusion should be explained in more detail.

In view of specific Community programmes, and taking into account the Community decision-making process over time, it is evident that the programmes prioritize technological areas in which Spain is not comparatively very well-provided in the area of research and in the number of national competitive producing companies, as in the case of the microelectronics and telecommunications fields. At the same time, in other sectors in which it has a greater comparative advantage in future-orientated sectors, such as agro-industry, fishing and catering, it receives little or no Community support.

Furthermore, the Plan Nacional de Investigacion Cientifica y Desarrollo Tecnico (National Plan for Scientific Research and Technological Development) was seen to be something of an incentive to the companies participating in international programmes. In conclusion, it may be stated that technological policies are relatively subordinate to Community decisions. However, it has been shown in this section that there is empirical evidence that the technological capacity of Spanish firms is increasing, as well as the penetration of MNCs in the most research-intensive sectors, and these MNCs are involved in assembly activities as well as in other activities that are more technologically orientated.

Finally, a useful indicator of technological capacity is the number of applications for patents. In this respect, applications for patents in Spain (domestic applications plus applications of foreigners) went up from 52,384 applications in the period 1981–5 to 116,468 in the period 1986–90. The international applications for Spanish patents went up from 6,762 in 1981–5 to 16,550 applications in 1986–90. Although the patents granted in the industrial property register were somewhat less than the number of applications, we have considered the latter data as a representative signal.[10] At the same time, the improvement of the Spanish technological capacity and competitiveness can also be seen from the complementary information in Table 8.17. This table shows the number of applications for European patents of Spanish origin during the period 1986–9, in which there is clearly a steady growth. European patents are subject to a more rigorous acceptance procedure than in most other countries. The table also confirms our earlier conclusions about the improved technological capacity and economic behaviour of Spanish industry.

Table 8.17   Number of applications for European patents of Spanish origin by sector

	1986	1987	1988	1989
Food & beverages	18	28	33	36
Transportation	24	33	38	48
Chemistry & metallurgy	15	21	27	38
Textiles & paper	5	15	9	7
Construction	6	9	11	12
Mechanics	9	22	10	26
Physics	18	9	24	13
Electricity & electronics	6	9	13	14
Others	1	3	12	4
Total	102	149	177	198

Source: Registro de la Propiedad Industrial.

8.7   LOCATIONAL FACTORS AFFECTING FDI IN SPAIN

The specialization and rationalization of production which has been taking shape in preparation for the creation of the EC in 1993 is to some extent modifying the comparative advantages of each country. In the case of Spain, some analyses (Martin, 1989) have tried to identify the most vulnerable sectors and those which will have significant comparative advantages. In the first case, in addition to the most protected sectors, we should single out those sectors with a high technological content and whose comparative advantage is basically determined by the locational decisions of the MNCs of the Triad (electronics, aerospace equipment, electromedicine, computers and office automation, some branches of chemicals and so on). In the second case, we might mention footwear, textiles, toys, sports equipment, ceramics, food, shipbuilding and motor vehicles and some materials for transport equipment. The two latter sectors, and to a lesser degree the food sector, are heavily penetrated by global MNCs. However, some of the labour-intensive sectors in which Spain has comparative advantages are undergoing heavy competition from some newly industrialized countries (especially South-East Asia) and particularly by France and Italy. In this context, an improvement may be expected in the competitive strategies of Spanish companies involved in technological and marketing activities (distribution and brand policies), as well as greater integration with French and Italian companies.

Despite a noticeable wage rise, there has been a sharp increase in FDI. This may be explained by examining three factors. In the first place, we must mention that the Spanish workforce has achieved an overall improvement in its qualifications and attitudes. As a whole, Spain has improved its supply of human capital. In addition pay rises imply increased purchasing power for the population, which in turn expands the market. This conclusion is in line with that reached by Culem (1988), on observing the increase in unit labour costs when FDI flows between the USA and the EC were analysed, along with intra-Community FDI.

Next, we must point out, with particular reference to the purchase of Spanish companies by MNCs, the appreciation in the value of Spanish companies. Spain's geographical location, as well as other factors of attraction such as the improvement in the supply of human capital, is a significant reason for its use by some MNCs as a base for their international expansion. Thus some MNCs have located their regional offices for part or all of Europe and North Africa in Spain, such as Arthur Andersen and Coca Cola, and Spanish subsidiaries are also being used as platforms for DI into Portugal, North Africa and Latin America, as for example in the case of Cristaleria Española, a subsidiary of the French MNC Saint-Gobain, and also several German companies.

Lastly, we must mention Spain's geographical, technological and economic position when considering the Mediterranean as a strategic area for future development. The competitive aspects of this location have been fortified by the effects of the Europe of 1993. In general, the greater liberalization and deregulation of the economy, the increase in technological capacity and human capacity, as well as greater stability and integration, constitute a favourable overall environment for the reception of FDI, and also help to produce Spanish direct investment abroad. If these factors occur to a considerable degree, and the local

Spanish economy is confronted by strong international competition, Spanish direct investment abroad will be generated in a significant manner. This has some quantitative and qualitative relevance in the Community period (1986–90), when the factors mentioned became more apparent. The intermediate and complementary nature of the technology of Spanish companies and the international distribution of their products encouraged their location abroad. Also, the financial sector is the top investor abroad, due to the flag strategy (emigrants, exports and DI) and because of their involvement in shares of capital of many domestic companies (Duran and Lamothe, 1991).

Some of the big Spanish public-service companies are especially dynamic in their internationalization processes. This is a phase of co-operation agreements (strategic alliances) and licences with European, American and Japanese companies, and clear DI action directed basically to Latin America. These companies are in the areas of telecommunications (Telefonica) and transport (Renfe and Iberia). In these, the direct investment cycle mentioned by Dunning and Cantwell (1990) has occurred, particularly in Telefonica. This company began as a subsidiary of ITT, then became a mixed domestic company (public and private capital) and is currently a major Spanish multinational company.

The model which corresponds to the Spanish economy must have the following characteristics:

(a) government policy integrating the science–technology–industry system by the efficient combination of the activities of MNCs and Spanish public and private companies;
(b) promote international technological co-operation;
(c) facilitate R&D efforts designed to adopt and apply international technology, developing national technological capacity;
(d) promote the internationalization of Spanish companies.

8.8 CONCLUSIONS

The uninterrupted and steadily increasing presence of FDI in Spain has been important not only in its effect on economic growth, but also in the transfer of technology. This transfer of technology has had a positive effect as a consequence of the adaptation of technology to the environment of the Spanish economy. In this context, the indicators show the operating improvement achieved in imported technologies. These conclusions are particularly striking as, during the period

1960–85, there was scant institutional and business response to the creation of a technology base which would be sufficient to generate leadership in the international competitiveness of Spanish companies, in specific global segments and market niches.

Even despite the significant efforts made over the last six years, a continuing emphasis must be placed upon the ongoing and considerable technological deficit suffered by the Spanish economy (in the entire 1960–90 period). This is another example of the structural dependence of Spanish companies on imported technology. The lack of R&D programmes, both public and private, until the beginning of the 1980s has also reduced the effectiveness of the transfer of technology, adversely affecting the competitiveness of the Spanish economy. Since the mid–1980s there has been a considerable increase in the research effort both by the public administration and by companies, although the desired efficiency has not yet been achieved due to a certain lack of co-ordination among institutions. The public companies as a whole have contributed more to Spanish technological capacity than have private companies. However, if a distinction is made in this case between subsidiaries of multinational companies and national companies, the multinational group becomes the first in innovative density, followed by the public sector and the local private sector respectively.

As a result of Spain's incorporation into the EC in 1986 and in anticipation of the creation of the European single market in 1993, the determinants of the location of investments have been positively modified. Institutional reforms (in the education system, improvement in infrastructures and in the public R&D system and the creation of new organizations), by improving the competitiveness of domestic companies and their ability to respond to rising inward investment have produced significant increases in Spanish direct investment abroad. The growth and competitive potential of the Spanish economy are illustrated by important increases in the economic value of businesses and corporate activity. The empirical evidence shows a clear interdependence between Spanish inward and outward direct investment.

The governmental and institutional strategy has been one of classic support for economic and technological development. The improvement in Spain's technological capacity is evident. However, so is the loss of efficiency which still occurs as a result of the lack of better articulation of the science–technology–industry system.

The dominant trend in business activity indicates that a large proportion of European companies engaged in production in Spain have

based their location on the differences in production costs. The technological levels involved are relatively low. On the other hand, the
degree of penetration has increased in sectors with great growth potential such as food, trade, banking and insurance and construction. The
greatest penetration by non-European MNCs, particularly Japanese
and American, has been partly caused by Spain's capacity to act as a
base for penetrating the EC. Finally, wholly Spanish companies have
become internationalized, seeking primarily a position in European
production and distribution networks; attempting not to subordinate
themselves hierarchically to other companies. To this end, they have
in some cases made purchases of companies abroad, and in others
strategic alliances have been formed. Overall the integration rate into
the EC, with Spain becoming part of the Triad since 1986, has been
growing every year.

The activity of Spanish companies in third countries follows two
basic directions. On the one hand, investment activity in Latin
America has recovered, and on the other hand, the Mediterranean has
been revitalized as a strategic area with great development potential.
Additionally, there is also a certain presence in Eastern European
countries, although not yet significant. In the two first cases, Spain's
attractive geographical location is an advantage for conducting international business with Latin America and the Mediterranean and
North Africa. Some MNC subsidiaries are using Spain as a regional
centre for international operations in these two geographical areas.

NOTES

1. Four key dates may actually be pinpointed at a worldwide level to define the
   relevant sub-periods after the creation of the Bretton Woods and GATT systems
   in 1944 and the OECD in 1948. First was the creation of the EC in 1958.
   Subsequently 1973, which represents the beginning of a new international environment which became a reality: an environment of great uncertainty (flexible
   exchange rates, volatile interest rates, effects on the world economy of changes
   in relative prices, and a strong boost for the development of international financial
   markets). Thirdly, 1982 with the recognition of the less-developed countries'
   foreign debt crisis, as well as the recovery and expansion of the industrialized
   countries. Lastly 1989–91 with the drastic changes in Eastern Europe and the
   USSR. Meanwhile the G–7 have been playing a role in the international system.
2. In the period 1950–80 for most countries inward and outward direct investment
   were regarded as two unrelated phenomena. The main exceptions to this were
   Japan, followed by South Korea, Singapore and Taiwan. Nowadays few countries
   follow a holistic approach although there seems to be a greater tendency to make
   allowance for the interaction between inward and outward investment (Dunning,
   1991).
3. According to this indicator, a country is an investor when it has ratios greater

than 0.33, it is a crossroad country when the values are between −0.33 and +0.33, and a receiver when the ratio is less than −0.33. The net receiver countries are Greece, Portugal, Spain and Ireland, and the net investors are the Netherlands and Germany. Over time, there has been a certain mobility between countries, particularly the United Kingdom, Italy and Holland (Muchielli, 1985; Molle and Morsink, 1990).

4. Before Spain joined the EC, the Spanish balance of payments showed an overall trade surplus, while after 1986 the deficit increased over time. After 1986 Spain had a trade surplus with France and the Netherlands in 1986–7 and with Portugal and Greece during the whole period 1986–90.

5. Regarding the complementary relationship between the FDI and exports, in the Spanish case the following may be consulted: Alonso and Donoso (1989); Duran and Lamothe (1990).

6. Generally speaking, there has always been a lack of interest (due to lack of information and training) by the Spanish businessman in patenting his discoveries. Thus it is estimated that less than 20 per cent of material requiring protection is patented. It is expected that only 3 per cent of discoveries patented in Spain in the coming years will be patented by Spaniards (Diario, *Cinco Dias*, 8 April 1991).

7. The resources dedicated to R&D in 1984 accounted for 0.4 per cent of the GDP, while this figure rose to 0.68 per cent in 1987 and with the development of the Plan Nacional de Investigacion Cientifica y Desarrollo Tecnico (National Plan for Scientific Research and Technological Development), it is expected to exceed 1 per cent of the GDP in 1992 (in 1990 it went up to 0.9 per cent).

8. Thus apparent annual consumption has gone from 1.7 per cent in the 1980–4 period to 14.57 per cent in the 1985–9 period. Along the same lines and for the same sub-periods, average annual growth has risen from 2.09 per cent to 13.28 per cent. The average annual rate growth for imports is about 13.5 per cent while for exports is 6.4 per cent.

9. Out of the top 20 importers, 12 are subsidiaries of MNCs and out of the top 20 exporters, 8 are subsidiaries of MNCs and 6 are public companies.

10. These data come from the Spanish Register for Industrial Property, which is a part of the Ministry of Industry. The patents acceptance rate during the whole period was about 50 per cent for Spanish applications for patents and 25 per cent for international applications of Spanish patents.

REFERENCES

Aliber, R.Z. (1971), 'The Multinational Enterprise in a Multiple Currency World', in J.H. Dunning (ed.), *The Multinational Enterprise*, London: Allen & Unwin.

Alonso, J.A. and Donoso, V. (1989), *Caracteristicas y Estrategias de la Empresa Exportadora Española*, Madrid: ICEX.

Baldwin, R. (1989), 'The Growth Effects of 1992', *Economic Policy*, **9**, October, 248–81.

Buesa, M. and Molero, J. (1991), 'La Empresa Española en la Internacionalizacion del Cambio Tecnologico', *Economistas*, (47), 376–84.

Burgenmeier, B. and Mucchielli, J.L. (ed.) (1990), *Multinationals and Europe 1992*, London: Routledge.

Cantwell, J.A. (1987), 'The Reorganization of European Industries after Integration: Selected Evidence on the Role of Multinational Enterprise Activities', *Journal of Common Market Studies*, **26**, December, 127–51.

Cantwell, J.A. (1989), *Technological Innovation and Multinational Corporations*, Oxford: Basil Blackwell.
Cantwell, J.A. (1990), 'The Technological Competence Theory of International Production and its Implications', University of Reading, *Discussion Paper in International Investment and Business Studies*, no. 149, November.
Castells, M. (1990), *El impacto de las Nuevas Tecnologias en la Economia Internacional. Implicaciones para la Economia Española*, Madrid: Informes del Instituto de Estudios de Prospectiva. Secretaria de Estado de Economia. Ministerio de Economia y Hacienda.
Caves, R. (1988), 'Exchange Rate Movements and Foreign Direct Investment in the United States', Harvard Institute of Economic Research, *Discussion Papers Series* no. 1383, May.
Cecchini, P. *et al.* (1988), *The European Challenge 1992: The Benefits of a Single Market*, Aldershot, Hants.: Wildwood House.
Circulo de Empresarios (1988), *Actitud y Comportamiento de las grandes empresas españolas ante la innovacion*, Madrid.
Cohen, W. and Levinthal, D.A. (1990), 'Absorptive Capacity: a New Perspective on Learning and Innovation', *Administrative Science Quarterly*, **35**, 128–52.
Culem, C. (1988), 'The Locational Determinants of Direct Investments among Industrialized Countries', *European Economic Review*, **32**, 885–904.
Dunning, J.H. (1981), *International Production and the Multinational Enterprise*, London: Allen & Unwin.
Dunning, J.H. (1988), 'The Eclectic Paradigm of International Production: a Restatement and Some Possible Extensions', *Journal of International Business Studies*, **1**(21), 1–31.
Dunning, J.H. (1991), 'Governments and Multinational Enterprises: From Corporation to Co-operation?', University of Reading, *Discussion Papers in International Investment and Business Studies*, no. 153.
Dunning, J.H. and Cantwell, J.A. (1990), 'Japanese Direct Investment in Europe', in B. Burgenmeier and J.L. Muchielli (eds), *Multinationals and Europe 1991*, London: Routledge.
Duran Herrera, J.J. (1987), 'Decisiones de inversion directa en el exterior de la empresa española 1979–1985', *Informacion Comercial Española*, (643), 73–86.
Duran Herrera, J.J. (1990a), 'Inversion directa y resultados de las empresas multinacionales españolas', *Papeles de Economia Española*, (39/40), 339–55.
Duran Herrera, J.J. (1990b), *Estrategias y evaluacion e la Inversion Directa en el Exterior*, Madrid: ICEX.
Duran J.J. and Lamothe, P. (1989), 'Caracteristicas y comportamiento economico-financiero de las empresas españolas vs. filiales de multinacionales, 1982–1986', *Papeles de Economia Española*, (39/40), 293–320.
Duran, J.J. and Lamothe, P. (1990), 'La internacionalizacion de la banca española', *Informacion Comercial Española*, April.
Duran, J.J. and Lamothe, P. (1991), 'International Banking in Spain: an Analysis Based in the Country of Origins', Working Paper, Centro Internacional Carlos V. Universidad Autonoma de Madrid.
Duran, J.J. and Sanchez, M.P. (1981), *La internacionalizacion de la empresa española. Inversiones españolas en el exterior*, Madrid: Ministerio de Economia y Comercio. Secretaria General Tecnica.

Franko, L.G. (1976), *The European Multinationals: A Renewed Challenge to American and British Big Business*, London: Harper & Row.

Graham, E.M. and Krugman, P. (1989), *Foreign Direct Investment in the United States*, Washington, D.C.: Institute for International Economics.

Iranzo, J. (1990), 'La inversion extranjera en España y el comercio exterior', *Revista de Economia* (5).

Itaki, M. and Waterson, M. (1990), 'European Multinationals and 1992', University of Reading, *Discussion Papers in International Investment and Business Studies*, series B, vol. III, no. 141.

Krugman, P.R. (1987), 'Economic Integration in Europe: Some Conceptual Issues', in I. Padua-Schiuppa (ed.), *Efficiency, Stability and Equity*, Oxford: Oxford University Press.

Lunn, J. (1980), 'Determinants of US Direct Investment in the EEC: Further Evidence', *European Economic Review*, **13**, 93–101.

Lunn, J. (1983), 'Determinants of US Direct Investment in the EEC: Revisited Again', *European Economic Review*, **21**, 391–3.

Martin, C. (1989), 'Spain's Foreign Trade and Industrial Structure: the Effects of EEC Membership and the Single European Market of 1992', CEPR and European Community Commission.

MINER (1987, 1991): 'Informe sobre la Industria Española', Madrid: Secretaria General Tecnica, Ministerio de Industria.

Molle, W., and Morsink, R.L.A. (1990), 'Intra-European Direct Investment', in B. Burgenmeier and J. Mucchielli (eds), *Multinationals and Europe 1991*, London: Routledge.

Mucchielli, S.L. (1985), 'Les firmes multinationales mutations et nouvelles perspectives', Paris: Economia.

OECD (1981), *International Investment and Multinational Enterprise*, Paris: OECD.

Sanchez, M.P. (1984), *La dependencia tecnologica española*, Madrid: Ministerio de Economia y Hacienda.

Sanchez, M.P. (1988), *La empresa española la exportacion de tecnologia*, Madrid: ICEX.

Scapaerlanda, A.E. and Balough, R. (1983), 'Determinants of US Direct Investment in the EEC Revisited', *European Economic Review*, **21**.

UNCTC (1988), *Transnational Corporations in World Development: Trends and Prospects*, New York: United Nations.

Yannopoulos, G.N. (1990), 'Foreign Direct Investment and European Integration: the Evidence from the Formative Years of the European Community', *Journal of Common Market Studies*, **28** (2).

Young, S., McDermott, M. and Dunlop, S. (1990), 'The Challenge of the Single Market', in R. Burgenmeier and J. Mucchielli (eds), *Multinationals and Europe 1991*, London: Routledge.

9. European Integration and the Pattern of FDI Inflow in Portugal

Vitor Corado Simões*

9.1 INTRODUCTION

European integration since the mid–1980s has gained a new momentum. The Single European Act and the accession of Spain and Portugal marked the start of another phase in the process initiated in the 1950s. Further impetus was achieved in the wake of developments in Eastern Europe and with the new targets of European economic and monetary union and the more-distant political union.

The Single European Act aims to build up a real internal market by establishing conditions for the free flow of goods, services, labour and capital within the European Community. According to the Cecchini Report (1988) the benefits to be generated by setting up the single market are very significant: around 210 billion Ecus for the whole EC at 1988 prices.

However, beyond being a final situation to be achieved on the first day of 1993, the single market is a process; a process of economic, but also political and social, integration; a process started well before 1993 and to be continued thereafter. This process has substantial implications for the countries and regions of the Community. It cannot be taken for granted that the benefits will be evenly spread. Some areas will gain while others may lose, generating new regional imbalances or deepening those already existing.

Implications for firms – both European and non-European – and their investment strategies are also evident. The relationships between the single market and international investment flows may be assessed at three levels: the world, the Community (or Europe in general), and specific countries or regions. It is well known that one of the purposes of the single market is to provide European multinationals

*The author acknowledges with thanks the comments of Daniel Van Den Bulcke, John Cantwell and Julien Savary on an earlier draft. The usual disclaimer applies.

(or 'European champions') with a larger basis in their global competition against their American and Japanese counterparts; intra-Triadic cross-hauling investments will continue to develop. At a European level three main movements can be identified: (a) intra-European restructuring and rationalization of manufacturing and trading activities, including mergers and acquisitions; (b) new investments by non-European firms to respond to what they perceive as the building up of 'fortress Europe'; and (c) further Europeanization of SMEs to tackle the whole single market, either through direct investment or through co-operative agreements. With regard to the country/regional perspective, an increased presence of foreign firms in most EC economies may be expected, especially in some regional poles with highly attractive conditions. The potential benefits to be captured from the setting-up of foreign affiliates will strengthen inter-country (and inter-regional) competition to court foreign investors; however, the occurrence from time to time of nationalistic waves as a reaction to the foreign control of former 'national champions' cannot be excluded.

The purpose of this chapter is to assess the likely implications of the process of European integration, namely the single market, on the trends and characteristics of inward investment in Portugal. Such an exercise has to be largely qualitative and speculative. It requires a 'holistic approach' (Hood and Young, 1987) to link multinational strategies, international investment trends, industry requirements and market structures, location determinants and the impact of different affiliates upon domestic economy. The focus will be placed on manufacturing industry.

The chapter is divided into four parts. The first provides a taxonomy of international corporate strategies and affiliate characteristics that will be used throughout the analysis. The second draws a brief picture of the main features of foreign direct investment (FDI) in Portugal, especially in the post-accession period. The next section deals with the heart of the matter: what kind of inward FDI may be expected in the years to come and what will be its contribution towards the development of the Portuguese economy, mainly from the technological standpoint. The last part summarizes the main conclusions and poses some policy suggestions.

9.2 CORPORATE STRATEGIES AND AFFILIATES' CHARACTERISTICS

International investment decisions are taken by firms. Internationalization is a sequential process, largely shaped by corporate history and

Table 9.1 Corporate strategies and affiliates' characteristics

Corporate strategy	Geographic configuration of activities					Coordination	Type of subsidiary
	Production	Marketing	Service	Technology development	Sourcing		
Exporting	Headquarters	Dispersed	Dispersed	Headquarters	Headquarters	Low for export-based strategies High for simple global strategies	Marketing satellite
Domestic with foreign production	Dispersed (in few countries)	Headquarters	Headquarters	Headquarters	Headquarters	High (foreign production is restricted to labour intensive activities and is tightly controlled)	Direct manufacturing platform
Multidomestic	Dispersed	Dispersed	Dispersed	Headquarters (with product adaptation in main markets)	Dispersed	Low (with the exception of a few strategic issues)	Domestic market orientated manufacturer
Resource-seeking	Dispersed	Dispersed	Dispersed	Headquarters	Dispersed (dependent on resource availability)	High (in most cases) to low	Resource-based affiliate
Multinational integration	Dispersed	Dispersed	Dispersed	Headquarters	Headquarters/ Dispersed	High	Integrated manufacturer (These affiliates may have a product and/ or a process specialization)

Corporate strategy	Geographic configuration of activities					Coordination	Type of subsidiary
	Production	Marketing	Service	Technology development‡	Sourcing		
Global on a product basis	Dispersed (by product)	Dispersed	Dispersed	Dispersed (by product)	Dispersed	High to medium (affiliates enjoy freedom within the context of their product mandates)	Product specialist
Global	Dispersed	Dispersed	Dispersed	Headquarters + Technology-strong affiliates	Dispersed	High to medium (Development of 'heterarchies')	Strategic majors

Note: This table must be read as an instrument to analyse firms' behaviour from the host country's standpoint. It is not intended to encapsulate all the possible strategies to be followed by multinationals, nor are strategies so clear-cut as assumed here.
Source: Developed on the basis of Porter (1986); Doz (1986); White and Poynter (1984); Young, Hood and Hamill (1988); and Bartlett and Ghoshal (1990). The term 'multinational integration' is taken from Doz (1986). The terms marketing satellite and product specialist are borrowed from White and Poynter (1984).

culture (Kogut, 1983 and 1990). Corporate behaviour is also influenced by country and industry factors (Dunning, 1988). The first concerns home and host country conditions and relative locational advantages. The second relates to industry patterns: market structures, technological progress, entry and exit barriers, economics of scale and scope, product characteristics, input requirements and so on.

Our purpose is to build up a taxonomy of corporate strategies and affiliate characteristics that could constitute a framework to forecast the future patterns of inward FDI in Portugal.

The work of Porter (1986) on international strategies will be our starting point. According to him, such strategies can be defined by taking account of two main criteria: the geographical configuration of activities (location of the different parts of firms' value chain) and intra-firm co-ordination of activities. However, Porter's approach does not fully address the characteristics and scope of subsidiaries abroad – a crucial subject from a host country perspective. It is therefore convenient to relate international corporate strategies to the corresponding affiliates' patterns, by identifying the segments of the value chain that are located abroad as well as the level of freedom enjoyed by those affiliates. The classification of affiliates developed by White and Poynter (1984) is also helpful in this regard, although it does not fully capture the whole range of situations that we are concerned with.

Seven main types of subsidiaries can be identified (see Table 9.1):[1]

(a) *'Marketing satellite'*, the objective of which is to sell goods manufactured centrally; its links with host country manufacturing and technological fabric tend to be weak.

(b) *Direct manufacturing platform*, without autonomy and directly linked to, and controlled by, the mother-company. Their activities are mostly labour-intensive, the majority of inputs being imported from headquarters (usually under a draw-back or similar regime) and the output also being shipped to them. This kind of subsidiary is relatively common in low-wage areas and in industries such as clothing, footwear, electrical appliances and simple electronic products.

(c) *Domestic market-orientated manufacturer*, producing and marketing some of the parent's product lines and/or similar goods in the host country and sometimes in adjacent countries. This kind of subsidiary is more prone to interact with the domestic manufacturing and technological fabric and may have limited product development activities; their domestic linkages may be gradually strengthened.

(d) *Resource-based affiliate*, aimed at exploiting local natural resources. The strategic freedom of this type of affiliate is variable: in most cases there is tight central co-ordination, especially when the subsidiary produces intermediate products to be further processed abroad; when it manufactures a final product and is entitled to market it worldwide, its independence is strongly increased. Similarly, its relationships with the local environment will vary, although its technological contribution tends to be limited.

(e) *Integrated manufacturer*, specializing in a specific stage of a product's manufacturing process (process specialization) or in the manufacturing of a limited part of the multinational group's product range, aiming at a multi-country or world market but whose marketing is centrally managed (product specialization). An integrated manufacturer's autonomy is, as a rule, scarce, although it may increase over time as a result of the building-up of technical and engineering know-how (Howells, Charles and Wood, 1991; Hakanson, 1990); using Bartlett and Ghoshal (1990) terminology, an evolutionary pattern might be envisaged in some product areas, whereby integrated manufacturers are given wider technological mandates, changing from 'implementers' to 'contributors' and later to 'leaders'. The life of subsidiaries is largely dependent on overall strategies and rationalization decisions taken by headquarters.

(f) *'Product specialist'*, when the subsidiary is responsible for developing, manufacturing and marketing a specific product (or a limited range of products) for world (or, in some cases, continental) markets. These subsidiaries have a larger ground to interact with the domestic technological fabric; in some instances they are set up in a given country due to the very dynamics of the local environment. Product specialists may also result from the acknowledgment of the capabilities of former integrated manufacturers, from the performance of domestic-market orientated manufacturers in specific product lines or from the strengths of resource-based affiliates.

(g) *Strategic major*, corresponding to subsidiaries that enjoy independence to develop new lines of business (similar to the 'strategic' independents of White and Poynter) or that perform the role of listening posts or technology scanners in the context of 'technological accumulation' approaches (Pavitt, 1987; Cantwell, 1989). As a rule, strategic majors have significant relationships with home country technological infrastructure but may also be instruments to 'suck' domestic technological innovations. This concept of strategic majors is not fully compatible with the traditional view of the multinational firm as a clear hierarchical structure and is more in line with new perspectives of multinationals as 'horizontal organizations' (White and Poynter, 1990) or 'heterarchies' (Hedlund, 1986).

This taxonomy must be used with care, especially when applied to the links between corporate strategies and subsidiary characteristics. There is not a one-to-one correspondence: a given strategy may lead to the setting-up of different types of subsidiaries; on the other hand, a single firm may follow different strategies, according to the characteristics of its products. Similarly, one subsidiary may simultaneously act as a 'marketing satellite', a domestic-market orientated manufacturer and an integrated manufacturer. The taxonomy is therefore an instrument to allow better understanding of and to interpret a given phenomenon but it cannot fully capture all the aspects of a multi-faceted reality.

9.3   PATTERNS OF FOREIGN INVESTMENT IN PORTUGAL

9.3.1   Historical Background

Since FDI is a sequential process, forecasting the future requires some knowledge of past trends and patterns. FDI inflows are not just the outcome of setting up green-field investments or takeovers; they are also a consequence of the behaviour of existing foreign subsidiaries. In Portugal a large share of FDI inflow has been accounted for by the reinvestments of existing foreign-owned firms.

The pattern and characteristics of inward FDI has changed historically in response to domestic and international factors. Paramount among the first were the overall cconomic cnvironment of Portugal and the policies and attitudes of the Portuguese authorities towards trade and investment flows. With regard to the second, international investment trends and determinants deserve recognition (Fernandes and Simões, 1988).

Almost half a century has elapsed since the end of the Second World War. In this period five main stages in FDI inflow in Portugal may be identified:

(a) *Nationalism*, lasting for the duration of the 1940s and 1950s, marked by an attitude of distrust towards foreign investors.

(b) *Opening-up*, characterized by some economic liberalization and by EFTA membership (and, in the early 1970s, by the trade agreement with the EC); this period extended from 1960 to 1974.

(c) *Post-April*, corresponding to the second half of the 1970s, a period of economic and political turmoil in Portugal and of international economic crisis.

(d) *Early 1980s*, marked by the recovery of a favourable foreign investment climate and the preparation for EC accession.

(e) *Late 1980s*, starting with entry into the EC on 1 January 1986, and characterized by a very significant FDI inflow.

A comparison of the most relevant features of FDI inflow in these periods (size of flows, types of subsidiaries, market orientation and main investment motivations) is provided in Table 9.2.[2]

For the purposes of this chapter it is convenient to stress the following aspects:

(a) The first *post*-war free trade experience (EFTA membership) gave rise to important FDI inflows, mainly translated into affiliates that were direct manufacturing platforms and integrated manufacturers. Investments were export-orientated and aimed to benefit from low wages. Investors were based either in other EFTA member countries (direct manufacturing platform-type subsidiaries by Swedish and Finnish firms) or third countries (namely, integrated manufacturers set up by US and original EC–6 firms to supply the British market).

(b) The evaluation of the outcome of the 1972 free-trade agreement with the EC is difficult because of the changes that occurred in Portugal in 1974–5. There are, however, indications that it had a positive impact on two grounds: first, the establishment of direct manufacturing platforms and integrated manufacturers by European firms (mainly German); secondly, the progressive export drive of former domestic market-orientated manufacturers.

(c) Investment patterns in the early 1980s resumed, to a large extent, the features prevailing in late 1960s and early 1970s: labour-intensive, export-orientated direct manufacturing platforms and integrated manufacturers. However, the automotive sector took the lead, instead of electronics. In parallel there were a few large

Table 9.2   Historical trends in the pattern of inward FDI in Portugal

Period	National environment	International investment conditions	Size	Main type of subsid.	Market	Main determinants	Addit. remarks
Nationalism (1945–59)	Inward orientated economic and political system. Law of Nationalization of Capitals (published 1943). 'Industrial conditioning' (limitations to the establishment of nationals and foreigners in several industries)	Post-war growth of investment flows. United States leadership; significant American investments in Europe following the creation of EC. Predominance of import substitution investments, to supply local markets	Small	(1) Marketing satellites (2) Domestic market orientated manuf.	Domestic	(1) Domestic market supply through imports (2) Import substituting	Some resource-based affiliates orientated towards foreign markets
Opening up (1960–74)	Creation of EFTA. Liberalization of FDI inflow (Decree 46312/1965). Softening of 'industrial conditioning'. Trade agreements with EC and CECA (1972)	Strengthening of the internationalization process, still under US leadership. Emergence of new investors (Germany and Japan). Starting of the transfer of some manufacturing activities towards low wage countries and of intra-European rationalization of production. International crisis: oil shock and US monetary crisis	Strong growth (annual average of 20% between 1964 and 1974)	(1) Manufacturing platforms (2) Integrated manufacturers	Foreign (Germany, UK, Scandinavia)	Profiting from low wages	Domestic market orientated manuf. continued to be set up. Resource-based affiliates in paper pulp and tomato paste
Post-April (1974–9)	Phase I: Democratization. Socio-political instability. Nationalizations.	Decline in international investment growth. Struggles between multinationals and nation states. Divestments.	Decline in absolute amounts of FDI. Slow recovery	(1) Marketing satellites (2) Domestic market orientated manuf	Domestic	(1) Domestic market supply through imports (2) Import substituting	Although domestic market orientated investments

Period	National environment	International investment conditions	Size	Main type of subsid.	Market	Main determinants	Addit. remarks
	Consolidation of democracy. Demand of accession to the EC. Economic liberalization of the rules of the game to attract/control FDI (Foreign Investment Code/ 1977)	1978. New forms of investment. Emergence of Third World multinationals. Development of cross-hauling investments. Starting of investments in the US					was not very clear-cut
Early 1980s (1980–5)	Gradual economic liberalization. Austerity policies. Opening to and courting foreign investors. Preparation for EC accession	Moderate growth. Reduction in internationally mobile investments, leading to increased competition among countries to attract FDI. Growing relevance of technology in the formulation and implementation of firms' investment strategies. Globalization of production and markets; mergers and acquisitions	Strong growth (annual average above 40%)	(1) Integrat. manufact. (2) Manufact. platform (3) Resource-based	Foreign	(1) and (2) profiting from low wages and incentives. (3) Exploit natural resources (mining and forestry)	
Late 1980s (1986–9)	EC accession. Significant economic growth. Improvement of infrastructures. Promotion of FDI inflow through investment incentives (cash grants).	Development of inter-firm co-operation. Increased concentration of investments within the Triad. Strong investments in the US. Further internationalization of Japanese firms	Very strong growth (annual average above 100%)	(1) Integrated manufact. (2) Domestic market orientated manuf. (3) Resource-based	(1) & (3) Foreign (2) Domestic	(1) Profiting from low wages and incentives (2) Respond to growth in domestic demand (3) Exploit natural resources	

investments in resource-based affiliates: paper pulp and copper mining.

(d)   After a wait-and-see period in 1986, foreign investors betted strongly on Portugal in the late 1980s: the FDI inflow in 1989 was close to 350 billion escudos as against 42 billion in 1985. However, the share of manufacturing was low, reaching only 28 as an average; services – mainly tourism and real-estate operations and banking and insurance – took the lead. Foreign manufacturing investments were mainly greenfield (especially in the automotive industry, where General Motors and Ford undertook significant investments), but acquisitions and reinvestments also reached high amounts.

To forecast future FDI trends a closer look at recent manufacturing investment patterns is needed. This will be the subject of the next section.

9.3.2   Characteristics of Manufacturing Investments in the Post-accession Period

The taxonomy of foreign subsidiaries will be used to analyse the biggest FDI projects in manufacturing recorded during the period 1986–9.

FDI statistics formerly published by the Foreign Investment Institute (and later by the Institute for Foreign Trade) included a specific reference to the biggest FDI projects, whose amount exceeded 200 million escudos. They provided, for each project, information on the foreign investors responsible, the expected value of FDI and the industry of investment. This source identified 89 manufacturing FDI projects in 1986–9. They correspond to less than 5 per cent of the total number of FDI projects recorded in that period, but reached over 75 per cent of the value of FDI in manufacturing.

Further information on these 89 projects was collected from several sources, including company reports, press articles and interviews with executives. It was thus possible to get a picture of the characteristics of most projects and sponsoring firms, to classify projects according to our taxonomy.

Each investment was classified under one of the relevant types of subsidiary.[3] Projects aimed at the exploitation and processing of natural resources were classified as resource-based affiliates, irrespective of their export orientation; several projects in food processing (canned fish, for instance), wood and cork, paper and pulp and non-metallic minerals were included under this heading. All the remaining projects whose export forecasts were below 50 per cent of total turn-over were classified as domestic-market orientated manufacturers. Finally, export-orientated projects (the remainder) were ascribed to one of the three export-driven types (direct manufacturing platform, integrated manufacturer and product specialist), bearing in mind its characteristics, in terms of intra-firm trade and the degree of autonomy and role of the subsidiary. None of the projects studied could be classified as a strategic major. The outcome of this exercise is presented on Table 9.3, where the FDI values of the 89 projects are broken down by type of subsidiary and manufacturing branch.

The procedure followed deserves two further remarks. First, it is recognized that FDI values are not necessarily the best indicator of project size and relevance. Furthermore, the definition of an investment minimum may lead to the under-representation of industries with lower fixed capital requirements, such as clothing and footwear. In spite of these difficulties, we think that the high coverage of our sample (accounting for at least 60 per cent of the total FDI amount in every two-digit ISIC industry) provides a good picture of the main features of FDI inflow in Portugal for 1986–9. The second remark relates to the fact that it would be better to classify plants or business units instead of subsidiaries, as we did. Unfortunately, the statistical data available concerned subsidiaries and did not permit a plant-level analysis. The bias due to the use of a subsidiary-type analysis is, however, small, because most foreign subsidiaries in Portugal have one plant only; those that have several plants manufacturing products whose export content differs are exceptions and, in these cases, additional information was sought to identify project characteristics more specifically.

The analysis of Table 9.3, together with the qualitative information obtained on the mode of foreign entry (by greenfield investment, acquisition or reinvestment) and on corporate investment strategies, suggests the following observations:

(a) *Export-orientated investments predominate over domestic market-orientated ones.* Almost two-thirds of the total value of FDI of our sample was due to export-orientated subsidiaries (resource-based, direct manufacturing platforms, integrated manufacturers and product specialists). This export emphasis was, however, mostly due to two very large (by Portuguese standards) integrated manufacturer investments in the automotive sector: one for producing car radios, under-

Table 9.3 Pattern of FDI in manufacturing (1986–9)

	Domestic market orientated manuf.	Resource based affiliates	Integrated manufacturers	Manufacturing platforms	Product specialists	Amount (10⁶ esc)	%
Food, drink & tobacco	12,462	6,578	–	–	–	19,040	15.2
Textiles, clothing & footwear	–	–	3,241	1,650	–	4,891	3.9
Wood & cork	–	2,995	–	–	–	2,995	2.4
Paper, printing & publishing	2,748	9,995	–	–	–	12,743	10.1
Chemicals	12,072	–	968	–	246	13,286	10.6
Non-metallic minerals	8,268	5280	–	–	–	13,548	10.8
Basic metals	–	–	870	–	–	870	0.9
Metal products, machinery & transport equipment	9,786	–	47,409	–	–	57,195	45.7
Other manufacturing	–	–	600	–	–	600	0.5
Total: Amount	45,336	24,848	53,088	1,650	246	12,5168	100
%	36.2	19.9	42.4	1.3	0.2		

Source: Own calculations, based on data provided by IIE and ICEP.

taken by Ford; and another by General Motors to manufacture ignition systems. Both generated high levels of employment.

(b) *Portugal is a manufacturing location that offers advantages for Europe-wide or global integration strategies.* Again, the two big automotive investments provide illustratious in this respect. Portugal simultaneously provided low production costs and generous investment incentives. The evidence available suggests that these investments may correspond to a qualitative leap forward *vis-à-vis* the traditional pattern of integrated manufacturers in Portugal, bearing in mind their higher technological requirements. However, much remains to be seen as to the extent of the linkages to be established with domestic component suppliers.

As a rule, the exploitation of wage gaps was one of the main incentives behind the setting up of integrated manufacturers. Portugal's EC accession, together with the prospects for the European single market, create the possibility of a better matching of regional and corporate integration. This generated a movement towards the establishment of labour-intensive (but not skill-demanding) activities to supply the European market, where non-EC investors have played a significant role (clothing, wire harnesses).

Another interesting feature of FDI was the integration of former contractual partners (namely licensees) into hierarchies; this happened mainly in fabricated metal products and non-electrical machinery. The removal of tariff barriers due to EC accession reduced the incentive for foreign firms to undertake licensing, and significantly increased the competitive pressures faced by the former Portuguese licensees; these problems were in some instances compounded by financial problems and the lack of management capacity. Foreign firms were mainly attracted by the tradition, skills and wages of the Portuguese workforce and by their mastery of current, non-sophisticated technologies. Former Portuguese licensees were allocated the manufacturing of standardized or medium-technology-intensive products; in some cases the manufacturing of such products in the major industrialized countries was discontinued and these production lines were transferred to Portugal, as happened in the case of the manufacture of water boilers by a division of a large German multinational.

The simultaneous accession to the EC of Portugal and Spain generated a strong upsurge in intra-Iberian intra-firm trade. In fact, multinational firms have been eager to exploit the possibilities for plant specialization within the Iberian Peninsula, especially in the automotive sector. In this regard, it is worth mentioning the assignment of 'Iberian mandates' for the production and marketing of some lines of domestic white-goods to the Portuguese affiliates of two Italian firms. This move was again stimulated by lower wages as an instrument for improving competitiveness in an industry where price competition is increasingly fierce.

(c)　*Investments in resource-based affiliates were clustered around three axes: sea, forestry and non-metallic minerals.* Canned-fish manufacturers were one of the main acquisition targets by foreign investors, especially from Spain and non-European countries (the United States and Kuwait). The interest of foreign firms in Portugal's forestry assets was felt well before EC accession, but regional integration appears to have provided a new impetus to investments in wood processing and wood articles. This also applies to the biggest operation undertaken in the 1980s: the purchase by Wiggins Teape of a share in Soporcel (paper pulp). The non-metallic minerals industry was, until the mid–1980s, scarcely penetrated by foreign capital. Since then investments have boomed, acquisitions being the preferred mode of entry. French firms were the most active, but Spanish and Kuwaiti investments were also substantial.

(d)　*Domestic-market orientated manufacturers still accounted for a significant share in total FDI.* Although export-orientated affiliates took the lead, the Portuguese domestic market also had some appeal for foreign investors. The main reasons for this were probably to take advantage of the opportunities opened up by growing demand, both in volume and sophistication; and to strengthen their presence in a market that is no longer marginal but, rather, a part of an increasingly integrated EC market. Investments were concentrated in four industries: food and drink; chemicals; metal products, machinery and transportation equipment; and non-metallic minerals.

(e)　*The near-absence of investments in product specialists and strategic majors.* Portuguese subsidiaries usually have very limited roles, mostly restricted to manufacturing, and marketing in the domestic market. Most exports are intra-group or closely controlled by international or regional marketing divisions, except in the case of a few resource-based affiliates. Technological development activities by Portuguese subsidiaries are also weak, despite a few examples of new product development. Therefore those subsidiaries are mostly 'implementers', enjoying limited autonomy.

9.4 THE SINGLE MARKET AND THE FUTURE OF INWARD FDI

9.4.1 The Single Market and International Investment

It is widely acknowledged that regional integration stimulates corporate integration (Dunning and Robson, 1987). The removal of barriers to the free movement of goods, services, capital and people within the EC will generate increased possibilities for matching firms with ownership advantages, which are internationally mobile, with country factor endowments and characterized by higher 'immobility' – although it should be remarked that the single market drive will also contribute to the reduction of the spatial 'immobility' of some factors.

The building-up of the Community's internal market has already largely impacted upon firms' strategies and investment decisions (UNCTC, 1990). The wave of mergers and acquisitions within Europe and the boom in inter-firm co-operation agreements are to some extent due to 'preparing for 1992'.

As Buigues and Jacquemin (1988) have shown, the single market will not affect all industries in the same way. Based on the Boston Consulting Group matrix of competitive systems, these authors concluded that specialized and volume competitive environments are the most likely to be influenced by the single market. On the other hand, an enlarged market does not mean that national or local markets will completely lose their attraction to international investors. Besides technological and organizational limitations to plant scale, there are socio-cultural (consumer patterns and preferences) and product-specific factors (transportation costs, perishability of goods) that militate against a complete centralization of production. Even in these cases the single market may have an impact, by providing an impetus to new patterns of intra-EC regional manufacturing and marketing integration that may not exactly fit with national borders.

The 1992 programme will have various effects on corporate strategies. These will not be confined to rationalization and restructuring by firms that already own several manufacturing affiliates throughout the Community. Smaller national firms, based in the various EC member countries, will be increasingly forced to 'think European'. And non-EC-based companies will react by setting up manufacturing facilities within the EC, to profit, as insiders, from the single market (Crespy, 1990; Young, McDermott and Dunlop, 1990; Ozawa, 1990). It may be argued that multinational firms of non-EC origin are likely to be among the main beneficiaries of the removal of non-tariff bar-

Table 9.4 Expected trends in investment determinants

Investment determinants	Types of subsidiary						
	MS	DM	MP	RB	IM	PS	SM
Location factors							
*Market size	++ −	++					+
*Market specificity and sophistication	+	++			+	++	++
*Market growth	++	++					
*Natural resources		+		++	+		
*Relative wages		−	−−		−−		
*Availability of skilled (and high-skilled) manpower		+			+	++	++
*Scientific and tec. capacity and dynamics of innovation					+	++	++
*Relative (non-wage) production costs		−	−−		−−	−	
*Setting-up costs		−		−	−	−	

Expected trends in investment determinants

Single market will lead to an enlargement of the market. Its impact will however vary according to the industries. Possible exploitation of regional markets (Iberian, Southern Europe). Domestic market will continue to be the most relevant for fragmented-environment industries.

Decline in Portuguese market specificity, due to harmonization of consumption patterns and European standards. Increased sophistication of domestic demand. The main demand centres, with higher sophistication and requiring stronger demand–design–production–marketing interaction will continue to be located in central, industrialized EC areas.

Domestic market is expected to show growth rates higher than EC average.

Increased interest in exploiting Portugal's endowment in natural resources. Control of main sources by big multinational firms.

Portuguese nominal wages will gradually approach EC average. Significant gaps will remain in the short/medium term, so that relative wages will continue to be among the leading motives to interest in Portugal. In parallel the trend towards the decline of direct labour costs in overall product's value will continue to hold.

Investments have been made in training, although the weakness in intermediate managers stemming from the closing of technical education in the 1970s still constitute a hindrance for Portugal; it is likely that its negative effects will gradually be less significant. The single market, increasing labour mobility, may generate some migration of skilled people and even a 'brain drain'. As a whole, it is expected that Portugal's weakness in skilled manpower might be reduced.

Despite the efforts now underway (including namely PEDIP and CIÊNCIA programmes) Portugal will show, in the short to medium term, a weak S&T infrastructure compared to most of her EC partners, with the exception of a few restricted excellency areas. Innovative capacity of domestic firms will probably remain limited. These factors will seriously hinder the establishment, or development, of a significant number of product specialists and strategic majors.

The single market, together with Portugal's development prospects, is likely to lead to closing the gap in comparative costs of production. However, except in industries with strong energy requirements, Portugal's costs will remain lower than EC average in the years to come.

The costs of setting up a manufacturing plant in Portugal, namely real-estate and construction costs are lower in Portugal than in other EC countries, although some traditional industrial areas are becoming crowded. The costs of creating a firm in Portugal will be gradually reduced, as red tape is cut down.

Investment determinants	Types of subsidiary						
	MS	DM	MP	RB	IM	PS	SM
*Physical infra-struct.		+	+		++	++	++
*Psychic distance	−−	−−			−	−	−+
*Tariff and non-tariff barriers to trade	−−	++	−−	−	−−	−−	
*Relative transportation costs	−−	++	−−	−	−−	−−	
*Public sourcing policies	+	++			+	+	+
*Investment incentives		+	++	+	++	++	
Ownership and internalization factors *Technological/marketing advantages	++	++	+	++	++	++	++
*Product-service marketing and after-sales service	++	++				++	

Expected trends in investment determinants

Strong investments are being undertaken, with the support of EC structural funds, especially in the areas of communications (roads and ports) and telecommunications. This is not enough, however, fully to bridge the gap between Portugal and industrialized EC countries (but Portugal might enjoy some advantages when compared to other peripheral economies).

Psychic distance has already been substantially reduced with Portugal's EC accession and will be further diminished as a result of the single market; investors' perception of the risk of investing in Portugal is declining. This phenomenon will have a positive effect on the establishment of replica affiliates and marketing satellites and will, on the other hand, contribute to differentiate Portugal from non-EC locations.

The elimination of tariff and especially non-tariff barriers to trade is at the heart of the single market programme. It is not realistic to expect, however, that all non-tariff barriers will be removed by the end of 1992. For non-EC based firms, particularly from those without significant manufacturing activities within EC, direct investment in one or several EC countries may be envisaged as a way to benefit fully from the internal market.

Transportation costs will be reduced due to the elimination (or alleviation) of border controls and the standardization of transport regulations within EC. Geographic location may, however, be a negative point for Portugal.

The single market will entail a substantial reduction in the freedom of national authorities to privilege domestic suppliers and thereby influence investment decisions. The enlargement of the market associated with the reduced fragmentation may stimulate the establishment of non-EC firms (as it happened with Brazilian construction firms).

In recent years Portugal has largely drawn upon investment incentives (namely cash grants) to attract foreign investors. The reform of structural funds to take place after 1992 may limit the availability of funds for incentives. Intra-EC competition to attract FDI will be increasingly fierce, and East European countries are entering the game.

Strengthening of corporate research and innovation effort, both in-house and through inter-firm co-operation. Technology (and trade-mark) driven acquisitions are likely to continue, although the pace may gradually slow down. EC R&D and technology policies will continue to bet on the development of 'European champions' to meet the Triadic challenge.

Development of complex products (product-system) with high service values, adapted to specific demands. After-sales service may be an important factor in product differentiation, particularly in 'specialized' competitive environments.

Investment determinants	Types of subsidiary						
	MS	DM	MP	RB	IM	PS	SM
*Oligopolistic market structures	+	++	+	++	+	++	++
*Scale and scope economies	++	——	++	+	++	++	+
*Economies of international segmentation and vertical integration of production		——	++	++	++	+	++
*Management control	+	+	++	++	++	++	+
*Contractual costs (partner search and negotiation)	+	++	++	++	++		
*Risks of contractual sourcing	++	++	++	++	++	++	++

Notes

(1) MS: Marketing satellite; DM: Domestic market orientated manufacturer; MP: Manufacturing platform; RB: Resource-based affiliate; IM: Integrated manufacturer; PS: Product specialist; SM: Strategic major

(2) ++ denotes a strong and direct relationship between the investment factor and the type of subsidiary concerned (+ denotes a less-strong relationship)
—— denotes a strong and negative relationship between the investment factor and the type of subsidiary concerned (− denotes a less-strong relationship).

Expected trends in investment determinants

The single market will generate a further oligopolization of market structures, with the swallowing of some former 'national champions'. Portugal will also suffer from this phenomenon, domestic firms being taken over by multinationals to strengthen their EC-wide base.

The single market will provide firms with a better environment to profit from economies of scale and scope. The overall trend towards flexible manufacturing and automation may in some ways reduce the importance of economies of scale in the years to come.

In those industries where the process of production may be segmented in different stages, the single market will further facilitate an EC-wide rationalization of production to profit fully from matching ownership specific advantages (internationally mobile) with relatively 'immobile' country endowments in factors of production. This will provide a new impetus mainly to integrated-manufacturer-type of subsidiaries, leading, on the other hand, to divestments.

Strengthening of intra-firm co-ordination at the European level. Internationalization of activities formerly developed on a contractual basis. Decline in the autonomy of affiliates, with the exception of product specialists and strategic majors.

Contractual searching costs will be reduced due to the removal of circulation barriers, the reduced psychic distance among EC countries and regions and the efforts of EC authorities to promote inter-firm collaboration, namely, through the establishment of EC networks. However, the increased difficulties in discriminating contracts by market may hinder negotiation. Furthermore, market enlargement and uniformization reduces the risks of going it alone.

This kind of risk is somewhat reduced due to the increased freedom of product circulation within EC and legal harmonization and standardization. Risks of transactional nature will however remain.

riers, since they have less institutional impediments in the way of locating their operations in a fashion better-suited to the new market conditions (Dunning, 1989; Dunning and Cantwell, 1991).

In overall terms, the single market programme might be expected to lead to a shift of FDI to the EC from other developed, and possibly even from developing countries (UNCTC, 1990). It is likely to foster the development of 'a closer network of manufacturing and service-based sectors across national boundaries (. . .) in which multinationals from within and outside the Community are the key players, but within which will be incorporated a host of smaller and more specialised firms' (Dunning, 1989).

9.4.2　Expected Trends in the Determinants of FDI in Portugal

Against the background provided above, what is the likely pattern of FDI in Portugal in the years to come and how will it interact with the domestic industrial fabric? To answer this question, we begin with an examination of the expected impact of the single market on the determinants of FDI inflow into Portugal, bearing in mind the taxonomy of subsidiary roles developed above.

Investment determinants can be organized in two groups: location factors and firm-specific or ownership/internalization factors (Dunning, 1988). Their relevance for each type of subsidiary was assessed. Finally, trends in these determinants were forecast, taking into account the future development of the single market and other environmental changes, at both Portuguese and international levels.

The main conclusions are summarized in Table 9.4. It suggests some observations on a few themes: domestic market appeal, psychic distance, the relationship between wages and worker skills, the use of investment incentives, the challenge of East European countries, and intra-firm co-ordination.

The strengthening of EC integration will entail a decline in the importance of Portugal's domestic market as a locational attraction to investment: firms will try instead to maximize economies of scale through concentration of their manufacturing activities (Buckley and Artisien, 1987). Furthermore, the domestic market is small, with low levels of sophistication and specificity. However, other factors need to be taken into consideration: strong market-growth prospects (as incomes increase); the need to integrate Portugal into European distribution networks; the decline in risk evaluations; and the scope for using Portugal as a platform to supply the whole Iberian market.

Statistical data show that domestic-market orientated manufacturers still accounted for a significant share of inward FDI in the 1986–9 period. Putting these arguments together, it seems that this kind of investment will continue to develop progressively, at least in the next few years.

Psychic distance is widely acknowledged as a major factor in investment decisions, especially for smaller firms in the initial phases of internationalization. Portugal's accession to the EC, together with the single market programme, gave the country a new image as a member of the 'Club of 12', thereby reducing the barriers to investment. EC membership is also a significant advantage for Portugal when facing the challenge of Eastern European countries courting foreign investors.

Technological development, and the success of other measures to raise company productivity, led to a decline in the share of direct labour costs in firms' value chains. The introduction of information technologies in manufacturing and new, more-integrated, innovation management systems, where synergies between R&D and production operations are stronger, generated in some industries a centralization of investments in the more industrialized countries.

These developments, compounded by a trend towards reducing wage differences throughout the Community, might generate a decline in the importance of wage levels in motivating investment. However, wage gaps will remain for a long time and the opportunities for Community-wide rationalization of multinational activities are increased by the internal market, so that investments in export-orientated subsidiaries will continue to develop, as the latest figures show. This entails a potential danger: the specialization of Portugal in low-skill, intensive, automation-resilient industries such as clothing, footwear and wire harness manufacturing. However, recent trends in the pattern of FDI suggest that the likelihood of such a danger has been reduced. In fact, the biggest FDI projects in the last three years have been concentrated in the automotive industry, including a huge investment by Ford and Volkswagen to manufacture in Portugal a new multi-purpose vehicle.[4] Although these projects were attracted by low wage costs and high financial incentives granted, their technological requirements are well above the average for FDI ventures in Portugal and this may be interpreted as the start of a qualitative upgrading of the foreign-owned sector. Despite this positive development, it is clear that there is a strong need for investments in infrastructure (going beyond improvements to the road system) to cope with the requirements of worldwide manufacturing networks, and investment in human resources to attract more skill-demanding industries.

In recent years Portugal used financial incentives widely to attract FDI. Investments in the automotive industry by Ford, General Motors and Ford/Volkswagen were heavily subsidized, since inter-country (or inter-regional) competition to get those projects was fierce. For instance, the huge Ford/Volkswagen project was granted incentives of 90 billion escudos, corresponding to around 20 per cent of the investment; cash grants provided to Ford Electronics and Delco Remy (General Motors) accounted for 41 per cent and 31 per cent, respectively, of the amount of planned investments. Such a policy was possible due to the substantial value of funds transferred to Portugal from the EC. However, the reform of EC structural funds which is planned after 1992 may limit the availability of funds for incentives. The use of investment incentives by the Portuguese authorities to attract foreign investors is therefore likely to decline in the future.

The opening-up of Eastern Europe (namely Hungary, Czechoslovakia and Poland) may lead to a diversion of international investments towards those countries. Their markets are eager for Western products. They have relatively skilled labour earning low wages. They are not far from the more-developed EC areas and may be granted privileged trade arrangements and EC funds that might be used to attract export-orientated investments. However, these countries also face serious difficulties. They are undergoing a period of political, institutional, economic and social instability that will take some time to resolve; risk assessment, especially for export-orientated investments, will be high, thereby discouraging investment decisions. Furthermore, they lack the infrastructures needed to attract the more technology-demanding projects.

Taking all these factors into account, it is our contention that Eastern Europe will not present, at least in the short to medium term, a serious challenge to the investment position of Portugal. As a matter of fact, Portugal enjoys significant advantages: a well-established market economy, EC membership, better infrastructures, a more highly developed domestic business tradition and social fabric, and a lower risk investment location. Portugal's main competitors will continue to be other less-developed areas within the Community.

The single market will also impact upon the conditions for intrafirm co-ordination: as was argued above, regional and corporate integration go in parallel. The single market is likely to strengthen inter-affiliate co-ordination, at least at a European level. The increase in central co-ordination will be higher for domestic-market orientated manufacturers that today enjoy relative independence (Martinez and Jarillo, 1988), but will be felt by all types of affiliate. This decline in subsidiary autonomy will also restrict the scope for nationally controlled or sponsored interaction between foreign affiliates and indigenous firms.

9.4.3 The Possible Pattern of FDI in the future

After assessing the possible trends in the determination of investment, we are now better equipped to answer the question raised at the beginning of the last section.

For reasons explained above, the analysis is not restricted to new investments but will encompass the foreseeable changes in existing subsidiaries as well. Trends in the investments of three different types of foreign company may be distinguished: (a) firms already established in Portugal; (b) firms without investments in Portugal, but with relevant manufacturing locations in the EC; and (c) non-EC-based firms without a significant manufacturing presence within the Community.[5]

Before entering into the heart of the matter, a word of caution is needed. FDI growth rates may be strongly influenced by the sporadic occurrence of very big projects, like the Ford/Volkswagen investment whose value is estimated to reach 450 billion escudos, a figure well above total FDI inflow for 1989. The occurrence of this kind of project cannot be forecast, so that our analysis will be restricted to 'current' projects, leaving aside these exceptionally large investments. It must be borne in mind, however, that larger projects may have a powerful 'dragging' effect, attracting a constellation of foreign suppliers and sub-contractors.

Our main conclusion is that, in general, FDI inflow in Portugal will continue to grow significantly, especially in the next couple of years. Afterwards, a slowdown in growth rates may occur, due to the combined influence of several effects: less funds for investment incentives; stronger competition (including competition from Eastern Europe); an increase in domestic national wages; and the achievement of the integration of Portugal into multinational companies' EC networks.

The analysis suggests that all types of subsidiaries are likely to increase in number in the short term. However, integrated manufacturers clearly appear to be the group with the greatest growth potential. In recent years the biggest foreign investments have been of this kind, and there are reasons to believe that this will continue to be true in the future, since Portugal offers significant advantages as a manufacturing location in the context of global or European strategies.

Table 9.5 *Future patterns of FDI in Portugal*

Type of subsidiary	Firms already established in Portugal	Firms with a relevant EC manufacturing base, but not established in Portugal	Firms not established in Portugal and without a relevant EC manufacturing base
Marketing satellite	*Expansion of existing firms. Strengthening of intra-firm co-ordination, with reduced autonomy. Launching of new products. »'Replica' affiliates: profiting from market growth. »»»Integrated manufacturer: profiting from attractive manufacturing conditions in the country.	**Strong trend in setting up marketing satellites to benefit from the decline of barriers to trade and psychic distance and to tap a growing market. (Those subsidiaries may later evolve to have manufacturing activities in Portugal.)	*Moderate movement in setting up marketing satellites (Japanese firms are likely to be the most active).
Domestic-market orientated manuf.	*Moderate growth. Strengthening of intra-firm coordination. Struggle towards increasing market shares, *inter alia* through taking over existing domestic competitors. Diversification and sophistication of product range (partly imported). »»»Marketing satellite: closure of manufacturing facilities to profit from economies of scale, Portuguese market being fully supplied through imports »»»Integrated manufacturer: particularly product specialization.	**Strong growth, as a consequence of internationalization of European SMEs and of increased psychic proximity. Entry may take place through acquisitions.	*The investment in new 'replica' affiliates aimed at supplying the Portuguese market only will be limited.

Type of subsidiary	Firms already established in Portugal	Firms with a relevant EC manufacturing base, but not established in Portugal	Firms not established in Portugal and without a relevant EC manufacturing base
Manufacturing platform	*Expansion in the short term, followed by a progressive slowing down. »»Integrated manufacturer: specialization products where low skilled labour costs account for a high share in total cost. »»Divestments, especially by electrical appliances and electronics firms (in a first phase) and by clothing and footwear firms (in the medium term). The size of divestments will depend on relative wages and technological trends.	*Moderate growth in new subsidiaries in clothing (in the short term). In the medium term growth rates will tend to decline. (Again the size of this kind of investment will be dependent on relative wages and technological developments, namely automation).	*Investments are likely to be low, except for EFTA-based firms.
Resource based affiliates	**Strong expansion, mainly through external growth (taking over domestic firms). Possibility of evolution of a few subsidiaries, in areas where Portugal has significant resource endowments, towards product specialists.	**Strong growth. Those groups without a presence in Portugal may invest, mainly through acquisitions, to get a hold in the resource field. Main target sectors might be food industries, non-metallic minerals, wood and cork, and mining.	**Strong growth, likely to be higher than for firms not established in Portugal, but with a relevant EC-base (see recent investments by Finnish firms).
Integrated manufacturer	***Very strong growth, mainly through setting up new production facilities (see, for instance, the new investments by Ford and General Motors and the expansion of Yazaky-Saltano). Possible up-grading of existing activities. Trend towards further integration of this kind of affiliates into	**Strong growth. The single market generates new opportunities for corporate integration and rationalized manufacturing strategies at EC-wide or regional levels, namely within the Iberian Peninsula.	***Very strong movement towards setting up EC affiliates to become insiders in what they perceive as 'fortress Europe'. Such a movement may have 3 main forms: (a) use of Portugal as a manufacturing basis to

Type of subsidiary	Firms already established in Portugal	Firms with a relevant EC manufacturing base, but not established in Portugal	Firms not established in Portugal and without a relevant EC manufacturing base
	corporate networks, thus reducing the scope of locally-decided subcontracting and linkage creating. Likely restructuration of activities in the context of European-wide rationalization decisions. »Product specialist: such a movement will remain limited in the short term. »Divestment: as a consequence of EC or global restructuring of activities and of wage increases.		penetrate EC markets; (b) integration of (future) Portuguese affiliates in the building-up of EC manufacturing networks; and (c) internationalization of suppliers (sub-contractors) following previous moves by their main clients. The prospects for new integrated manufacturers, especially from Japan, will generate a fierce competition among EC countries (and regions) to attract them.
Product specialist	*There are very few product specialists. Future cases of evolution of other types of subsidiaries (mainly resource-based and integrated manufacturers) may be envisaged, but as a whole they will remain limited.	*The ex-novo setting up of product specialists is not probable. Only in a few cases might the assignment of Iberian (or Southern Europe) product mandates – with limited R&D activities – be envisaged.	*The setting-up of product specialists is unlikely. The only exception might come from Brazilian firms.
Strategic majors	The evolution of other types of subsidiaries towards strategic majors has a very low probability, since Portuguese environment will remain strategically unimportant.	The setting-up of the strategic majors in Portugal is not foreseeable in the short/medium term.	The setting-up of strategic majors in Portugal is not foreseeable in the short/medium term.

Notes
*** Growth prospects range from *** (very strong) to * (moderate).
»» denotes the probability of a strong movement of transition towards other types of subsidiary (» denotes a less important movement).

A more-detailed presentation of the forecasts, by type of subsidiary and characteristics of investing firms, can be found in Table 9.5. A brief comment on the trends identified for each type of subsidiary follows.

Marketing satellites
The number of affiliates of this type is likely to grow as a response to the increase in the size and sophistication of domestic demand. Firms that already have a significant European base will take advantage of the removal of non-tariff barriers by setting up subsidiaries in Portugal to market goods manufactured elsewhere in the Community; and the expansion in franchising operations recorded in 1986–91 may continue. The single market programme is encouraging non-EC-based firms to build a stronger foothold in the Community, undertaking some manufacturing activities there. These firms will endeavour to spread their marketing channels across the EC and they may therefore set up marketing satellites in Portugal. Previously established affiliates are likely to expand further, but more moderately than in the past, since macroeconomic projections suggest a slowdown in domestic demand.

Manufacturing platforms
The evolution of investments of this type appears to be more dependent on relative wage trends and on technological innovation than on the single market. As the manager of a German subsidiary put it, '1992 already exists for us' (Simões, 1989).

In the short to medium term, the increased freedom in the movement of goods, and especially the continuation of a wage gap between Portugal and her more-industrialized EC partners is likely to lead to the setting up of new direct manufacturing platform subsidiaries. This move will take place mostly in the context of defensive strategies by firms in automation-resilient industries, faced with increased competition from the NICs; EC- and EFTA-based companies appear to be the most likely promoters of such investments. With regard to affiliates of this kind already established in the country, some growth may be also envisaged in the short term, since many of them, especially in footwear and clothing, were set up recently.

The likely reduction in the gap in nominal wages between Portugal and the Community; the decline in the pool of unskilled local labour; the enhancement in the investment climate of Eastern Europe; and technological developments may lead, in the medium term, to a slowdown, or even a decline, in the setting-up of manufacturing platforms in Portugal, and to divestment by established firms. Firms may close existing plants, transferring the production towards low-wage Mediterranean countries or Eastern Europe (clothing and footwear) or towards the home countries of the parent companies (especially in the electrical and electronics industries). A shift in the role of existing affiliates from manufacturing platforms to integrated manufacturers, specializing in standard, low value added products, might also be envisaged – although plain divestment decisions seem more likely.

Domestic-market orientated manufacturers
It was shown above that, despite the single market, the Portuguese domestic market will retain some appeal for the setting-up and development of manufacturing subsidiaries.

New investments (green-field or acquisitions) will possibly be undertaken mainly by medium-sized European firms specialized in their own market niches. Some integration of former contractual partners into hierarchies may also occur as contracts reach their term; this process is likely, however, to run its course eventually.

Existing affiliates will continue to expand, though at a slower pace than in 1986–9, due to the slower growth expected in domestic demand. Domestic-market orientated manufacturers will be more tightly integrated into their multinational groups, as a consequence of the drive towards more uniform products and marketing approaches throughout the Community. The expansion of existing firms will probably take two principal forms: external growth, by taking over Portuguese competitors as a means of increasing market shares; and the widening of product ranges, simultaneously promoting and responding to a more-sophisticated demand.

In contrast, the removal of non-tariff barriers to trade and the progressive harmonization of consumption patterns may generate an intra-EC concentration of manufacturing activity, leading as a consequence to the transformation of domestic-market orientated manufacturers into marketing satellites. Although this has not happened so far to any significant extent,[6] it may do so in future. Another possible evolution is a shift towards rationalized manufacturers, particularly in the context of trans-European (or Iberian) product-specialization strategies. This restructuring may have some advantages from the Portuguese standpoint: it avoids the closure of plants, stimulates exports (to be set against increased imports) and may facilitate the formation of potential future product-specialist subsidiaries. On the other hand it is not without drawbacks: the lower level of industrialization of Portugal together with her lower wages may result in the specialization of Portuguese subsidiaries in mature, standardized products, with lower quality and manufacturing skill requirements.

Resource-based affiliates
Investments in resource-based affiliates are likely to sustain their current growth. The configuration of activities to be undertaken in Portugal will be mainly influenced by international competition and the interrelationships between oligopolists. Government pressures and incentives may also play a role either in attracting investments or in preventing undesired moves.

Existing subsidiaries are expected to grow through: (a) the strengthening of existing business lines, expanding present activities and the control over resources (in many cases by taking-over domestic firms) and/or (b) diversification of their range of activities. In a few cases there is a trend towards increased local processing of raw materials in the country, and engaging in more value-added activities; however, as a rule, the more skill-demanding and value-added-generating production stages are not located in Portugal. An evolution of resource-based affiliates towards product specialists might be envisaged, particularly in those cases where Portugal has significant and specific resource endowments – as in the case of wine. However, this possibility appears to be constrained by two factors: the lack of relevant domestic R&D infrastructure and technological capabilities, and the strategies of production chain segmentation and R&D concentration followed by resource-based multinationals.

New investments will continue to occur. Acquisitions will be the preferred route (sometimes the only one available) to control resources and challenge the position held by incumbent competitors; joint ventures may also be a way to get access to limited resources. Investments will mostly be undertaken by non-EC firms, since the most important EC resource-based multinationals are already present in Portugal. Data on the second half of the 1980s show the interest of Japanese, Arab and Finnish groups in these sectors.

Integrated manufacturers
Integrated manufacturers are undoubtedly the leading type of FDI establishment in manufacturing industry, as is clearly shown by the figures provided in the last section. Recent developments, particularly the Ford/Volkswagen investment to manufacture a new multi-purpose vehicle, have strengthened existing trends. The building-up of the single market creates improved conditions for this type of investment and opens up new opportunities for intra-Community integration of

manufacturing activities for both European and non-European multinationals.[7]

The development of integrated manufacturers in Portugal seems to
depend on four factors. First, technological innovation, namely, the
spreading of automation and robotics to further stages of production,
and the trend towards a reduction in the share of wages in cost
structures. Secondly, the new possibilities for the segmentation of
production processes and the balancing between central co-ordination,
production process logistics, and the dispersion of manufacturing sites
and marketing requirements (van Tulder, Ruygrok and Baven, 1991).
Thirdly, the trends in oligopolistic competition and the key factors
influencing firms' competitive advantage. Fourthly, Portugal's assets
as an investment location. These assets need to be envisaged in comparative terms (as against alternative locations) and go beyond relative
wage levels to include, for instance, infrastructural conditions, skilled
labour availability and industrial services. Furthermore, investment
incentives play a significant role in shaping firms' choices between
competitive locations; in recent years cash grants have been widely
used by the Portuguese authorities to attract FDI projects.

The likely increase in nominal wages may lead to several divestments. But it may also entail a technological upgrading and a higher
skill content in manufacturing activities.[8] This movement will, of
course, depend on environmental and infrastructural (physical and
human) conditions and on the provision of investment incentives to
reduce switching costs.

It seems likely that the biggest investments in this type of subsidiary
will be undertaken by firms already established in the country (but
not necessarily as extensions of existing activities, as the recent investments by Ford and General Motors show) and by firms without a
relevant manufacturing base within EC. In this latter case investments
may stem from three basic motives: (a) the use of Portugal as a
manufacturing base to penetrate the EC market, profiting from relatively low wage-levels and cultural and psychic proximity (Brazil) or
geographical complementarity (Scandinavian firms); (b) the building-
up of EC-wide manufacturing networks in the context of product or
process specialization strategies, as happened with American firms in
the 1950s and '60s, who may be followed by Japanese firms in the
1990s to respond to the challenge of the single market; and (c) the
internationalization of subcontractors following previous moves by
their main clients, especially in the automotive, electronics and electrical machinery industries where client-supplier links are strong and a
significant share of components is contracted out (a good example is

the successful Yazaki–Saltano joint venture that Ozawa (1990) refers to in his analysis of Japanese multinationals and 1992).

The strengthening of European integration does not *ipso facto* entail a significant change in the technological capability of integrated manufacturers. Analysis of the largest investments undertaken in the last two years suggests a significant upgrading in the technological content of projects; however, such projects were given substantial incentives (non-reimbursable cash grants) and it is unclear whether linkages with domestic counterparts to stimulate technology diffusion were given enough consideration. The evidence available seems to support the contention that in future integrated manufacturers will be more technology-intensive than in the past, but it cannot be taken for granted that stronger links with domestic firms will result.

Product specialists and strategic majors
In the short to medium term, the setting-up in Portugal of these types of affiliates will remain very limited. The weakness of Portuguese scientific and technological infrastructure and industrial fabric is a serious hurdle to the feasibility of a policy aimed at attracting this type of subsidiary. In the foreseeable future product specialists may arise more as a consequence of the evolution of resource-based affiliates and integrated manufacturers than through their establishment as *ex-novo* affiliates. With regard to strategic majors, the probability of occurrence is even smaller. Borrowing Bartlett and Ghoshal's (1990) words, the 'strategic importance' of the Portuguese environment is too low to host this kind of subsidiary.

9.4.4   The Interaction Between FDI and Indigenous Firms

Having sketched probable developments in the general pattern of manufacturing FDI in Portugal, a more specific issue will be now addressed: the interaction between FDI and indigenous firms. The taxonomy of subsidiaries presented above constitutes the reference point.

Unfortunately, there are very few empirical studies of the role of FDI in Portugal's technological development. One study, commissioned by the Ministry of Industry and Energy, on the technological profile of a sample of 23 majority-owned foreign affiliates concluded that the prevailing profile is characterized by 'an "off-shore" positioning, taking advantage of low cost labour'.[9] This is, in our opinion, an overstated conclusion, presumably influenced by the sample's composition. It is true that most manufacturing platforms and some integrated manufacturers are 'enclave-type' subsidiaries, fully dependent on the parent company headquarters and having little relationship with the local environment. In spite of this, we think that an overall assessment of the matter leads to a more positive judgement: foreign investment has, in general, played a positive role as a vehicle for technology inflow (Simões, 1987). We agree, however, that things could have been much better: the record of interaction between FDI and domestic manufacturing and scientific and technological networks falls below what might be considered desirable. Foreign investors are not the only source of blame for this situation; the weakness of Portugal's industrial and technological fabric, poor management, the technological insufficiencies of domestic firms and inadequate government policies have also played a role.

Additionally, Portuguese firms have generally not participated in the wave of technology-based co-operative agreements that characterized the 1980s. We have commented elsewhere that this finding may be interpreted as indicating that Portuguese companies are still technologically too weak to be regarded as interesting partners for this kind of co-operation (Simões, 1991).

What about the future, though? The first point to stress is that the building-up of the single market, together with the globalization of multinational firms' strategies, is likely to reduce small recipient countries' room for manoeuvre in promoting horizontal and vertical linkages between foreign-owned and domestic firms. In the context of multi-domestic investments and protectionism, national governments could make the setting-up of foreign affiliates conditional on the establishment of linkages with domestic suppliers and on local performance requirements. By the same token, the domestic market might be used by national firms and governments as a bargaining tool in the negotiation of joint ventures and other co-operative arrangements; even for projects with a significant export content, privileged access to the domestic market might play a major role in attracting FDI, as the example of the Renault project in Portugal clearly shows.

But when barriers to trade are lifted and investment strategies become more global, the situation is drastically changed. This puts a further burden on small, technologically weak countries, such as Portugal, to implement policies aimed at fostering the creation of linkages between FDI and domestic firms.

Another probable consequence of the single market will be a further centralization of purchasing decisions at the European level (Martinez and Jarillo, 1988). This process will affect all types of subsidiaries, not only the export-orientated but also the traditionally more independent domestic-market orientated manufacturers.

Taking these factors into account, let us provide some thoughts on the likely interaction between the most common types of manufacturing subsidiaries and the local economic environment in years to come.

The characteristics of manufacturing platforms seriously limit the extent of their linkages with the domestic environment. They are often 'enclave-type' affiliates, whose contribution towards the upgrading of the local industrial fabric is minor: transactions are almost exclusively with companies located abroad; the affiliate's management is fully dependent on the parent company's decisions; and labour is mostly unskilled. The main positive contribution of this kind of investment has been employment generation; and a few demonstration effects in administrative systems and manufacturing procedures. However, Portugal enjoys today a very low unemployment rate, so that the creation of unskilled jobs is not valued highly. Similarly, the scope for demonstration effects is shrinking. In a scenario of increasing labour costs, Portugal will gradually become a less-attractive location for this kind of investment – a development that seems desirable if Portugal wishes to upgrade its image as an investment location.

Domestic-market orientated manufacturers are among the types of subsidiary that exhibit a higher propensity to interact with indigenous firms. Enjoying, in some cases, significant levels of autonomy in decision-making, these subsidiaries have followed an incremental approach towards building-up a reliable network of domestic suppliers. However, the trend towards a further centralization of purchasing at the European level and the likely transformation of some domestic-market orientated manufacturers into integrated manufacturers (specialized in mature, standardized products) will curtail the possibilities for interaction. On the other hand, the likely development of the domestic industrial fabric may work in the opposite direction, generating new opportunities for local sourcing, and in some instances supplying other European affiliates. The outcome of these opposing forces is likely to be a specialization in local sourcing, thereby reducing the density of linkages but increasing the extent of sourcing from selected suppliers.

The interaction between resource-based affiliates and the local environment depends very much on the strategies of foreign multinationals and on the specificity of Portugal's resources. Several such affiliates undertake R&D activities in Portugal, on the development of new trees and winestocks and on the characteristics and applications of minerals; in a few cases these activities were undertaken in co-operation with local research centres. Nevertheless, the scope of these activities has remained limited, and the results are tightly controlled to prevent diffusion. Among recent investments there is an interesting case of a diversified food multinational that set up in Portugal a base for supplying the European canned-fish market; this affiliate was granted some marketing autonomy and looks likely to forge significant domestic linkages.

Integrated manufacturers are probably the more complex case since this designation encompasses a wide range, from 'enclave-type' affiliates to investments considered 'centres of excellence', such as the Philips unit in Ovar which might be classified in its output of certain products as a product specialist.

Technological sophistication of integrated manufacturers is therefore highly variable. Some have significant technological requirements, use the most modern technologies, have large pools of skilled people and have undertaken relevant product-development activities (Simões, 1989). Others, by comparison, are concentrated in low-skill-demanding areas. Taking into account that wage levels are among the main attractions for investment, it comes as no surprise to learn that the latter are much more common than the former. As a rule, R&D activities performed in Portugal, if any, are limited and of little relevance to their respective multinational groups.

In the most recent years there are signs of an upgrading in the technological content of the integrated manufacturers established in Portugal. Recent investments in the automotive industry, namely the Ford/Volkswagen project, already have a significant technological sophistication and will employ a large share of skilled people.

The establishment of linkages between integrated manufacturers and indigenous firms is limited by their very characteristics: being part of European or global networks they are obliged to follow very strict, centrally defined standards. Therefore, linkages with the local industrial and technological fabric are not very strong and take place mainly through component sourcing (including subcontracting), training and co-operative projects with Portuguese research institutions (Simões, 1987).

The trend to centralize purchasing decisions, mentioned earlier, will further restrict the scope for local linkages. Moreover, the current sourcing strategies of multinational firms tend to be shifting from multi-sourcing toward strategic long-term single-sourcing relationships; these save costs and time for the assemblers/purchasers, while they require suppliers to have product development capabilities and to meet short delivery schedules, in return for stronger purchasing guarantees.

The thresholds needed for purchaser-supplier (or main assembler-supplier) linkages are significantly increased, since the requirements placed on suppliers are much higher than they used to be.

This is likely to have a significant impact on the interactions between integrated manufacturers and indigenous firms. Portuguese companies that are suppliers of global or regional networks of MNCs are increasingly facing a dilemma: to grow, strengthening their manufacturing and product-development capabilities, and to internationalize their operations – or to give up. On the other hand, policies aimed at attracting integrated manufacturers should be given a wide scope. More attention must be given to the support of the technological and marketing development of local component suppliers, enabling them to meet the conditions required by the central purchasing divisions of MNCs. To capture fully the potential benefits of foreign subsidiaries, a systemic approach would be needed, so that support (and financial incentives) might be granted not only to foreign investors but also to their would-be domestic suppliers, leading to the development of sound inter-firm networks.

9.5   CONCLUSIONS AND POLICY ISSUES

Taking into account the likely impact of the single market upon the various types of subsidiaries and the attractiveness of Portugal as an investment location, it is possible to foresee a growing trend for inward FDI in Portugal. Investments will be undertaken not only by non-established firms but also by those that already have interests in the country, confirming the sequential nature of FDI. Growth prospects are still better for integrated manufacturers.

An important topic is the interaction between foreign subsidiaries and domestic firms. It is widely acknowledged that FDI may play a very positive role in creating technological upgrading and the modernization of the domestic industrial fabric, as well as in promoting domestic entrepreneurship, especially through linkages, training and demonstration effects. Some examples of the positive contribution of FDI have been provided elsewhere (Simões, 1985 and 1987). Such a contribution cannot, however, be taken for granted.

As a matter of fact, the logic of the single market itself may strengthen the specialization of central and peripheral Europe: the first as the locus of technology-intensive, high-value-added projects; the second as the place for less skill-demanding, cost-cutting investments. To recall Cantwell (1987): 'in locations where innovation is strong, success breeds success in the form of a virtuous circle, while countries whose firms have a lower capacity for innovation fall further and further behind and are gradually driven out of world markets in a vicious circle of cumulative decline'. If such a process is to take place it will seriously undermine another of the main objectives of the Community: economic and social cohesion. A coherent and strong effort should therefore be taken by EC authorities to provide peripheral regions with the conditions they need to attract more skill-demanding and technology-intensive investments – an effort that clearly exceeds the boundaries of structural funds and that must continue after 1992.

The major role, however, has to be played by the Portuguese government itself through three types of measures: (a) generic actions to upgrade infrastructures and foster domestic innovation; (b) foreign investment policies; and (c) support for the internationalization of domestic firms.

Infrastructural development should be seen in a broad perspective, encompassing not only physical infrastructures, but also 'human capital' and a network of support services. Infrastructure is of paramount importance in attracting FDI and in shaping FDI promotion policies. Policies should pursue clear and realistic targets, always having in mind the need to foster linkages between FDI and local firms. A minimum level of congruence between the characteristics of foreign investment and the technological capabilities of domestic firms is needed for a country to reap the expected benefits from the relative technological advancement of foreign firms (Simões, 1987). Finally, the single market requires a quantum leap in the internationalization of domestic firms. To face the increased competition they need to go abroad, not only through traditional exports but also through direct investment to strengthen their presence in foreign markets and to enlarge their control over the value added chain; international co-operation with other firms should be promoted as well.

Seen from the Portuguese perspective, the steps that lie ahead in the process of European integration (the single market and economic and monetary union) will certainly increase the role of FDI in the national economy. Inter-country (and inter-regional) competition to court and attract foreign investors is likely to become increasingly fierce, particularly among less-industrialized areas. Promoting the interplay between foreign and local firms requires further attention, having in mind the limited freedom of integrated manufacturers and the reduced scope for countries to impose performance requirements on foreign investors.

These are mostly speculations about future behaviour. Time, that great master – to recall Marguerite Yourcenar's words – will show how right we are.

NOTES

1. The terms 'marketing satellite' and 'product specialist' are borrowed from White and Poynter (1984).
2. A more-detailed analysis of historical FDI trends may be found in Simões (1985); Fernandes and Simões (1988); and Taveira (1984).
3. The analysis was restricted to projects classified as manufacturing; marketing satellites were not included.
4. The final decision on this project was taken when most of the article was already written. The Ford/Volkswagen investment may have a very important role in fostering FDI inflow, due to the attraction of suppliers and to the significant improvement of the country's image as an investment location.
5. The need to take into consideration the existing activities of non-EC firms within the Community has been acknowledged by other authors; see, for instance, Young, McDermott and Dunlop (1990); and Rugman and Verbeke (1990).
6. Some multinationals with domestic-market orientated manufacturers as affiliates in both Portugal and Spain have preferred to follow a product-specialization approach rather than concentrating all production in just one subsidiary and transforming the other into a marketing satellite.
7. See, on this topic, Cantwell (1987); Dunning and Cantwell (1991); Dunning and Robson (1987); Young, McDermott and Dunlop (1990); Ozawa (1990); Buckley and Artisien (1987); Crespy (1990); Savary (1989); and Martinez and Jarillo (1988).
8. As a matter of fact, several managers of foreign firms pointed out to us that existing wage levels discourage the introduction of more-sophisticated machinery.
9. Quoted from *Expresso*, 2 February 1991.

REFERENCES

Bartlett, C.A. (1986), 'Building and Managing the Transnational: the New Organizational Challenge', in Michael Porter (ed.), *Competition in Global Industries*, Boston, Mass.: Harvard Business School Press, 367–403.

Bartlett, C.A., Doz, Y. and Hedlund, G. (eds) (1990), *Managing the Global Firm*, London: Routledge.

Bartlett, C.A. and Ghoshal, S. (1990), 'Managing Innovation in the Transnational Corporation', in Bartlett, Doz and Hedlund (1990).

Buckley, P.J. and Artisien, P. (1987), 'Policy Issues of Intra-EC Direct Investment: British, French and German Multinationals in Greece, Portugal and Spain, with Special Reference to Employment Effects', *Journal of Common Market Studies*, **26** (2), 207–30.

Buckley, P.J. (1988), 'The Limits of Explanation: Testing the Internalization Theory of the Multinational Enterprise', *Journal of International Business Studies*, **19** (2), 181–94.

Buigues, P. and Jacquemin, A. (1988), '1992: Quelles stratégies pour les entreprises europeènnes?', *Revue Française de Gestion*, (69), 5–15.

Burgenmeier, B. and Mucchielli, J.-L. (eds) (1991), *Multinationals and Europe 1992*, London: Routledge.

Cantwell, J.A. (1987), 'The Reorganization of European Industries after Integration: Select Evidence on the Role of the Multinational Enterprise Activities', *Journal of Common Market Studies*, **26** (2), 127–52.

Cantwell, J.A. (1989), *Technological Innovation and Multinational Corporations*, Oxford: Basil Blackwell.

Cecchini, P. (1988), *1992 – Le Défi: nouvelles données économiques de l'Europe sans frontières*, Paris: Flammarion.

Crespy, G. (ed.) (1990), *Marché unique, marché multiple*, Paris: Economica.

Doz, Y. (1986), *Strategic Management in Multinational Companies*, Oxford: Pergamon Press.

Dunning, J.H. (1981), *International Production and the Multinational Enterprise*, London: Allen & Unwin.

Dunning, J.H. (1988), 'The Electric Paradigm of International Production: a Restatement and Some Possible Extensions', *Journal of International Business Studies*, **19** (1), 1–31.

Dunning, J.H. (1989), 'Foreign Direct Investment in the European Community: a Brief Overview', *Multinational Business*, (4), 1–9.

Dunning, J.H. and Cantwell, J.A. (1987), *The Changing Role of Multinational Enterprises in the International Creation, Transfer and Diffusion of Technology*, University of Reading Discussion Papers, no. 107.

Dunning, J.H. and Cantwell, J.A. (1991), *Japanese Direct Investment in Europe*, in Burgenmeier and Mucchielli (1991).

Dunning, J.H. and Robson, P. (1987), 'Multinational Corporate Integration and Regional Economic Integration', *Journal of Common Market Studies*, **26** (2), 103–26.

Encarnation, D. and Wells, L.T. Jr (1986), 'Competitive Strategies in Global Industries: a View from Host Governments', in: Michael Porter (ed.), *Competition in Global Industries*, Boston, Mass.: Harvard Business School Press, 267–90.

Fernandes, I. and Simões, V.C. (1988), *Foreign Investment in Portugal: Trends and Characteristics, unpublished.*

Hakanson, L. (1990), 'International Decentralization of R&D: the Organizational Challenges', in Bartlett, Doz and Hedlund (1990).

Hedlund, G. (1986), 'The Hypermodern MNC: an Heterarchy?', *Human Resource Management*, Spring.

Hood, N. and Vahlne, J.-E. (eds) (1988), *Strategies in Global Competition*, London: Croom-Helm.

Hood, N. and Young, S. (1987), 'Inward Investment and the EC: UK Evidence on Corporate Integration Strategies', *Journal of Common Market Studies*, **26** (2), 193–206.

Howells, J., Charles, D. and Wood, M. (1991), 'Global Production Systems', paper presented to the MONITOR/FAST Meeting on 'Globalization of Economy and Technology', Brussels.

Kogut, B. (1983), 'Foreign Direct Investment as a Sequential Process', in C.P. Kindleberger and D. Audretsch (eds), *The Multinational Corporation in the 1980s*, Cambridge, Mass.: MIT Press.

Kogut, B. (1990), 'International Sequential Advantages and Network Flexibility', in Bartlett, Doz and Hedlund (1990).

Martinez, J.I. and Jarillo, J.C. (1988), 'La Respuesta de las multinacionales ante el reto de 1992', *Información Comercial Española*, Oct., 71–82.

Mascarenhas, B. (1986), 'International Strategies of Non-dominant Firms', *Journal of International Business Studies*, **17** (1), 1–26.

Ozawa, T. (1991), 'Japanese Multinationals and 1992', in Burgenmeier and Mucchielli (1991).

Pavitt, K. (1987), 'International Patterns of Technological Accumulation', in Hood and Vahlnc (1987).

Porter, M. (1986), 'Competition in Global Industries: a Conceptual Framework', in M. Porter (1986).

Porter, M. (ed.) (1986), *Competition in Global Industries*, Boston, Mass.: Harvard Business School Press.

Rugman, A.M. and Verbeke, A. (1991), 'Competitive Strategies for Non-European Firms', in Burgenmeier and Mucchielli (1991).

Savary, J. (1989), 'Des strategies multinationales aux stratégies globales de groupes en Europe', paper presented to the Seminar on Industrial and Financial groups and European Integration, Toulouse.

Simões, V.C. (1985), 'Portugal', in J.H. Dunning (ed.), *Multinational Enterprises, Economic Structure and International Competitiveness*, Chichester: J. Wiley.

Simões, V.C. (1987), 'Foreign Investment and Technological Development: a Portuguese Approach', in D. van den Bulcke (ed.), *International Business Issues*, Proceedings of the 13th Annual Meeting of EIBA, Antwerp.

Simões, V.C. (1989), *German Direct Investment in Portugal*, Lisbon: IED, mimeo.

Simões, V.C. (1991), *Globalisation and the Small Less Advanced Countries in the E.C.: Portugal*, Report to the FAST/MONITOR Programme, Lisbon.

Taveira, E. (1984), *Foreign Direct Investment in Portugal: The Present Structure, Determinants of Future Evolution after the Accession to the EEC*, Doctoral Thesis, University of Reading.

UNCTC (1990), *Regional Economic Integration and Transnational Corporations in the 1990s: Europe 1992, North America, and Developing Countries*, *UNCTC Current Studies*, series A, no. 15, New York: UNCTC.

van Tulder, R., Ruygrok, W. and Baven, G. (1991), 'The Globalisation or Glocalisation of the Car Complex?', paper presented to the MONITOR/FAST meeting on 'Globalisation of Economy and Technology', Brussels.

White, R.E. and Poynter, T. (1984), 'Strategies for Foreign-Owned Subsidiaries in Canada', *Business Quarterly*, Summer.

White, R.E. and Poynter, T. (1990), 'Organizing for World-wide Advantage', in Bartlett, Doz and Hedlund (1990).

Young, S. (1986), *The Internationalization of Business*, SIBU Working Papers 86/8, Glasgow.

Young, S., Hood, N. and Hamill, J. (1988), *Foreign Multinationals and the British Economy*, London: Croom Helm.

Young, S., McDermott, M. and Dunlop, S. (1991), *The Challenge of the Single Market*, in Burgenmeier and Mucchielli (1991).

10. Cross-Investment in the EC Banking Sector

P.A. Campayne*

10.1 INTRODUCTION

The EC single market directives, by permitting free trade in banking services and the right of establishment throughout the EC, have the potential to reshape the current structure of banking in the EC.[1] The directives could stimulate classical trade in banking services, that is, the cross-border movement of services based on comparative advantage, and/or foreign direct investment (FDI): the establishment, growth or takeover of foreign branch networks, subsidiaries or alliances (in which there is some measure of control). The expectation is that increased competition resulting from the implementation of the directives and the increase in FDI and trade, will raise the efficiency and lower the prices for banking services by as much as 0.7 per cent of EC GDP according to the Cecchini report.[2]

The theories of international production have traditionally viewed the locational decisions of multinational banks (MNBs) as a choice between FDI or exporting from the home country. They suggest that the greater the FDI undertaken by the banks' customers, the more likely are the banks to also engage in FDI. However, this traditional type of analysis may be of less relevance today, particularly in the EC context. The reduced segmentation of financial markets brought about by the EC directives could potentially create a regional banking

*This work has benefited greatly from my participation at two conferences: first, Multinational Investment in Modern Europe, at Cargese, Corsica, May 1991; and secondly, the annual Danish Summer Research Institute, at Gilleleje Denmark, August 1991. Whilst thanking all the participants at these conferences for their comments I would particularly like to single out John Cantwell, Juan Jose Duran Herrera, Heather Hazard and Art Stonehill for their very helpful suggestions and advice. I have also benefited from discussions with many of my colleagues, in particular Jonathan Elven, Robert Heath and Hugh Simpson. The views expressed in the chapter are purely personal, however, and are not necessarily those of the Bank of England. All errors and omissions are, of course, my sole responsibility.

market. In such an environment the major forces determining the configuration of banks' European operations could differ from that of simply following their customers. It is therefore necessary to introduce other concepts into the analysis, such as that of strategic competition.

The purpose of this chapter is to investigate the current level and pattern of FDI in banking and the impact of Europe-wide competition on strategic thinking, in order to assess the potential consequences of the EC directives on the location and mode of provision of banking services within the EC. Section 10.2 briefly outlines the structure of European banking and the pressures stimulating FDI and trade. Section 10.3 provides a stylized model of bank multinationalization. An analysis of the level and pattern of FDI by banks in the EC is then undertaken in section 10.4. The strategic responses of the major banks to the single market are examined in section 10.5. An assessment of possible future developments is made in the conclusion.

10.2 AN INTEGRATED EUROPEAN BANKING MARKET

10.2.1 Regulatory Changes

The passage of the Single European Act in 1986 called for the creation of the European Community internal market by the end of 1992. One goal of the single market programme is the creation of an integrated, competitive European banking market. The regulatory framework to foster this goal was based on a few general principles:

(a)   free movement of capital;
(b)   harmonization of minimum regulations;
(c)   mutual recognition; and
(d)   home-country control.

The main directives were as follows:

(a)   *The Capital Movements Directive (June 1988)*, which removes all foreign exchange and capital controls to permit the free movement of capital throughout the Community (with a few specific derogations).
(b)   *The Own Funds Directive (April 1989)* and the *Solvency Ratio Directive (December 1989)*. These harmonized the definition of the capital of credit institutions within the EC and their solvency

ratios, respectively. The risk-weighted ratios are similar in definition to the BIS capital-adequacy ratios, with banks having to
meet the minimum 8 per cent ratio.

(c) *The Second Banking Co-ordination Directive (December 1989)*,
which permits the right to establishment and to the provision of
cross-border banking services throughout the EC for an institution authorized in any one member country. The institution
does not need separate authorization in each member state,
whether the provision of its services is through cross-border trade
or location in the country. This is the so-called single banking
licence. In broad terms, authorization and supervision of credit
institutions remains in the hands of the home country authorities.

The new directives represent changes in the competitive environment for European banking at the structural and macro level. At
present, the sector may be regarded as having a dual structure, and
the competitive strategies of the banks will in part depend on the
segments and individual activities in which they are seeking to participate.

10.2.2   Retail Markets

One segment of the European banking market consists of a collection
of relatively separate national retail markets, some of which have been
heavily regulated and protected from foreign competition and where
there have been high margins and sizeable inefficiencies. The degree
of concentration in most national banking sectors is quite high, with
only Germany, the UK, Spain and Luxembourg having modest concentration ratios, although in every country there is a well-established
core group of banks that are the market leaders. In many EC countries
recent domestic deregulation has increased the level of competition
and degree of contestability by reducing cartel-like arrangements and
widening the range of activities in which different types of financial
institutions can compete. Yet, in most, the potential entry of foreign
predators into the retail market is thought to pose only a modest
threat in a contestable framework (although as shown in section 10.5
even this modest threat has stimulated consolidation in some countries). This is because these domestic retail markets are characterized
by a high degree of customer loyalty and high set-up costs which
typically cannot be recovered in the case of later withdrawal. These
act as barriers to entry by establishment for both domestic and foreign
firms. In addition, the European retail market remains fragmented

and contestability low because of the perceived managerial difficulty of operating an EC-wide retail banking network; this is combined with the possible reluctance to see extensive foreign ownership of major institutions because of the scarcity of large-scale retail networks available for purchase due to the large public ownership of banks in some countries.[3]

Yet these very factors that make entry into retail markets by FDI difficult, whether through establishment or takeover, at the same time help to explain why such access may be necessary for the competitive success of the bank. The distinguishing feature of the banking industry and markets described above suggest that the comparative advantage of a bank is not primarily embodied in a particular product or production process, but in information, reputation, confidence and customer proximity. FDI, at present, is therefore a necessity at the retail level as it will be easier for banks to obtain trust, confidence and reputation in a market if they are in geographical proximity to their customers (Neven, 1990). In addition, even under roughly constant returns to scale, some European banks may opt for a European dimension for a number of possible reasons, including the following:

(a) Under constant returns to scale the choice of scale is undetermined. Hence, power and prestige considerations could encourage many bankers into growth- or scale-maximization strategies (Gilibert and Steinherr, 1989).

(b) European scale can provide some increase in risk diversification (Gilibert and Steinherr, 1989) and, particularly if differences in the pattern of country business cycles remain, may lead to less-volatile growth in earnings.[4]

(c) In an environment of Europe-wide competition, banks may engage in strategic games in which FDI is undertaken either aggressively to increase profits, or defensively to protect home markets by, for example, providing competition in the foreign competitor's home market and hence slowing down the rate of expansion of the competitor into the domestic bank's home market.

(d) National, oligopolistic interdependence means that internationalization by one or two banks from a particular country may appear as a breach of the status quo or established equilibrium in the home country and compel other competitors to adopt a 'follow-the-leader, loss-minimising' strategy (Metais, 1990).

Foreign entry into retail markets can also take place through cross-border trade, and this may well increase as new technologies potentially permit bank services to be supplied without the need for FDI. For example, the home banking systems with which some banks are experimenting could be extended across borders. Also, some institutions are trying to establish European credit card businesses with the minimum of FDI. As the regulatory and cultural barriers to such approaches are removed, the level of trade in retail banking services could be increased. However, a strategy of relying on production of the service in one country and cross-border trade still calls for a distribution network in the foreign country which, given the need for confidence and reputation, means the bank may want an equity stake in its partner in the foreign country.

10.2.3   Wholesale Markets

The other part of the European banking market comprises the international, wholesale and corporate banking markets, in which competition is very intense, margins are thin and there already exists considerable freedom of entry. Typically, in comparison to the retail sector, the activities undertaken in these markets are more complex, benefit from external economies of scale and agglomeration economies, and are locationally concentrated in the leading financial centres. Campayne (1992) showed how the interaction between the characteristics of these activities and the locational attractiveness of different financial centres give rise to a hierarchical international division of activities consisting at a global level of:

(a)   local centres in which a few lower order activities are undertaken by MNBs, directed towards the local market, primarily to service the needs of their home country clients;
(b)   regional centres in which a much wider range of activities is undertaken, to serve the needs of not only the local but regional market, for example, Zurich, Toronto, Hong Kong and Frankfurt;
(c)   a few specialist centres, in lower- and higher-order activities, that serve their regional market and possibly the global market as well, for example, Chicago and Singapore;
(d)   the global centres, London, New York and Tokyo, undertaking the full range of activities, but in which the higher-order activities are concentrated, servicing the local, regional and global market.

For the European banks in the study the hierarchies were little different from that overall and are shown in Table 10.1. The strategies of banks participating in the international, wholesale and corporate banking markets reflect the nature of this international division of activities and at the same time facilitate it. FDI is stimulated by the need to locate in the major financial centres in which the activities are concentrated. At the same time, trade out of these centres is encouraged and made possible by the fact that some of these activities generate products that are transferable across national boundaries by means of modern technology. Theoretical models and the experience of the industrial sector when trade barriers have been lowered both suggest that, given present technology, deregulation in the European banking industry could further reinforce the incentives for banks to organize an international division of activities, concentrating into fewer financial centres the most complex activities that require liquid markets and benefit from external economies of scale, while dispersing those more bound to the location of the consumer (that is, the retail markets described above).

10.3 A SEQUENTIAL MODEL OF BANK MULTINATIONALIZATION

To help in the analysis of the restructuring process underway in the European banking market it is useful to have a stylized model of bank multinationalization. Yannopoulos (1983), Cho (1985) and Campayne (1990) are among those who have argued that Dunning's eclectic paradigm is the most appropriate framework to explain the existence of MNBs. The gist of the paradigm is the 'juxtaposition of the ownership specific advantages of firms contemplating foreign production or an increase in foreign production, the propensity to internalise the cross-border markets for these, and the attractiveness of a foreign location for production' (Dunning, 1988, p. 5). In other words, the bank possesses specific competitive (ownership) advantages which its competitors do not – be they of a tangible/intangible asset or transaction type – which it decides is in its best interest to transfer across frontiers within its own organization, and which it thereby exploits in conjunction with indigenous resources of the foreign country.[5]

The first step in the multinationalization process for a bank and the lowest level of international involvement is analogous to the exporting activities of industrial firms. The domestic bank conducts its operations from its home country and supplies its banking services abroad via a bank domiciled in the foreign country. The most common mechanism

Table 10.1   The international division of activities for European banks[1]

Hierarchy of financial centres		Hierarchy of activities		
	TS^2 NA^3		TS^4	NL^5
London	278 26	Foreign equity underwriting	35	14
New York	220 26	Foreign bond underwriting	36	12
Zurich	168 26	Euro equity underwriting	41	15
		Trust banking	42	21
Singapore	133 26	Traded options	47	15
Frankfurt	116 26	Global fund management	48	14
Tokyo	100 26	Euro equity sales	49	15
Paris	100 26	Euro bond underwriting	49	15
Hong Kong	97 26	Domestic bond underwriting	52	16
Luxembourg	76 24	Domestic equity underwriting	53	15
Sydney	75 26	International research	53	22
Amsterdam	62 26	Foreign equity sales	55	15
Milan	39 25	Domestic equity sales	57	18
Toronto	36 22	Domestic research	71	23
Rio de Janeiro	29 23	Retail banking	76	26
Chicago	29 11			
Copenhagen	28 24	Mergers and acquisitions	54	22
Madrid	23 12	Financial futures	60	15
Antwerp	19 10	Foreign bond sales	62	15
Jakarta	15 9	Euro bond sales	70	16
Buenos Aires	14 11	Euro syndicated credits	74	24
Stockholm	14 9	Swaps	80	23
Cayman Islands	13 7	Trade finance	103	25
San Francisco	12 8			
Bahrain	9 7	Foreign exchange	128	25
Lagos	8 7	Currency deposit/lending	138	27
Mexico City	5 3	Money market deposit/lending	145	28
Bahamas	3 2			

Notes
1. A questionnaire survey was conducted to discover which of 26 activities banks undertook in 33 different financial centres. By summing across the respondents and undertaking cluster and regression analyses, it was possible to construct a hierarchy of both centres and activities. Higher-order activities were defined as those that the banks would do least across all centres, due to regulatory reasons and the complexity or nature of the activity. The top centres were defined as those in which the most banks operated and the widest range of activities were undertaken, and in which the highest order activities were concentrated.
2. Sum of no. of activities undertaken by all banks in the location.
3. No. of activities undertaken by at least one bank in the location.
4. The sum over all banks of the number of locations in which they are represented, for each activity.
5. No. of locations in which at least one bank undertakes the activity.
Source: Campayne (1992).

through which the services are provided is that of the correspondent network, with the correspondent bank primarily acting as the payment/ settlement agent. Complementary to this are the representative offices the bank may establish abroad. These serve as points of contact for providing information to head office on the local business conditions and for establishing business connections. They also provide advice to clients who wish to develop their business relationships in the home or host country.

The second stage, and the point at which the bank becomes multi-national, is when it engages in FDI by establishing branches and subsidiaries abroad. These investments are usually initially aimed at servicing the requirements of home-country customers, and are in themselves stimulated by FDI on the part of the bank's clients. Indeed, most authors suggest that the major factor prompting the postwar development of MNBs has been the growth of their multinational enterprise clients (for example, Fieleke, 1977; Terrell and Key, 1977; Goldberg and Saunders, 1981; Sabi, 1988). Khoury (1980) put it most succinctly when he stated that 'the multinationalisation of the manufac-turing corporation brought about the multinationalisation of their banks, whose commitment to long-term relationships with their clients, and to multi-dimensional service packages, produced a multi-locational strategy for the provision of these services'.

Follow-the-customer type FDI by the banks is in part undertaken because the services provided are profitable in their own right. Initially these tend to be primarily an extension of those undertaken through the correspondent network, namely, trade finance, forex and some local money-market activities. However, more importantly, the FDI is in response to a strategic recognition of the potential threat to the domestic relationship that could emerge if the foreign business of home customers represented a significant part of the customers' activi-ties, and were that business to be won by another bank, particularly a home country competitor. The link between the multinationalization of corporate business and that of the banking industry has been par-ticularly strong in the case of American banks, and much of the empirical research showing the presence of MNEs to be statistically related to branch bank activity has been conducted for US banks (for example, Fieleke, 1977; Nigh, Cho and Krishnan, 1986; and Sabi, 1988). In addition, the link has also empirically been shown to be important in the case of other nationalities, for example, Canada (Kamath and Tilley, 1987), Japan (Fujita and Ishigaki, 1986) and Denmark (Vastrup, 1983).

Within this second stage of multinationalization there are two subsets of note. First, alongside the locational pattern of investments of their MNE customers and as their involvement in international and multinational banking activities grows, banks will tend to undertake or increase their FDI in the major international financial centres. These centres provide access to the global capital and credit markets. They are also centres in which the provision and demand for particular services and activities tend to concentrate and the location for skills, knowledge and innovation that the bank may wish to tap. This type of investment could broadly be seen as a form of resource-based FDI. The second subset is where the FDI is undertaken to service a retail market – that is, individual customers or small and medium-size business clients – but aimed at nationals from the home country who are resident abroad. There are many instances of banks entering the US market in particular to service home-country nationals. In addition, in postwar Europe, French and British banks, and to a lesser extent Dutch and Belgian ones, had already established overseas retail branch networks, but in a colonial framework in which they primarily serviced home-country nationals or *de facto* constituted the banking system of the country.

The third phase of multinationalization for banks active abroad is usually to diversify away from their domestic customer business. One way is to take the import-substituting route to its logical conclusion and tackle the host market. Some banks, seeing the prospect of profitable local business, will extend their activities to try and capture the business of indigenous customers in the host markets. This is particularly the case where they are able to participate in profitable domestic cartels and oligopolies (Giddy, 1983), or the sophistication of the local banks is not adequate to accommodate a rising demand for financial services. In addition, as well as seeking the business of indigenous customers, banks may attempt to use their location in an international financial centre as an export platform to win the business of foreign firms from and in any other geographical location. This third phase tends therefore to be a more difficult level for banks to operate at, as the strategies they may be pursuing bring them into direct competition with their foreign counterpart seeking to preserve its core home customer relationships.

The fourth stage is one of rationalized investment, in which the banks configure their operations to service the global or regional market. The reduced segmentation of financial markets brought about by technological progress, deregulation and financial innovations have made possible a more globally or regionally optimal locational pattern of banking activities. It means that strategic considerations can first be taken into account and from this global or regional perspective the decision can be made on how best to configure operations to serve the market as a whole. 'The decision as to where to undertake FDI and where to export is then a secondary one to the attractiveness of different competing locations and the competitive advantage that can be gained by locating certain activities in particular locations' (Campayne, 1990). The single market programme makes possible, in theory, such a strategy of rationalized investment in all EC banking markets, particularly in the context of the international division of activities described above.

10.4 THE CURRENT LEVEL AND PATTERN OF FDI IN THE EUROPEAN BANKING SECTOR

10.4.1 Overall

To date, there has been little empirical analysis of the level and pattern of FDI by European banks because of data limitations. Some indication of the overall pattern of FDI in the European banking sector in recent years can be gauged from data collected by Eurostat (Table 10.2). First, these reveal a redirection of direct investment flows towards other EC countries and away from the rest of the world. The intra-EC share of total EC DI flows in finance and banking have increased significantly, from a net disinvestment position in 1984 to 70.4 per cent of DI flows in 1988, while cumulative intra-EC DI during 1987 and 1988 was more than twice that in the previous three years. Secondly, the EC has become a more-attractive location for DI from non-EC countries, with the extra-EC outward/inward (O/I) DI ratio falling sharply, and the cumulative flow of inward DI increasing in the latter part of the period. Thirdly, the readjustment and redirection of DI flows has been more significant for the finance and banking sector than for industry, where the intra-EC share of total DI was relatively flat over 1985–8, and the EC remains a large net outward investor. This may be a reflection of the greater barriers to trade and investment in the EC financial and banking sector than in the industrial sector that existed prior to the single market programme. These trends are also brought out by analysis of national data.

Table 10.2   European Community direct investment flows

	1984	1985	1986	1987	1988
(a) Intra EC as share of total (%)					
All sectors	19.6	31.3	36.0	29.1	38.3
Finance and banking	−206.7	51.3	52.4	62.4	70.4
Industry	51.9	26.4	32.1	25.8	22.4
(b) Intra-EC/extra-EC (%)					
All sectors	26.6	45.5	56.3	41.1	62.1
Finance and banking	−67.3	105.5	110.1	165.8	238.1
Industry	107.8	35.9	47.3	34.8	28.8
(c) Extra-EC O/I (%)					
All sectors	281.6	272.3	324.0	244.7	215.1
Finance and banking	−140.9	1186.6	90.9	36.3	58.6
Industry	125.3	719.7	994.2	238.9	223.9

	1984–86		1987–8	
(d) Cumulative intra-EC (Ecu mns)				
All sectors	24,081		31,722	
Finance and banking	3,488		8,170	
Industry	9,829		9,108	
(e) Cumulative extra-EC (ECu mns)				
	Outward	Inward	Outward	Inward
All sectors	54,908	18,654	61,491	26,856
Finance and banking	7,997	5,134	3,923	8,395
Industry	18,696	3,932	29,013	12,608

Source: Eurostat.

10.4.2   The United Kingdom

The level and pattern of outward DI of UK banks reflects the historical trading and colonial relationships of the UK, and the fact that many British banks have a long tradition of international banking because of the previous importance of sterling in world trade and finance, the extensive activities of UK exporters and importers, colonial and Commonwealth links, and the importance of London as a financial centre. At end 1987 the total stock of outward DI stood at £7.5 bn, whilst that of inward DI was £5.5 bn (Table 10.3). The major recipient and source of DI was the US, accounting for around one-third of outward and one-fifth of inward DI. The EC accounted for under a quarter of both inward and outward investment. Over 80 per cent of the outward investment to the EC was accounted for by three countries (Table 10.4), the Netherlands (54.1 per cent), France (18.7 per cent) and Germany (10.3 per cent), while 65 per cent of inward investment came from France (24.7 per cent), Belgium/Luxembourg (22.7 per cent) and Germany (17.8 per cent).[6] Although at end 1987 Japan was a relatively minor partner for UK FDI, the rapid growth seen in inward investment from Japan both between 1984–7 and subsequently, will have pushed its share of inward DI significantly higher, and probably depressed its O/I ratio even lower than the 14 per cent registered in 1987.

Table 10.3   Distribution and rate of growth of UK bank direct investment

| | Direct investment stock in 1987 | | | Average annual rate of growth 1984–7 | |
	Outward (%)	Inward (%)	O/I (£mn, %)	Outward (%)	Inward (%)
Western Europe	31.7	38.6	111.0	34.6	17.7
EC–12	24.5	22.4	147.8	n.a	15.9
Switzerland	7.0	7.3	129.6	n.a	77.8
North America	37.8	25.7	199.4	−2.1	33.5
Japan	0.6	5.9	14.0	n.a	32.0
World	100.0	100.0			
World (£mn)	7,485.6	5,534.4	135.3	7.1	23.7

Source: Bank of England.

The pattern of outward DI of UK banks closely mirrors that of the manufacturing sector, and a simple regression reveals a significant positive relationship, in line with the bank multinationalization model above.[7] However, the pattern of inward investment is different, with the share accounted for by EC countries twice as great for the banking

Table 10.4   *UK bank direct investment in (from) the EC–12 (% distribution by member country)*

	Direct investment stock in 1987			Average annual rate of growth 1984–7	
	Outward (%)	Inward (%)	O/I (£mn, %)	Outward (%)	Inward (%)
Belgium/ Luxembourg	4.7	22.7	30.4	46.3	17.0
Denmark	0.0	7.2	n.a	n.a	25.2
France	18.7	24.7	112.1	39.0	11.8
Germany	10.3	17.8	85.6	2.2	34.3
Greece	0.0	0.0	n.a	n.a	n.a
Ireland	2.8	3.2	130.7	−12.2	−21.9
Italy	1.2	8.8	20.4	11.2	12.5
Netherlands	54.1	8.5	945.9	80.9	1.6
Portugal	1.2	0.9	196.5	n.a	64.5
Spain	5.4	5.2	151.2	n.a	236.5
Unallocated	1.6	1.1	-	-	-
EC–12	100.0	100.0			

Source: Bank of England.

sector as for manufacturing, where the US has an overwhelming dominance (share of 61 per cent). Another difference between manufacturing and banking is in the respective rates of growth of outward and inward DI. In the case of the banking sector, the rate of growth of outward DI between 1984 and 1987 was only one-third that of inward DI (7.1 per cent and 23.7 per cent respectively). This reflects the increased attractiveness of London as a financial centre resulting from the 'Big Bang' deregulation of UK financial markets. In marked contrast, manufacturing inward investment grew at a rate of 8 per cent per annum over the period, while that of outward investment rose 17.4 per cent per annum. Overall, the UK is more of a net outward investor in manufacturing (O/I ratio of 151 per cent), than in banking (O/I ratio of 135.3 per cent), in part reflecting the greater attractiveness of the UK as a location for financial activities than for manufacturing.

Another trend that is clearly suggested by the data is the redirection of UK banks' outward DI away from the US and towards Western

Europe and the EC in particular. The average annual rate of growth
of DI to Western Europe between 1984 and 1987 was 34.6 per cent,
and its share of total outward investment more than doubled over the
period. By contrast, the stock of UK banks' DI in the US actually
contracted by 2.1 per cent per annum over the period, reflecting the
problems that UK, and other, banks experienced in the US market
at this time. The impact of the single market proposal may be seen
in the flow data, with the EC accounting for 63.4 per cent of the
cumulative annual DI flow over 1987–9, after actually contracting
between 1984 and 1986 (Table 10.5). The major beneficiary over this
time was Spain, reflecting its accession to the EC in 1986. By comparison, multinational banks from other EC countries have not shown the
same degree of interest in investing in the UK. Inward investment
from these countries grew at 17.7 per cent per annum over 1984–7,

*Table 10.5 UK bank cumulative direct investment flows (% distri-
bution)*

| | Outward | | Inward |
	1984–6	1987–9	1988–9
EC–12	−292.9	63.4	21.5
Belgium/Luxembourg	0.0	2.5	6.2
Denmark	0.3	0.0	0.0
France	12.8	11.6	1.2
Germany	4.1	5.8	5.1
Greece	0.0	0.0	0.0
Ireland	2.8	1.1	0.9
Italy	−1.5	5.1	−0.6
Netherlands	−321.0	10.0	2.1
Portugal	0.0	1.0	−0.5
Spain	8.6	24.8	6.0
Switzerland	14.7	1.8	−0.3
Canada	27.4	−0.4	3.5
USA	83.3	15.3	19.7
Japan	6.7	3.1	31.2
Rest of world	227.0	16.8	27.1
World	100.0	100.0	100.0
World (£mns)	700.6	1,144.5	2,281.6

Source: Bank of England.

or around half the rate of growth of investment from North America or Japan. As a result, the share of total inward investment accounted for by EC countries actually declined over the period, and may have continued to decline as its share of cumulative inward flow over 1988 and 1989 was 21.5 per cent compared with 19.7 per cent and 31.2 per cent for the US and Japan respectively.

10.4.3   Germany

The stock of outward direct investment of German credit institutions at end 1989 was DM16,030 mn (£5.9 bn). Although a strict comparison with UK figures cannot really be made, due to differences in definition, most commentators would agree that the stock of outward DI of German banks is lower than that of UK or US banks. The locational pattern of DI also differs between German and UK banks with, in the German case, the EC accounting for the overwhelming share of German outward investment (67 per cent) and the US playing a much smaller role as a recipient (9 per cent) (Table 10.6). Moreover, while around 30 per cent of UK banks' outward DI stock was outside the EC, North America, Switzerland and Japan, due to historical links, the comparable figure for Germany is around 17 per cent. In part the very high share of investment to the EC reflects the greater degree of integration and higher share of German trade and manufacturing investment with the EC. In addition, however, the figures for the credit institutions are slightly distorted by the high level of DI into Luxembourg. Most of this is for regulatory reasons, with Luxembourg mainly used as an offshore centre and a substitute for business that could otherwise be undertaken in Germany. British banks have less need to make use of Luxembourg, given the liberal regulatory regime in the UK. Yet, even if one made the heroic decision simply to subtract Luxembourg from the statistics, the EC would still account for around half of German credit institutions' DI.

When a comparison is made with the pattern of investments by German manufacturing firms two features stand out. First, the DI of the credit institutions is concentrated in a few countries (between them, the UK, US and Luxembourg account for nearly 60 per cent), while that of the manufacturing sector is relatively more dispersed. Secondly, the role of London as the major international financial centre clearly stands out. Its share of credit institutions' DI is more than twice that of the manufacturing sector. Conversely, the US has a remarkably small share, given New York's position as a financial

Table 10.6 Distribution and rate of growth of outward German direct investment

	Direct investment stock in 1989 (%)		Average annual rate of growth 1986-9 (%)	
	Credit inst.	Manuf. sector	Credit inst.	Manuf. sector
EC-12	67.0	41.9	15.5	12.4
Belgium	0.5	5.2	9.2	15.2
Denmark	n.a	0.7	n.a	5.1
France	3.9	11.3	13.7	11.7
Greece	n.a	0.4	n.a	4.7
Great Britain	13.7	6.1	34.6	13.4
Ireland	3.1	0.6	n.a	17.4
Italy	4.6	5.0	n.a	12.2
Luxembourg	35.7	0.4	6.6	16.6
Netherlands	2.7	4.6	30.0	5.9
Portugal	n.a	0.6	n.a	15.1
Spain	2.5	7.0	51.0	16.6
Switzerland	5.1	2.1	4.1	−0.5
Canada	1.0	2.0	21.6	9.2
USA	9.1	28.0	10.1	3.6
Japan	n.a	2.9	n.a	18.7
World	100.0	100.0		
World (DM mn)	16,030.0	113,475.0	15.0	7.3

Source: Deutsche Bundesbank, *Appendix to the Statistical Supplement to the Monthly Report of the Deutsche Bundesbank*, various issues.

centre and the 28 per cent of German manufacturing investment located in the US.

Over the period 1986-9 the overall rate of growth of German credit institutions' outward DI was twice that of the manufacturing sector, although for the EC subset the two rates were much closer: 15.5 per cent and 12.4 per cent respectively. Interestingly, although the rate of growth was fairly uniform across the EC for manufacturing, for the credit institutions this was not the case. The pace of investment was particularly rapid into Spain (51.0 per cent per annum), reflecting its accession to the EC, and into the UK (34.6 per cent per annum), reflecting German interest in 'Big Bang'. Hence, it is not so much that German credit institutions have redirected investments to the EC, as the EC's share has always been high, rather that there has been a further consolidation or concentration of these investments. The continuing high rate of DI flowing to the UK lends weight to the argument that deregulation reinforces the international division of activities, as nearly all the investment is said to have been directed towards the international, wholesale, corporate and securities markets in London.

The analysis of inward investment in Germany is made difficult by the fact that the data only consists of primary DI, thereby underestimating the real value of foreign activities, and that the data is not very disaggregated. Nevertheless, it suggests that the EC is a much smaller source of inward investment to Germany than it is a recipient, with the role played by the US increasing and indeed holding the dominant share of manufacturing investment (Table 10.7). Also, the role of the Japanese increases significantly, to become the largest single national group of inward investors in the banking sector.

Table 10.7   Distribution and rate of growth of inward German direct investment

	Direct investment stock in 1989 (%)		Average annual rate of growth 1986–9 (%)	
	Credit inst.	Manuf. sector	Credit inst.	Manuf. sector
EC–12	38.8	29.9	13.0	7.1
France	7.4	4.0	6.8	5.6
Great Britain	5.2	7.2	9.7	−8.2
Netherlands	11.7	14.6	4.2	19.8
Switzerland	4.7	13.5	20.3	2.1
USA	19.9	45.9	−4.1	−2.1
Japan	26.3	2.2	15.9	25.9
World	100.0	100.0		
World (DM mn)	9,741.0	49,142.0	8.0	2.5

Source: As for Table 10.6.

10.4.4 France

Unlike the cases of the UK and Germany, stock figures on French DI were not available. However, some indication of the recent pattern and trend in investment can be gauged from an analysis of the Eurostat flow data. The main feature revealed by the data is that since 1984 the EC has become a more important source and recipient of French DI, particularly in the finance and banking sector. For example, in 1987 and 1988 the EC's shares of total outward DI in the finance and banking sector were 66 per cent and 95.2 per cent respectively, a significant jump from an average of around 30 per cent over 1984–6 (Table 10.8). Since 1987 France has become a significant net outward investor in finance and banking to other EC countries, and in 1988 became a net inward investor for non-EC countries.

Table 10.8   French direct investment flows

	1984	1985	1986	1987	1988
(a) Outward to EC as share of total outward (%)					
All sectors	35.0	19.0	33.8	53.9	63.4
Finance and banking	31.1	28.8	30.2	66.0	95.2
Industry	32.6	15.5	41.0	38.1	44.4
(b) Inward from EC as share of total inward (%)					
All sectors	50.5	42.8	50.7	48.8	70.1
Finance and banking	60.6	54.7	63.7	57.7	70.1
Industry	54.0	39.9	32.9	35.3	68.6
(c) Extra-EC O/I (%)					
All sectors	126.0	141.9	245.6	169.4	218.3
Finance and banking	292.6	264.2	295.0	178.2	48.1
Industry	101.8	107.7	220.4	159.2	302.3
(d) Intra-EC O/I (%)					
All sectors	66.3	44.6	126.2	207.4	160.6
Finance and banking	86.1	88.3	72.5	254.7	402.4
Industry	41.9	29.9	312.0	180.0	110.2

Table 10.8 Continued

	1984–6		1987–8	
	Outward	Inward	Outward	Inward
(e) Cumulative extra-EC (Ecu mns)				
All sectors	7,657	4,451	7,440	3,869
Finance and banking	2,064	725	811	680
Industry	2,114	1,455	4,405	1,995
(f) Cumulative intra-EC (Ecu mns)				
All sectors	3,301	4,098	10,925	6,235
Finance and banking	886	1,100	4,198	1,229
Industry	1,100	1,108	3,185	2,498

Source: Eurostat.

10.4.5 Denmark

To provide a small-country example, figures on the flow of Danish FDI were utilized (Tables 10.9 and 10.10). Danish banks started going international by establishing subsidiaries and branches abroad about the mid–1970s. Vastrup (1983) suggests that they essentially followed their customers abroad in order to maintain their relationships and to provide a lower cost of funding based on their knowledge of the creditworthiness of their clients. In addition, Danish official foreign-exchange regulations, at that time, prevented Danish banks from providing more than a small amount of foreign funds to Danish customers through their domestic offices. Hence the backbone of the banks' foreign networks is Danish-related business: trade finance, forex, financing Danish companies, and private banking for Danish expatriates.

Most outward DI by Danish banks in recent years has been to other EC countries, about 59 per cent of the flow between 1987 and 1989, a figure close to the 54.1 per cent for industry. As with the German credit institutions, the UK share of banking investment (33 per cent) far exceeds that for the manufacturing sector (17.8 per cent), with most of the investment said to be directed towards the wholesale and corporate markets. The inflow of DI to Denmark over the period was much lower than the level of outward DI, reflecting both the smaller size and degree of concentration of the Danish retail market, and Copenhagen's position as an international financial centre. It is interesting that, despite a significant trading relationship with the Nordic countries, Norway, Sweden and Finland, and a high share of

Table 10.9   Cumulative outward Danish direct investment, 1987–9

	All sectors (%)	Industry (%)	Banking (%)	Other financial (%)
EC–12	68.1	54.1	58.7	91.4
Belgium	0.7	2.1	0.0	0.0
Luxembourg	0.9	0.2	2.6	3.9
France	10.1	9.6	0.0	42.4
Germany	10.5	10.3	20.8	3.7
Great Britain	23.2	17.8	33.3	40.8
Greece	0.00	0.00	0.00	0.00
Ireland	0.1	0.4	0.0	0.0
Italy	0.1	0.2	0.0	0.0
Netherlands	18.3	3.9	0.0	0.5
Portugal	0.5	0.4	0.0	0.5
Spain	3.6	9.2	2.0	0.0
EFTA	11.4	14.5	2.9	2.4
Switzerland	2.3	1.9	2.9	1.5
North America	10.6	20.3	14.0	4.0
USA	9.7	17.9	14.0	4.0
Other developed	1.4	3.3	0.0	0.7
Rest of world	8.6	7.8	24.4	1.5
World	100.0	100.0	100.0	100.0
World (DKr mns)	29,244.0	6,944.0	2,986.0	4,389.0

Source: Danmarks Nationalbank.

manufacturing investment flows, the DI banking flows between these countries and Denmark were negligible, probably due to implicit co-operation agreements between the Scandinavian banks not to enter each others' markets directly. With regard to outward Danish DI flows, this distortion of the expected relationship was probably due to strict regulations on foreign ownership of financial institutions in the Nordic countries.[8] However, it is not clear why there were no inward flows.

Table 10.10   Cumulative inward Danish direct investment, 1987–9

	All sectors (%)	Industry (%)	Banking (%)	Other financial (%)
EC–12	32.3	32.2	61.2	57.7
Luxembourg	0.7	0.0	30.0	0.7
France	16.3	0.7	18.9	56.1
Germany	2.5	5.6	0.0	0.2
Great Britain	5.1	5.9	0.8	0.5
Netherlands	7.6	19.9	11.6	0.2
EFTA	53.1	54.8	0.0	22.9
North America	10.2	8.4	38.8	19.3
World	100.0	100.0	100.0	100.0
World (Dkr mn)	23,887.0	5,942.0	397.0	5,970.0

Source: Danmarks Nationalbank.

10.5   THE STRATEGIC RESPONSE TO THE SINGLE MARKET PROGRAMME

The catalyst provided by the single market programme has already stimulated the restructuring of European banking activity, as can be seen from the FDI data above. The strategies pursued by the major European banks have been varied, but underlying the different approaches are the twin aims of protecting the home market and expanding into the enlarged European market. For some EC banks the attainment of these goals corresponds with two distinct phases: secure home first, expand afterwards; while others seem to be attempting to achieve both goals simultaneously.

The first and most important goal for EC banks has been to protect their home markets and reinforce their sources of competitive advantage. In all countries, banks have sought to reduce their operating costs, particularly by streamlining their branch networks and cutting back on staff, and by selling off non-core business. In addition, they have tried to get a better grasp of the underlying cost of provision of individual services so that pricing decisions can more fully reflect the marginal cost of the inputs involved, including a normal profit-level for the capital employed.

Alongside operational and organizational changes, in some countries banks have sought to protect their home market and improve their competitive position through local mergers and acquisitions, and this has led to consolidation in national banking markets (route A in Figure 10.1). The declared rationale behind this domestic consolidation has been the need to rationalize overbanked markets, generate economies of scale, and produce large banking groups of sufficient size to compete in the post–1992 European market. Good examples of this type of strategy are provided by the creation of AMRO-ABN in The Netherlands, Unibank and Den Danske Bank in Denmark, and Banco Bilbao Vizcaya in Spain. This process of domestic consolidation has also included linkages with non-banking financial groups, particularly insurance companies, giving rise to the terms '*Allfinanz*' or '*Bancassurance*'. Examples include the links between BNP and UAP of France, Dresdner and Allianz in Germany, and the merger of NMB Postbank and Nationale Nederlanden in The Netherlands. For the banks such links have, in part, been established because they enable economies of scope to be exploited, for example, the sale of insurance products through the branch network, and, in addition, because the non-banking groups were capturing an ever-larger share of the savings of the banks' customers. While such large-scale domestic consolidation was not perhaps the expected outcome of the single market, it is not a very surprising reaction to a perceived foreign threat, however limited the reality of that threat may have proved. Moreover, it should also be recognized that while the process of consolidation may well in the long run generate the reduction in costs and increased international competitiveness its proponents suggest, such mergers, by reducing the number of banks available for takeover and increasing the size of the remaining ones, make foreign entry on any significant scale more difficult.

The second goal of most banks in the restructuring process is to expand into the enlarged European market (route B in Figure 10.1). For many, the decision to establish abroad and the choice of location is not that of an individual act of FDI on each occasion but part of a strategy of being or becoming a 'European bank'. The aim is to make the foreign market not just an extension of their domestic market but an integral part of their sphere of operations. By so doing, it in turn reinforces the protection offered to the home base, for example, through the acquisition of new skills or products, a diversification of risk and the profit cycle, by protecting its home-country customer base in the foreign market, or by attacking a foreign competitor in its home market and lessening its ability to enter the banks' home market.

One method of entry into foreign markets is simply *de novo* estab-

Figure 10.1 FDI and strategic business expansion

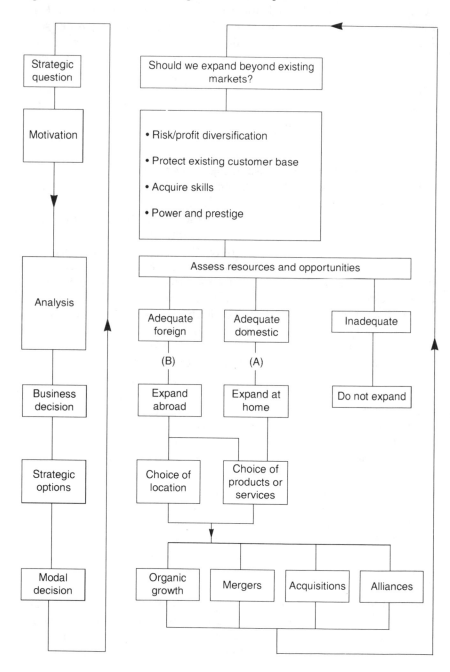

lishment and organic growth. This may well be a viable proposition in certain niche markets, for example, Barclay's move into the credit card business in Germany. However, the high set-up costs and substantial barriers to entry on a significant scale make the prospects of success for such an entry route rather limited. Some banks have sought to build up operations they already have in other EC countries but, at least prior to 1987, as few foreign banks already had significant shares of the business in other countries this strategy tends to be seen as a minimalist approach.

The most common strategy to enter other European markets and deal with the post–1992 market has been the creation of strategic cross-border alliances and co-operation agreements. There have been many such arrangements established, the most notable being those between Royal Bank of Scotland and Banco Santander, Dresdner and BNP, and the longer-running Europartners grouping of Crédit Lyonnais, Commerzbank, Banco di Roma and Banco Hispano. There are a number of reasons for the popularity of such arrangements, the most important being that they provide instant access into a foreign country through the partner bank's distribution network, and that they are an easier and cheaper option than engaging in large-scale mergers and acquisitions. In addition, there is a perception that by placing equity in friendly hands, these agreements can make a hostile takeover more difficult.

Yet these strategic alliances and co-operation agreements are in many cases merely a more-advanced form of the correspondent relationship outlined as the first step in the multinationalization model, simply involving a more-extensive and deeper relationship and/or equity stake.[9] The nature of these relationships still leaves unanswered the most basic question: where are they leading? Some banks may be content to remain at the level of small-scale agreements. But for the larger banks in particular, while the approach may provide a mechanism through which they can come closer together and integrate their activities, eventually, either as the level of business grows or the ambitions of one of the partners increases, the issue of whether to merge or not is raised. At present, large cross-border mergers seem unlikely, as witnessed by the failure of the proposed Generale Bank–AMRO merger. In the meanwhile, the inevitable tensions of maintaining such an alliance, particularly as the partners may start to act independently of each other, puts the agreement at risk.

Another approach has been to enter foreign markets through cross-border acquisitions.[10] Most of the major acquisitions have been by French, British and German banks, with those from other countries as yet more preoccupied with domestic consolidation or strategic alliances. A large proportion of these acquisitions have been targeted at entering niche markets rather than full-service banking, particularly in the leading financial centres. For example, a number of UK fund managers have been taken over (by, amongst others, Indosuez, Dresdner, and Crédit Commercial of France), and a number of French and Spanish brokerage houses have been acquisition targets. In some cases these foreign acquisitions have also been used as a means to bring specific skills back to the home country, to protect or enhance the position of the acquiring bank in its home market. An example of this is Deutsche Bank's takeover of the UK's Morgan Grenfell. For Deutsche, the Morgan Grenfell acquisition was a major step towards its goal of becoming an investment banking force in Europe and, indeed, worldwide. Though it had a significant presence in the Eurobond market, the German bank needed the boost to its corporate finance, cross-border M&A, and fund management operations that Morgan Grenfell will provide. Hence the acquisition enabled it to enhance its position in the domestic UK market, at the same time increase its competitive position in the global market by using London as an export platform and finally, by bringing the specific skills and reputation of Grenfell to Germany, enhance its position in the German market.

By contrast, there can be said to have been relatively few acquisitions made with the aim of entering the broad range of banking activities in the foreign market, although some banks seem to be trying to establish European banking networks for high-net-worth customers (for example, Barclays' takeover of L'Européenne de Banque in France and Merck Finck in Germany). The most notable retail acquisitions have been Deutsche Bank's takeover of Banca d'America d'Italia and controlling stake in Banca Commerciale Transatlantico of Spain; and the string of commercial bank acquisitions by Crédit Lyonnais in The Netherlands, Belgium, Italy and Spain as it seeks to achieve its stated goal of being a pan-European bank. The reasons for the fewer foreign retail acquisitions are not hard to see: few available targets, high cost of acquisitions, legal and cultural problems. As a result, the present structure of European retail banking, consisting of national markets in which a few domestic firms tend to dominate, is likely to remain for some time.

The responses of non-EC banks to the single market programme have varied. Other European banks seem to have accepted that there will be one pan-European banking space in which they will be forced to compete. Their strategies have echoed those of the EC banks, namely, domestic consolidation and cross-border alliances and acquisitions. By contrast, many of the US banks have cut back on their international expansion due to their domestic difficulties (Figure 10.2). Indeed, it has been the subsidiaries of US banks that have provided many of the acquisition targets for European banks wishing to build up their European networks. Security Pacific, Bank America, Chase and Chemical are among the institutions that have pulled out of or greatly reduced their European operations, relinquishing ambitions to challenge the top European institutions on their home ground.

Japanese financial institutions have generally been expanding their overseas networks and the size of their overseas operations. Many have been attracted to the major international financial centres and have tended to follow their MNE customers abroad. Their lack of investment in retail banking in the EC, compared for example with California, may be explained by the tiny Japanese community in the EC. Throughout the EC, Japanese banks as a whole currently operate around 109 business outposts (branches, representative offices and subsidiaries), whereas European banks have 125 equivalents in Japan (Ozawa, 1990). In recent years around 40 per cent of Japanese direct investment into the EC has been to the UK. While it is likely that the UK will continue to receive a substantial proportion of Japanese direct investment, Japanese companies have indicated that they will in the future diversify their investments in the EC more widely. This could encourage Japanese banks to extend their branch networks more widely through Europe, although maintaining their wholesale activities in London.

10.6 CONCLUSIONS

It is clear that the single market programme has already stimulated a restructuring process in the European banking sector. The FDI data available reveal a reorientation or reinforcement of intra-EC DI and increase in inward DI from non-EC countries. The major European banks have taken a variety of approaches, both aggressive and defensive, to create the critical mass of alliances they believe necessary to survive in the new competitive environment. Given the close relationship between banks and their major corporate customers, it seems likely that customer-following strategies may form the basis for a part of the FDI undertaken in the single European banking market. However, it is probable that such strategies will decline in importance over time. FDI may increasingly be driven by a desire to break into

Figure 10.2   FDI and strategic business contractions

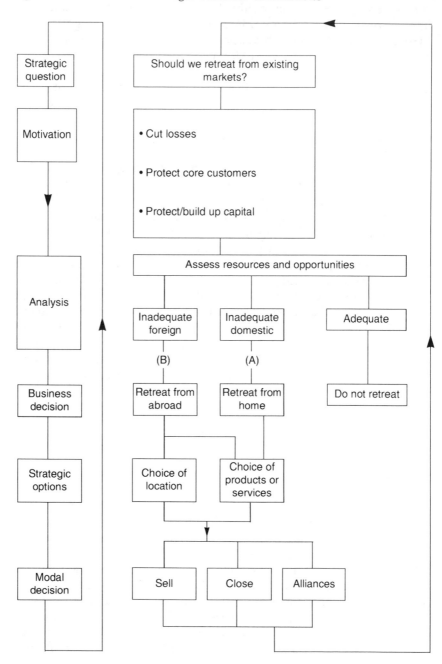

domestic markets, in which event it could be directed to the largest markets, those with the most profit potential or those for which the opportunity to enter arises as target banks become available. Banks may wish to enter the domestic market for a number of reasons, including prestige or as part of a game of strategic competition. If they already have operations in the foreign country they may further expand if their home-country clients grow slower than local businesses in the foreign market, prompting diversification in order to remain profitable. One note of caution is that experience suggests that diversifying away from a home-country client base can often involve lending to higher-risk clients in order to break into the domestic market. If this is not prudently managed it can result in serious problems. For example, the recent deregulation in Australia permitted foreign banks to expand their operations. Many have subsequently made large losses through their dependence on higher-risk clients who ran into difficulties.

Neven (1990) suggests that in the long run any movement towards a more competitive and integrated European retail banking structure is more likely to be brought about by, and at the same time facilitate, FDI. Yet, with cultural and economic barriers to entry still remaining, an increase in the DI activities of foreign banks in national retail markets could be a long and slow process. Many institutions are instead placing a greater emphasis either on co-operation agreements and alliances or on organic growth in their established foreign offices. Nevertheless, certain institutions have publicly expressed the desire to become pan-European banks in a broad range of activities, and a few could emerge as dominant, broad-based competitors in the enlarged European markets. It seems probable that other competitors will have to narrow either the scope of services they supply or concentrate on selected geographical markets or both. The resulting industry structure, at both European and national level, could therefore be one of greater concentration in terms of broad-based suppliers and greater segmentation into product and regional specialists.

NOTES

1. The main EC directive of relevance to this paper is the Second Banking Co-ordination Directive. This permits the right to establishment and to the provision of cross-border banking services throughout the EC for an institution authorized in any one member country. The institution does not need separate authorization for each member state, whether the provision of its services is through cross-border trade or location in the country.

2. However, as many authors have pointed out, competition is likely to remain imperfect, due to the presence of important economic and cultural barriers to entry, and this will yield an upper bound for the integration benefits lower than the competitive benchmark estimated in Cecchini.

3. Molyneux (1989) estimates that of the 162 European banks in the *Banker* top 500 for 1987, 67 were owned by central or local governments. These 67 accounted for 26 per cent of the total assets of the 162 banks. In addition there were 26 co-operatives and mutuals, accounting for 43 per cent. Gardener and Molyneux (1990) calculated that the share of total banking assets accounted for by public and mutual banks in 1988 exceeded 50 per cent in France (62.4 per cent), Germany (66.2 per cent), Italy (84.7 per cent) and Portugal (89 per cent).

4. This reason for FDI would be reduced in importance, however, if the securitization of European assets developed on a significant scale. If foreign banks were to recognize that domestic banks have a comparative advantage in loan origination and deposit collection in retail markets, and that the price of entry into such markets would be exorbitantly high, then instead of establishing a European retail network they would simply buy the bundles of securitized foreign assets they required. Indeed, this may be the most efficient way for banks to make use of their capital. However, this presumes that the foreign bank has little to offer the domestic market in the way of new skills or products, and/or that the demand for bank services is being adequately met by the domestic banks. Moreover, there are many other reasons why banks may want to enter a foreign retail market. It is also important to recognize that one consequence of the European market developing in this way is that there would be very little foreign competition at the retail level and hence lower welfare gains than have been suggested by Cecchini.

5. Campayne (1990) spells out more fully the various sources of locational, ownership and internalization advantages a bank may have.

6. However, the real importance of The Netherlands as a recipient of DI is probably overstated. Due to special advantages in the tax and legal regime, UK banks may set up separate subsidiaries in The Netherlands or Netherlands Antilles for capital-raising purposes, before channelling the funds elsewhere. These investments are recorded as being Dutch in the official statistics. Interestingly, the level of DI by UK banks into branches in the Netherlands is of a comparable size to that of most other EC countries, and its rate of increase between 1984 and 1987, at 0.7 per cent per annum was actually slower than most EC countries and half the West European average.

7. The dependent variable was the total FDI of UK banks. The measure for UK business presence was the end-year book-value of UK manufacturing firms FDI. The analysis was conducted across 25 countries or regional groupings. R^2 equalled 0.7295 in 1987 and 0.7443 in 1984. The β values equalled 0.2071 in 1987 and 0.2072 in 1984. The t statistic was significant at the 1 per cent level in both years.

8. Recently the Nordic countries have begun to open up their markets, partly to attract foreign capital, and partly to come closer to the EC regulatory structure.

9. Indeed, although there have been many alliances established, most do not qualify statistically as FDI as they do not involve a large enough equity stake. The UK definition for FDI is that there must be a minimum 20 per cent equity stake or that the UK firm must be able to demonstrate management control of the host country firm.

10. To date there have been no major cross-border mergers, with the failure of the proposed merger between AMRO and Generale indicative of the considerable problems associated with integrating two major commercial banking networks across borders.

REFERENCES

Bisignano, J.R. (1989), 'Banking in the EEC: Structure, Competition and Public Policy', Geneva: Bank For International Settlements, *mimeo*.

Campayne, P.A. (1990), *The Impact of Multinational Banks on the International Location of Banking Activity and the Global Hierarchy of Financial Centres*, Reading University, unpublished PhD thesis.

Campayne, P.A. (1992), 'The Impact of Multinational Banks on International Financial Centres', in M. Casson (ed.), *International Business and Global Integration*, London: Macmillan.

Cho, K.R. (1985), *Multinational Banks: Their Identities and Determinants*, Ann Arbor, Mich.

Davis, E.P. (1990), *International Financial Centres: An Industrial Analysis*, Bank of England Discussion Paper.

Dermine, J. (1990), *European Banking in the 1990s*, Oxford: Basil Blackwell.

Dunning, J.H. (1988), 'The Eclectic Paradigm of International Production: a Restatement and some Possible Extensions', *Journal of International Business*, **29** (1), 1–31.

Fieleke, N. (1977), 'The Growth of US Banking Abroad: an Analytical Survey', in *Key Issues in International Banking*, Boston, Mass.: Federal Reserve Bank of Boston.

Fujita, M. and Ishigaki, K. (1986), 'The Internationalisation of Japanese Commercial Banking', in M. Taylor and N. Thrift (eds), *Multinationals and the Restructuring of the World Economy*, London: Croom-Helm.

Gardener, E.P.M. and Molyneux, P. (1990), *Changes in Western European Banking*, London: Unwin-Hyman.

Germidis, D. and Michalet, C.A. (1984), *International Banks and Financial Markets in Developing Countries*, Paris: OECD.

Giddy, I. (1983), 'The Theory and Industrial Organization of International Banking', in R.G. Hawkins, R.M. Levich and C.G. Wihlburg (eds), *The Internationalisation of Financial Markets and National Economic Policy*, New York: JAI Press.

Gilibert, P.L. and Steinherr, A. (1989), *The Impact of Financial Market Integration on the European Banking Industry*, European Institute of Banking Papers, no. 8.

Goldberg, L.G. and Saunders, A. (1980), 'The Causes of US Bank Expansion Overseas: the Case of Great Britain', *Journal of Money, Credit and Banking*, **12** (4), 630–43.

Goldberg, L.G. and Saunders, A. (1981), 'The Growth of Organisational Forms of Foreign Banks in the US', *Journal of Money, Credit and Banking*, **13** (3), 304–74.

Grubel, H.G. (1977), 'A Theory of Multinational Banking', *Banca Nazionale del Lavoro, Quarterly Review*, (123), 349–64.

Haley, J.C. and Seligman, B. (1983), 'The Development of International Banking', in W. Baughn and D. Mandich (eds), *The International Banking Handbook*, Illinois: Dow Jones.

Jain, A.K. (1986), 'International Lending Patterns of US Commercial Banks', *Journal of International Business Studies*, **17**, 73–88.

Kamath, S. and Tilley, J.R. (1987), 'Canadian International Banking and the Debt Crisis', *Columbia Journal of World Business*, **22** (4), 75–85.

Khoury, S.J. (1980), *Dynamics of International Banking*, New York: Praeger.

Metais, J. (1990), 'Towards a Restructuring of the International Financial Services Industry', in E.P.M. Gardener (ed.), *The Future of Financial Systems and Services*, London: Macmillan.

Molyneux, P. (1989), 'An Analysis of the Structure and Performance Characteristics of Top EC Banks and the Strategic Implications for 1992', *Revue de la banque*, **53** (6), June.

Neven, D.J. (1990), 'Structural Adjustment in European Retail Banking: Some Views from Industrial Organisation', in J. Dermine (ed.), *European Banking in the 1990s*, Oxford: Basil Blackwell.

Niehans, J. (1983), 'Financial Innovation, Multinational Banking and Monetary Policy', *Journal of Banking and Finance*, **7**, 537–51.

Nigh, D., Cho, K.R. and Krishnan, S. (1986), 'The Role of Location-related Factors in US Banking Involvement Abroad: an Empirical Examination', *Journal of International Business Studies*, **17**, 59–72.

Ozawa, T. (1990), 'A Case Study on Japanese Direct Investment', submitted to UNCTC, *mimeo*.

Pecchioli, R.M. (1983), *The Internationalisation of Banking*, Paris: OECD.

Sabi, M. (1988), 'An Application of the Theory of Foreign Direct Investment to Multinational Banking in LDCs', *Journal of International Business Studies*, **19** (3), 433–9.

Terrell, H. (1979), 'US Banks in Japan and Japanese Banks in the US: an Empirical Comparison', *Federal Reserve Bank of San Francisco Economic Review*, 18–30.

Terrell, H. and Key, S.J. (1977), 'The US Activities of Foreign Banks: an Analytical Survey', Board of Governors of the Federal Reserve System, *International Finance Discussion Paper*, no. 113.

Vastrup, L. (1983), 'Economic Motives for Foreign Banking: the Danish Case', *Kredit and Kapital*, **16** (1), 117–25.

Yannopoulos, G.N. (1983), 'The Growth of Transnational Banking', in M. Casson (ed.), *The Growth of International Business*, London: Allen & Unwin.

11. Multinational Corporations and the Single European Market

George N. Yannopoulos

11.1 INTRODUCTION

The process of economic integration in Western Europe has stimulated considerable activity by multinational corporations. The formation of the European Economic Community in the second half of the 1950s has attracted considerable direct investment flows into the six original member states. Similar trends have also been observed in EFTA. The subsequent enlargements of the European Community appear also to have attracted clearly identified responses by multinational corporations originating either from inside or outside the EC (Yannopoulos, 1990: Dunning, 1991). The measures initiated in 1985 to complete the internal market of the EC have also coincided with an expansion of the activities of multinational corporations within the EC involving both new, green-field investments, acquisitions, restructuring operations and joint ventures and alliances. The extent to which the acceleration in the growth of foreign direct investment in the EC and from the EC to the rest of the world is directly related to the single market programme or associated with broader trends in the world economy is a key issue in assessing the role of European integration on the activities of the multinational corporation.

This chapter examines the strategic responses of multinational corporations to the changes in the business environment that will inevitably result from the elimination of the non-tariff barriers in the internal market of the EC. The first section discusses the impact of the measures of the single market programme on the key determinants that influence the decision of a multinational corporation as to how to serve a particular market – in this case, the single European market. Following the OLI paradigm of the theory of international production the section examines how the single market programme is expected to influence the size of the locational advantages associated with the choice of production sites within the EC, the strength and nature of the

ownership advantages of multinational firms originating or operating in
the EC and the costs of common governance of spatially separated
units operating within the same hierarchy. In the following section the
strategic responses open to multinational firms for each type of change
identified earlier are specified together with the kind of investment
activity that they are likely to stimulate. The third section looks at
the trends in foreign direct investment, especially since 1985, and in
other activities associated with the strengthening of the position of
multinational firms inside the single market. The changing position of
the EC as a host and home region in the world economy is emphasized
together with an emerging trend towards the 'regionalization' of EC
industry. In the fourth section merger and acquisition activity inside
the European Community is examined, together with its policy implications. Finally, this chapter uses a number of selected case studies
to focus more directly on the patterns of response adopted by multinational corporations in advance of the single market.

11.2   THE IMPACT OF THE SINGLE MARKET MEASURES ON THE DETERMINANTS OF FOREIGN DIRECT INVESTMENT

The measures of the EC's single market programme will affect both
inward investment into the Community and the size and structure of
outward investment from the Community.

The major impact on inward investment comes from the increase
in the locational advantages of the internal market. Indeed, the measures of the single market programme will bring about a significant
global redistribution of the locational advantages of alternative host
regions to foreign direct investment.

(a)   The elimination of the host of non-tariff barriers to trade in the
internal market of the Community will discriminate positively in favour
of those trading inside the Community. The removal of the physical
barriers to trade, the reduction in the technical barriers to trade and
the elimination of financial barriers, such as exchange market controls,
will bring benefits to both insiders and outsiders trading in the Community. But on balance there will be a margin of preference in favour
of the trader from the internal market. This is even more obvious in
the case of the removal of market-entry barriers such as public procurement policies or the creation of a European financial area. The
size of the differential reduction of costs in favour of those trading

from production facilities inside the European Community is a matter of specific quantitative analysis in each sector.

In general, the reduction in the trading and other costs from the elimination of non-tariff barriers in intra-Community trade will be, on balance, larger for members than for non-members. Companies serving the internal market through exports from production facilities located outside the EC will find that their relative competitive position is eroded. Import substituting, defensive, direct investment to serve the market from within is one option open to restore the relative competitive position of the third-country trader.

(b)   Another factor contributing to changes in the distribution of locational advantages between the EC and alternative host regions for foreign direct investment is the uncertainty about the future course of the common external commercial policy of the integration region. When tariff barriers are eliminated inside a customs union and are replaced by a common external tariff, the level of the new external barrier faced by third countries is clearly identified and, as it is under the discipline of the GATT, it is subject to the rules of the international trading system. When integration takes place through the elimination of non-tariff barriers, one deals with a number of 'grey-area' trade policy measures for which the GATT rules are either inadequate or nonexistent. In such cases the common external commercial policy is surrounded by fluidity and uncertainty about its future course. An example is the case of nationally based and imposed voluntary export restraints. In a single market such measures cannot be policed effectively and must thus either be abolished or 'communitized'. 'Communitization' has the danger of excluding the third-country exporter from future demand growth (Yannopoulos, 1991).

These side effects and the uncertainty generated by the harmonization at the Community level of 'grey-area' trade policy instruments increase the attraction of producing inside the single market. Related to this is the fear generated by the possible use of the external commercial policy to cushion the internal adjustments of market liberalization. The use of product-specific rules of origin in the case of chips or the application of the anti-dumping policy have strengthened these fears. The danger that import trade restrictions may be used to this effect is an additional factor that increases the perceived advantages of supplying the internal market through local production rather than through exports from outside. This uncertainty effect from the fluidity of the common external commercial policy will stimulate defensive, import-substituting foreign direct investment.

(c)   Locations inside the single market may also become more attractive particularly for international sourcing by multinational corporations as a result of the efficiency gains expected from further economic integration. The costs of intermediate products may be lowered as a result of economies of scale in the industries supplying these inputs or as a consequence of the intensification of competition, particularly in highly fragmented markets. Examples of this kind can be found in the manufacturing of components, the telecommunications industry and the host of financial services industries. Depending on how strong these cost reduction effects are, they may stimulate inward rationalized direct investment.

(d)   A major consequence of the removal of non-tariff barriers to intra-EC trade is the stimulus to growth to be provided by the dynamic gains of integration. The one–off output expansion effects from the completion of the internal market will raise the output-capital ratio of the economy which in turn will generate a permanent increase in its sustainable growth rate. This increment in the rate of growth will be larger and will last longer if there are economy-wide increasing returns to scale. Baldwin (1989) has shown that when the medium-run growth effects of the internal market programme are taken explicitly into consideration, the output expansion effects of the Cecchini report (ranging between 2.5 and 6.5 per cent) would roughly double with half of this additional medium-run growth effect to be realized in the first ten years following the completion of the internal market. All in all, the EC growth rate will be lifted permanently by between one-quarter and nine-tenths of one percentage point.

This expected growth in market size adds further to the locational advantages of the EC as a host region with the potential effect of stimulating offensive import-substituting investment aimed at the servicing of market growth from production locations inside the EC. This type of foreign direct investment will be stronger in sectors where presence near the consumer is an important element of the marketing strategy of the firm.

(e)   The single market programme is expected in addition to generate a redistribution of locational advantages *inside* the common market. The removal of a number of market-entry barriers (for example, in the provision of financial services, in public procurement and so on) will enhance the locational attraction of those member states whose firms are best at providing specific services or supplying specific goods. Reorganization of investment is expected to take place in such cases with the regrouping of production in the most profitable locations and the servicing of the rest of the market from these locations. But the opening up of some markets previously reserved for nationals may not necessarily generate investment of the traditional type as the cost of acquiring the required knowledge about the local market may be high. In such cases alternative forms of market penetration may be adopted, such as joint ventures or alliances.

The intensification of competition inside the single market will also induce firms to concentrate in their core businesses, that is, in the activities they are best at. This will tend to reverse the trend towards conglomerate businesses based on product diversification, and encourage instead geographic diversification through the acquisition of assets in other member states primarily in the firm's core business. It is worth noting that intensification of competition from the removal of market segmentation can lead firms from inside the single market to hive off part of their production processes outside the single market in search of more-favourable costs. Thus further integration in the single market will stimulate outward direct investment too.

The analysis up to this point has focused on inward direct investment in the single market stimulated by the changes in the distribution of locational advantages either globally or within the single market. It is also possible that the process of market integration will exert an impact on the ownership-specific advantages of multinational firms originating or simply operating inside the single market. The channel through which ownership-specific advantages may be created or simply strengthened is via the impact of the unification of markets on the exploitation of economies of scale and scope and particularly through the more rational utilization of the firm's R&D resources and the stimulus to innovative activities. Such developments may strengthen the ownership-specific advantages of firms operating inside the single market. This will then tend to improve their competitiveness not only inside the single market but also in the rest of the world *vis-à-vis* competing firms. This is another route through which further integration inside the European Community can encourage more outward direct investment as well.

It is not clear whether the strengthening of ownership-specific advantages will benefit indigenous firms exclusively or whether it will include the multinational firms already operating inside the single market. Indeed, it may be argued that further integration in the single market will strengthen the ownership advantages possessed already by the multinational firms producing inside the EC, given the lower marginal costs enjoyed by the latter.

Integration of hitherto fragmented markets facilitates the exploitation of any economies of common governance by firms. Removal of the location-specific market imperfections enables firms to tackle more-effectively intrinsic market failures through the development of appropriate hierarchical structures. The opening-up of new opportunities for exploiting the economies of common governance gives EC-based firms time to build up new experiences in the governance of multidivisional, geographically separated units. This enables them to accumulate knowledge that will assist their penetration of non-EC, third-country markets.

11.3   PATTERNS OF STRATEGIC RESPONSE

Given the complexity of the 1992 legislative programme, its exact impact on specific enterprises will be a function of industry structural factors and corporate strategies. The elimination of the technical barriers to intra-Community trade will affect most those industrial sectors where the incidence of these barriers is regarded as high: pharmaceuticals, motor cars, electronics and so on. The deregulation of the road haulage transport industry as part of the measures to eliminate physical barriers to intra-Community trade will benefit the distribution trade more extensively. A considerable part of the effects of the single market programme is thus sector specific (Young *et al.*, 1991).

In addition, the type of response more appropriate to coping with changes in the business environment is related to current corporate strategies of servicing markets. A multinational corporation exporting to the single market from production facilities outside the EC will attempt to defend its market share by undertaking defensive import-substituting investment. A multinational enterprise with production facilities already inside the single market will engage in reorganization investment or, in other cases, in rationalized investment. Finally, a multinational firm neither trading with nor producing inside the single market may decide to build a market share, given the inducement from the growth effects of the internal market programme.

The analysis in section 11.2 suggests the following propositions with regard to the possible strategic responses of multinational corporations to the European single market programme:

(a)   The internal market programme will stimulate both inward investment into the Community (either of a defensive import-substituting type to defend existing market shares by firms exporting to the EC or of the offensive type aiming at tapping expected market growth) and outward investment as a consequence either of the search for lower costs (rationalized investment) or of the strengthened position of the EC-based firms. Rationalized investment may also be undertaken inside the EC by multinational corporations from non-EC countries eager to exploit the new opportunities for sourcing that arise from changing cost structures in intermediate products industries.

(b) Direct investment inside the single market will be undertaken either for offensive import-substituting purposes or for the purpose of reorganization or as rationalized investment to better exploit differences in input costs (for example, lower labour costs in the peripheral nations). Offensive import-substituting investment will be undertaken especially in sectors where market-entry barriers have been substantial up to now, such as in banking and insurance, or in construction and building engineering where public procurement practices have favoured local firms. Reorganization investment will be either in the form of divestment from certain countries and restructuring in others or in the form of expansion to form larger manufacturing units in order to compete successfully in the single European market. The first type of reorganization investment will be practised by multinational firms which in the past were obliged, because of government policies on market-entry controls and purchasing by the public authorities or the state-owned companies, to produce inside the fragmented national markets in order to sell. This will be the case in pharmaceuticals, for example, in power generating equipment or railway stock.

The second type of reorganization investment will be undertaken by enterprises in industries where scale economies are of some importance and which have operated especially from small markets but under conditions that assured indirectly a certain level of protection from competition from larger outside firms. This has been popularized as the idea of building industrial locomotives to compete successfully in the single market. This form of reorganization investment is likely to take place through mergers of national firms, especially in the smaller countries. In January 1989 three leading Danish firms in the food and beverages industry (De Danske Sukkefabrikker, De Danske Spiritfabrikker and Danisco) with a combined turnover of $1.8 billion announced an agreed merger. Subsequently, the two leading pharmaceutical producers in Denmark (Novo and Nordisk Gentofte) merged to form Novo-Nordisk. In both cases the explanation given was the need for a larger group to meet competition in the internal market.

Similar examples in different sectors can also be found from other EC countries. In the Netherlands the five big banks have been reduced to three with the mergers of NMB–Postbank and ABN–Amro. In Italy the second largest savings bank, Cassa di Risparmio di Roma, bought in 1990 Banco di Spirito Santo and acquired 65 per cent of Banco di Roma. These investments are not strictly speaking foreign direct investments but they can be regarded as the first step to subsequent expansion outside the home country, that is, in the rest of the Community. An interesting example of this two-stage strategic move is the merger in 1990 between Amev, the third largest Dutch insurer, and VSB, the largest Dutch savings bank group. Amev/VSB later merged with the Belgian insurance firm AG to create the multinational group Fortis.

(c)   As the changes that the single market programme will bring to the business environment are likely to be far more extensive for firms operating inside the Community, one would expect that intra-EC direct investment will grow during the period up to the effective completion of the internal market at rates faster than those involving extra-EC direct investment. The unification of the Community markets, especially in sectors where unique national tastes or high transport costs are not regarded as serious impediments to manufacturing integration, will encourage the pursuit of a regional core network strategy, that is, the building-up of integrated networks of affiliated units in each of the principal markets of the EC. This will lead to the regionalization of EC industry with the emergence of companies which look to the Community rather than to their home country as their principal market and relevant investment reference point.

This type of strategy leading to the 'regionalization' of European industry will be pursued by both third-country multinationals that operate already inside the EC and indigenous Community firms. This will force the latter to accelerate their moves towards becoming global competitors. In many cases this will induce EC-based multinationals to accelerate their investments in other world regions, for example, in the US or other developed countries, in an effort to gain the critical mass necessary to create the capacity to compete effectively with large American and Japanese multinational enterprises. The single market programme will strengthen these trends which were already in process in the early 1980s (UNCTC, 1991). It is clear that outward investment from the EC will not be reduced because the single market programme will strengthen the move towards 'regionalization' of European industry. The opposite seems to be more likely as firms of Community origin will be more exposed to global competition in the single market.

(d)   The new competitive environment in the EC will encourage more product and process specialization within the Community market. Firms will attempt to extend their geographical sphere of operations by buying up firms in other member states in their core business, that is, in the activities that they are best at. Cross-border takeovers, strategic stake-building and joint ventures will be more expedient forms to acquire first-mover advantages in the opening markets previously closed to non-nationals. In sectors where presence near the customer and knowledge of the local conditions is vital to compete effectively, alliances with local firms, mergers or the building of strategic stakes will be the best strategic move to exploit the new opportunities rather than 'green-field' investment. Cross-border holdings have been extensively built up by French and German construction and building companies. Such alternatives to green-field investments have also been used extensively in banking. In 1990, for example, only 9 per cent of cross-border banking transactions in the EC involved new investment. Acquisitions and mergers accounted for 35 per cent of these transactions, strategic share holdings 23 per cent, joint ventures 22 per cent, whilst the remaining 11 per cent involved principally market agreements and alliances (*The Financial Times*, 14 February 1991). In a number of sectors, therefore, non-traditional forms of direct investment will tend to dominate the intra-EC patterns of direct investment activity which are stimulated by the single market programme.

11.4   THE PATTERN OF DIRECT INVESTMENT ACTIVITY IN THE 1980s

This section examines the trends in inward and outward direct investment in and from the EC and assesses the role of the single market programme in shaping these trends. The difficulty in analysing such a complex phenomenon like the patterns of foreign direct investment is to disentangle the importance of the many different influences that operate on it simultaneously.

Before we look into the trends in the activities of the multinational corporations in the EC it is important to examine the worldwide developments in the activities of multinational corporations. Foreign direct investment has been growing very rapidly at 28.9 per cent per annum between 1983 and 1989. Foreign direct investment has been growing during this period at much faster rates than either world output (which was expanding at 7.8 per cent yearly) or world exports (which were growing at 9.4 per cent per annum). The world total of foreign direct investment was growing during the 1980s three times as fast as world output, becoming an increasingly larger proportion of world GDP. Thus one observes that worldwide foreign direct investment had already been going through a phase of fast expansion a few years before the launching of the single market programme in 1985. New trends in global competition and the strategies of multinational corporations from US, EC and Japan (the 'Triad') to build up integrated network affiliates in each of the Triad regions (UNCTC, 1991) are the principal explanations of the resurgence in the growth of foreign direct investment since 1983.

How does inward direct investment in the EC and outward direct investment from the Community compare to these world trends during this period? Table 11.1 provides information for both inward and outward investment in both stocks and flows. Total inward foreign direct investment (FDI) to the EC reached 33 per cent of world direct investment flows during 1985–9 from the 30 per cent share of the period 1980–4. This may be taken as an indication of how the internal market programme has affected the size of the inward flows of direct investment into the Community. However, this trend of an increased share of world inward direct investment and a rising position as a world host region should be interpreted carefully, given the contrasting trends in the stock shares. In terms of the value of stocks of world inward foreign direct investment, the EC share went down to 33 per cent in 1988 from the higher level of 40 per cent attained in 1980. However, the stock data extend only up to 1988 and this time-span may be regarded as insufficient in assessing the impact of the single market programme.

When inward investment flows are subdivided between extra-EC and intra-EC, one can see that the rising position of the Community as a host region for FDI flows is due entirely to the accelerated growth in intra-EC direct investment flows. Extra-EC flows declined to 16 per cent of world inward direct investment during 1985–9, compared with 20 per cent during 1980–4.

It appears that the single market programme created a new impetus towards the 'regionalization' of EC industry and the emergence of new multinational business strategies of rationalizing production operations on a European scale. This is a strong trend clearly identified by the data in Table 11.1.

Table 11.1   Foreign direct investment to and from the EC

	Flow data in US $ billions (annual averages)				Stock data in US $ billions			
	Inward		Outward		Inward		Outward	
	1980–4	1985–9	1980–4	1985–9	1980	1988	1980	1988
Extra-EC	10	19	18	39	143	239	153	332
(percentage of world total)	(20)	(16)	(38)	(31)	(28)	(20)	(29)	(32)
Intra-EC	5	21	4	20	45	160	50	160
(percentage of world total)	(10)	(17)	(8)	(16)	(9)	(13)	(10)	(16)
EC total	15	40	22	59	188	399	203	492
(percentage of world total)	(30)	(33)	(46)	(47)	(40)	(33)	(39)	(48)

Source: UNCTC, *Directory of Transnational Corporations*, New York: UNCTC, 1991.

These data underline another important trend regarding the position of the EC as a home region of multinational corporations. Here the trend is uniform, irrespective of whether one looks at stocks or flow data. The EC has become by the end of the last decade the most important home region or source of outward direct investment, surpassing the importance of the US. By 1988 the US accounted for 33 per cent of the world (including intra-EC) stock of outward direct investment (down from 42 per cent in 1980). In the case of the EC, its share in the world stock of outward direct investment has risen from 39 per cent in 1980 to 48 per cent in 1988. In terms of flow data, the position of the US declined from 29 per cent of world outward total (inclusive of intra-EC flows) during 1980–4 to only 14 per cent during 1985–9. For the EC the corresponding shares are 46 per cent and 47 per cent respectively. One is tempted, therefore, to say that, especially since 1985, the European multinationals pursued simultaneously strategies of 'regionalization' aiming at the rationaliz-ation of their production operations inside the EC and strategies of building-up integrated networks of affiliates worldwide in an effort to reach the critical mass required for effective global competition. It would appear that both strategies are mutually reinforcing and that EC multinationals view both moves as complementary strategies in global competition.

Evidence on intra-Community direct investment (Spanneut, 1990) shows more clearly the growing trend towards 'regionalization' in the investment and production strategies of Community-based corporations – especially since the mid–1980s (see Table 11.2). Intra-Community investment (irrespective of whether it is taken from balance of payments records of investing countries or from similar sources of the receiving countries) has increased by approximately five times between 1984 and 1988. It is notable that the major upwards deflection of the trend in the recorded flows occurred in 1986 – the year of the Single European Act.

Table 11.2   Intra-Community direct investment (million Ecu)

Declared by:	1984	1985	1986	1987	1988
Investing countries	−4265	−6987	−12469	−12646	−19076
Receiving countries	4358	5666	10354	11722	22976

Source: Eurostat, Provisional Report by Christine Spanneut on *Direct Investment of the European Community*, Luxembourg, August 1990, p. 15.

This twin-track strategy of rationalization operations inside the EC and integrated network-building worldwide is further demonstrated by comparing these trends in intra-Community direct investment with the corresponding trends in EC outward direct investment in other parts of the world. In 1984 Community-based corporations invested one Ecu in the Community for every four invested outside the EC. In 1988 Community-based corporations invested 2 2/3 Ecus inside the EC for every four Ecus invested in third countries outside the Community (Spanneut, 1990).

In terms of investing countries (home countries), the UK and France have accounted for nearly 50 per cent of the intra-EC direct investment flows. Indeed, six countries (Belgium, France, Germany, Italy, The Netherlands and the United Kingdom) have accounted for between 70 and 90 per cent of the direct investment flows generated inside the EC during 1984–8. Spain has also become an important home country of direct investment flows generated inside the EC. If her share is added, then these seven EC countries account for well over 90 per cent of the direct investment flows generated in the EC during 1984–8. However, it is not clear from the data whether the upward trend in intra-EC direct investment flows observed since 1985 has also led to important changes in the distribution of these flows by investing countries. The countries that acted as home countries for intra-EC multinational corporate activity continued to show an important presence in the restructuring and reorganization investment generated post–1985 (Table 11.3). The only obvious change has been the growing importance of the Netherlands as a source of intra-EC direct investment flows.

Table 11.3   *Intra-EC direct investment flows by home member country (percentage distribution; three-year moving averages)*

	1984–6	1985–7	1986–8
Belgium-Luxembourg	13.0	7.3	11.0
Denmark	0.3	0.0	0.3
France	19.3	13.0	14.3
Germany	9.3	5.0	3.7
Greece	1.0	1.3	0.6
Ireland	2.6	2.3	1.6
Italy	13.0	7.0	6.6
Netherlands	−11.3	14.0	17.0
Portugal	2.0	2.0	1.6
Spain	10.3	9.7	10.3
UK	37.0	37.7	30.7
Unallocated	3.0	0.3	1.3

Source: As for Table 11.2.

During this period intra-EC direct investment flows have been directed in proportions exceeding 95 per cent to the same six countries that we identified above as important sources of intra-EC direct investment flows (Table 11.4). Most of the restructuring and reorganization investment by Community-based multinational corporations was taking place in these six countries. France and the Netherlands in particular have received increasing shares of this type of investment.

Thus, unlike the distribution of intra-EC direct investment flows by origin, which indicates that the trends of higher direct investment activity inside the EC have not changed the relative importance of

*Table 11.4   Intra-EC direct investment flows by host member country
(percentage distribution; three-year moving averages)*

	1984–6	1985–7	1986–8
Belgium-Luxembourg	9.7	7.3	7.7
Denmark	2.3	1.7	1.3
France	12.0	15.3	18.7
Germany	19.0	18.0	13.7
Greece	0.0	0.0	0.0
Ireland	0.6	0.6	0.6
Italy	7.0	5.0	5.3
Netherlands	15.0	16.3	22.3
Portugal	0.0	0.0	0.0
Spain	0.3	0.6	1.0
UK	33.0	34.0	27.7
Unallocated	1.0	1.0	1.3

Source: As for Table 11.2.

the different sources from member states, the distribution of intra-EC direct investment flows by host (receiving) country suggests some changes in the relative importance of different host member states. France and the Netherlands have become increasingly more-important recipients of the reorganization and restructuring direct investment flows generated from within the EC, whilst the UK maintained more or less intact its position as recipient of about 30 per cent of the intra-EC direct investment flows.

It is interesting to examine the sectoral distribution of these flows to establish whether the restructuring and reorganization direct investment flows generated from within the EC are channelled towards specific sectors. Data on a broad sectoral distribution of intra-EC direct investment flows in the major five recipient member states (Table 11.5) show that in France, Germany and Italy more than 50 per cent of such investment flows were directed to service activities (banking and other financial services, trade and so on). Indeed, in Germany all the intra-EC net direct investment flows in 1986–8 were invested in service activities whilst the proportion in Italy was 79 per cent. The Netherlands appears to be the exception, with around 60 per cent of intra-EC direct investment flows channelled to the Dutch economy invested in manufacturing. The UK data are inconclusive due to the large size (59 per cent) of sectorally unallocated items.

Table 11.5   *Sectoral distribution of intra-EC inward direct investment flows (percentage distribution of cumulative total, 1986–8)*

	Manufacturing	Energy	Construction	Services	Unallocated
France	35.9	0.9	0.0	57.8	5.4
Germany	7.0	NA	NA	100.9	−7.9
Italy	12.2	8.8	NA	79.0	0.0
Netherlands	60.1	NA	NA	38.6	1.3
UK	11.4	NA	NA	29.1	59.5

NA = Not available
Source: As for Table 11.2.

Thus most of the intra-EC direct investment flows that were chan-nelled during this period to the five principal host countries of the Community have been absorbed by those sectors that are expected to face more-intense competition following the measures of the single market programme: sectors such as financial services where market entry barriers have been significant, and distribution and similar activi-ties where the removal of physical barriers to trade and other non-tariff barriers is likely to have an impact on costs.

It is instructive to compare the above trends in the late 1980s with corresponding trends in the early 1980s. Information on these latter trends can be found in Molle and Morsink (1991) and Morsink and Molle (1991). From this period the Netherlands, Belgium/Luxembourg and the United Kingdom have increasingly become the most important host countries within the EC, receiving more than 50 per cent of the intra-EC net direct investment flows. Germany and France, on the other hand, have increasingly lost share in the total inward net direct investment flows generated during 1980–4. The trend in France has been reversed since 1985. The United Kingdom and the Netherlands during this period have simultaneously become more-important sources of the net direct investment flows generated within the EC. Italy has also risen as a country of origin but from a low base. Four EC countries, namely the Netherlands, the United Kingdom, Germany and France, accounted for more than three-quarters of the net direct investment flows generated within the EC during 1980–4. This trend has continued during the second half of the 1980s.

Information on inward FDI into the Community from third countries is more detailed to enable us to see whether the patterns of manufac-turing investment in the EC by third-country multinational cor-porations have been changing in response to the single market pro-gramme (Buiges and Jacquemin, 1991). From Table 11.6 one can see that the United States multinationals have attempted to consolidate their production basis in sectors like transport, chemicals and machinery (including computers and related data processing equipment) and to some extent in food products. Interestingly, these are sectors where US export performance in the Community markets also appears strong. Whilst US multinationals tried during this period to reinforce their strong positions in the above sectors, they attempted a relative withdrawal from sectors like metal products and electrical and electronic equipment where their position was already weak in terms of both investment and exports. The exception here is the semiconductor industry where, following the modification of the rules of origin for chips which required that the diffusion process in the production of wafers must take place within the EC, both Texas Instruments and Intel announced plans in 1989 to build semiconductor chip manufacturing plants in southern Italy and the Republic of Ireland respectively.

Table 11.6   Changes in the EC share of direct investment originating from the United States, 1984–7

Sector	Percentage change
Chemicals and related products	+11.3
Machinery and data processing equipment	+10.8
Transport equipment	+10.6
Other manufactures	+ 9.9
Food products	+ 7.6
Metals	− 0.2
Electrical/electronic equipment	− 1.1
Industrial average	+ 9.1

Source: *Survey of Current Business*, various issues.

The Japanese pattern of penetration of EC markets suggests that Japanese multinationals are strengthening through the investment undertaken during 1984–7 their positions in electronic and electrical equipment, machinery and data processing, transport equipment and chemicals. During this period one observes a relative contraction of the presence of Japanese multinationals in ferrous and non-ferrous metals and in pulp and paper – sectors in which the Japanese firms are not strong internationally. In pulp and paper the Scandinavian firms have extended their presence in the EC through a series of acquisitions.

The data in Tables 11.6 and 11.7 suggest that as the competitive pressures from the single market programme intensify, third-country multinationals in the EC attempt a consolidation of their position in the sectors where they are competitively strong. In those sectors where international competitiveness is weak, both US and Japanese multinationals are going through a phase of relative contraction within the EC.

Table 11.7   Changes in the EC share of cumulative flows of direct investment originating from Japan, 1984–7

Sector	Percentage change
Chemical products	+3.8
Food products	+2.5
Textiles	+2.3
Transport equipment	+2.2
Machinery and data processing equipment	+1.6
Electrical/electronic equipment	+1.6
Pulp and paper	+0.2
Ferrous/non-ferrous metals	−0.4
Other manufactures	−6.2
Industrial average	+1.6

Source: Ministry of Finance, Tokyo.

11.5   CROSS-BORDER MERGER ACTIVITY IN EUROPE

In section 11.3 it was argued that cross-border mergers and aquisitions as well as other forms of non-green-field investments will be used extensively to respond to the changes in the business environment brought about by the single market programme. In this section we look in more detail into this type of strategic response by multinational corporations either from the EC or from non-EC countries. In evaluating the evidence, it is important to note that the growth in mergers and acquisitions is a worldwide phenomenon that precedes the launching of the internal market programme.

The globalization of markets, the need to enhance market positions and the opportunities offered by the availability of firms suffering from the aftermath of the economic recession of 1979–81 have brought about an intense merger and acquisition activity in all developed market economies. The internal market programme has provided an additional stimulus as firms across the Community attempt to enhance their market position in preparation for the stronger competition they are likely to experience in their own domestic market. At the same time they need to explore new market openings by acquiring a secure base in segments of the Community market not familiar to them. Acquisitions and mergers provide a fast method to establish the required sales network in order to penetrate unfamiliar market segments and also a secure way of entering markets, since it minimizes the risks for product development and marketing. Acquisitions are also helping in attaining economies of scale. With the merger wave in full swing, firms enter into the process of acquisitions and takeovers simply to avoid being raided themselves.

Evidence on the level of merger activity in Europe does suggest that the challenge of 1992 has acted as a key factor in its intensification throughout the Community. The number of cross-border acquisitions and mergers taking place by firms originating from the United States exceeded in 1985 the combined total of all cross-border takeovers recorded in France, Italy and the United Kingdom taken together. By 1987 this picture has changed, with cross-border takeovers in these three EC member states nearly trebling (487 compared to 165 in 1985), thus dwarfing those recorded in the United States (142 in 1987 compared to 175 in 1985). Companies both inside and outside the Community have been induced by the prospects of the completion of the internal market to take part in cross-border mergers. The data in Table 11.8 provide information on two types of merger activity: takeovers by companies from three EC countries and the USA, and takeovers in five Community countries by companies from other EC member states. The number of takeovers in Community countries in which the acquiring company originated from France increased from 31 in 1985 to 121 in 1987, a fourfold increase. The takeovers in the countries of the European Community in which the acquiring company originated from Italy also increased substantially from 14 in 1985 to 40 in 1987. On the contrary, takeovers in the countries of the European Community in which the acquiring company is from the United States have declined during the same period.

Table 11.8   Number of takeovers involving member states of the EC

Country	1980	1982	1985	1986	1987
Acquiring companies from:					
France	-	-	31	75	121
Italy	-	3	14	22	40
United Kingdom	12	10	15	13	68
United States	64	57	101	94	82
Acquired companies in:					
France	-	-	46	72	102
Italy	-	13	15	26	51
United Kingdom	6	4	3	5	5
Germany	112	71	86	-	-
Netherlands	16	15	19	-	-

Source: UNCTC, *The Process of Transnationalisation and Transnational Mergers*, New York: UNCTC, 1988.

11.6   CONCLUDING REMARKS

Early evidence from the activities of multinational corporations in the EC following the launch of the single market programme indicates that the measures under this programme have acted as an additional stimulus to enhance the position of the EC both as a host and as a home region of foreign direct investment. The most noticeable trend is the growing regionalization of European industry, as shown by the growing importance of intra-EC FDI both as a proportion of total inward investment in the EC and as a share of world total inward FDI flows. The Europeanization of EC multinationals has also been accompanied by increasing outward investment in other Triad regions or Triad-dominated regions in an effort to strengthen their global competitive position through the acquisition of the appropriate critical mass for this task. Thus a twin-track strategy of regionalization and global network-building seems to have been adopted by EC-based multinationals in their effort to strengthen their overall competitive position.

Both EC multinational corporations and multinationals from the US and Japan have engaged in reorganization with the aim of strengthening their positions inside the EC in those activities in which they are already strong internationally and to contract relatively in sectors of weak performance. This will tend to reverse previous trends in product diversification and conglomerate structures in favour of geographical diversification. The rising proportion of mergers and acquisitions as opposed to green-field investments raises important policy questions regarding the strength of competition in the internal market (Porter, 1991).

REFERENCES

Baldwin, R. (1989), 'The Growth Effects of 1992', *Economic Policy: A European Forum*, no. 9, 247–81.
Buiges, P. and Jacquemin, A. (1991) 'Effects of the Pull Exerted by the Single Market on United States and Japanese Exports and Direct Investment', paper presented at the Conference on Foreign Direct Investment in Europe, Louvain.
Dunning, J.H. (1991), 'European Integration and Transatlantic Foreign Direct Investment: the Record Assessed', in G.N. Yannopoulos (ed.), *Europe and America, 1992: US–EC Economic Relations and the Single European Market*, Manchester: Manchester University Press, 153–74.
Molle, W.T.M. and Morsink, R.L.A. (1991), 'Intra-European Direct Investment', in B. Bürgenmeier and J.L. Mucchielli (eds), *Multinationals and Europe 1992: Strategies for the Future*, London: Routledge, 81–101.
Morsink, R.L.A. and Molle, W.T.M. (1991), 'Direct Investment and European Integration', paper presented at the Conference on Foreign Direct Investment in Europe, Louvain.
Porter, M. (1991), 'Europe's Companies after 1992: Don't Collaborate, Compete', *The Economist*, 9 June, 23–6.
Spanneut, C. (1990), *Direct Investment of the European Community: 1984–1988*, Eurostat provisional report, Luxembourg: Eurostat.
UNCTC (1991), *The Triad in Foreign Direct Investment*, United Nations: Commission on Transnational Corporations, E/C. 10/1991/2.
Yannopoulos, G.N. (1990), 'Foreign Direct Investment and European Integration: the Evidence from the Formative Years', *Journal of Common Market Studies*, **28** (3), 235–59.
Yannopoulos, G.N. (1991), 'Trade Policy Issues on the Completion of the Internal Market' in G.N. Yannopoulos (ed.), *Europe and America, 1992: US–EC Economic Relations and the Single European Market*, Manchester: Manchester University Press, 9–23.
Young, S., McDermott, M. and Dunlop, S. (1991), 'The Challenge of the Single Market', in B. Bürgenmeier and J. L. Mucchielli (eds), *Multinationals and Europe 1992: Strategies for the Future*, London: Routledge, 3–21.

12. Multinational Investment in the EC: Some Policy Implications

John H. Dunning*

12.1 INTRODUCTION

This chapter seeks to analyse some of the implications of European economic integration, and particularly the completion of the internal market in 1992, for the policies adopted, both by the leading EC nations and by the European Commission, towards inward and outward direct investment and the activities of multinational corporations (MNCs).

We shall limit our analysis to two main time periods. First, the early postwar years through the establishment of the European Economic Community (EC) on 1 January 1958, to around 1975; and secondly, from that date to the present day. While the first period was mainly characterized by an inflow of US MNC activity into Europe, the latter saw both a widening of the sources of inward investment and a shift in its nature from primarily import substituting to efficiency or strategic asset seeking. In addition the latter years of the second period saw a marked increase in inward investment in anticipation of EC 1992, and a liberalization and harmonization of both national and regional policies towards such investment.

12.2 FDI AND THE MACROECONOMIC ORGANIZATION OF NATION STATES: SOME CONCEPTUAL ISSUES

12.2.1 The Issues Identified

Until recently, the ways in which individual European countries organized their economic activities had little to do with the presence or

* I am indebted to Professors Durán Herrera and Julien Savary and Dr V. Simões for providing me with some data in the preparation of this chapter.

349

absence of foreign-owned firms in their midst or with the outward investment of their own MNCs. Essentially, the macro-organizational policies of governments were addressed to fostering their macro-economic and social objectives; and primarily reflected the political ideology and the value judgements of alternative modes of organization of the governments in power. All the Western (but not the Southern) European countries, which are now members of the EC, operated mixed economies in which the role of the State in affecting the workings of the free market varied along a spectrum from near-centralized planning to near-*laissez faire*. However aware governments may have been of the impact on their economic and political goals of outbound or inbound MNC activity, there is no evidence that it had any direct effect on the macro-organization of economic activity.[1]

This is not to say that governments had no policy towards MNC activity or that, in certain areas of micro-organization (such as anti-trust legislation, regional development and investment incentives) their strategies were not modified in the light of the special features of MNCs or their affiliates. But, in general, government actions specifically directed to foreign direct investors were designed to ensure that the latter's conduct and performance enhanced rather than inhibited the success of *existing* macroeconomic and organizational policies. It then follows that, as long as MNCs were perceived to effect national objectives no differently than national firms, government policy would be neutral. If, for good or bad, their behaviour was distinctive, then measures might be taken either to encourage or to discourage their activities – or, more likely, to discourage the adverse micro-organizational impacts, while encouraging (or not deterring) the beneficial impacts.

For the most part, the philosophy of all European governments led either to no specific macro-organizational policies on MNC activity or to a number of very specific measures designed to achieve quite particular micro-organizational or macroeconomic objectives. Before considering these actions, however, it is worth observing that there are several different kinds of motives for FDI; and the economic consequences of each of these is quite distinctive.

The literature[2] identifies four main types of FDI: *natural resource seeking, market seeking, rationalized (or efficiency) seeking* and *strategic asset and capability seeking*. For the most part, EC countries have attracted and continue to attract direct investment of the three latter types.[3] Outward direct investment from EC countries is of all four kinds.

12.2.2 Inward Direct Investment

Each kind of MNC activity has its distinctive policy implications. Let us take inward investment first. *Market-seeking* investment, as its name implies, is investment designed to produce goods for the market in which the investment is made. Essentially, it occurs because foreign firms perceive that they can best service a particular market by being physically present in that market, rather than by exports from their home countries (or other host countries); or by licensing local producers to manufacture the products on their behalf. Historically, the main impetus for market-seeking investment has been the restrictions imposed by host governments on imports of foreign-made goods. In this event, there is a deliberate attempt by governments to switch the location of production and/or to protect their indigenous sectors against foreign imports.

The distinctive consequences of such market-seeking investment arise from the resources and capabilities transferred by the investing company and the way in which these resources and capabilities are utilized and managed. This resource-providing and organizational function of MNC activity may impinge upon both the host country's macroeconomic goals, for example, employment, interest rates, balance of payments, inflation, and upon its macro- or micro-organizational goals, such as industrial restructuring, competition, the environment, industrial relations, research and development (R&D) strategy and so on.

Governments have tended to try to protect themselves against the possible adverse consequences of inbound investment by imposing certain conditions of entry on the investing firms and by insisting on certain patterns of behaviour from them. Thus, a country in balance of payments difficulty might require a foreign subsidiary to buy a high proportion of its inputs from local sources or to export a certain proportion of its output. Another country which is suffering from regional unemployment may steer its foreign investors to the areas most seriously affected. FDI in particular sectors may be welcome in some countries but not in others, according to its industrial structure and the competitiveness of its indigenous firms. Because, then, of the different differential impact of FDI on host countries, and because of differences in the perceived needs and concerns of governments, it follows that the policies will also vary. Such policies may also vary according to whether the inward MNC activity takes the form of a green-field investment or an acquisition or merger of an existing domestic company.

The purpose of *rationalized* or *efficiency-seeking* investment is primarily to restructure – and sometimes expand – existing MNC activities so as to enhance the efficiency or global competitiveness of the investing corporation. Such investment is almost always 'sequential', that is, additional to existing investment.[4] Its impact on the host country is likely to be different from market-seeking investment (which it often complements) in that rather than, or in addition to, providing its affiliates with resources, technology and management capabilities, it provides them with cross-border organizational direction. Indeed, sequential investment captures much of the distinctive characteristics of modern-day MNC activity. While initially a firm's main ownership-specific advantages tend to lie in its privileged possession of (or access to) particular assets (which it makes available to its affiliates),[5] sequentially, it is the cross-border organization of these assets, that is, the advantages of (efficient) multinationality *per se*, which may predominate. At the same time, these organizational advantages[6] may enable a firm to sustain or enhance the kind of proprietary rights which made possible the initial investment.[7]

Nevertheless, rationalized production affects the structure of economic activity of the host country by locking it into the international corporate strategy of the investing companies. Whether or not this is to the benefit of the host nation depends on (a) how far its interests are best served by being part of an international division of labour, which implies some delegation of sovereignty – either to foreign markets or hierarchies; and (b) how far the ownership and control of that division of labour by MNC hierarchies benefits the host country *vis-à-vis* some alternative organizational pattern.

The more the government of a country perceives its interests as coincidental to those of the world economy (and especially to those of the countries with whom it trades), and the more MNCs are forced to behave as if they were operating in a competitive environment, the more it is likely to welcome MNCs for the cross-border organizational direction they provide. The more a government wishes to pursue a policy of economic autonomy and is concerned lest inbound MNC activity forces on it an unacceptable division of labour and/or reduces its bargaining or negotiating capabilities, the more it will seek to introduce specific policy instruments to control the level, direction or behaviour of foreign MNCs.

Unlike market-seeking investment, cross-border rationalized investment can only occur where there is relatively free trade between the countries which are host to the subsidiaries of MNCs. While market-seeking investment often responds to government-imposed market distortions and/or is undertaken to counteract the actions of competitors, rationalized investment flourishes where there are no structural market distortions but where, because of endemic market failure, the benefits of the common governance of economic activities and the transactions arising from these are substantial.

From the perspective of the investing company, rationalized investment is a response to the imperative of technological developments on the one hand and the liberalization of cross-border markets on the other. It tends to occur in capital- or technology-intensive sectors in which the advantages of both intra-industry and intra-firm trade are the most prevalent. These are the sectors in which the economies of scale, scope and geographical specialization can best be reaped, and where firms tend to differentiate their products as a form of competitive advantage. They include motor vehicles, consumer electronics, pharmaceuticals and telecommunications in the manufacturing sector, and finance, banking and insurance, consultancy and construction in the services sector. These are also the sectors which tend to be among the most footloose in their value added activities and which, in a Western European context at least, are less influenced in their location strategies by the availability of national resources and size of local markets and more by that of technological, educational, transport and communications infrastructure. Each of these latter variables have been shown to be critical to minimizing the costs of governance and maximizing the benefits of cross-border corporate integration (Dunning, 1991b).

Partly because rationalized investment is sequential – even though, currently, Japanese MNCs setting up subsidiaries in Europe are pursuing market-seeking FDI as part of a regionally integrated strategy – partly because its output is not primarily destined for the local market, and partly because the product and production configuration of rationalized affiliates is likely to be different from that of their local competitors, not only does government policy need to be different than is the case with market-seeking investment, but governments require to recognize that the responsiveness by rationalized or efficiency-seeking affiliates to any action taken by any set of policy instruments is also likely to be unique.

In a seminal contribution Yves Doz (1986) distinguished between three types of foreign affiliates which might operate in Western Europe. The first he classified as *nationally responsive* affiliates. These are entities which are similar to their indigenous competitors in all major respects except their privileged access to the assets and capabilities of the foreign corporations of which they are part. They tend to be truncated versions of their parent companies which treat them as part of a polycentric organization. These are also the foreign affiliates, the conduct of which host governments are most easily able to influence, although the nature and direction of such influence varies according to structure of the host economies and their objectives; while their *power* to influence the behaviour of the affiliates, or extract the maximum economic rent from them, rests on their bargaining capabilities.[8]

The second kind of affiliate identified by Doz is one which is part of an MNC which pursues a regionally or globally rationalized strategy. In such cases, host governments perceive the benefits to be those which arise from integration; but the costs are a reduction in the flexibility to enforce certain policies to ensure that affiliates behave in the national interest. Doz refers to a trade-off between the MNC not exploiting all the benefits of integration to be a good citizen; whereas the government accepts that the benefits of integration may not be achieved without some costs. Such costs may include the MNC purchasing a higher percentage of its inputs from foreign sources so that it can maintain the quality standards on output destined for international markets.

The rationalized affiliate is likely to be part of a geocentrically orientated investing company, and to engage in a considerable amount of intra-firm trade. Because they are less tied to a particular location, MNCs can (and often do) react to unwelcome government policies by relocating their activities. MNCs are usually more anxious to retain full equity control of efficiency-seeking affiliates than they are of market-seeking affiliates. *Inter alia*, this is shown by their greater reluctance to conclude joint equity ventures in the latter than in the former.[9] Consequently, the leeway for action by governments is likely to be less than in the case of market-seeking investments; although much again will depend on the balance between the rents earned on the resources transferred, on the one hand, and the benefits which arise from cross-border integration on the other.

Doz classifies most value added activities by MNCs as being some kind of balance between the degree of national responsiveness (or local citizenry), on the one hand, and international integration (or world wide citizenry), on the other. He acknowledges that most foreign MNCs operating in Western Europe fall somewhere in the middle. Such companies, he suggests, pursue a multifocal strategy by which management assesses the appropriate trade-off between responsiveness and integration for each decision-taking (or functional) area separately. Thus a MNC may behave as a nationally responsive company in the arena of labour relations or where (within a country) it locates its plant; but, as far as its sourcing, marketing and R&D strategy is concerned, it may operate as a regionally or globally integrated company.

Certainly, too, the balance between integrated and nationally responsive MNCs will depend on the countries in which they locate their activities and the countries from which they originate. As we have already seen, it will also vary between sectors. Thus, even within a regionally integrated area one might expect there to be a higher proportion of nationally responsive MNCs in countries which have large and prosperous markets, good supply capabilities, and whose governments exercise a critical and selective eye on the costs and benefits of economic interdependence. By contrast, in smaller countries which practice an export-orientated industrial strategy, one might find the ratio of efficiency to market-seeking investments rather higher. Examples of the latter group of EC countries are Belgium, Luxembourg, the Netherlands, Portugal, Ireland and Denmark. Examples of the former are West Germany, Italy and France. Spain and the UK, each for very different reasons, fall between these groups.

We now turn to consider the fourth kind of FDI in Western Europe, which has only recently been given explicit attention by economists and business analysts.[10] This investment we have called *strategic asset-seeking* investment. Its purpose is essentially to protect, sustain or advance the *global* competitive position of the investing company *vis-à-vis* its major national and international competitors. Such investment has been almost solely concentrated within Western Europe and in the US. It is directed chiefly to globally-orientated sectors,[11] whether these be growing or stagnating. European firms have acquired assets in the US mainly to strengthen their competitive position *vis-à-vis* US and Japanese MNCs, and US firms have acquired European firms to strengthen their position *vis-à-vis* European and Japanese MNCs and to re-configure their investments in preparation for EC 92. Meanwhile, Japanese firms have tended to use this strategy to acquire assets either in international sectors in which they are comparatively disadvantaged, such as pharmaceuticals, or in those which there is surplus capacity on the world markets, for example, Sunitomo's acquisition of Dunlop; or in those which offer complementary technologies or market access, such as Fujitsu's takeover of ICL. We have suggested that the intended effect of asset-acquiring investment is to benefit the global portfolio of the investing company. Often, this will mean a restructuring of the acquired firm's value added activities. This may take various forms, including a divestment of resources and capabilities unrelated to the core assets of the business, a slimming-down of the operations and a change in the organization of production.

The consequences of asset-acquiring investment for the host country are not easily predictable. Much depends on the characteristics of the firms involved and their positioning in international markets. The benefits include the injection of new capital, technology, markets, entrepreneurship and ideas, and perhaps the resuscitation of a declining industry. In others, there is a strengthening of the international posture of the acquired firm, even if it is now foreign-owned and integrated into the global network of activities. The costs are that the focus of control may be changed to the disadvantage of the host country. A company which was nationally responsive and integrated into the domestic economy may now become more responsive to global corporate objectives. There may even be a hollowing-out of the assets and markets of the acquired firm. This is likely to be most likely where its innovatory capabilities are transferred back to the new foreign owners and absorbed into their domestic R&D facilities.

Governments often have much less leeway to control or influence the outcome of an inward investment after it has been made, except where the effects are so widespread and far-reaching that it pays governments to modify their general macro- or micro-organizational policies. Generally speaking, until the mid–1980s, European governments were generally sceptical about the benefits of foreign acquisitions or takeovers, primarily because they feared that these might increase the concentration of foreign ownership, reduce indigenous and technological capacity, or close particular foreign markets (which the acquiring firm may prefer to service from one of its other subsidiaries). For many years now, the main policy instrument used by governments to thwart hostile takeovers has been monopoly and anti-trust legislation, which has been implemented with greater or lesser vigour by all European administrators.

In the last decade, however, attitudes towards cross-border mergers and acquisitions have become more relaxed, even though both individual national governments and the EC still view as unacceptable certain types of 'restrictive business practices'. This is partly due to the opening-up of domestic European markets to outside competition, and partly to the increasing belief that inward direct investment (or involving foreign partners' alliances) can, by its provision of new assets, capabilities and organizational direction, aid the competitiveness of the host countries. This latter claim is yet to be substantiated. Certainly, in some instances it has dubious validity, as exactly the same argument is advanced by home countries about the benefit of some kinds of outward direct investment.

In summary, depending on the type of inward direct investment, the extent of the existing foreign investment stake, the sectors in which it is made, the conditions under which it is made, and the home and host countries involved, its policy implications are likely to differ. However, one generalization is, perhaps, permissible. Over the last 20 years or more, the economic significance of inward direct investment to most EC countries has steadily risen (UNCTC, 1991; Dunning, 1992(a)). So indeed, has that of outward direct investment. The result is that the MNC intensity of economic activity (measured as the percentage of inward plus outward investment stake to GNP) has risen from being generally of marginal significance to being of very considerable significance. In 1988, for example, in the UK and the Netherlands, the MNC intensity was over 40 per cent, in Belgium it was 30 per cent and in Germany, Greece and Ireland it was more than 15 per cent. Most of these percentages are at least double those of 20 years ago. This index alone (and there are others which tell a similar story[12]) suggest that the time is coming when governments will need to take account more explicitly of the specific role of both domestic and foreign MNC activity in the formulation of their micro- and macro-organizational policies (and indeed, some of their macro-economic policies as well[13]) and the very specific contributions made by such companies to national economic objectives.

But as section 12.3 of this chapter will suggest, there is little evidence that this is being done – at least, not in an EC context. Indeed, early in 1991 the author was informed by a senior official of the EC Secretariat that the nationality of the owners of firms producing in the EC was of little or no interest to the European Commission. This is in stark contrast to the Japanese perception of the significance of inward and outward direct investment, where since the mid 1960s it has not only been explicitly incorporated into their industrial, trade and technology policies but in recent years has come to dominate increasingly these policies[14] (Ozawa, 1989). But before taking these comparisons further, we turn to consider some effects of outward investment on the policy formation of the capital-exporting countries.

12.2.3 Outward Direct Investment

For much of the twentieth century, most western European MNCs have been actively involved in both *resource* and *market-seeking* outward investments. Because of intra-European tariff barriers (including cultural and political barriers) and their inability or unwillingness to exploit the economies of cross-border activities, they have lagged behind US MNCs in developing both horizontal and vertical *rationalized* investments.[15] There are signs that Europe 1992 is producing a major change in the attitude of European MNCs, who at the same time are engaging in more aggressive *strategic asset-acquiring* investment both within Western Europe and in the US and Japan. However, rather than repeat (in mirror fashion) the approach of the previous section to analysing the policy implications of outward investment, we shall examine two or three of the major policy areas by which such investment has been evaluated. We shall then relate the shift in priority given to these areas to the changes in the international economic scenario, and in the attitudes of home governments towards the costs and benefits of outbound MNC activity.

The national output and the balance of payments of the home country

As has been demonstrated elsewhere (Dunning, 1992b), the initial post–1945 concern of most European governments was about the effects of outward MNC activity on the balance of payments. Many European currencies, including the £, were not fully convertible until the early 1960s while, for most of the rest of that decade the (current) balance of payments of European countries with the exception of Germany was in deficit; and much macroeconomic policy was directed to correcting this deficit. In addition, governments of the era, (and particularly that of the UK) were concerned about the consequences of outward investment on the real national output, as at the time academic research was showing that the *direct* social rate of return of foreign direct investment was less than the social rate of return of domestic investment.[16] However, outbound investment sometimes led to *indirect* benefits to the home country. Among the most important of these identified by economists in the 1960s were the additional demand for goods produced by the home country and a feedback of technical knowledge resulting from foreign production (Reddaway, Potter and Taylor, 1968; Hufbauer and Adler, 1968).

As with inward investment, the effects and policy implications of outward investment rest crucially on the kind of investment being made and the assumptions made about what would have happened in the absence of such investment – the so-called 'counterfactual' or 'alternative' position. For example, most *market-seeking* FDI is likely – to some extent at least – to be export-replacing. However, if, in the absence of such FDI, MNCs from other countries had made the investment, it is possible that exports would have fallen even more.

Moreover, if government macroeconomic policy is successful in filling the investment 'gap' opened by the capital exports, this will have very different consequences for the national output and the balance of payments than if there is no compensatory investment.[17]

By contrast, *resource-seeking* outward investment is less likely to be substitutable for domestic investment or exports from the investing country; indeed, it may be complementary to them. Much resource-based investment by developed industrialized countries is undertaken to safeguard sources, lower the prices or improve the quality of minerals, energy supplies, raw materials and agricultural products used by domestic manufacturing firms, and to protect or advance their supply capabilities *vis-à-vis* those of their competitors. At the same time, the extent to which such investment benefits the capital exporting country is likely to depend, first, on whether or not in its absence some other firms would have made the investment; and secondly, on how far it is at the expense of other kinds of domestic capital formation, or indeed, of the efforts of the purchasing companies to seek alternative sources of primary products or to economize on their use. It may also partially rest on the extent to which home governments are prepared to protect their investors from the uninsurable risks of FDI (for example, the possibility of nationalization or expropriation of their foreign assets), by some kind of investment insurance or guarantee schemes.

Governments' strategic options may differ according to their perception of the likelihood and the costs and benefits of these alternative scenarios. But one thing is clear: the opening-up of opportunities for FDI in resource-based sectors implies some kind of policy response on the part of the home government – even though this may result in no action being taken.

The attractions of *rationalized* outward investment to capital-exporting countries rest largely on the extent to which the *raison d'être* for such investment is consistent with the economic goals of the home countries. In general, assuming that the home country accepts the benefits of economic interdependence and that MNCs are operating within a (reasonably) competitive international environment, it is to be expected that they are. A division of labour forged by MNCs from West Germany or the UK, provided it is in response to market forces rather than to government-imposed distortions, is likely to create structural changes, and secure an economic rent which will accrue to the benefit of the home country. The main policy challenge posed by rationalized investment is how best to minimize the costs of structural adjustment arising from it. Such fragmentary research as has been undertaken on this subject (OECD, 1985) suggests that MNCs tend to respond to changes in the external business environment more speedily than their uninational competitors and that this could exacerbate the short-run problems of resource reallocation. Certainly, outward investment, which is designed to take advantage of low labour costs (a form of resource-based investment but one which is motivated by efficiency-seeking considerations) by US MNCs in Mexico and some Asian industrializing countries, has been loudly condemned by those in the home countries who attribute to it their loss of jobs. At the same time, it is likely that, in the absence of such investment, European and latterly Japanese MNCs would have captured at least some of the markets supplied by US firms.

If rationalized investment is broadly consistent with the long-term output and trading goals of home countries, the effects of *strategic-asset-acquiring* investment are more difficult to assess, simply because the conditions for such investment and the rationale behind it are so firm-specific. And yet, in some ways, since very large capital exports are involved, this kind of investment is directly substitutable for domestic investment; indeed, for reasons which we shall soon discuss, it has the potential to be the most socially costly form of FDI. At the same time, the possible social benefits are also quite significant. Much again depends on whether other kinds of domestic or inward foreign investment can fill (or would have filled) the gap vacated by the outward investments.

Long term competitiveness and technological capability

The last two decades have seen a noticeable change of emphasis in the evaluation of outward direct investment by most countries. Except in the case of some Asian countries, however, it is still too early to identify the policy changes which can be specifically attributed to this reconfiguration of values. Basically, attention has switched from judging outward investment by its direct effects (for example, the profits it earns) to assessing its wider consequences on the resources and capabilities of the investing country, and the efficiency with which these resources and capabilities are organized. This explicitly or implicitly assumes that FDI, like trade, can (depending on the conditions in which it is made) either advance or retard a nation's competitive advantages. Action taken to further this objective may range from eliminating internal structural market distortions to introducing or strengthening a variety of measures designed to facilitate domestic resources and competences to better deal with and react to market forces, including those requiring changes in the direction of resource allocation and the organization of resource usage.

However, national policy might go well beyond that specifically directed to outbound MNCs. It could, for example, encompass actions taken against other countries which pursue strategic trade (and/or other) policies to protect or advance the interests of their national champions (Stegemann, 1989). Domestic policy may also extend to other areas of macro-organization which are affected by, or affect, the ability and willingness of domestic companies to be competitive in global markets. Of these, education and training, science and technology, transport and communications and environmental policies are perhaps the most important. These directly affect the willingness and ability of a country's firms to upgrade the quality of indigenous resources and the way in which these are organized, both at home and abroad.

Using this criterion, outward direct investment is assessed by the way in which it contributes to the long-term competitiveness of a nation, not only by advancing the efficiency of its own resources but by accomplishing this goal more effectively than its competitors. To this extent, governments, and particularly governments of advanced industrial nations which are at a similar stage of economic development and producing broadly similar products, are increasingly implementing organizational strategies not unlike those pursued by their indigenous firms.

Such a strategic or holistic approach to outbound MNC activity tends to require a very different set of policy measures than those described earlier. Moreover, ideally, governments should adopt policies which take domestic investment by indigenous firms, domestic investment by foreign firms and foreign investment by indigenous firms as part of the same package of resource usage and allocation.

We have not the space to take this argument much further. It is, in any case, further developed by the author in several recent contributions.[18] However, it may be useful to illustrate our contentions by reference to the contemporary debate on the role of MNCs and generators, organizers and utilizers of technological capacity. To what extent is outward direct investment likely to assist or inhibit the achievement of this goal?

There seem to be a number of arguments both in favour of and against government intervention in outbound MNC activity. The main argument in favour of such activity is that (whether it be *market*, *resource*, *efficiency* or *strategic asset* seeking) it may help the investing firms to acquire resources, capabilities or markets which will help them sustain or advance their competitiveness in world markets and to engage in more higher-value-added activity in their home countries. R&D is becoming increasingly expensive and needs either global markets to help finance it or for its costs to be shared with other firms.[19] According to the protagonists, foreign and domestic investment are complementary ingredients of the global competitive strategy of firms and of the upgrading of domestic resources and as such should be supported rather than discouraged by home governments.

The main arguments put forward against FDI – especially in high-technology sectors – are twofold. First, firms may be transferring technology to foreign countries at too low a social price. This is thought particularly likely where the importing countries are potential competitors to the exporting country. This argument is sometimes coupled with another, which is that, in pursuance of their defensive oligopolistic strategies, MNCs may transfer some of their ownership-specific advantages to a foreign location, at the cost of eroding the competitive advantage of domestic resources. Secondly, the strategic or security-related concern is that, having assisted a foreign country to become economically strong – particularly in defence-sensitive sectors – should that country then become unfriendly, it could rebound to the detriment of the home nation. The validity of both these arguments depends on the extent to which the host countries are able to obtain the technology being exported by the MNC either from other countries or by other routes, for example, export, licensing arrangements and so on. They also tend to assume that there would be no retaliations from the country adversely affected by restrictions on technological exports and to underestimate the technological gains it may be receiving from *inward* investment.

While it would be difficult to deny there are some cases where FDI is to the long-term technological disadvantage of the investing country, in general, a combination of the convergence in the technological abilities of the major investing countries and the two-way flow of MNC activity in high-technology sectors seems to suggest that the case for a neutral – if not a (market) supportive – government policy towards outward direct investment and the complementary restructuring and upgrading of domestic resources and capabilities is more desirable than a restrictive policy.[20]

12.3 POLICY MEASURES

With these analytical underpinnings in mind, let us review the evolving national and regional (that is to say, EC) policies towards inbound and outbound MNC activity in the EC. Because the focus of this volume is very much on the impact of contemporary and likely future events in intra EC investment patterns, we shall only refer to past policies in so far as they help us understand the current policies and the changes which have occurred in the actions of governments over the past three or more decades.

12.3.1 Phase 1: The Postwar Period – up to 1975 or Thereabouts

Prior to the establishment of the European Economic Community there was no harmonization of policies of governments of the future member states towards inward or outward direct investment. Almost all the inward investment until the late 1950s was *market-seeking*, although in some cases investment in one country was used to service other European countries and, in the case of the UK, the non-$ Commonwealth markets. Outbound MNC activity was predominantly *resource-seeking* and mainly directed to the rich Commonwealth or developing countries. The exception was some *market-seeking* investment in the US and in other parts of Europe.

Most countries used foreign exchange control measures to ensure that both inward and outward MNC activity did as little damage as possible to their balance of payments; while, especially in countries which pursued or had pursued socialist economic policies and promoted the state ownership of industry (such as France and the UK), there were strict limitations on the participation of foreign firms in 'key' or strategically sensitive sectors. The identification of these key sectors varied between countries,[21] as did the attitude of the authorities to the acquisition of local firms by foreign MNCs, the access of foreign investors to local capital markets, the restriction of official aid, subsidies and public purchasing to nationally owned firms, and discriminatory legal treatment of foreign affiliates.[22] Outward investment was disallowed or discouraged to hard-currency areas. At the same time, apart from the UK, Switzerland, Sweden and the Netherlands, MNCs generally lacked the ability or the incentive to engage in new foreign value-added activities – apart from those which were export-promoting.

Of the European countries, France had the most explicit general policies towards inward investment which, after the publication of Jacques Servan Schreiber's treatise *Le Défi Americain* in 1968, became more restrictive. It is also fair to say that, by this time, France had evolved the most aggressive and distinctive policies towards technological development, as most noticeably witnessed by its efforts to maintain a French presence in the computer and related high-technology sectors. The French authorities also much preferred green-field to foreign investment, and generally resisted proposals for new investment (which had to be registered with the Ministry of Economics and Finance) which were likely to be highly competitive with those of local firms or interfered with their own plans to restructure industry (Safarian, 1983).

At the other end of the policy spectrum was the Federal Republic of Germany. Even in the early years of the postwar period few sectors were closed to foreign participation, although until recently a number of sectors, such as telecommunications, have been subject to strong governmental control. Neither has there ever been any authorization or screening of forms of entry or of foreign takeovers, although Germany currently operates one of the most stringent anti-trust policies in Europe. In the 1950s and '60s the UK occupied a midway position between Germany and France in its attitudes towards MNC activity. Generally taking a welcoming stance, the main policy instruments used by successive UK governments were foreign exchange control regulations[23] and such agencies as the Industrial Reorganisation Corporation set up in the 1960s to help rationalize and restructure some key industrial sectors. Debates in the House of Commons, recorded by Hansard,[24] suggest that on frequent occasions there were calls for more control on both inbound and outbound capital movements. In addition, certain sections of the UK community, such as the Trades Union Congress, were particularly critical of certain kinds of MNC activity. At the same time, despite its liberal stance, the UK government has, from time to time, intervened to support indigenous firms in competition with foreign affiliates, noticeably in the motor vehicles, microelectronic and computer industries. Other critical measures which the UK government was able to use to influence FDI were the Monopolies and Restrictive Practices Act (1965) and the City Panel on Takeovers and Mergers. However, these facilities were not *specifically* directed to foreign companies and there is no reason to suppose that they were used in a discriminatory way either in favour of or against such companies.

The Italian attitude to FDI was similar to that of Germany. However, the 1956 law on foreign investments stated that such participation in Italian industry was welcome only in so far as it might be expected to lead to the establishment of new 'productive' corporations or help existing productive corporations to expand. The result of the law is that since 1956 such designated or approved foreign-owned firms have, for all intents and purposes, been treated as domestic firms. The only exception is that foreign firms do not have complete freedom of access to Italian financial and capital markets. Italy, like France, also has a substantial public sector in which in the 1960s and '70s foreign firms were not allowed to invest. Finally, for many years the government of Italy has also reserved the right (infrequently used) to block an acquisition of a major Italian firm by a foreign MNC (after 1958 a non-EC MNC), but, to the best of our knowledge, this prerogative has never been used.

Until the 1950s, the policy of the Irish authorities was to keep control of its industry and to discourage inward foreign investment. This policy was dramatically reversed in the 1960s. Since that time Ireland, along with Belgium, has developed a very extensive range of incentives to foreign investors, some of which have since drawn the critical attention of the European Commission. Both Belgium and Ireland are examples of countries which, from the start, have tried to attract rationalized or export-orientated inward investment; but both countries have also used such MNC activity as a means of fostering regional development. In both countries, too, the foreign-owned manufacturing sector has recorded impressive productivity and growth performances; although in the case of Ireland, at least, not all scholars agree that the impact of inward investment has been an unalloyed benefit (O'Hearn, 1990). Finally, for many years, the foreign sector has played such a dominant role in both Belgium and Ireland that the macro-organizational policies of these countries cannot but have been strongly influenced by their presence. These have included anti-cyclical policies, bearing in mind that, in years of domestic economic strain, foreign firms tend to cut back their foreign investments earlier than their domestic investment.[25]

Like Ireland and Belgium, the Netherlands is also heavily reliant on inward investment. None the less, for many years past the Netherlands has been an important capital exporter.[26] It is not perhaps surprising, then, that in spite of the export-orientation of her major inward investors, Dutch policies towards MNC activity have been generally comparable to the UK which, *par excellence*, is the world's leading international investor.[27] Except in broadcasting, military production and aviation, foreign-owned affiliates are treated exactly the same as domestic firms. The rules on acquisitions and mergers are also non-discriminatory. As with other governments, the Dutch have tried to steer foreign firms into areas suffering from above-average unemployment. They were one of the first European countries to stimulate both foreign and domestic investors in energy conservation and to make use of alternative energy sources and pollution preventatives. The Dutch have never operated any screening mechanism for foreign investment.

Portugal, Spain and Greece did not join the EC until the 1980s. In the mid–1960s and the 1970s they took a somewhat more selective, though generally welcoming, attitude to foreign investment. In Spain, for example, there was no democratically elected government until 1975, and, prior to that date, the economy was highly protectionist. Even in the late 1970s, FDI was vetted in most high-technology sectors and those with approved industrial conversion plans (for example, automobiles, shipbuilding, household appliances and textiles). The Spaniards also had quite complex administrative procedures for inward investors, and several government ministries, including the Council of Ministers (the Spanish cabinet) were usually to be consulted. The authorities also exercised dividend limitations up to early 1981.

In the past, Portugal has imposed quite extensive requirements on foreign investors. As recently as the early 1980s, not only were some sectors barred to foreign MNCs altogether, but in others, such as mining and quarrying, fishing and international road transport, only a 49 per cent foreign shareholding was permitted. The conditions under which acquisitions were authorized were also laid down. Repatriation of dividends and profits required Bank of Portugal approval, while Portugal's main watchdog on foreign investments (the Foreign Investment Review Agency) carefully evaluated and monitored all technology transfer agreements and was apt to view unfavourably any efforts by a foreign firm to integrate the production and marketing strategy of its Portuguese affiliates with that of the parent company. To a greater extent than in Spain, FDI in Portugal was encouraged towards sectors in which Portugal had, or was striving to achieve, a comparative trading advantage (Simões, 1985).

Although Spain and Portugal were not major outward investors prior to the mid–1980s, both countries operated fairly strict exchange control regimes. Of all the current members of the EC, perhaps Greece has historically viewed inward investment with the greatest caution. Though the attitude of successive governments has been generally cordial, since 1953 foreign investment has been expected to meet certain conditions not required of domestic firms. Like several developing countries, it has valued MNC activity as a means of importing technology, creating jobs and promoting exports: such investments are classified as productive investments. Along with quite generous

investment incentives, the Greek authorities also laid down fairly stringent performance requirements which foreign firms were expected
to meet before they could freely remit any profits and dividends
earned.

Acquisitions of Greek companies were generally not eligible for
investment incentives. All investments had to be approved by the
Minister of National Economy on the recommendation of the appropriate consultative committee. In general, the Greek attitude towards
inward investment, which was a mixture of *resource-* and *market-
seeking*, was similar to that of many developing countries of the time.

In summary, in the period prior to and during the early years of
European integration, there was no harmonization of national policies
towards MNC activity. Attitudes and actions varied according to the
political complexion of the government in power, the macro-organization policies it pursued and its attitude towards economic interdependence. Policies tended to be most liberal in the smaller industrialized
countries which relied heavily on international transactions for their
prosperity and least liberal in the less-developed and less-integrated
economies. In the larger developed countries, much rested on their
role as international investors in the world economy and the extent to
which governments intervened in the management of their economies.

12.3.2 Phase II: The Later Years and Preparing for EC 1992

The new economic climate for MNC activity
With the increasing integration of Western European economies and as
MNCs have come to view the EC as a single market, the geographical
distribution of FDI between the member countries has become increasingly based on an *efficiency-seeking* rather than a (national) *market-*
or *resource-seeking* kind. The restructuring of MNC activity in the
EC between 1957 and the mid-1980s has been well-documented, for
example, by Cantwell (1989, 1992), and the UNCTC (1992b); and
there is considerable evidence to suggest that at least the larger and
more-experienced US foreign investors are engaging in a regional
division of labour in the EC. Foremost among this evidence is the
quite dramatic increase in intra-firm EC trade undertaken by US
MNCs (US Department of Commerce, v.d.; UNCTC, 1991). In 1985
56.1 per cent of the sales of US subsidiaries in the EC were sold to
other US affiliates,[28] compared with 21.5 per cent in 1966. Between
1985 and 1988 these sales rose by 74.7 per cent compared with local
sales of 47.4 per cent.

Yet coupled with this efficiency-seeking investment, since the early

1980s there has been a surge of 'first-time' MNC activity by medium and smaller US firms, by Japanese firms, by some third world MNCs and, perhaps most interestingly of all, by EC MNCs in other EC countries (that is, intra-EC direct investment). Much of this investment, at least since 1986, has been 'pulled in' by expectancies about EC 1992. It is in part defensive or protective and in part aggressive and opportunistic. Part, too – especially that undertaken by the Japanese MNCs – can be thought of as traditional *market-seeking* investment – most certainly so if one takes the EC as a single market in its own right; while part – and one suspects this particularly applies to intra-European investment – has more the characteristics of *strategic asset-acquiring* investment, as firms aim to sustain and advance their global competitive positions. One response of EC firms to this new thrust of inbound MNC activity has been to step up their own intra-EC direct investment and strategic alliances. Indeed, apart from Asian FDI, this is the fastest growing form of cross-border activity now being undertaken within the EC.

Quite apart from changes in the motives for and character of MNC activity in and out of the EC, governments of EC countries have also been reappraising their economic objectives and re-evaluating the means by which they can best achieve these objectives. In particular, there has been a wholesale revamping of macro-organizational policies, as witnessed, for example, by the liberalization and privatization of many markets and the reduced role of government as an organizer of economic activity. The liberalization and reform of financial markets has also led to a spectacular increase in the cross-border mobility of capital. It has also resulted in a phasing-out of all forms of exchange control. At the same time, added to national government policies, there are now EC policies on a whole range of economic matters, including that specifically directed to MNC activity.

A review of national policies recently undertaken by OECD (1991) reveals a general removal of obstacles to both outward and inward MNC value-added activity and a relaxation in the performance expectations of foreign affiliates. At the same time, it is clear that some sharp differences are emerging as to the *kind* of inward investment that is most welcome. These differences are particularly marked between the smaller and larger and between the more- and less-developed EC. There is also a growing divergence of attitude – particularly on the part of France and Italy – towards inward investment according to its country of origin. Japanese inward investment, for example, is often viewed more as a Trojan Horse than is either intra-EC investment or North American investment.

At the same time, the kind of FDI policies now being pursued by European governments are best considered as part and parcel of macro-organization strategies which, directly or indirectly, are being increasingly influenced by the globalization of economic activity. But before discussing these broader strategies, let us identify the main changes in the attitudes and actions of EC governments towards inward and outward investment.

Inward investment

The changing attitudes and actions towards inbound MNC activity may be summarized under eight headings:

(a)   There has been a general warming of attitudes and relaxation of policies towards inward direct investment and the removal of restrictions and obstacles to most kinds of capital imports. Foremost among the liberalizing countries in the later 1980s have been France, Spain and Portugal; and in the early 1990s Greece is following a similar path.

(b)   Many countries have replaced fairly detailed and multifaceted authorization procedures for inward investment by simple notification or verification devices. Authorization procedures are now normally confined to very large transactions and/or acquisitions; and in most cases only one authorizing ministry or agency is involved. The greatest progress towards liberalization has been made by Portugal, Spain and France.

(c)   Many sectoral restrictions have been lifted or greatly reduced. Sectors which used to be wholly denied to foreign investors have now been opened up. However, most EC countries still limit and/or regulate conditions for non-EC foreign investment in: the finance and insurance sectors (see (e) below); basic telecommunications services (Spain); broadcasting (Spain, the UK and France); publishing (France); nuclear power and oil-related activities (France); airlines (Spain, Italy, the UK, Ireland, Luxembourg); maritime transport – and particularly the registration of ships and the access of foreign-owned vessels to cabotage (most EC countries); fishing (Italy, Ireland, Denmark and France); and armaments manufacturers (Denmark, Spain, France and the Netherlands).

(d)   The reduction or elimination of all exchange controls on inward investment. Here the most radical reforms have occurred in France,

Spain, Portugal and Greece. There is now a virtually free international capital market in the EC, although there are still some restrictions imposed on non-EC investment by France, Portugal and Greece.

(e)   Restrictions on the local financing of capital expenditure by non-residents have also been markedly reduced. Those which remain relate mainly to some general provisions on the access by non-residents to local capital markets, currently imposed by Italy, Portugal and Spain.

(f)   Provisions maintained by member countries on essential national security and public-order grounds, however, remain extensive and some have even been strengthened, especially in the strategic economic and 'cutting-edge' technology sectors.

(g)   There has been rather less progress made on the liberalization of FDI in services. Reciprocity conditions, linking the recipient country's treatment of a foreign investor to that granted to the recipient country MNCs in the investor's country of origin are still frequently imposed, particularly on US and Japanese MNCs. For example, in the banking sector reciprocity conditions are being applied by Belgium, Germany and the UK; in the insurance sector, by Luxembourg and Portugal; and in other financial services, by Denmark and Portugal.

(h)   In spite of the general loosening of controls on inbound MNC activity, many countries, including those which otherwise adopt a most welcoming stance, still encourage, or even insist that, foreign investors should accept certain performance requirements. Often the adherence to these requirements is the price extracted by host governments for tax concessions and other incentives. To this extent – unwisely in the view of some economists – EC countries have taken a leaf out of the books of developing countries by intervening in the normal market process. The two requirements[29] most widely imposed – even by the most liberal-minded governments – are, first, that over a certain period of time a certain pre-agreed proportion of the value of a good sold by a foreign subsidiary in an EC country will be produced in the EC (the local-content requirement); and secondly (and this is linked to the first), that an investing firm will, by an agreed date, undertake at least some of its higher-value-added activities in its European subsidiaries. Both these provisions are particularly directed to Japanese investors. The particular concern is lest Europe should simply become a low-value-added base servicing the higher-value-added activities of Japanese firms in their home country.

Outward investment

According to the OECD (1991), there are practically no restrictions on outward direct investment currently imposed by EC countries, either in authorization procedures or in financing. It would seem that as the balance of payments constraints of the leading investing countries have become less severe (or the measures taken to influence outward investment for this reason have proved ineffective or inappropriate), policy towards outbound MNC activity has become more relaxed. Moreover, the liberalization of both exchange and capital markets, together with a more congenial climate towards inward investment, has mellowed the attitude of most authorities towards capital exports.

At the same time, over the past decade or more domestic unemployment has risen in all EC countries, while the need to increase investment in competitive enhancing domestic activities has become more urgent. Certainly, labour unions have continued to be vocal against the export of capital in labour-intensive sectors to developing countries; while some commentators believe the large outflows of capital by MNC conglomerates to acquire US assets do little to help the restructuring and wealth-creating activities of domestic industry.

However, in general there would appear to be much less concern in most European countries than there is in the US about the possible adverse effects of outward investment on domestic competitiveness and technological capacity. Partly this may be because most EC MNC activity (outside the EC) is not made to exploit a cutting-edge technology in countries lower down the innovating 'pecking order'; nor is it directed to potential competitors. There is comparatively little EC high-technology investment in Japan; while that undertaken in the US is intended to acquire a competitive advantage rather than to exploit an existing one. Any concern of national governments over exporting Europe's technological heritage to its competitors would seem to be outweighed by the belief that both *efficiency-* and *strategic-asset-seeking* by European firms are ways of strengthening their global competitive position; while, in the US and Japan, *market-seeking* investment, along with exports and a range of co-operative agreements are intended to gain an entrance to the two wealthiest countries in the world.

Contemporary national policies of EC governments towards inward and outward investment are being increasingly dominated by the perceived need of their firms and resources to benefit from the liberalization of world markets, on the one hand, and from EC 1992 and the exciting opportunities opening up in Central and Eastern Europe, on the other. The outcome has been not only a general unshackling of controls over all forms of MNC activity but a more positive recognition of the benefits likely to arise from such activities.

At the same time, we would observe that such a change in national policies towards FDI has resulted in a shift from being one of 'negative' interventionism to one of 'no' interventionism. Positive interventionism to use inbound or outbound MNC activity, in the restructuring or upgrading of domestic resources, is generally absent throughout EC countries. Since any kind of government interventionism in macro-organization is generally out of keeping with the current philosophy of most European governments, this should come as no surprise. Certainly, all EC governments have a long way to go before they approach the holistic approach of the Japanese government as it seeks to incorporate its policies towards both outward and inward direct investment into its wider macro-organizational strategy.[30]

Elsewhere, we have argued the case for a new macro-organizational approach by Western governments which is not specifically directed to MNC activity but rather to all areas of policy germane to determining the competitiveness of a country's resources and firms in the global market place (Dunning, 1991a, 1991b, 1991c). As suggested earlier in this chapter, it is our contention that governments, like firms, need to take a strategic perspective to the organization of the resources under their jurisdiction or influence. At the very least, this means monitoring the macro-organizational strategies of foreign governments, particularly those micro-organizational policies which either facilitate markets or distort market signals. While some of the arguments for strategic trade policies are not as persuasive as was first thought (Stegemann, 1989), there is still an important complementary role for governments to play in assisting the market economy and encouraging the response of their firms to be effective.

This, indeed, is the central message of the World Bank in its latest development report (World Bank, 1991). Though addressed mainly to developing countries, it is no less applicable to developed countries. The Bank hypothesises that the countries which most efficiently manage this particular form of co-operation or complementarity are those most likely to prosper over the next decade or more. And, since the interaction between governments and MNCs is becoming more important all the time, the need to devise positive and constructive policies which optimize the benefits from such activity are an integral part of this task.

12.4 THE EC DIMENSION

The completion of the internal market by the end of 1992 is the second of the major efforts of the European Commission to achieve economic integration among its member states. The first, which marked the initiation of the Community in 1958, was the removal of intra-EC tariff barriers and import controls. The second, which began in the mid–1980s and is described in the Cecchini Report (1988), is to remove the major non-tariff barriers by 1 January 1993.

The European Commission does not have a policy towards MNC activity *per se*. As described earlier, the 'revealed' philosophy of its Secretariat is to downplay the significance of the nationality of ownership as a factor influencing the efficiency of intra-EC resource organization and utilization.[31] But through its various economic and social programmes, as agreed by the member countries, it can and does greatly influence the conditions affecting MNC activity.

Considerable research has already been done in assessing the impact of the first phase of European integration on the volume and direction of MNC activity[32] while, elsewhere in this chapter, we have examined how it affected both the motives for and organization of such activity. Much less work has been done on the impact of pre–1992 EC integration on the policies of individual member states towards inward or outward investment. In its recent study, the OECD (1991) identified the EC as one of the factors making for a more liberalized climate towards MNC activity, although it observes that the main changes in policy have occurred only in the last quarter of the Community's existence (that is, over the last eight years or so).[33] However, although the EC has not produced dramatic results on the FDI policies of national governments, it has affected the costs and benefits of different kinds of MNC activity and the opportunity costs of that activity. This has forced national governments, particularly of smaller countries, to be more competitive in their bidding for inbound investment and to shape their general economic policies accordingly.[34]

The more-pronounced competitive environment for MNC activity so far fostered by European integration is likely to be reinforced by EC 1992 which liberalizes even further both markets and the opportunities open to MNCs. Since, too, EC directives and regulations have led to a harmonization of many national policy instruments and measures which otherwise might have affected the locational decisions of firms, purely commercial considerations, particularly those to do with the underlying supply capabilities offered by individual countries – many of which are strongly Government influenced (Porter, 1990)

– will be of greater importance (Dunning, 1991a). It is, then, the way in which countries respond to regional integration in their resource organization and utilization policies, as much regional integration *per se*, that will determine their success or failure both in attracting new inward investment and in providing the opportunities and incentives for competitive enhancing outward investment.

But there are also other aspects of European integration which affect the intra-EC distribution of MNC activity. One of these is the social programme of the European Commission[35] which, in the 1960s and '70s, considerably affected the attitudes of foreign MNCs towards investing in the EC. Another is the attempt by the Community to help the poorer regions of the Community to develop their resource potential and also assist in the restructuring of other regions suffering from above-average unemployment. To promote these latter two objectives, the Community provides grants or loans, known as 'fiscal transfers', which are financed by the more-prosperous member states.

Such fiscal transfers are, quite intentionally, discriminatory in their consequences. They are used by the recipient countries in various ways, some of which are likely to affect their relative attractions to foreign investors. Thus structural adjustment funds may be used to upgrade infrastructure of less-prosperous EC countries in such a way as will attract *efficiency-seeking* MNC activity which might otherwise have been located in more-prosperous EC countries. Or they might be used to assist domestic firms in the upgrading of their technological capabilities, which may help to improve their competitiveness *vis-à-vis* other European firms in the markets in which they both compete.

Thus, by a variety of means designed to help the poorer regions of the EC to become more productive, the Commission can affect the level and geographical composition of both inward and outward direct investment. But other policies – such as those which aim to stimulate the innovatory capacity of EC-based firms in cutting-edge technologies – are likely to favour the wealthier member states, as it is from these countries that MNCs in advanced-technology sectors are most likely to come. A study of the membership of government-funded research-based consortia and of the recipients of grants from the various EC-funded science and technology initiatives (Mytelka and Delapierre, 1988) reveals that these are mainly located in the high-income EC nations. Such subsidies, then, will tend to enhance the ability of countries to be outward investors, and by upgrading domestic resource capability, add to their locational attractions for inward investment.

More generally, the completion of the internal market will most certainly affect the relative competitiveness of EC firms *vis-à-vis* non-

EC firms and the attractions of a European location for investment by all kinds of firms. Because some of the main beneficiaries of the removal of non-tariff barriers are likely to be in the service sectors, one would expect an increase in *efficiency-seeking* and *strategic-asset-seeking* MNC investment in the years to come. Also, through the increase in intra-European competition, one might also expect to see the emergence of a leaner and fitter group of European MNCs, better equipped than their predecessors to penetrate global markets.

At the same time, the policy of the Community towards import barriers to non-EC countries is as yet unclear. This will clearly affect the amount of EC market-seeking investment, particularly of newer Japanese MNCs. Here, of course, the policy of the Community is intimately tied up with the progress of the GATT negotiations; but it is this area of policy which the Community *qua* Community is most likely to influence.

At a micro-organizational level, the European Commission, through the provisions of the Rome Treaty, can and does impact on the actions of both domestic and foreign-based MNCs. Foremost among these are a wide range of regulations designed to reduce monopolistic practices and encourage competition in the Community; for example, as laid down in Article 85 of the Treaty, the EC's labour law programme, which is especially directed to advancing employment protection and worker participation,[36] as outlined in the Fifth Directive of the Commission; the directives on corporate responsibility and group accounts; the harmonization of aids to inward investment (Articles 92–94 of the Treaty) and a variety of directives and rulings on environmental, safety and health matters. One particularly good example of a regional ruling directly affecting inward investment is that made by the Commission in July 1991 about the local content of a 'European-made' car produced in the Community by Japanese-owned firms. Cars with that amount of local (EC-made) content can then trade freely in the EC without any barriers. At the same time, the Community pegged the level of imports of Japanese cars at the 1990 level until 1998 when all quotas are to be abolished. It is by such decrees or directive measures that the EC may have a direct impact on MNC activity, on the level and direction of MNC activity and on the policies of individual member states.

In summary, although the European Commission may have few distinctive policies towards MNC activity *per se*, many of their macro-organizational actions affect, for good or bad, both the total amount of foreign direct investment in the EC and its distribution among member states. Take, for example, environmental standards and regulations. If these are kept at too high a level, they will not only divert MNC activity to non-EC countries (as an EC location will become less competitive), but, within the EC, they will redirect it from low-wage, low-productivity countries to high-wage, high-productivity countries. These latter countries are also those which tend to have high tax rates and social expenditures along with more stringent environmental standards (Sweeney, 1991). By contrast, a reduction in domestic content requirements, or in other non-tariff barriers, is likely to lead to more foreign investment in the EC, in which all EC countries should benefit to a greater or lesser extent.

More generally, the EC can opt for two contrasting mixes of policies. The one is to force poorer EC members to adopt a social charter, for example, in respect of wages, welfare and environmental standards, closer to the levels of the higher-income members. This is likely to put poorer countries at a disadvantage and divert the flow of inward investment from them to their wealthier neighbours, as well as possibly reducing the total amount of FDI in the EC.[37] At the other extreme, the EC may choose to implement policies that do not attempt to keep investment from being diverted from high- to low-income member states. The outcome of this strategy might be that high-income countries would unilaterally reduce their tax rates or lower their social transaction costs so as to make themselves more competitive with the rest of the EC – and, indeed, the rest of the world. In this event, the net result would be an increase in both domestic and foreign investment and a reduction in structural employment (Sweeney, 1991).

12.5   CONCLUSIONS

In the future it is likely that the European Commission will play a more active role in setting the ground rules which member states will be expected to follow in their policies towards MNC activity.

However, notwithstanding a likely trend towards more-harmonized policies, we believe that the role of national governments in influencing both the locational attractions of their countries to foreign direct investors and the competitive advantages of their own MNCs is likely to become more, rather than less, important.

Moreover, there is a world of difference between a convergence of national policies (Safarian, 1991) and that of the ability of governments to organize efficiently and monitor these policies. In their attempts to promote the economic wellbeing of their citizens, individual EC governments are likely to be paying more attention to their macro-organizational policies because, central to these policies, is the role played by international direct investment and cross-border collaborative alliances. In this respect, it may be that the 1990s will see a new era of co-operation between governments and firms, as the role of the former is steered increasingly towards compensating for market failures that inhibit the latter from achieving their full economic potential.

All this is not to ignore the economic powers ceded to the European Community or the Commission, by the individual member states. These will not only have the effect of largely neutralizing inter-country, structurally distorting, national policies, but will also considerably influence patterns of individual development, particularly those of peripheral regions. The EC is also likely to play a more important role on the harmonization of intra-EC technical standards and of sectoral regulations and restrictions, particularly in the services sectors.

Finally, perhaps most importantly, in the light of the strategically orientated trade and investment policies of the US and Japan, the EC *qua* EC is likely to strengthen the negotiating hand of individual European Governments in international fora. Barring completely unforeseen events, by the year 2000, for most practical economic purposes, the economic space of Western Europe, and particularly the EC, will be very similar to that of the proposed North American Free Trade Area. Yet, within these regional blocs, national Governments and regional authorities (for example, US States), will continue to devise strategies both to promote their own national champions, and to encourage the appropriate investment by firms from outside their countries or regions. Competition between countries and regions will co-exist with cooperation between countries and regions. Each will both affect and be affected by the level, structure and geographical distribution of MNC activity; and it is this interaction and the opportunities and tensions it brings, which is likely to offer a fruitful area of research for international business scholars for many years to come.

NOTES

1. By macro-organization policy, we mean the instruments available to and chosen by governments to affect the overall organization of the production and transactions of resources. As compared with macroeconomic policy, it is designed to bring about a certain system of resource allocation (i.e., a means towards an end) rather than to achieve certain goals (employment, stable exchange rates, economic growth etc.). We shall use the term micro-organization to refer to specific aspects of macro-organization policy such as subsidies to assist training grants, R&D subventions, patent regulations, anti-trust legislation, environmental controls, investment incentives etc.).

2. As set out most recently in Chapters 4 and 5 of Dunning (1992a).
3. The exception is in Southern Europe where some investment is undertaken to take advantage of a plentiful and cheap supply of labour.
4. For analysis of the distinctive characteristics of sequential investment, see Kogut (1983).
5. Elsewhere referred to as O_a (the ownership of specific assets) advantages (Dunning, 1988).
6. Elsewhere referred to as O (the ownership of the ability to organize assets to minimize transaction costs and maximize productive efficiency).
7. For example, efficient organization may lead to cost reductions in the price of products, which may lead to an increase in sales, which may raise profits and which may enable a firm to spend more on R&D to create new products or production methods.
8. Which in turn rested on the balance between the respective opportunity costs of the bargaining parties.
9. Though there is less reluctance by foreign MNCs to conclude some kinds of non-equity ventures, e.g., strategic alliances, for specific purposes.
10. See Dunning (1991d and 1992a).
11. That is, those who record an average proportion of their sales (whether by export or FDI) outside their national boundaries.
12. Such as the % of domestic corporate profits accounted for by the foreign activities of domestic MNCs plus those of foreign subsidiaries, the % of domestic output and employment accounted for by the same two groups of activities. Ratios on these are currently being calculated by the UNCTC and will appear in UNCTC (1992a).
13. For example, the effects of a currency devaluation or revaluation which fails to take account of the (likely) very different pricing policies of domestic firms and foreign subsidiaries may fail to achieve its purpose.
14. See also chapter 2 by Terutomo Ozawa in this volume.
15. With the notable exception of a few large MNCs, such as Philips of Eindhoven and Electrolux of Sweden.
16. Defined as the average income earned on FDI less taxes paid to foreign governments, as compared with the earnings on domestic investment gross of tax. For an analysis of the UK situation, see Chapters 2 and 3 of Dunning (1970) entitled 'The Costs and Benefits of Foreign Direct Investment to the Investing Country: the UK Experience' and 'Further Thoughts on Foreign Investment'.
17. For analysis of the likely impact of outward direct investment on the UK and US balance of payments according to the assumptions made, see Dunning (1969).
18. See especially Dunning, 1991(a), 1991(b), 1991(c).
19. Hence the growth of joint ventures and strategic alliances particularly in high-technology sectors. See Gugler and Dunning (1992).
20. We do, however, accept the argument that, in some cases, firms contemplating FDI (or an expansion in FDI) as a means of promoting their competitive position might be better advised to use the resources to improve the efficiency of their domestic activities and/or engage in more R&D.
21. Usually they tended to be defence and related high-technology sectors, those which were nationalized or closely regulated (e.g. transport and banking) and those which were identified with the maintenance of national culture (e.g., newspapers and broadcasting). For further details, see Safarian (1983) and OECD (1982).
22. Including denial of work permits or professional cards to technical and managerial staff and restriction of shareholder voting rights to nationals.
23. The Exchange Control Act gave the Treasury wide powers to influence the amount and pattern of both inward and outward investment. Exchange control permission was, for example, required for any change in the control of a UK company passing to a foreign resident. So far as the Treasury was concerned, the main objective

of the Exchange Control Act was that FDI should have a favourable impact on the foreign currency reserves.

24. Some of these are summarized in Hodges (1974).

25. For some examples of plant closures in Ireland and Belgium in the 1970s, see OECD (1985), van den Bulcke (1985).

26. For example, some 33.0% of manufacturing employment in Belgium in 1985, and 42.8% of that in Ireland in 1987, is accounted for by foreign-owned firms.

27. As measured, for example, by the ratio between the accumulated inward and outward direct capital stake and the GNP of the country.

28. The exact proportion sold to other EC affiliates is unknown, but it is believed to be very substantial indeed.

29. It is not always easy to distinguish between a request, a tacit agreement and a contractual obligation imposed on a foreign direct investor as, *de facto*, very rarely do negotiated settlements between national governments and foreign MNCs have any binding force.

30. For a somewhat different view which argues that Japanese policy – at least towards inward investment – was more influenced by the actions and bargaining power of foreign MNCs, see Encarnation and Mason (1990).

31. For example, hardly any mention is made of the role of outward or inward direct investment in the Cecchini report.

32. For a review of this work, see Dunning and Robson (1988), Yannopolous (1990) and UNCTC (1992b).

33. In particular, it is possible that countries like the UK, Germany and Italy would have adopted less-liberal policies towards inward investment in the absence of their membership of the EC. This is simply because MNCs would have had less opportunity to engage in efficiency-seeking investment. In other words, their affiliates would most likely have been more responsive to domestic government policies.

34. For a discussion of the impact of different kinds of MNC activity on the framing of national economic policies, see Panic (1991). An interesting perspective on the (positive) role played by US MNCs on the (limited) liberalization of inward investment policy in Japan is contained in Encarnation and Mason (1990).

35. As described, for example, in Robinson (1983).

36. Which included the contentious Vredling initiative which, *inter alia*, was designed to enforce foreign MNCs to disclose information about their worldwide operations to labour representatives bargaining with their European affiliates.

37. This diversion might be prevented if the wealthier countries, through such institutions as the Regional Development Fund, encourage the poorer countries to upgrade their standards.

REFERENCES

Cantwell, J.A. (1988), 'The Reorganisation of European Industries after Integration', in J.H. Dunning and P. Robson (eds), *Multinationals and the European Community*, Oxford: Basil Blackwell.

Cantwell, J.A. (1989), *Technological Innovation and Multinational Corporations*, Oxford: Basil Blackwell.

Cantwell, J.A. (1992), 'The Effects of Integration on the Structure of Multinational Corporation Activity in the EC', in M. Klein and P.J.J. Welfens (eds), *Multinationals in the New Europe and Global Trade*, Berlin and New York: Springer-Verlag.

Cecchini, P. *et al.* (1988), *The European Challenge 1992: The Benefits of a Single Market*, Aldershot, Hants.: Wildwood House.

Doz, Y. (1986), *Strategic Management in Multinational Corporations*, Oxford: Pergamon Press.

Dunning, J.H. (1969), 'The Reddaway and Hufbauer/Adler Reports', *Bankers Magazine*, May, June and July 1969.

Dunning, J.H. (1970), *Studies in International Investment*, London: Allen & Unwin.

Dunning, J.H. (1988), *Explaining International Production*, London and Boston, Mass.: Unwin Hyman.

Dunning, J.H. (1991a), 'Governments – Markets – Firms: Towards a New Balance', *CTC Reporter*, no. 31, 2–7.

Dunning, J.H. (1991b), 'Governments and Multinational Enterprises: from Confrontation to Cooperation', *Millenium Journal of International Studies*, **20**, 223–44.

Dunning, J.H. (1991c), 'Governments, Organization and International Competitiveness', in L.G. Mattson and B. Stymne (eds), *Corporate and Industry Strategies for Europe*, Amsterdam: Elsevier Science Publishers.

Dunning, J.H. (1991d), 'The Eclectic Paradigm of International Production: a Personal Perspective', in C.N. Pitelis and R. Sugden (eds), *The Nature of the Transnational Firm*, London and New York: Routledge, 117–36.

Dunning, J.H. (1992a), *Multinational Enterprises and the Global Economy*, Reading (Mass.) and London: Addison Wesley.

Dunning, J.H. (1992b), 'The Political Economy of International Production', in P. Buckley (ed.), *New Directions in International Business*, London: Edward Elgar.

Dunning, J.H. and Robson, P. (eds) (1988), *Multinationals and the European Community*, Oxford: Basil Blackwell.

Encarnation, D.J. and Mason, M. (1990), 'Neither MITI nor America; the Political Economy of Capital Liberalisation in Japan', *International Organisation*, **44**, 25–54.

Gugler, P. and Dunning, J.H. (1992), 'Technology Based Cross-border Alliances', in R. Culpan (ed.), *Multinational Strategic Alliances*, New York: Haworth Press (forthcoming).

Hodges, M. (1974), *Multinational Corporations and National Governments: A Case Study of the United Kingdom Experience*, London: D.C. Heath.

Hufbauer, G. and Adler, F.M. (1968), *Overseas Manufacturing Investment and the Balance of Payments*, Washington, D.C.: US Treasury Department, *Tax Policy Research Study no. 1*.

Kogut, B. (1983), 'Foreign Direct Investment as a Sequential Process', in C.P. Kindleberger and D. Audretsch (eds), *The Multinational in the 1980s*, Cambridge, Mass.: MIT Press.

Mytelka, L.K. and Delappierre, M. (1988), 'The Alliance Strategies of European Firms in the Information Technology Industry and the Role of ESPRIT', in J. Dunning and P. Robson (eds), *Multinationals and the European Community*, Oxford: Basil Blackwell.

OECD (1982 and 1987), *Controls and Impediments Affecting Inward Direct Investment in OECD Countries*, Paris: OECD.

OECD (1985), *Structural Adjustment and Multinational Enterprises*, Paris: OECD.

OECD (1991), *Measures Affecting Direct Investment in OECD Countries*, Paris: OECD.

O'Hearn, D. (1990), 'TNCs, Intervening Mechanisms and Economic Growth in Ireland: A Longitudinal Test and Extension of the Bornschier Model', *World Development*, **18**, 417–29.

Ozawa, T. (1989), *Japan's Strategic Policy Towards Outward Investment*, Fort Collins: Colorado State University, *mimeo*.

Panic, M. (1991), 'The Impact of Multinationals on National Economic Policies', in B. Bürgenmeier and J.L. Mucchielli (eds), *Multinationals and Europe, 1992*, London and New York: Routledge, 204–32.

Porter, M. (1990), *The Competitive Advantage of Nations*, New York: Basic Books.

Reddaway, W.B., Potter, S.J. and Taylor, C.T. (1968), *Effects of UK Direct Investment Overseas*, Cambridge: Cambridge University Press.

Robinson, J. (1983), *Multinationals and Political Control*, Aldershot, Hants.: Gower.

Safarian, A.E. (1983), *Governments and Multinationals: Policies in the Developed Countries*, Washington, D.C.: British-North American Committee.

Safarian, A.E. (1991), 'Firm and Government Strategies', in B. Bürgenmeier and J.L. Mucchielli (eds), *Multinationals and Europe, 1992*, London and New York: Routledge, 187–203.

Simões, V. (1985), 'Portugal' in J.H. Dunning (ed.), *Multinational Enterprises, Economic Structure and Competitiveness*, Chichester and New York: John Wiley.

Stegemann, K. (1989), 'Policy Rivalry among Nation States: What Can We Learn from Models of Strategic Trade Policy', *International Organisation*, **43** (1).

Sweeney, R.J. (1991), *The Competition for Foreign Direct Investment*, Washington, D.C.: Georgetown University, *mimeo*.

UNCTC (1991), *World Investment Report*, New York: UN.

UNCTC (1992a), *The UNCTC Directory of Statistics on International Investment and Production*, New York: UN (forthcoming).

UNCTC (1992b), *European Integration and Investment by Transnational Corporations*, vol. 1, New York: UN (forthcoming).

US Department of Commerce (various dates), *Survey of Current Business*.

van den Bulcke, D. (1985), 'Belgium', in J.H. Dunning (ed.), *Multinational Enterprises, Economic Structure and International Competitiveness*, Chichester: John Wiley, 249–80.

World Bank (1991), *World Development Report*, Washington: World Bank.

Yannopolous, G.N. (1990), 'Foreign Direct Investment and European Integration: the Evidence from the Formative Years of the European Community', *Journal of Common Market Studies*, **28**, March.

Young, S., Hood, N. and Hamill, J. (1988), *Foreign Multinationals and the British Economy*, London and New York: Croom Helm.

Index

References in the text to individual companies and particular industries are indexed under the heading 'companies (named)' and 'industries (named)'